ARUBA

ROSALIE KLEIN

Contents

Discover Aruba................ **12**
5 Top Experiences............... 16
Planning Your Trip............... 22
The Best of Aruba 27
Best Water Sports 32
Romantic Rendezvous 35
Explore the Outback............. 38

Beaches **40**
Oranjestad..................... 42
Eagle Beach and Manchebo Beach... 45
Palm Beach, Malmok, and Noord 47
North Coast.................... 49
San Nicolas, Savaneta, and Pos
   Chiquito 52

Recreation..................... **55**
Water Activities 57
Land Tours..................... 68
Hiking and Running 77
Golf and Tennis 79
Spas and Yoga.................. 80

Sights **83**
Oranjestad..................... 85
Palm Beach, Malmok, and Noord 89
North Coast.................... 91
Santa Cruz, Paradera, and Piedra Plat . 94
San Nicolas, Savaneta, and Pos
   Chiquito 99

Food **102**
Oranjestad..................... 104
Eagle Beach and Manchebo Beach... 116
Palm Beach, Malmok, and Noord 122
North Coast.................... 132
Santa Cruz, Paradera, and Piedra Plat . 132
San Nicolas, Savaneta, and Pos
   Chiquito 135

Entertainment and Events **138**
Nightlife 140
Shows and Concert Venues........ 148
Festivals and Events 150

Shops **158**
   Oranjestad 160
   Eagle Beach and Manchebo Beach . . . 168
   Palm Beach, Malmok, and Noord 169
   North Coast 175
   Santa Cruz, Paradera, and Piedra Plat . 175

Where to Stay **176**
   Oranjestad 181
   Eagle Beach and Manchebo Beach . . . 183
   Palm Beach, Malmok, and Noord . . . 187
   Santa Cruz, Paradera, and Piedra Plat . 193
   San Nicolas, Savaneta, and Pos
      Chiquito 194

Background **198**
   The Landscape 198
   Environmental Issues 200
   Plants and Animals 203
   History 208
   Government and Economy 218
   People and Culture 219

Essentials **227**
   Transportation 227
   Visas and Officialdom 235
   Conduct and Customs 238
   Health and Safety 238
   Travel Tips 241
   Information and Services 245

Resources **248**
   Papiamento Phrasebook 248
   Suggested Reading 249
   Internet Resources 251

Index **255**

List of Maps **259**

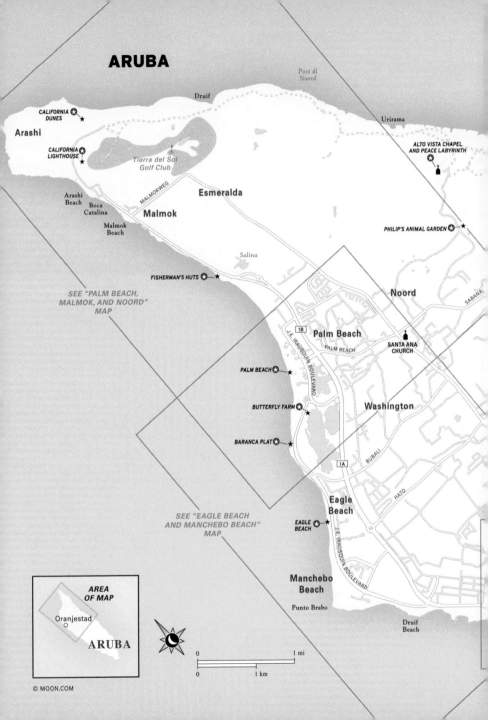

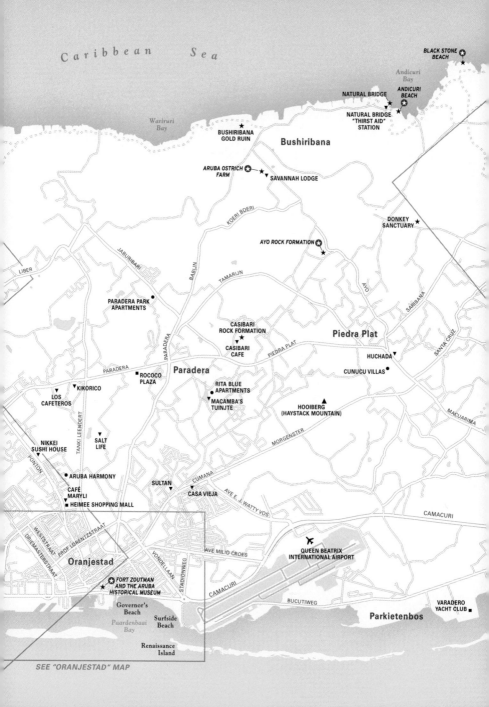

Caribbean Sea

Andicuri Bay

BLACK STONE BEACH ✪ ★

Wariruri Bay

NATURAL BRIDGE ▼

ANDICURI BEACH ✪ ★

NATURAL BRIDGE "THIRST AID" STATION ▼

BUSHIRIBANA GOLD RUIN ◆

Bushiribana

ARUBA OSTRICH FARM ✪ ★

SAVANNAH LODGE ▼

Koeri Boeri

DONKEY SANCTUARY ▼

Jaburibari

AYO ROCK FORMATION ✪ ★

LIBER

Babijn

Tamarijn

Ayo

Sabiana

Santa Cruz

PARADERA PARK APARTMENTS ◆

Paradera

CASIBARI ROCK FORMATION ★

CASIBARI CAFE ▼

Piedra Plat

Piedra Plat

HUCHADA ▼

CUNUCU VILLAS ◆

Paradera

ROCOCO PLAZA ■

KIKORICO ▼

RITA BLUE APARTMENTS ◆

MACAMBA'S TUINJTE ▼

HOOIBERG (HAYSTACK MOUNTAIN) ▲

Macuarima

LOS CAFETEROS ▼

Tanki Leendert

SALT LIFE ▼

Morgenster

NIKKEI SUSHI HOUSE ▼

Ponton

ARUBA HARMONY ●

CAFÉ MARYLI ▼

HEIMEE SHOPPING MALL ■

SULTAN ▼

Cumana

CASA VIEJA ▼

Ave E. J. Watty Vos

Camacuri

Weststraat

Driemasterstraat

Prof Lorenitzstraat

Ave Milio Croes

✈ QUEEN BEATRIX INTERNATIONAL AIRPORT

Camacuri

Bucutiweg

VARADERO YACHT CLUB ■

Oranjestad

Yondellaan

Stadionweg

FORT ZOUTMAN AND THE ARUBA HISTORICAL MUSEUM ✪

Governor's Beach

Surfside Beach

Paardenbaai Bay

Camacuri

Parkietenbos

Renaissance Island

SEE "ORANJESTAD" MAP

★ BLACK STONE
BEACH

Daimari
Beach

⊕ CONCHI
(NATURAL POOL)
✦ Conchi

Dos
Playa

Boca
Prins

★ FONTEIN CAVES

Arikok

⊕ MADI'S MAGICAL
TOURS

ANGOCHI

■ RANCHO LOCO

⊕ Arikok National Park
★ SAN FUEGO ENTRANCE/
COFFEE SHOP

National

SAN FUEGO

**Santa
Cruz**

PICARON

▼ URATAKA
CENTER

Park

MACUARIMA

BALASHI

▼ B-55

SABANA   BASORA

CAMACURI

SEROE ALEJANDRO

● THE HIDEAWAY

● CLUB ARIAS
BED AND BREAKFAST

Savaneta

Pos Chiquito

POS CHIQUITO

▼ ANTESALA

FORTUNA ●
VILLA

● ARUBA
OCEAN
VILLAS

● ARUBA KAYAK
ADVENTURES

**Mangel
Halto**

FLYING ▼
FISHBONE

▼ SERENE BY
THE SEA

■ BALASHI
BEER GARDEN

▼ MARINA
PIRATA

▼ SEABREEZE
APARTMENTS

⊕ MANGEL
HALTO

Santo
Largo

Savaneta
Beach

▼ ZEEROVER

▼ ARUBA REEF
APARTMENTS

● VISTALMAR

■ VARADERO
YACHT CLUB

*Commandeurs
Bay*

Caribbean

ARUBA
(CONTINUED)

SEE
"ARIKOK NATIONAL PARK"
MAP (P. 97)

★ QUADIKAKIRI
CAVES

Caribbean Sea

Rincon Bay

Grapefield Beach

Boca Grande

Bachelor's Beach

Sabana Lodo

Sero Grandi

WEG FONTEIN
WEG SEROE BLANCO
BRASIL
PALISIAWEG

SEROE COLORADO

★ LOURDES GROTTO/
SEROE PRETO CITY OF LIGHTS

WEG FONTEIN

Esso Heights

FORTHEUVEL STRAAT

Lago Heights

Seroe Colorado

Lagoville

CAYA JOSE GEERMAN
WEG BRASIL

PASTOR HENDRIK STRAAT

Essoville

★ MUSEUM OF INDUSTRY

★ CHARLIE'S BAR

ROGER'S BEACH

RUM REEF BAR

★ BABY BEACH

San Nicolas Bay

JADS DIVE SHOP

PASTOR HENDRIK STRAAT

★ O'NIEL CARIBBEAN KITCHEN

★ SAN NICOLAS COMMUNITY MUSEUM

San Nicolas

★ ROYAL DUTCH MARINE CAMP

Sea

0   1 mi
0   1 km

ARUBA

Oranjestad

AREA OF MAP

© MOON.COM

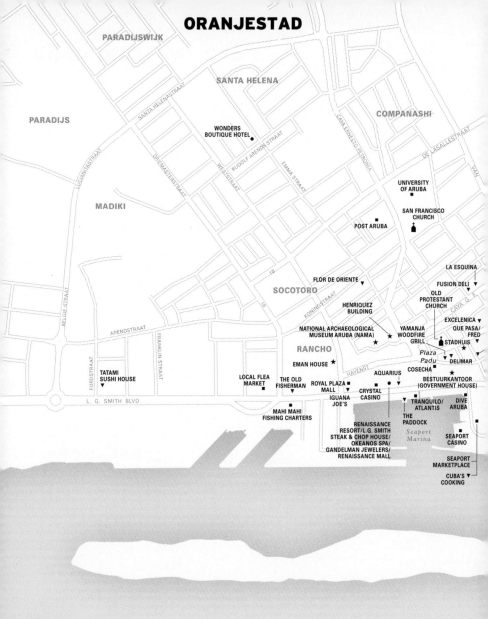

ORANJESTAD

PARADIJSWIJK

SANTA HELENA

COMPANASHI

PARADIJS

MADIKI

Santa Helenastraat

Driemastersstraat

Luciandastraat

Belgiestraat

WONDERS
BOUTIQUE HOTEL

Rudolf Arends Straat

Wesstraat

Emma Straat

Caya Ernesto Petronia

De Lasallestraat

Van

UNIVERSITY
OF ARUBA

SAN FRANCISCO
CHURCH

POST ARUBA

SOCOTORO

FLOR DE ORIENTE

Koningstraat

18

19

LA ESQUINA

FUSION DELI

OLD
PROTESTANT
CHURCH

Caya G. F.

EXCELENICA

QUE PASA/
FRED

HENRIQUEZ
BUILDING

NATIONAL ARCHAEOLOGICAL
MUSEUM ARUBA (NAMA)

YAMANJA
WOODFIRE
GRILL

STADHUIS

RANCHO

EMAN HOUSE

*Plaza
Padu*

DELIMAR

Arendstraat

Franklin Straat

Fordstraat

TATAMI
SUSHI HOUSE

LOCAL FLEA
MARKET

THE OLD
FISHERMAN

ROYAL PLAZA
MALL

Havenst.

COSECHA

AQUARIUS

BESTUURKANTOOR
(GOVERNMENT HOUSE)

CRYSTAL
CASINO

IGUANA
JOE'S

TRANQUILO/
ATLANTIS

DIVE
ARUBA

L. G. SMITH BLVD

MAHI MAHI
FISHING CHARTERS

RENAISSANCE
RESORT/L.G. SMITH
STEAK & CHOP HOUSE/
OKEANOS SPA/
GANDELMAN JEWELERS/
RENAISSANCE MALL

THE
PADDOCK

*Seaport
Marina*

SEAPORT
CASINO

SEAPORT
MARKETPLACE

CUBA'S
COOKING

Caribbean   Sea

| 0 | | 0.25 mi |

| 0 | | 0.25 km |

© MOON.COM

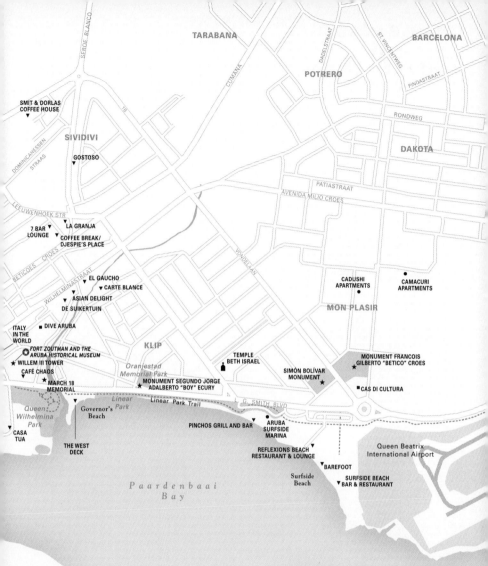

TARABANA

BARCELONA

POTRERO

RONDWEG

DAKOTA

SMIT & DORLAS
COFFEE HOUSE

SIVIDIVI

GOSTOSO

PATIASTRAAT

AVENIDA MILIO CROES

7 BAR
LOUNGE

LA GRANJA

COFFEE BREAK/
DJESPIE'S PLACE

CADUSHI
APARTMENTS

CAMACURI
APARTMENTS

EL GAUCHO

CARTE BLANCE

ASIAN DELIGHT

DE SUIKERTUIN

MON PLASIR

ITALY
IN THE
WORLD

DIVE ARUBA

FORT ZOUTMAN AND THE
ARUBA HISTORICAL MUSEUM

WILLEM III TOWER

CAFÉ CHAOS

KLIP

Oranjestad
Memorial Park

TEMPLE
BETH ISRAEL

SIMÓN BOLÍVAR
MONUMENT

MONUMENT FRANCOIS
GILBERTO "BETICO" CROES

MARCH 18
MEMORIAL

MONUMENT SEGUNDO JORGE
ADALBERTO "BOY" ECURY

CAS DI CULTURA

Linear
Park

Linear Park Trail

G. SMITH BLVD.

Queen
Wilhelmina
Park

Governor's
Beach

CASA
TUA

THE WEST
DECK

PINCHOS GRILL AND BAR

ARUBA
SURFSIDE
MARINA

Queen Beatrix
International Airport

REFLEXIONS BEACH
RESTAURANT & LOUNGE

BAREFOOT

Surfside
Beach

SURFSIDE BEACH
BAR & RESTAURANT

Paardenbaai
Bay

Renaissance
Island

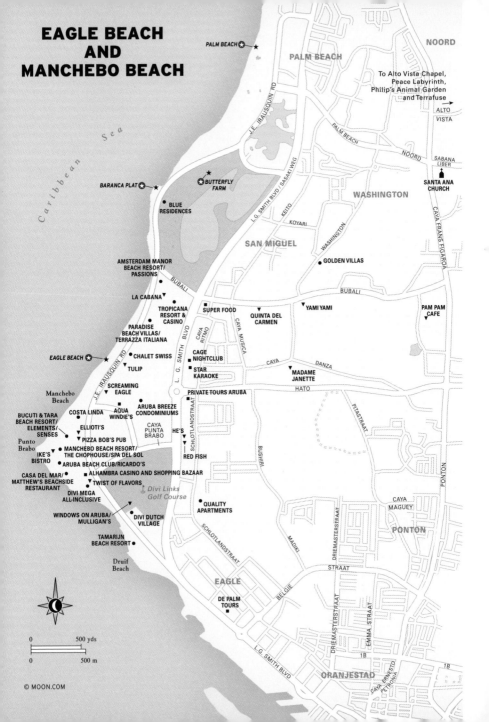

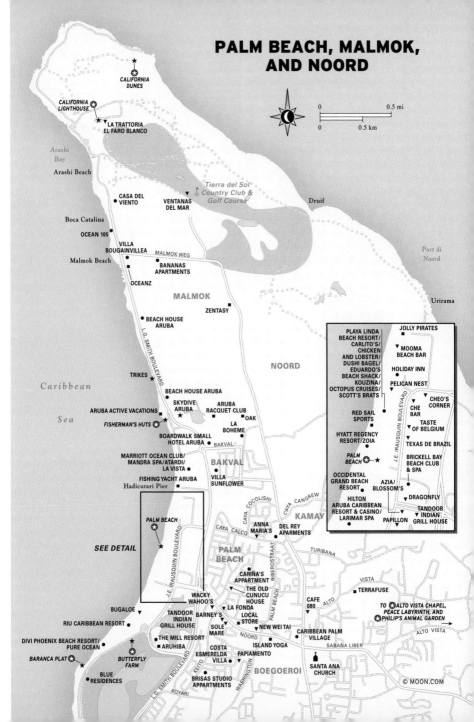

PALM BEACH, MALMOK, AND NOORD

0   0.5 mi

0   0.5 km

CALIFORNIA DUNES

CALIFORNIA LIGHTHOUSE

LA TRATTORIA EL FARO BLANCO

Arashi Bay

Arashi Beach

Tierra del Sol Country Club & Golf Course

Druif

CASA DEL VIENTO

VENTANAS DEL MAR

Boca Catalina

OCEAN 105

VILLA BOUGAINVILLEA

MALMOK WEG

Malmok Beach

BANANAS APARTMENTS

OCEANZ

Post di Noord

MALMOK

ZENTASY

Urirama

BEACH HOUSE ARUBA

Caribbean Sea

NOORD

TRIKES

BEACH HOUSE ARUBA

ARUBA ACTIVE VACATIONS

SKYDIVE ARUBA

ARUBA RACQUET CLUB

FISHERMAN'S HUTS

OAK

LA BOHEME

BOARDWALK SMALL HOTEL ARUBA

L.G. SMITH BOULEVARD

BAKVAL

MARRIOTT OCEAN CLUB/ MANDRA SPA/ATARDI/ LA VISTA

BAKVAL

FISHING YACHT ARUBA

Hadicurari Pier

VILLA SUNFLOWER

PALM BEACH

SEE DETAIL

J.E. IRAUSQUIN BOULEVARD

CAVA COCOLISHI

CAVA CANGREW

KAMAY

CAVA CALCO

ANNA MARIA'S

DEL REY APARMENTS

PALM BEACH

TURIBANA

CARIÑA'S APPARTMENT

THE OLD CUNUCU HOUSE

VISTA

TERRAFUSE

WACKY WAHOO'S

BARNEY'S

LA FONDA

LOCAL STORE

CAFE 080

ALTO

TO ALTO VISTA CHAPEL, PEACE LABYRINTH, AND PHILIP'S ANIMAL GARDEN

BUGALOE

TANDOOR INDIAN GRILL HOUSE

SOLE MARE

NEW WEI TAI

PALM BEACH

NOORD

CARIBBEAN PALM VILLAGE

RIU CARIBBEAN RESORT

COSTA ESMERELDA VILLA

ISLAND YOGA

SABANA LIBER

DIVI PHOENIX BEACH RESORT/ PURE OCEAN

THE MILL RESORT

PAPIAMENTO

ARUHIBA

BARANCA PLAT

BUTTERFLY FARM

BRISAS STUDIO APPARTMENTS

SANTA ANA CHURCH

BOEGOEROEI

BLUE RESIDENCES

KEITO

KOYARI

WASHINGTON

© MOON.COM

Detail inset

PLAYA LINDA BEACH RESORT/ CARLITO'S/ CHICKEN AND LOBSTER/ DUSHI BAGEL/ EDUARDO'S BEACH SHACK/ KOUZINA/ OCTOPUS CRUISES/ SCOTT'S BRATS

JOLLY PIRATES

MOOMA BEACH BAR

HOLIDAY INN

PELICAN NEST

RED SAIL SPORTS

CHEO'S CORNER

CHE BAR

TASTE OF BELGIUM

HYATT REGENCY RESORT/ZOIA

TEXAS DE BRAZIL

PALM BEACH

J.E. IRAUSQUIN BOULEVARD

BRICKELL BAY BEACH CLUB & SPA

OCCIDENTAL GRAND BEACH RESORT

AZIA/ BLOSSOM'S

DRAGONFLY

HILTON ARUBA CARIBBEAN RESORT & CASINO/ LARIMAR SPA

PAPILLON

TANDOOR INDIAN GRILL HOUSE

DISCOVER

Aruba

Look out the window when coming in for a landing on Aruba, and you'll be struck by the contrast between the intense blue of the Caribbean Sea and the snowy white of the beaches. "Aruba is right next door to heaven," is how one longtime visitor describes it.

Some of the most stunning beaches in the Caribbean line the west coast of the island, with turquoise waters as calm as any lake at spots like Palm Beach and Eagle Beach. Lined by resorts from the intimate to the grand, these areas offer a wealth of eateries, shops, and casinos.

But a visit to Aruba isn't complete without exploring beyond the beaches and hotels. Adventures await in every direction. At Arikok National Park you'll find hiking trails, native species, and incredible geological formations, including Conchi (Natural Pool), a dramatic spot for swimming created by cooled lava rock. On the north coast you'll encounter a lunar landscape of coral rock and pillow basalt, while spume from the crashing waves surges high. Also rife for exploration are the island's caves, dunes, rock formations, and coves.

The best part about Aruba is that there's little divide between island dwellers and visitors. Don't be surprised to find a table of islanders sitting right next

Clockwise from top left: street art by Benno Anaya in Oranjestad; brilliantly hued flamboyan flowers; iguana; scarlet macaw; cocktail; kayakers.

to you at a resort restaurant or casino any night of the week. This congenial relationship with vacationers has made Aruba the most popular repeat destination in the Caribbean.

Aruba can be a tranquil respite from the hustle and bustle of everyday existence, or each day can offer exciting new natural and cultural experiences. The richness and variety of this "One Happy Island" can fulfill the vacation needs of honeymooners, singles, families, and adventurers. This is a place where modern luxury and the rugged landscape exist side by side. Your Aruban vacation can be whatever you want it to be—the choice is yours.

Clockwise from top left: Aruban sunset; flamingos on Renaissance Island; kitesurfer; Aruban architecture.

5 TOP
EXPERIENCES

1 **Bask on the Beach:** Aruba's soft sands and turquoise waters will take your breath away (page 41).

2 **Plan Your Romantic Rendezvous:** With secluded retreats, waterfront restaurants, spectacular sunsets, and relaxing diversions, Aruba offers the ideal getaway for lovers (page 35).

>>>

3 **Explore Arikok National Park:** Aruba's largest national preserve occupies 18 percent of the island and encompasses numerous trails, caves, the island's highest point, native flora and fauna, and attractions (page 96).

>>>

4 **Engage in Local Culture:** Celebrate with locals at festivals like **Carnival** and dine on delicious **cuisine** drawing from Aruba's Caribbean roots and diverse communities (pages 31 and 109).

5 **Get Active in the Water:** From kitesurfing to snorkeling, scuba diving, and deep-sea fishing, the island offers a water activity for everyone (page 32).

Planning Your Trip

Where to Go

Aruba measures only 186.5 square kilometers (72 square mi), merely a speck on a map of the Caribbean. A single main road, **1A,** allows visitors to drive from the **California Lighthouse** on its northwest point to **Baby Beach** at the southeast tip. An ordinary rental car will suffice for traveling to these easily accessible sights, but if you're planning to take in more rural spots on the island, such as **Conchi (Natural Pool)** or **Andicuri Beach,** a 4WD vehicle will serve you better and enhance the experience. Allow at least a day for touring the main sights, and two if you want to see everything. Organized tours provide an introduction to the island and the lay of the land, but there is much to see beyond their limited schedules.

If you plan to stay at the major hotels in **Eagle Beach-Manchebo Beach** and **Palm Beach** and travel no farther than **Oranjestad,** then **Arubus,** the mass transit system, is the way to go. Nearly every hotel has a bus stop that will take you to the main terminal in town. Service is frequent and the vehicles are modern, clean, and comfortable.

Oranjestad

Aruba's capital offers visitors a taste of **authentic island life.** Playa, as it is also known, boasts quaint side streets interwoven with major shopping avenues. Right next to **malls with designer shops,** town residents still live in **homes from the 18th century.** Aruba's history and culture are on display here in museums such as the **National Archaeological Museum Aruba**

Oranjestad

(NAMA) or the **Aruba Historical Museum.** Wind down your day with **superb dining** and **casino play.**

Oranjestad also features a harbor filled with **deep-sea fishing** boats; the major **Renaissance Resort;** and many attractive **guesthouses.** Some local beaches, like **Surfside and Druif,** are practically deserted during the week and fill up with islanders on weekends.

Eagle Beach and Manchebo Beach

This resort area offers a **tranquil getaway.** Miles of beaches are shaded by large copses of sea grape. In many spots, at certain times of day, a visitor can settle down, look around, and not see a soul. The apartment-style resorts are **well suited to families.** The **Divi Links golf course** is surrounded by a beautiful resort, so golfers can roll out of bed to an early tee time. Organized activities for kids, such as arts and crafts, scavenger hunts, pool games, and contests keep the whole family happy. Close proximity to Oranjestad

allows history buffs and shoppers **easy access to museums and designer stores.**

Palm Beach, Malmok, and Noord

Palm Beach is one of the most popular places on the island for **lounging on the beach** and **nightlife.** Restaurants, casinos, and clubs sit next to **glamorous resorts.** It is the center of every water activity imaginable: **sailing, snorkeling, scuba diving** off the *Antilla* shipwreck, **tubing, deep-sea fishing, parasailing, windsurfing,** and *Seaworld Explorer.* Family fun is close by at the exhilarating **Butterfly Farm** and **Philip's Animal Garden.**

North Coast

The dramatic, craggy north coast sharply contrasts Aruba's tranquil western shores. Follow the **spectacular coast trail** in a 4WD vehicle or UTV to find **secluded coves for surfing.** Off-road adventurers enjoy traversing the **Aruban outback** for a trip back in time. **Horseback tours,** provided by stables such as **Rancho Loco,**

snorkeling Aruba's waters

California Lighthouse

Aruba's Carnival parade

weave through the dramatic coastal formations. Befriend a giant bird at the **Aruba Ostrich Farm** or do some **rock climbing at Ayo** and explore the **Bushiribana Gold Ruin.**

The challenging **Tierra Del Sol Country Club and Golf Course** borders the coastal road. A beacon to the northwest point, the **California Lighthouse** can be visited by car and on **mountain bike** and **Segway tours.**

Santa Cruz, Paradera, and Piedra Plat

Aruba's inland residential areas of Santa Cruz, Paradera, and Piedra Plat are home to interesting **rock formations, native architecture,** and **inexpensive guesthouses,** all allowing visitors to immerse themselves in authentic island life. Santa Cruz borders Aruba's national park, protecting indigenous flora and fauna.

Hikers find just what they love on the trails of **Arikok National Park.** Make the trek to Aruba's highest point, **Seroe Jamanota,** or visit **Conchi (Natural Pool),** within the preserve, the best example of the dramatic lava rock formations on

Aruba. This is horseback and UTV country. Easy **spelunking** can be found in **Quadirikiri and Fontein Caves** on the far side of the park. Meet local fauna at the **Donkey Sanctuary** or go **rock climbing** among formations at **Casibari.** Collectors can sift through **antiques at Rococo Plaza** in Paradera.

San Nicolas, Savaneta, and Pos Chiquito

The unspoiled and **secluded coves** of Aruba's eastern end are favorite spots for **kitesurfers, sunbathers,** and **snorkelers.** The south side is known for **pristine beaches** with stunning turquoise seas. A barrier reef following the coast is home to some of the island's **best scuba spots.**

Meet and interact with islanders at **authentic local fish restaurants** along the shore. The **Museum of Industry** and **San Nicolas Community Museum** provide fascinating glimpses into, respectively, the economic development of San Nicolas and its multicultural community. On the outskirts of the town is the spiritually atmospheric **Lourdes Grotto.**

Before You Go

High and Low Seasons

Unlike resort destinations at more northern latitudes, Aruba has the advantage of eternal summer, with little change between the seasons. The most expensive peak travel time is December 15-April 15. This is also when the island is most crowded. Room rates are lowest in September and early October, when visitors can walk into any restaurant without a reservation and enjoy a deserted beach. Other surprisingly quiet times are the 10 days before Christmas and the week after New Year's. The spectacular pageantry of Carnival dominates Aruba from the first weekend in January until Ash Wednesday (Feb.-early Mar.). The last two weeks in particular are filled with parades and musical events.

Passports, Visas, and Vaccinations

Valid current passports are required for visitors from the United States and Canada. Aruban immigration requires that officials see a return ticket upon arrival. An Embarkation-Disembarkation form, or ED-Card, is issued to visitors on the plane prior to arrival to fill in and give to Aruban immigration. Nationals of most countries are required to have a visa to enter Aruba. Besides the United States and Canada, exemptions are made for the European Union's Schengen countries, the United Kingdom, Ireland, and Colombian and Jamaican nationals coming from the United States with valid U.S. residence permits or U.S. visas.

Transportation

Aruba's Reina Beatrix International Airport has daily flights from the United States and Canada. Several cruise ship lines include Oranjestad Harbor on their agenda. Once on the island, visitors will find ample, if pricey, taxis. It

cruise ship

is easy to rent **mopeds, cars,** and **jeeps,** or arrange minibuses to chauffeur large groups. Some are equipped for people with disabilities. None of the major hotels provide airport shuttle service, so taxis are the most common means of transfer. A strip of **car rental agencies** is just outside the airport arrivals terminal. The **public bus system, Arubus,** also serves major resorts and residential areas. Buses stop frequently in front of the hotels to take visitors to Oranjestad. For touring, readily available options are **UTVs, 4WDs, Segways,** and Harley-Davidson **motorcycles.** For visits over major holiday weeks, make car rental reservations well in advance. If you plan to spend your week relaxing on the beach, it is not really necessary to rent a car; nightlife and diverse dining options are within easy walking distance of most resorts.

Baby Beach

enjoying drinks at Bugaloe beach bar and grill

The Best of Aruba

Aruba's principal attractions are its gorgeous beaches and azure waters. Still, it is worth traveling beyond the beaches to explore the unique topography of the island and its culture. Main tourist areas offer myriad choices for dining and nightlife, but you will also find excellent eateries in less-trafficked places. Free musical entertainment can be had at several venues. The most stunning show, however, is the colorful sunset along Aruba's western shore. Hotel beach bars and independent lounges offer happy-hour prices while you enjoy this spectacle, which can segue into a romantic dinner right on the beach.

Day 1

After you have settled into your accommodations, run down to the beach to savor the sunset while taking advantage of happy hour. Look for 2-for-1 cocktails at most hotel bars and nearby cafés. If you're staying in the Palm Beach area, try **Bugaloe** at the end of the **De Palm Pier.** If you're staying in the Manchebo Beach area,

enjoy a gourmet fresh fish entrée beachside at **Ricardo's** in the **Aruba Beach Club.**

After hours, take in some free live music at Palm Beach's **Arawak Gardens, Fusion Wine and Piano Bar** in the **Alhambra Shopping Bazaar,** or at the bandstand by the water at the **Renaissance Marketplace** in Oranjestad. If it's a weekend, find a great band and fun crowd at **Café Chaos** across the street from Renaissance Marketplace or at **South Beach Lounge** in Palm Beach.

Day 2

On Sunday, check out the luxurious brunch at **Windows on Aruba** at the **Divi Links** or all you can eat waffles and pancakes at **Ché Bar** in Palm Beach. Enjoy an exhilarating morning stroll or jog along the paths parallel to Eagle Beach or following the shore from the Marriott to Malmok. If you prefer, refresh your chi with yoga on the beach at the **Manchebo Beach Resort.** For a true introduction to pampering and relaxation,

Okeanos Spa will take you out to Renaissance Island for a treatment in their private cove.

After breakfast, head over to the Butterfly Farm in Palm Beach for your first real outing—it won't be your last visit; all subsequent trips to the farm for the week are free. Butterflies are most active in the morning. Those eager to learn to snorkel or dive should join a sailing and snorkeling tour. Dive operators like Dive Aruba will have you exploring under the water in a few short hours. Quick morning courses allow novices to dive at one of the easier dive sites around the west coast, or snorkelers can enjoy a trip to the *Antilla* shipwreck and Arashi Beach.

Share a romantic dinner on the beach at Elements at the Bucuti & Tara Beach Resort, or book a private sail and dinner for two on the *Tranquilo.* Afterward, stroll along the Palm Beach promenade for some souvenir shopping. Stay until late to party at Gusto.

Day 3

Catch a bus to Oranjestad for the day. Explore the landmark buildings that house the National Archaeological Museum Aruba (NAMA) and the Aruba Historical Museum located within Fort Zoutman.

Check out a charming lunch spot with a view of the harbor at The Paddock, or meet island movers and shakers at their favorite power lunch restaurant Aquarius. Break up the day by indulging in an underwater adventure on the *Atlantis* Submarines. For dinner, enjoy authentic regional cuisine at Excelencia, or a romantic meal on the water at Pinchos Grill and Bar.

Day 4

Today, get away from both beach and town and do some touring with Madi's Magical Tours, a highly personalized, unique safari tour with a dawn trip to Conchi (Natural Pool) on the north coast. From there, Madi can take you on an outback adventure lasting all or part of a day.

You can also choose to rent a 4WD vehicle to tour on your own: Start the day by watching the sunrise from the California Lighthouse. From there, head down the north coast road, or make your way back to Noord and take in such sights as

the Butterfly Farm

historic buildings in Oranjestad

Conchi, the Natural Pool

fish course at Senses

Alto Vista Chapel, Philip's Animal Garden, and Santa Ana Church. Venturing farther along the coast in a 4WD, follow the gravel road to the Bushiribana Gold Ruin and the Aruba Ostrich Farm. After scrambling around the Ayo Rock Formation, explore the countryside even further on horseback with Gold Mine Ranch.

Unwind from an exhausting day of touring with a sunset "toes in the sand" dinner at Pure Ocean at the Divi Phoenix Beach Resort in Palm Beach.

Day 5

Enjoy a day of hiking or horseback riding in Arikok National Park and the caves and coves beyond. A hearty but inexpensive breakfast of arepas can be had at Cheo's Corner in Paseo Herencia Shopping Mall in Palm Beach before you venture out into the wilds. Paved roads within the park allow exploration by car, or park rangers can guide you on various hiking paths, such as Cunucu Arikok Trail, or to the summit of Seroe Jamanota. A trek to Conchi (Natural Pool) will take up a morning or nearly the entire

day. Enjoy a lunch of authentic Aruban cuisine at Urataka Center on the road leading to the park. Call Rancho Loco if you'd prefer to take the tour on horseback.

If you booked online months in advance, you can savor a gourmet dinner at Senses, in the Bucuti & Tara Beach Resort. This is a long, full, and entertaining evening of socializing with the chef and sommelier while watching them prepare a delicious dinner.

Day 6

Try one of Oranjestad's many early-morning eateries, such as Smit & Dorlas Coffee House. Drive to San Nicolas to soak in the scenery of "Sunrise City" and experience a real Caribbean town. Take a dip at Baby Beach or Roger's Beach, two of the most beautiful inlets on Aruba. You can also set up diving or snorkeling trips in this area with JADS Dive Shop. While in San Nicolas, don't miss out on an excellent lunch at the picturesque O'Niel Caribbean Kitchen.

On the way back from San Nicolas, stop at

Zeerover, on the water in Savaneta, for fresh fish island-style, an authentic Caribbean experience. From there, you can easily stop at Mangel Halto for a relaxing swim. For a full day of water fun, families can skip the excursion in favor of the Aruba Waterpark off the Oranjestad-Santa Cruz road. They have a nice kitchen featuring local cuisine and barbecue.

Returning from the south side of the island takes you past the Orange Mall on the Sasaki Highway, which houses Red Fish restaurant, an affordably priced haven for fresh-caught fish and island cuisine.

Day 7

Dig into a buffet breakfast at La Vista to fuel up for windsurfing or kitesurfing lessons with Aruba Active Vacations. For a real thrill, try Skydive Aruba in the field across the road from the windsurfing center. Scuba is a no-no less than 24 hours before departure, but sailing and snorkeling are always an option. Try something really different by exploring the south shore with Aruba Kayak Adventures, which includes lunch, or opt for a customized surfing tour with Aruba Surf School.

In the evening hours you can pick up some last-minute souvenirs and explore the hot spots at Arawak Gardens. It is also a good time to give in and buy that pair of earrings that caught your fancy at Gemstones International on the Palm Beach strip or go back for one of the exquisite handcrafted accessories at The Village mall's flea market. Combine shopping with some island history and culture while enjoying the Waltzing Waters at Paseo Herencia Shopping Mall. Finish the day at Kalin's in Palm Beach Plaza for tasty Mexican food, giant drinks, and some of the friendliest staff on the island.

Baby Beach

festive scene at The Village mall flea market

Local Culture

Islanders love to share their culture and traditions with visitors, particularly around holidays and during Carnival season.

MUSEUMS

National Archaeological Museum Aruba

A number of digs has resulted in a huge collection of ceramics and artifacts linked to the prehistoric inhabitants of Aruba (page 85).

Aruba Historical Museum

This museum is housed in Fort Zoutman and provides an overview of the cultural development of the island through prehistoric, colonial, and modern times (page 87).

Museum of Industry

In one of Aruba's landmark water towers, this museum houses artifacts and interactive exhibits to portray the island's economic development and the individuals who contributed to it (page 99).

San Nicolas Community Museum

Located inside the picturesque Nicolaas Store, a protected island landmark, this museum is dedicated to the multicultural nature of Aruba's "Sunrise City," San Nicolas (page 99).

FESTIVALS AND EVENTS

Carnival

Lasting from early January to Ash Wednesday, Carnival season includes spectacular parades and original music, flaunting island culture at its loudest and most jubilant (page 150).

Betico Day

January 25 is the birthday of one of Aruba's most celebrated statesmen, Gilberto Francois "Betico" Croes, and features a show in Plaza Betico Croes accompanied by food and handicrafts (page 151).

Himno y Bandera Day

Celebrating Aruban independence means a flurry of festivities for days prior to the March 18 event (page 151).

Aruba Historical Museum

Caribbean Sea Jazz Festival

The last weekend in September means two nights of local, regional, and international artists performing innovative music at bargain prices (page 154).

Paseo Herencia Shopping Mall Cultural Shows

Six nights a week, Paseo Herencia in Palm Beach hosts a free cultural show beginning at 8pm, with each night highlighting some aspect of local modern or folkloric dance and music (page 150).

Bon Bini Festival

Every Tuesday evening at Fort Zoutman, the Bon Bini Festival provides a taste of Carnival, with a focus on folkloric dance, music, and traditions (page 150).

Best Water Sports

Sailing and Snorkeling Cruises
OCTOPUS CRUISES
As the only tour boat in Aruba without a motor, Octopus Cruises offers an authentic sailing experience, with snorkeling stops at sites where the fish flock as well as one of the most impressive wrecks in the Caribbean, the *Antilla,* when conditions permit (page 58).

TRANQUILO
Enjoy "toes in the water" sailing on the beautiful ketch *Tranquilo,* which tours Aruba's south side snorkel sites. This is one of the few boats that runs all-day trips—and the only one offering the personal expertise and congenial presence of Captain Anthony and his family (page 58).

Scuba Diving
DIVE ARUBA
Personal service, customized to experience and ability, is the Dive Aruba trademark. Veteran dive master Clive Paula takes experienced divers to out-of-the-way sites (page 60).

JADS DIVE SHOP
JADS provides courses for novices and regularly scheduled tours for certified divers. The instructors and dive masters are friendly and capable (page 61).

Windsurfing, Kitesurfing, and Surfing
ARUBA ACTIVE VACATIONS
Develop a windsurfing obsession with the congenial instructors at Aruba Active Vacations, one of

Octopus Cruises offers various boating options.

Skilled kitesurfers jump the sandbars.

the best outfitters on the island, with a large inventory of equipment designed for surfers of all abilities (page 66).

ARUBA SURF SCHOOL
Instructor Dennis Martinez is passionate about surfing and customizes lessons to his students' abilities and experience, scouting out the best surf on any given day (page 67).

Parasailing, Tubing, Banana Boats, and WaveRunners
FUN 4 EVERY 1
In front of the Riu Palace resort, Fun 4 Every 1 has four boats for tubing, parasailing, and banana boat rides (page 67).

NATIVE DIVERS WATERSPORTS
Native Divers Watersports pays attention to safety while providing a fun time for the whole family, whether you're interested in a banana boat ride or parasailing (page 67).

Deep-Sea Fishing
The principal departure points for fishing boats are Oranjestad Harbor and Hadicurari Pier, at the north end of Palm Beach. Crews clean your catch and take it to a recommended restaurant to have it prepared for your dinner.

DRIFTWOOD FISHING CHARTERS
Driftwood is named after the owner's popular seafood restaurant, where they will cook your catch. Captain Herby has a passion for the sport, and since he has to provide the catch for the restaurant's dinner menu, he's highly motivated to find the fish (page 65)!

MELINA CHARTERS
Melina departs from Hadicurari Pier, close to the Palm Beach resorts. Captain Piet is an amiable host with a love of the sport and keen knowledge of the best fishing grounds (page 66).

ACCOMMODATIONS

Villa Sunflower
The vibrant art of the hostess adorns every aspect of this cozy guesthouse in Bakval, a peaceful home close to Palm Beach with the opportunity to learn the art of mosaic (page 187).

Beach House Aruba
On the water at the outskirts of Palm Beach, the friendly hosts at this delightful guesthouse are central to its charm. Convenience, great rates, and a casual atmosphere give this house a true island feel (page 187).

Seabreeze Apartments
A charming complex of studio apartments minutes from Mangel Halto Beach, Seabreeze offers an escape from the Palm Beach crowds (page 194).

FOOD

Cuminda criollo (local cuisine) is admittedly heavy on starches and fried food, but you will always go home full without walloping your wallet. For health-conscious yet affordable dining, stick to fresh-caught local fish and stews.

Casa Vieja
The most authentic Colombian restaurant on Aruba, Casa Vieja, on the eastern outskirts of Oranjestad, serves huge mixed-meat platters. Eat and drink like royalty for pennies (page 111).

Terrazza Italiana
Enjoy a romantic meal on this terraced restaurant within the Paradise Beach Villas. Centrally located, Terrazza Italiana offers spectacular views and great pizza and pasta without the high prices (page 120).

Zeerover
Everyone's favorite place for fresh fish and shrimp, Zeerover is a glorified fish shack right on the water in Savaneta. Dine on the dock or under the canopy with ice-cold beer, pool tables, and TVs showing the latest soccer matches (page 135).

meal at O'Niel Caribbean Kitchen

O'Niel Caribbean Kitchen
For regional fare, this restaurant is unquestionably Aruba's best. Superb fresh fish, revelatory oxtail stew, and other excellent food makes it worth the trip to San Nicolas (page 136).

ENTERTAINMENT

Renaissance Marketplace
The bandstand at the waterside in Renaissance Marketplace in Oranjestad features various bands: classic rock, folk, pop, Latin, reggae, mellow, or metal (page 141).

Arawak Gardens
Singers and musicians take the stage in a centralized gazebo at Arawak Gardens in Palm Beach. Five different restaurant terraces allow patrons to linger over dinner or drinks in this amiable alfresco setting (page 144).

Romantic Rendezvous

Beaches
PUNTO BRABO
This wide stretch of beach north of the Costa Linda Resort is filled with large clusters of sea grape and greenery offering plenty of private spots to cuddle up and watch the sunset (page 45).

Cruises
TRANQUILO
In addition to day trips, the *Tranquilo* offers a private catered dinner for two with champagne at sunset (page 58).

RED SAIL SPORTS DINNER CRUISE
Sample an elegant dinner with wine and a champagne toast while cruising the coast and watching the sunset (page 64).

Spas
OKEANOS SPA
Couples can have a massage session in a private cove on Renaissance Island, with stunning views of the sea (page 81).

ZOIA
At the Hyatt Regency Resort in Palm Beach, ZoiA has a special room for couples, with a giant bath and private terrace with a beautiful view (page 81).

Waterfront Restaurants
PINCHOS GRILL AND BAR
On the water at Surfside Beach, Pinchos was designed to stoke romantic embers, with couches and hammocks for two along with sunset views (page 106).

relaxing on Renaissance Island

Aruba Ocean Villas

LA PLAYA TORCHLIGHT DINNER AT THE HILTON ARUBA CARIBBEAN RESORT

With one of the longest stretches of sand in Palm Beach, the Hilton is a sweet spot from which to watch the sunset, and offers the most reasonably priced private beachside dining (page 124).

LA TRATTORIA EL FARO BLANCO

Next to the California Lighthouse, La Trattoria El Faro Blanco offers spectacular sunset views from a charming terrace overlooking the northwest coast (page 132).

ZEEROVER

Although this is a family restaurant, tables out on the dock of this waterside spot offer an escape from the crowds, where you can enjoy fresh seafood and stunning sunsets (page 135).

Waterfront Accommodations

ARUBA REEF APARTMENTS

Book the ultimate island fantasy: These waterside apartments offer seclusion and a private beach to make honeymooners (or honeymooners at heart) feel like they are the only people in world (page 195).

ARUBA OCEAN VILLAS

Six thatched-roof beachfront bungalows—some perched on the water—along with a gorgeous bar and restaurant make this an ideal island retreat (page 197).

Family Fun

SURFSIDE BEACH

With a shoreline sheltered by a barrier reef, Surfside Beach has extremely quiet, shallow waters. An adjacent restaurant sports a kiddie pool and provides service on the beach (page 43).

PALM BEACH

Wave action is negligible and the shallow water is ideal for youngsters. It's also close to the resorts, beach toys, refreshments, and restrooms (page 47).

BABY BEACH

The breakwaters at Baby Beach create a tranquil lagoon rimmed with a circle of soft sand. Public *palapas* are scattered along the shore for shade. Vendors rent beach chairs and sell snacks (page 52).

ARUBA WATERPARK

Eminently affordable, this collection of slides ranges from kiddie to killer. It also has a great place for lunch. There is a playground for a change of pace (page 67).

BUTTERFLY FARM

The Butterfly Farm amazes kids and adults alike with an entertaining introduction to the beautiful world of exotic insects (page 89).

PHILIP'S ANIMAL GARDEN

Become intimately acquainted with exotic animals saved from neglect at this nonprofit refuge (page 91).

ARUBA OSTRICH FARM

An encounter with the world's largest birds at the Ostrich Farm in Matividiri is informative, fun, and always surprising (page 92).

family jumping into the ocean

DONKEY SANCTUARY

Enjoy a hands-on session with the residents of Aruba's wild donkey population in Bringamosa. The staff allows children to share in the animals' care (page 94).

DREAM BOWL

At the Palm Beach Plaza mall, Dream Bowl has eight lanes with neon-glowing gutters and balls, complemented by arcade games, air hockey, and foosball tables (page 144).

WALTZING WATERS

The free *Waltzing Waters* show in the Paseo Herencia Shopping Mall goes on four times nightly on the half-hour, 7:30pm-10:30pm (page 150).

Explore the Outback

Exploring Aruba's wilds is an interesting proposition, especially when trying to follow directions or looking for road signs, which are in short supply. Ensure a frustration-free day with the must-see sights by taking a tour with an enthusiastic and knowledgeable guide.

Safari Tours

PRIVATE TOURS ARUBA

Feel like a VIP while you explore in an air-conditioned SUV, choosing from fixed or customized itineraries (page 69).

MADAGASCAR ARUBA ADVENTURE

Madagascar is a small tour operator with a friendly guide, Alfredo, who doesn't hurry passengers and takes them past the most interesting sights (page 70).

Motorcycle, All-Terrain Vehicle, and Trike Tours

Fun and funky modes of transport make getting to the tour sights as exciting as the destinations themselves.

TRIKES

The ultimate car-motorcycle-ATV hybrid, trikes allow passengers and drivers complete comfort while touring in style. Trikes can cover tough terrain, and heads will turn wherever you go (page 71).

ARUBA MOTORCYCLE TOURS & RENTALS

The thrill of zipping along island roads on these giant Harley-Davidson motorcycles is great fun, and their ability to traverse some of the worst trails provides one of the best touring experiences (page 71).

ATV tour

atop Aruba's highest point, Seroe Jamanota

Horseback Tours

Aruba's principal mode of transport from colonial times is still one of the best ways to explore off the beaten track.

RANCHO LOCO

Ideally located close to Arikok National Park and some of the most dramatic trails, Rancho Loco picks up and returns guests to their resorts by van. Tours can take you to spots such as Conchi (page 75).

GOLD MINE RANCH

Riding enthusiasts encounter alternate trails and sights within Arikok National Park on the menu of Gold Mine Ranch. Guides take riders to sites along the coast or inland (page 75).

Hiking Trails

Arikok National Park is Aruba's hiking center, where trails have been groomed, timed, and measured for degree of difficulty. Rangers are on hand to lead groups for a nominal fee.

CUNUCU ARIKOK TRAIL

This popular trail offers a chance to study endemic flora and fauna along with a genuinely restored landmark farmhouse (page 77).

NATURAL POOL TRAIL TO CONCHI

Two trails can take hikers to Conchi. Find forest trails, dramatic rock formations along the coastline, and secluded beaches for a cooling swim (page 77).

SEROE JAMANOTA TRAIL

Aruba's highest point, Seroe Jamanota, offers two access routes: Reaching the summit can be a relaxing morning stroll or a hard-core adventure. Either way, the reward is stunning vistas (page 78).

Beaches

Oranjestad............42

Eagle Beach and Manchebo
    Beach 45

Palm Beach, Malmok, and
    Noord 47

North Coast...........49

San Nicolas, Savaneta, and
    Pos Chiquito.........52

Caribbean islands are synonymous with beauti-ful beaches, but veteran travelers will tell you that Aruba's are exceptional. Aruba has been hailed as one of the top beach destinations in the world. Its soft, snowy white sands (a composition of coral and shells crushed into a fine powder over eons) and the breathtaking blue waters make sunbathing, beachcombing, and swimming popular pastimes here. Although the temperature is consistently warm, Aruba's beaches are never too hot for a barefoot stroll, even at noon.

Palm Beach and Eagle Beach are the most raved about on the island, with fine accommodations along their shores. The uninterrupted miles of sand are the main attraction for both visitors and developers. Unquestionably, the nature of Aruba's beaches has dictated the

Highlights

Look for ★ to find recommended sights, activities, dining, and lodging.

★ **Eagle Beach:** Eagle Beach is one of the best beaches on the island and offers many of the same amenities as Palm Beach—with fewer people and slightly bigger waves (page 45).

★ **Palm Beach:** Aruba's principal playground has every manner of amenity and activity available within a few steps of your beach lounge. It also has the quietest waters of the long beachfronts (page 47).

★ **Baranca Plat:** You'll enjoy calm waters, snowy white sands, and the feeling of having a special place in the sun all to yourself at this cozy little cove, a short walk from the big resorts (page 47).

★ **Fisherman's Huts:** Relax among the dunes and take in the colorful sails speeding across the water at this windsurfing beach (page 47).

★ **California Dunes:** This expansive area is scenic and private—great for long walks and topless sunbathing (page 49).

★ **Andicuri Beach:** Dramatic terraces of limestone formations surround this secluded beach. The wave action here is perfect for body surfing (page 49).

★ **Black Stone Beach:** Named for the lava stones found along the shore, this beach also has natural rock bridges that make for beautiful photo ops (page 50).

★ **Baby Beach and Roger's Beach:** Two of Aruba's most beautiful beaches are within the remains of the old Lago Colony. Both have artificial lagoons great for swimming, surrounded by long stretches of white sands, and are bordered by greenery and carved stone cliffs (page 52).

★ **Mangel Halto:** Lush greenery surrounds this secluded beach, a series of interconnected coves that are perfect for getting away from the crowds (page 54).

degree of development of resort areas as well as their character. It was long ago decided that Palm Beach offered the "best beachfront," though, of course, vacationers who return to Manchebo Beach and Eagle Beach year after year are confident that they're staying at the best.

Along Palm Beach, the shallow water extends almost a half mile from the shore with negligible wave action, ideal for families with young children. The extremely shallow water is perfect for a baby's first encounter with the sea. Swimming areas are well-marked, patrolled, and maintained.

Eagle Beach is not quite as maintained and patrolled as Palm Beach, but all the resorts in Aruba take responsibility for the safety of their beachfronts. As more resorts crop up, more cordoned-off swim sections will appear. There is stronger wave action at Eagle Beach, and particularly Manchebo Beach, as the bottom suddenly drops off very close to shore. The current at Punto Brabo, where the southern shore meets the west and various currents collide, also contributes to bigger waves. This makes it very popular with surfers and bodyboarders. Other great spots favored for bodyboarding or waveboarding are Andicuri, Dos Playa, and Urirama, all on Aruba's north coast, where heavy winds from the northeast result in strong waves.

Oranjestad

Oranjestad's beaches are artificial, carved from the harbor and created by dumping sand in the early 1950s. Jetties have established some very calm coves and small stretches of beachfront.

DRUIF BEACH

The relatively wide, public **Druif Beach** (J. E. Irausquin Blvd. at the western outskirts of town) is an extension of the beachfront from the Tamarijn Beach Resort. It provides a great deal of greenery, shade trees, and areas cleared for small campfires or grills. You will likely find island families here on weekends. The water is shallow and quiet, nice for small children. A cautionary note: Before you lay out a towel on the grass, check for patches of plants with tenacious thistles, common during the dry season.

In 2018, the abandoned remains of the Bushiri Beach Hotel, which bordered Druif Beach, were finally torn down, and Druif Beach was radically extended. The area is now a public park, and there are plans to construct toilets, benches, and possibly a volleyball court in the area. Across the road from the beach are two supermarkets with restrooms and snack and drink options. Behind them is Ling & Sons, a supermarket with a café offering fresh smoothies, sandwiches, and a salad bar.

GOVERNOR'S BEACH

Just past the Renaissance complex is a bridge over a lagoon that divides Oranjestad's commercial area from the residential neighborhoods. This headland is informally named **Governor's Beach** (L. G. Smith Blvd. by Lagoonweg, on the east side of Wilhelmina Park) because it sits across from the traditional residence of Aruba's governor. It has some thatched *palapas* for shade, a restroom, and a boardwalk. Overlooking the waterfront is a charming restaurant called West Deck. In the middle of the beach is a striking monument dedicated to local fishers lost at sea. The area marks the beginning of a long stretch of narrow beach extending east along L. G. Smith Boulevard to Surfside, interspersed

---

Previous: Eagle Beach; Baby Beach; Arashi Beach.

Free Use of All Beaches

By law, all of Aruba's beaches are public within 20 meters (65 ft) of the waterline. This includes all the beaches along Palm Beach and Eagle Beach, regardless of the resorts. Blue pillars signal the dividing line. Resort personnel cannot prevent anyone from sitting on a public beach, though they can evict you from the lounges, which belong to the resorts and are reserved for guests. Interlopers are usually detected by their towels.

The thatched *palapas*, or "chikies," along the shore are maintained by the resorts. By law, if they are on the public section of the beach, then technically they are available to anyone without charge. Anyone can lay out on the sand or use a *palapa* for shade as long as they are within 20 meters of the waterline, except at De Palm Island and Renaissance Island, where the owners have the legal right to limit access. Homes that are situated on the water, such as in Malmok or Savaneta, have to respect the same 20-meter rule, and homeowners cannot claim the entire shorefront.

This practice ensures that the beaches belong to the Aruban people and island guests. It is only fair that islanders should not be prohibited from enjoying the natural assets that are their heritage. Beaches are a way of life for Arubans, accessible at all hours. Beach tags and usage fees are never required—beaches are always free to all.

with limestone terraces and ending at the airport runways.

The L. G. Smith beachfront is exceptionally quiet and shallow, good for little ones. There are lots of shade trees along the shore masking the area from L. G. Smith Boulevard and its busy traffic. Many locals come to this beach to set out on their boats or Jet Skis.

SURFSIDE BEACH

In front of the Talk of the Town Resort is the Plaza Turismo, the main plaza of the first section of the **Linear Park** (beach entrance is around either side of the plaza between the airport and Reflexions, at the east end of L. G. Smith Blvd.). The miles of dirt paths bordering L. G. Smith Boulevard have manicured jogging and cycling lanes, gardens, and periodic restrooms and open-air showers. This area and its beachfront have had a number of incarnations but are still referred to as **Surfside.**

The beach is a wide curving cove of white sand and very quiet waters. This is often where sailboats go for safe harbor when the western shore turns rough. Since this beach is popular with Europeans, you may encounter some topless sunbathers. Everything you need for a luxurious day at the beach are here: two nice restaurants and bars as well as a small pool.

The Surfside Café is a pleasant and economical place for a meal and exotic drinks. There is a small splash park with various mini slides.

The chic **Reflexions Lounge** (L. G. Smith Blvd. 1A, 297/582-0153, www.beach-aruba.com, 10am-10pm daily) features a shaded interior dining room that opens to the sea and a sunny terrace. Food and drink service is available to sunbathers on their beach lounges.

RENAISSANCE ISLAND

Guests at the Renaissance Resort have unlimited access to **Renaissance Island** (300 m/330 yd off Aruba's south shore, just north of the airport, 800/421-8188 or 297/583-6000, www.marriott.com, access only by boat, nonguest day pass $100), one of Aruba's nicest beaches. There are two sections connected by boardwalks, with mangroves and palm trees providing privacy. **Flamingo Beach,** on the western side, is adults-only. Since it is secluded, topless sunbathing is allowed. The flamingos that gives the beach its name keep guests entertained and are quite tame. The eastern half of Renaissance Island offers a large beach for families. The tranquil lagoon is perfect for toddlers. There are also a snack bar, a volleyball court, and a dock for paddleboats.

Water taxis to the island leave from three locations about every 15 minutes: the lobby of

the Marina Tower of the Renaissance Resort; waterside in the harbor, next to the underpass that goes under the L. G. Smith Boulevard; and next to the harbor heliport. Day passes for nonguests include lunch at the very charming Papagayo restaurant, a drink, and beach towels. The day pass also allows a choice of one activity: Visitors can snorkel, kayak, or use a paddleboat.

Okeanos Spa (297/583-6000, www. okeanosspaaruba.com) has an outlet adjacent to Flamingo Beach called The Cove. Purchasing a massage at this spa also gives you access to the island, but no other amenities. There is an additional charge ($25 pp) if you are not a guest of the resort.

Eagle Beach and Manchebo Beach

These two shore areas border the southwestern curve of Aruba and are renowned as one of the longest beachfronts in the Caribbean. Condominium complexes are rapidly taking over Eagle Beach, but there are still some areas that remain deserted. Large clusters of greenery offer both privacy and shade.

These beaches are an important nesting area for local and visiting sea turtles early spring to late autumn. During turtle season, you might see a giant leatherback lay her eggs or new hatchlings struggling to the sea. The local foundation TurtugAruba keeps an eye on these events and takes steps to protect them from disruption. Visitors are asked to report any turtle activity to them.

MANCHEBO BEACH

The wide expanse of **Manchebo Beach,** on the southwestern point of the island, is lined with small resorts that provide sunbathers with plenty of space. Unlike at larger hotels, you will not feel crowded or packed together. Holiday weeks are busy everywhere, but here you can still enjoy an isolated island getaway. Most of the shorefront resorts are only two stories high, and there are rooms directly on the beach. The smaller resorts have a well-established European clientele, but the timeshare beaches are primarily frequented by North Americans and Latin Americans.

PUNTO BRABO

Huge old sea grape trees stand along the shore just where Manchebo and Eagle Beaches meet at **Punto Brabo or "Rough Point"** (access via the south lane of J. E. Irausquin Blvd.), a very wide beach that fronts the Bucuti and Costa Linda Resorts. This southwest curve of the island has strong currents, and the bottom drops off close to shore. The beach is a stunning expanse of brilliant white sand. Visitors often mention the great wave action for body surfing. Care should be taken with young children. Green areas offer shelter and secluded spots to string up a hammock or set up a grill—which islanders will frequently do on weekends. There is ample parking just north of Costa Linda Resort. A cute little day café with restrooms is just north of the Costa Linda Resort.

★ EAGLE BEACH

The sea is quiet on **Eagle Beach** (J. E. Irausquin Blvd. between La Quinta Beach Resort and the north end of Amsterdam Manor Beach Resort), which is nearly deserted. The far northern edge is marked by Aruba's famous twin fofoti trees, a popular photo site.

Since the resorts along Eagle Beach are all across the street, the wide shorefront of soft sugary sand is sparsely populated, as many guests stay on the pool decks. On weekends, however, it is busy with island residents. The past scarcity of resorts meant Eagle Beach

---

1: Flamingo Beach on Renaissance Island; 2: bar at Surfside Beach

was considered a "local" beach, with parking along the shore. It is not unusual to find families or groups camping here. During Easter vacation, called Semana Santa, the beach is filled end to end with islanders' tents.

Resorts do have a presence on the sand, however. The La Cabana and Amsterdam Manor hotels have set up beach bars at the northern end of Eagle Beach. Some condos along this stretch have erected *palapas* for shade. Resorts have amenities along the shore for their patrons, such as lounges and shade structures. Passersby can often find unused and unattended *palapas* and lounges on the beach. Snack wagons are set up around the lunch hour.

Palm Beach, Malmok, and Noord

One of the most famous beaches in the world, Aruba's Palm Beach offers lakelike waters and every convenience imaginable. This is the center and departure point for 90 percent of water activities on the island. Except for the all-inclusive resorts of Riu Palace, Riu Antillean, and Barceló, the beach hotels welcome passersby to their beachfront restaurants, shops, and bars. Clean modern restrooms are always close at hand.

★ PALM BEACH

Palm Beach (from south of the Divi Phoenix Beach Resort to the north end of the Ritz-Carlton) is truly a world-class dream beach—an endless stretch of soft white sand and gentle surf. It's Aruba's principal playground, which makes it a busy, crowded place, and a perfect spot to make friends and socialize. The water is the calmest of Aruba's large beaches, so it's a favorite for families.

★ BARANCA PLAT

Just south of Palm Beach is a small cove called **Baranca Plat or "Flat Stone"** (turn off on the water side where the road divider begins on J. E. Irausquin Blvd., just north of the Blue Residences complex). Find seclusion among the sea grape trees, with the conveniences of Palm Beach a five-minute walk away. It's a tranquil option for a break from the busier beaches. The surrounding jetties produce quiet water and no waves, with the shallow depth making it excellent for little children. Pelicans and gulls fill the jetties for an entertaining show. No signs mark this beach; you'll know it by a platform where WaveRunners are tethered. It is just minutes south of the main resorts and across from Blue Residences.

★ FISHERMAN'S HUTS

North of Palm Beach, beyond the Ritz-Carlton, is the windsurfing and kitesurfing capital of Aruba, with a number of operations teaching both, along with places for refreshments and shade. This stretch, **Fisherman's Huts** (L. G. Smith Blvd. across from Bakval), is named for the tiny huts of generations of fishing families; the name remains but the huts were removed to make way for a resort. This beach is popular with islanders. Spend the day watching colorful sails whipping through the waves and the aerial acrobatics of the kitesurfers. Beach access is marked with a sign on L. G. Smith Boulevard, and there is ample parking.

MALMOK BEACH

Malmok Beach (L. G. Smith Blvd. north of Fishermen's Huts) is a short stretch that fronts some of the guest houses along the Malmok strip, south of Boca Catalina. It is marked by the remains of a shipwreck close to the water. Most of it is quite rocky, interspersed with a few sandy areas. Entry to the sea here is also rocky, and the water is shallow for some distance. The ocean is busy with windsurfers and kitesurfers, so care is advised when

1: Eagle Beach; 2: Baranca Plat

Water Safety at the Shore

snorkeler at Boca Catalina

- **Stay in the swim zone:** Before the tourism boom, beachfronts were vast and the population was small. Easygoing islanders rarely gave much thought to safety. As the number of resorts grew, resorts marked off protected areas of the sea for the safety of guests. Today, swim-area markers are maintained by a company that contracts with the hotels. Swimmers and snorkelers should avoid areas beyond the swim zone due to the frequent boat traffic.

- **Keep off the ropes:** Avoid sitting on or clinging to swim-zone barrier ropes. Although they are cleaned regularly, soft corals grow on them that can sting and cause an irritating rash. If you accidentally run into them, a topical steroid can relieve the pain and itching.

- **Be aware of the breeze:** Aruba's cooling offshore breezes have a drawback: They tend to blow objects out to sea—beach balls, floats, and water toys. The gentle wave motion on the water's surface from these breezes is often not noticeable but still steadily moves away from shore. Keep a close eye on youngsters in swim rings and lightweight floats. The outbound surface surge gets stronger the farther you get from shore.

- **Don't fall asleep on a float:** It's is not unheard of for people to wake up far from land. Most small-craft operators keep a rescue boat handy for such events. But even if you don't float away, falling asleep in the Caribbean sun may prove distressing. It is no fun being stuck in a hotel room with a sunburn.

- **Use the buddy system:** Scuba divers are trained never to dive alone. This commonsense rule applies to most water activities. Don't go off by yourself to snorkel; take a buddy and inform someone where you are going and when to expect you back. Dive operators and snorkel charters can provide buddies and keep an eye on patrons. If you are trying a water activity for the first time, having supervision is a good idea.

swimming; it is a better venue for sunbathing. The rocky formations that abut the beach are popular with local fishermen, so snorkelers should watch for fishing line and hooks, and stay close to the beach.

BOCA CATALINA

Bordered by limestone formations, **Boca Catalina** (L. G. Smith Blvd. 501 and 2a/2b Rd., Malmokweg) offers some nice snorkeling. The beach is small but the water is quiet. Boca Catalina is popular for large sailboats to stop during their charter runs.

The road here ends at the south end of the final cluster of waterfront homes. There is a wooden stairway entry at the northern point. Although it is bordered by Malmok's luxurious homes, the beach is public. There are some shaded tables but no facilities. There is limited parking, and it can get busy with islanders on weekends.

ARASHI BEACH

The last beachfront house of Malmok ends at the start of serene **Arashi Beach** (L. G. Smith Blvd., north of the waterfront homes), tailored for the public. A manicured parking lot with chemical toilets, shaded picnic tables, and benches is adjacent to the beach. Every day a colorful wagon selling snacks and snow cones sets up here. Several thatched *palapas* on the beach are maintained by the government, and it is usually crowded with locals on weekends; many islanders take advantage of the amenities for birthday parties and other events. The southern section of the shallow cove is quieter than the northern side, where the waves tend to break with more force.

North Coast

Many coves are scattered along Aruba's north shore, and many are suitable for a beach break while touring the outback, although swimming is not recommended, as riptides are rampant. Body surfing is not recommended due to the heavy waves, although some athletes indulge in it. Keep in mind there are no lifeguards, and help would have to come from far away. Children should be kept out of these waters.

★ CALIFORNIA DUNES

A long, rolling area of Sahara-like dunes, generally referred to as the **California Dunes** (from the turnoff from the west point and paved road, follow the start of a gravel road along the north coast to the base of the lighthouse), is a nice change of scenery from other shorelines. The dunes follow the coast for about a mile in line with the mount of the lighthouse and end at a rough shore not suitable for swimming. In the past it was popular for nude sunbathing, and a few isolated areas offer shelter for that pursuit.

DRUIF AND URIRAMA BEACHES

On the nameless north coast road are **Druif and Urirama Beaches** (Druif is about 2 km/1.2 mi past the California Dunes; Urirama is another 2 km/1.2 mi past Druif). Aside from waveboarders, these beaches attract anglers who have built driftwood shacks on the sand to clean fish and shelter from the sun. Islanders picnic here, but the swimming is not good. Dramatic photo ops of rugged seas crashing onto the cliffs are worth the trip.

★ ANDICURI BEACH

Andicuri Beach (down the winding road leading directly to the sea via the left fork from Ayo Rock Formation) is a wide, pristine beach flanked by dramatic limestone formations and stark trees. Large waves are fun for body surfing. Good swimmers will enjoy the surf, but it may be too much for children. Andicuri is only accessible with an off-road vehicle, and getting here is a scenic journey in itself.

★ BLACK STONE BEACH

From Andicuri Beach, a gravel road along the coast leads to **Black Stone Beach** (1.5 km/1 mi past Andicuri Beach), where a dramatic rock formation has two natural bridges carved from the cliffs. Where the sea meets the shore, the land is covered with the lava pebbles that give the beach its name. These were formed millions of years ago from magma bubbling up in the deep sea. The magma quickly cooled and fragmented, and the waves have made them smooth. It's a fun climb down to the shoreline, and easy enough for youngsters. Waves crash against the shore with great force; this is definitely not a place for swimming.

DAIMARI BEACH

The large and secluded **Daimari Beach** area has two separate coves divided by cliffs. The beaches can be accessed via the Natural Pool Trail in Arikok National Park. Once on the trail, continue north past the Natural Pool for about 500 meters (550 yd) to reach the beach. While parts of the cove have calm waters that little ones can enjoy, most of the beach is better for body surfing. The entire area covers about 100 meters (110 yd) of shore, and conditions vary depending on the wind and the time of year.

DOS PLAYA

Dos Playa are dual coves divided by rock formations, featuring rolling dunes and nice waves. A favorite spot for local bodyboarders, it is not recommended for children, and care should be taken if you are not a strong swimmer. Within Arikok National Park, Dos Playa is also a popular hiking tour destination (Rooi Tambu Trail, 5.5 km/3.4 mi, 2-3 hours round-trip from park welcome center via Mira Lamar pass).

To get here by car, follow the Mira Lamar pass gravel road and signs pointing to Dos Playa through the park for 4 kilometers (2.5 mi) to the crest of a hill, where you can see the beach. From here it is a five-minute walk.

BOCA PRINS

Boca Prins is an enormous cove with a wide beach circled by limestone terraces and outcroppings. Quite secluded, it can be accessed through Arikok National Park (via Rooi Prins Trail ending at Phantage, 5.5 km/3.4 mi from the visitor center), not far from the caves on the eastern end of the island. The sea at Boca Prins is deceptive, with treacherous riptides; don't go too far from shore. Better to sunbathe and enjoy the scenery.

By car, come via Mira Lamar pass. The clearly marked path, paved but winding and narrow, parallels the hiking route to the shore, leading to the eastern end of the park and the caves. Take a break and grab a cold drink from the little snack bar across the road.

1: Dos Playa; 2: natural bridges at Black Stone Beach

San Nicolas, Savaneta, and Pos Chiquito

The eastern and southern coasts feature quiet beaches and excellent swimming. The southern side is rimmed by protective sandbars and reefs, assuring calm waters and some nice snorkeling.

BOCA GRANDE

The name, "Large Mouth," tells you something about this big cove off the northeastern shore. It has a semicircle of soft white sand to work on a tan while watching the colorful kitesurfers jump the waves. Take the same route as to Baby Beach to get to **Boca Grande** (drive through San Nicolas heading east past all the settlements and out toward the former Lago Colony). The beach is by the large red anchor that marks the entry to Lago Colony. On weekends it fills with kitesurfers, which discourages swimming.

★ BABY BEACH AND ROGER'S BEACH

Two of Aruba's loveliest beaches are within the former Lago Colony. A paved road leads to the island's eastern tip, forking at the Rum Reef Bar. To the left is the entrance to Baby Beach, and to the right is Roger's Beach, named for Captain Robert Rogers, who convinced oil company executives to choose Aruba as the place to build their Caribbean refinery.

Baby Beach is a prime swimming destination. The artificial lagoon inside the breakwaters is perfectly still, shallow, and ideal for young children—hence the name. A long, clean circle of white beach surrounds the water, with cliffs of greenery rising to the Lago housing above. It is popular with tours but big enough to provide quiet areas for private sunbathing or swimming. The area is popular with islanders on weekends and is a favorite camping spot during holidays.

The area boasts stunning reefs beyond the breakwater, but the seas that far out are dangerous. The best of the reef is a few hundred yards from shore. Close in, there is a wide barrier of staghorn and elkhorn coral that sometimes breaks the surface. It is easy for the uninitiated snorkeler to get lost within. Coral scrapes are painful and easily get infected. Be watchful not to drift out past the breakwater. Unfortunately, there is little to see within that limit. It is better to arrange a trip to the reef by **JADS Dive Shop** (Seroe Colorado 245E, 297/584-6070, http://jadsaruba.com, $55-95).

Roger's Beach, right next door, is generally ignored by visitors because it stands in the shadow of the refinery. That is a mistake—it is clean and beautiful, with shallow water and snowy sand, and far less traffic than Baby Beach. A few picturesque native fishing boats are moored at the docks at the eastern end of the cove.

SAVANETA BEACH

A road parallel to the main highway between Oranjestad and San Nicolas follows the southern shoreline and allows access to the southside beaches, such as **Savaneta Beach.** To get to the beaches, you cross little wooden bridges placed periodically over the pipes from WEB, Aruba's water plant. Follow the main highway (1A) past the Pos Chiquito rotunda and continue on to Savaneta, then turn right at the gas station and head toward the water. Turn at the first right, which is a paved road. When you are 200 meters (220 yd) past the turn, take a left over a cement crossing over the pipes. The shore is dotted with mangrove clusters, limestone outcroppings, and a secluded stretch of snowy white sand. This beach has quiet crystal-clear water and nice

1: Baby Beach; 2: Savaneta Beach

Easter Week Camping

A time-honored way to celebrate Semana Santa on Aruba is to pack up the family and head to the beach. Islanders set up temporary homes on the shore in anything from pup tents to elaborately outfitted trailers powered by generators. The latter are frequently air-conditioned, with full-size refrigerators and giant plasma TVs. First-time visitors are often under the mistaken impression that this is how islanders live.

Camping on the beach is popular during summer vacation, Christmas, and the school break in the first week of October. This creates traffic snarls at Eagle Beach and Arashi Beach, two favored campsites on the west side of Aruba. Baby Beach and Roger's Beach are lined with camping tents and trailers, and parking in these areas becomes much more difficult.

With more campers comes more trash. The government puts out chemical toilets and extra waste bins to reduce the impact. Ecologically minded organizations and the local waste-removal company Ecotech have made inroads, and a contest for the cleanest campsite at the end of the week yields cash prizes and weekend stays at major resorts.

snorkeling. It is generally ignored, except by the residents of the neighborhood.

★ MANGEL HALTO

The tranquil, sheltered beach of **Mangel Halto** in Pos Chiquito features a series of connected coves with a barrier reef not far from shore. Pass through a break in the mangroves at the far right of the main beach for the best swimming experience. Beyond is an expansive swimming area that starts at standing depth but suddenly drops into a deep bowl before going shallow again. The mangrove roots create a tunnel you can pass through when the waters are low to some even more secluded beaches beyond the main area;

they are not always accessible when the tide is high. Mosquitoes are abundant in the mangroves, so coat yourself in repellent. Shaded tables and *palapas* are available for a picnic and beach day.

To get to Mangel Halto, turn toward the ocean at the Balashi traffic light on Highway 1A. Go to the end of the road at the T-intersection at the water and power plant. Turn left and cross the small bridge over Spaanslagoen. Turn right at the second road past the bridge, where there is a sign for Marina Pirata. Follow this road to the end and turn left. The beach entrance is clearly marked 500 meters (550 yd) farther along Spaanslagoenweg, the road bordering the sea.

Mangel Halto

Recreation

Aruba is a playground for all ages. A primary reason visitors give for returning to Aruba is that "whatever you like to do, Aruba has it all." Clear tropical waters and a lush marine environment are perfect for scuba diving, snorkeling, and every other water sport. Resorts and independent venues host excellent facilities for tennis and golf. Arikok National Park provides a range of hiking and biking options. The best part is that the constant reliable climate lets visitors enjoy their favorite activities in any season.

Tour companies offer a head-spinning number of ways to discover the Aruba outback and major sights. Entrepreneurial islanders are always on the lookout for original ways to show off their homeland. In addition to bus and safari tours, there are trikes (motorcycle-car

Water Activities 57
Land Tours 68
Hiking and Running 77
Golf and Tennis 79
Spas and Yoga 80

Highlights

Look for ★ to find recommended sights, activities, dining, and lodging.

★ **Octopus Cruises:** Enjoy smooth sailing on a wide, three-hulled sailboat (page 58).

★ *Tranquilo:* For sailing fanatics who enjoy the thrill of leaning into the wind, all-day trips on the *Tranquilo* deliver (page 58).

★ **Dive Aruba:** Dive with Clive for smaller groups and out-of-the-way dive spots (page 60).

★ **JADS Dive Shop:** The only dive operator in the Baby Beach area, JADS offers safe dives at a vibrant reef (page 61).

★ **Private Tours Aruba:** Tour the outback in your own luxurious, air-conditioned SUV with a guide, for less than an ATV tour and with a meal included (page 69).

★ **Tours By Locals:** Connect with a local guide and customize your tour itinerary (page 69).

★ **Trikes:** These motorcycle-car hybrids are a popular and fun way to tour the island (page 71).

★ **Rancho Loco:** Outback adventures are even more enjoyable on horseback, a great way to get to Conchi (Natural Pool) and other spots in Arikok National Park (page 75).

★ **Skydive Aruba:** A thrilling and adventurous way to see Aruba is a skydiving trip with an experienced instructor (page 75).

hybrids), Harley-Davidson treks, all-terrain vehicles, and horseback tours. For a journey that is as exciting as the destination, try a 4WD "safari" adventure, with a guide or on your own. Guides can provide knowledgeable commentary while ensuring you see those hard-to-find spots. As with snorkeling and diving, it is always advisable to explore a new area with an experienced guide to get the lay of the land.

Aruba's steady trade winds provide wonderful sailing. Experienced sailors can rent Sunfish sailboats and two-person cats for cruising the coast. Charter boats ply the waters for snorkeling or sunset sails daily. Scuba companies offer novice resort courses as well as dive trips. The island is also a top destination for windsurfing and kitesurfing, and if there is a way to play in the waves, you'll find it within a few steps of major resorts. Aruban waters are marlin country, and deep-sea fishing is available on full- or half-day trips on boats from several locations.

Golfers will delight in two vastly different courses close to the major resorts. Both employ veteran pros and offer clinics. Aruba's gusty winds are an interesting challenge; with a tailwind, some golfers report record drives.

Vacation is also the time to sample day spa treatments, from sumptuous to simple.

Water Activities

Seeing the tropical marine environment for the first time, whether snorkeling or on a scuba dive, has literally changed lives. It can elicit conservation attitudes or dedication to a fascinating pastime. Snorkeling and other water tours are easily arranged through independent booking agents on the beach in front of most resorts.

SNORKEL SITES

Aruban waters provide a variety of dive and snorkel sites. Aside from reef areas, there are wrecks, some purposely placed, such as the *Jane Sea* and the Sonesta airplanes. These soon become havens for fish. Dive operations have mapped out 39 dive spots around Aruba, though many are not appropriate for the casual vacation diver. The most commonly visited sites are popular for calm waters, safe and enjoyable for divers with limited experience. Those with expertise should look to smaller private operators for custom trips to remote locations. Aruba has a few appealing offshore snorkeling sites along the west coast, not far from Palm Beach. It is always advisable to snorkel with a buddy, a required practice for scuba divers. Renting an inflatable snorkel vest is also advisable.

BOCA CATALINA

Bordering Boca Catalina (north of Palm Beach on the west coast, close to Malmokweg), the coastline is a coral wall, rampant with a variety of sealife and a great spot for snorkeling. You don't have to swim far to enjoy the schools of grunts, copperheads, and silversides that shelter under the limestone outcroppings. There are two entry points, but the most interesting sealife is where steps have been carved into the stone, where the houses on the water side begin. Swim north or south of this point.

MANGEL HALTO

Aruba's south side has an extensive reef formation bordering the mangrove reefs along Pos Chiquito, the midpoint of the island. The inner lagoon has some sealife but a sandy bottom. It is enclosed by an extensive outcropping of elkhorn and staghorn coral. The areas facing into the lagoon provide interesting

Previous: Aqua Donut boat via Octopus Cruises; snorkeling cruise; owners and baby foal at Rancho Loco.

snorkeling. Traveling through the reef to the outer areas and the drop-off reefs is best done with an experienced guide who knows the route, as it requires snaking through sharp coral that skims the surface.

SNORKELING CRUISES

★ OCTOPUS CRUISES

One of the longest-running sailing outfitters on Aruba, **Octopus Cruises** (Seroe Janchi 31, departs from Playa Linda beach, 297/560-6565, www.octopusaruba.com, 9am-noon, 1pm-4pm, and 5pm-7pm or 4:30pm-6:30pm daily, $50-70) has a 40-foot trimaran sailboat. Now operated by a congenial family from Holland, the previous owner, Jethro, is still captain. Jethro has been sailing Aruba's waters for decades, and his crew is patient with novice snorkelers. Fish are accustomed to the crew's daily visits and do not shy away.

A champagne brunch trip includes food and drinks along with two snorkel stops, including the *Antilla* shipwreck. Shorter afternoon trips are mostly spent snorkeling at a reef and the wreck, with a snack of Dutch cheese baguettes and fresh fruit. Relaxing sunset sails feature cocktails and snacks but no snorkel stops. An open bar is included for all trips. Wine aficionados may want to look into the three-hour sunset cruise (4:30pm-7:30pm Mon.). The sommelier is Monrick Croes, proprietor of the Wine Room, who selects three wines to showcase, paired with various tapas.

Octopus also offers self-driven Aqua Donut boat rentals ($200-360 per hour). These large circular inflatables, with an outboard motor and expansive sun roofs, come in three sizes, for 2-10 people. You can also rent a personal propulsion device ($50) from Octopus when taking one of its tours. It's a fun way to traverse the water, particularly if you aren't a strong swimmer.

★ TRANQUILO

All-day trips on the 43-foot *Tranquilo* (Alto Vista 34K, departs from Renaissance Harbor, 297/594-2173, www.tranquiloaruba.com, 10am-3pm Tues. and Thurs.-Fri., $85) were made popular decades ago by Captain Mike, a local sailing legend. His son Anthony has kept up the tradition. Offering the only regularly scheduled full-day trips to Aruba's south side, the *Tranquilo* provides toes-in-the-water moments at some of the windier points along the coast. The single keel affords heeling well into the wind, and a real sailor's adventure on the water.

Trips include a secluded snorkel stop at an attractive reef in the Mangel Halto formation, affectionately referred to as "Mike's Reef." A platform on one of the sandbanks facilitates entry and exit. The *Tranquilo* has a regular clientele who come back for the Dutch pea soup that Anthony's mom, Celia, makes for lunch. *Tranquilo* also offers a Romantic Dinner for Two tour (book well in advance, $475), which includes a champagne toast, wine, and a customized menu.

FULL THROTTLE TOURS

Full Throttle Tours (L. G. Smith Blvd. 4, 297/741-8570, U.S. 480/626-0775, www. fullthrottletoursaruba.com, 9:30am-noon and 1:30pm-4pm daily, $67 adults, $52 ages 6-12, charters $600) is an apt name for this hardcore snorkeling outfit. Hosts Tammy and Jay provide the only snorkel tour from Oranjestad Harbor, a great convenience for cruise ship passengers. Full Throttle's 10-person inflatable speedboat is a fast, wild ride up the coast to the *Antilla* shipwreck and Arashi reef area. Captain Bhompi and mate Diego are pleasant company, and Bhompi's knowledge of the *Antilla* wreck is entertaining. The ride back to the south side and Barcadera reef, a beautiful and pristine snorkel spot, is even wilder—the reef is vibrant and healthy, unlike many of the more trafficked areas.

This is a great trip for experienced snorkelers, with currents and surge. Bhompi and Diego are in the water with you to lend a hand if need be, but this is not for the timid or novices. Water, fruit punch, and rum punch are

---

1: Red Sail Sports cruise; 2: Aruban marinelife

offered after each stop. Equipment and instructions are included, along with a souvenir water bottle.

JOLLY PIRATES

With a name like **Jolly Pirates** (J. E. Irausquin Blvd. 230, 297/586-8107, www. jolly-pirates.com, 9am-1pm, 2pm-5pm, and 5:30pm-7:30pm daily, $32-60), the mood is already set for a trip on picturesque old-style wooden schooners. Captain Harold and his lively crew deliver on those expectations. The ships are also famous for their rope swing. Trips depart from the Hadicurari Pier by MooMba Beach. Jolly Pirates runs two stylish ships, each taking up to 65 passengers. Morning trips include snorkeling, a barbecue lunch, an open bar, and fresh fruit; afternoon snorkel trips and sunset sails offer the bar only.

DIVING

Snorkeling is an easy and quick way to explore the marine environment, but to really study the reef and wrecks in detail, learn how to scuba dive. PADI-certified dive shops are plentiful on Aruba, mostly along the Palm Beach boardwalk. Some go beyond scuba lessons and offer sailing trips with snuba. With scuba, each diver has a breathing unit; snuba deploys what is known in the diving community as a "hookah." Four divers are attached to one tank, which floats on the surface, and divers descend to a maximum of 6 meters (20 ft). Since the air tank is shared, time underwater is limited. Snuba divers still have to get some instruction and learn a few scuba techniques.

Resort courses, devised and approved by PADI, provide enough background information and preliminary training for novices to perform a shallow supervised dive. The actual use of scuba equipment is not very complicated or difficult to learn. Becoming a fully certified diver involves training to plan and perform dives without supervision, and that requires much more knowledge, but you can learn enough in a resort course to get a taste of the sport. Full certification courses are offered by the dive shops. They cover an intense four days of classes, pool sessions, and dives. It is essential to contact a dive shop prior to your trip to arrange a class, since all the lectures, pool work, tests, and dives that would normally be conducted over a five-week period are compressed into a few days. Be prepared to commit nearly the entire day, every day, to complete the course.

Certifying organizations allow you to do the class and pool work over several weeks in the United States or Canada and then travel to a tropical destination to fulfill the dive requirements. Proof that this class and pool work was successfully completed must be in hand before Aruban dive shops can administer the four qualifying dives. The dives are underwater exercises and tests. PADI-affiliated dive shops on Aruba offer package prices for this service and should be contacted prior to arrival. A signed form from a doctor confirming the diver's fitness for the sport is also required. Pregnant women and individuals with chronic conditions requiring daily medication, such as diabetes, high blood pressure, heart disease, asthma, epilepsy, or having had recent major surgery are usually not eligible for these activities. A bad cold or congestion will also disqualify you, since this can result in serious damage to the sinuses or eardrums.

★ DIVE ARUBA

One of the island's most experienced PADI Open Water instructors, Clive Paula, operates **Dive Aruba** (Williamstraat 8, 297/582-7337, www.divearuba.com, Mon.-Sat., dives and classes by appointment, resort course $85, full certification $425), a small personalized operation out of Oranjestad, taking out only seven divers at a time. Dive trips are geared to certified divers, so if you're seeking a novice resort course, book ahead. Departing from the town harbor, his superfast boat can quickly access remote sites. Trips include hotel pickup and return. This is the only dive operation with the added perk of obtaining a cool "Dive with Clive" souvenir T-shirt.

Night Diving

Aruba is the perfect place for night diving. As beautiful as the underwater world is during the day, once night has fallen, a rarely seen environment is exposed. The deeper a diver descends during the day, the more color is lost. Bright corals and fish take on a bluish cast. The bright lights used at night reveal the brilliant hues of sponges and corals. Diurnal fish get sleepy at night, so they are not so quick to dart away.

The most daunting aspect for novice night divers is keeping oriented to the dive boat or entry point. Particularly over a reef area, divers can get confused. For this reason, the *Antilla* is a superb choice for an inaugural nocturnal dive. It is a huge object, the dive is not too deep, and it offers an enormous diversity of sealife within a limited area. Its structure orients you so you can relax and enjoy the fascinating experience.

Dive shops tend to schedule night dives when they have enough participants. **Aruba Watersports Center** and **Dive Aruba** put together night dives; contact them via email prior to arrival. **JADS Dive Shop** also holds regularly scheduled night dives to reef areas, as does **Aqua Windie's Watersports Center,** which visits the *Antilla* wreck. Advance booking and payment are required.

★ JADS DIVE SHOP

The only dive shop in Lago Colony and next to Baby Beach, **JADS** (Seroe Colorado 245E, 297/584-6070, http://jadsaruba.com, resort course $99, full certification $425) offers the best way to dive some of Aruba's most stunning reefs. No other operator has the advantage of this location, with boats taking divers to remote spots on the east side in record time. Patrons will find this PADI facility very conscientious and the staff personable and informative. JADS is located on the far end of the island from the resort areas, but they do hotel pickup and return.

AQUA WINDIE'S

Just across the street from Aruba's hospital is a large complex called **Aqua Windie's** (Dr. Horacio E. Oduber Blvd. no. 4, 297/583-56693, www.aquawindies.com, 8am-5pm Mon.-Sat., 8am-1pm Sun., resort course Mon.-Sat. $103, Open Water $455). One great advantage over other dive operators is its Olympic-size pool, where lessons are held. Many find this a more comfortable way to practice new skills. This congenial family operation, run by Windie and her husband, Rene, and their son as instructor, has a nice dive shop on the premises. Windie's pool is also available for lap swimming and hosts water aerobics classes at 9am

daily, some deploying special hydrobikes. It's a short walk to the Manchebo and Eagle Beach hotels.

ARUBA WATERSPORTS CENTER

Between the Hilton and Barceló hotels is **Aruba Watersports Center** (J. E. Irausquin Blvd. 81b, 297/586-6613, www.arubawatersportcenter.com, 9am-5pm daily, resort course Mon.-Sat. $107, Open Water $455, bicycle rental $25), a reliable family operation offering diving and small-craft activities, plus Sunfish and Beachcat boat rentals. There are two capable and personable PADI-certified instructors known as J. T. and Jake. The complex also offers a shop on the boardwalk for beachwear and sundries. It's a good place to pick up watertight beach boxes, sunblock, and other small items.

UNDERWATER TOURS

Family-oriented excursions provide a memorable experience for all ages and nonswimmers.

ATLANTIS SUBMARINES AND *SEAWORLD EXPLORER*

Two of the most unusual transports for touring the marine landscape are the *Atlantis* **Submarines** and *Seaworld Explorer*

(L. G. Smith Blvd., 800/609-7374, 297/582-4545, www.depalmtours.com, *Atlantis:* 11am, noon, 1pm daily, 90 minutes, $105 adults, $79 children, under age 4 not allowed; *Seaworld Explorer:* 11:30am daily, $44 adults, $29 children, free under age 2). *Atlantis* takes passengers past drop-off reefs and a few small wrecks on the south side, reaching depths of 46 meters (150 ft). Passengers look out portholes that line the sides of the sub. The impossible-to-miss ticket office and logo retail shop at Oranjestad Harbor is the embarkation point. *Seaworld Explorer* is a semi-submarine: the top half stays above the surface. The underwater portion has wide all-around picture windows for a panoramic view. It departs from the De Palm Pier in Palm Beach, taking passengers over the *Antilla* shipwreck and west-side reef areas. If you begin to feel a little claustrophobic down below, you can go up top to enjoy the wide vista.

DE PALM TOURS

De Palm Tours (L. G. Smith Blvd. 142, 297/582-4545, www.depalmtours.com) offers alternatives to going beyond snorkeling without taking the scuba plunge. **Sea Trek** ($49 adults, $36 ages 8-12) offers an interesting underwater experience that requires no swimming ability. You'll be outfitted in hard-hat helmets like divers of old, but with space-age design, allowing you to walk on the ocean floor tethered to the surface. No special training is required. As a bonus, staff film you during the trek and you can buy the DVD as a souvenir. **Snuba** ($49 adults, $36 ages 8-12) employs a hookah system: a single tank attached to several hoses and mouthpieces, allowing a family to share an underwater experience. The typical maximum depth—the length of the hose—is 6 meters (20 ft). Unlike snorkeling, some of the complexities of scuba are present with snuba, for example the effects of pressure on ears and sinuses. Instruction regarding equalizing pressure and other techniques is required.

Sea Trek is only available at **De Palm Island** (Balashi z/n, 9am-6pm daily, $99 adults, $69 children, with round-trip transport by bus), a family-oriented destination offering a mini waterpark, organized activities, and free snorkel gear, as well as free (if mediocre) food and drink. Note, however, that the Sea Trek experience costs extra. Snuba is also available at De Palm Island, so the same cost factors apply, although it can also be purchased as an add-on activity to De Palm Tours' snorkeling or sailing cruises ($69-89 adults, $52-64 ages 8-12) that leave from De Palm Pier in Palm Beach.

SAILING

Families and groups will appreciate the many large catamarans and trimarans in Aruba. They have a stability that guarantees smooth sailing in heavy winds. Their wider breadth also makes it easier to move around and stretch out. Day trips include snorkel stops, instruction, equipment, light meals, and beverages. Guests have the option of exploring the reefs or simply relaxing on board and working on their tan.

Palm Beach has the greatest concentration of water activities, including sailboat departures. Three large piers provide boarding and debarkation points for most trips. Pier operators are large water sports companies that offer diverse services and usually have a few sailboats. They also have contracts with visiting cruise ships, resulting in days when the trips are not available to independent bookings. An alternative to these larger companies are smaller owner-operated boats. The love of sailing is often passed down through the generations, and captains who run their own boats for sailing or deep-sea fishing are dedicated to the art. The atmosphere on these boat trips can feel like spending a day on the water with friends in a personalized experience.

In addition to offering snorkel sails, **Octopus Cruises** (Seroe Janchi 31, departs from Playa Linda beach, 297/593-3739, www.octopusaruba.com, 9am-noon Wed.-Fri.,

---

1: plying the coastline in sailboats; **2:** surfing; **3:** kayaking Aruba's clear waters

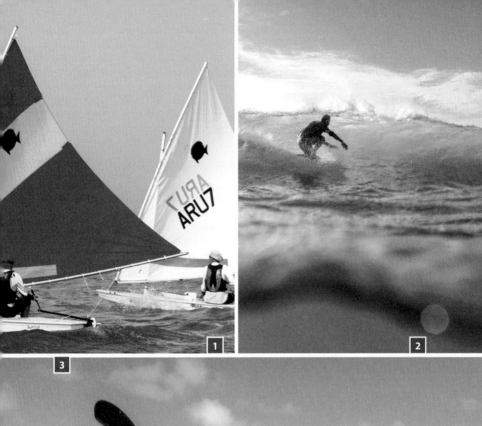

1

2

3

1pm-4pm Mon.-Fri., and 5pm-7pm Tues. and Thurs., $50-70) offers sunset sails with cocktails and snacks. The *Tranquilo* (Alto Vista 34K, departs from Renaissance Harbor, 297/594-2173, www.tranquiloaruba.com, 10am-3pm Tues. and Thurs.-Fri., $85) offers a Romantic Dinner for Two tour ($475), which includes a champagne toast, wine, and a customized menu, arranged in advance by email. **Jolly Pirates** (J. E. Irausquin Blvd. 230, 297/586-8107, www.jolly-pirate.com, 9am-1pm, 2pm-5pm, and 5:30pm-7:30pm daily, $32-60) offers sunset sails with an open bar in addition to their snorkel trips.

RED SAIL SPORTS DINNER CRUISE

Regularly scheduled dinner cruises depart every Wednesday from the **Red Sail Sports pier** (J. E. Irausquin Blvd. 348 A, 297/586-1603, U.S. 305/454-2538, www.aruba-redsail.com, 5:30pm-8:30pm Wed., $109 adults, $59 children) next to the Hyatt. Take the island fantasy dinner to a new level without being too hard on the wallet. The *Rumba* has a limit of 38 passengers for its sunset cruise and includes a buffet dinner catered by the Hyatt, known for its quality cuisine, and an open bar.

PADDLING

ARUBA KAYAK ADVENTURES

Aruba Kayak Adventures (Ponton 88, 297/582-5520, www.arubawavedancer.com, 8:30am-2:30pm Mon.-Sat., Sun. on request for groups, $83) runs memorable nature tours. Congenial entertaining guides Rosendo and Carlos take novice to experienced kayakers through the rich biodiversity of the mangrove preserves of Mangel Halto and the south side. Guests are picked up at their resorts and transported to this pristine location. There is a declared limit of 18-20 kayakers per tour, with varying routes for repeat guests. After snorkeling, lunch is at the quaint Balashi Beer Gardens.

CLEAR KAYAK ARUBA

Clear Kayak Aruba (Savaneta 42, 297/566-2205, www.clearkayakaruba.com, 2-hour tours 9am-8pm daily, $60-70) takes its name from the Lucite-bottomed kayaks used on its tours. This ingenious advance allows you to enjoy a lovely view of the reef and fish beneath while wending your way along Aruba's south coast. Tours begin in Savaneta and head west to finish at Mangel Halto, a vibrant reef area. The maximum number of two-person kayaks on any given tour is six.

Clear Kayak also offers a unique evening adventure from Arashi Beach, near the island's northwest point. Kayaks are equipped with LED floodlights that illuminate the underwater world. A fascinating range of nocturnal marinelife becomes active once the sun sets. Transportation to the pickup points can be arranged for an additional fee. Tours include fresh fruit, iced tea, and water.

FUTS ACTIVITY CENTER

At the south end of the Divi Resort is Fun Under the Sun, or **FUTS** (L. G. Smith Blvd. z/n, 297/560-7915, 9am-6pm daily), where you can rent water gear including SUPs ($25 per day) and banana boats or tubing gear ($25 per half hour) in the Manchebo Beach area. It's a small family operation, and Serge and his wife Milenne are very personable. FUTS also acts as an agent for a wide variety of other operators and can arrange activities from snorkeling and sailing to scuba trips without additional fees. The center also arranges land activities, including ATV and UTV rentals and 4WD tours.

DEEP-SEA FISHING

Deep-sea fishing can be arranged through concierge desks, major water sports companies, or many of the tent operators along Palm Beach; all have fishing boats on their roster. If you're serious about fishing, head down to the piers to watch the boats come in and see who is catching. Talk to the crew and the anglers. An amiable captain and crew adds enjoyment to the day. Several boats are moored at Hadicurari Pier, between MooMba Beach and the Marriott Surf Club in Palm Beach, or in Oranjestad Harbor. Charter rates vary

Tips for the Active Traveler

- **Hydrate:** Aruba's intense sun and temperatures can be extremely taxing, even for the fit. Continual rehydration is necessary, whether you are playing beach volleyball or just lying on the beach. Any strenuous activity should be accompanied by bottles of water or frequent stops for refreshments.

- **Cover up:** If you're touring in open vehicles, especially mopeds, don't make the mistake of wearing skimpy clothing. Aruba's roads can accumulate sand, which can be like driving over ice, particularly on curves. If you skid out, there is the potential for a nasty road rash. You are also likely to run into foliage, where you can expect cacti with sharp thorns. Dress as you would for riding a motorcycle at home: in protective jeans, shirts with sleeves, and, of course, lots of sunblock on exposed areas. Be sure to use the helmet provided.

- **Stay mindful:** Tropical temperatures pose the threat of heatstroke or heat exhaustion when engaging in physical activity, particularly if it is not part of your regular routine. Think twice about biking long distances at midday or any physically demanding activity you're not used to. A completely new sport, or hiking into dry deserted landscape, should not be done alone or without a guide.

- **Don't lose your wedding ring:** Perhaps due to fingers slicked up by sun lotion, there isn't a week that goes by without a story of some newlywed losing a shiny new ring in the sea. It might happen on a snorkeling excursion or swimming offshore. Crews on pleasure boats have gotten pretty good at finding lost rings, since they get quite a bit of practice, but why take that chance? Beach boxes will hold your rings, or lock them away.

RECREATION
WATER ACTIVITIES

widely depending on the size of the boat and length of the trip.

Oranjestad Harbor
DRIFTWOOD FISHING CHARTERS
Enjoy your catch for dinner after fishing with **Driftwood Fishing Charters** (Oranjestad Marina, 297/592-4040, www.driftwoodfishingcharters.com, 8am-noon and 1pm-5pm daily, $400-800). Fanatical angler Herby Merryweather will see that the catch gets cooked for no charge that same night at Driftwood, his Oranjestad restaurant. He has two boats; the *Driftwood II* is available only for all-day charters. Merryweather knows where the fish are and provides fish for his two restaurants, Driftwood and Red Fish.

MAHI MAHI FISHING CHARTERS
Equally fanatical guides are at **Mahi Mahi Fishing Charters** (Oranjestad Marina, 297/594-1181, www.arubamahimahi.com, hours vary, $400-1,100). Three boats for charter are the *Kepasa* and the *Mahi Mahi,* both 42-foot Hatteras, and the *Sea-iesta,* a 54-foot

Bertram. The congenial crew will clean and prepare 30 percent of the catch for you to take with you. If you don't have kitchen facilities, Barney's restaurant in Palm Beach will prepare your catch; you only pay for accompaniments.

TEASER FISHING CHARTERS
A consistent winner during annual fishing contests, **Teaser Fishing Charters** (Oranjestad Marina, 297/593-9228, www.teasercharters.com, $400-1,000) runs two 35-foot Bertrams: *Teaser* and *Kenny's Toy.* The captain and crew love the sport and the excitement of the catch. Teaser participates and places regularly in the annual international billfishing tournament in the fall, and has a top-of-the-line all-day billfishing run. Half-day to full-days tours are available.

Hadicurari Pier
FISHING YACHT ARUBA
Marcelino and Demian of **Fishing Yacht Aruba** (Hadicurari Pier, 297/737-4477 or 297/594-3717, www.fishingyachtaruba.com,

flexible hours, half-day $350-900) are living their dream. As they say, "Are you ready to catch some bad boys out there, or what?" They offer deep-sea and bottom fishing as well as a special tour for big game fish on *The Caroline* and *Persistence*. Patrons praise them especially for how well they work with novices and children. Full-day trips include snacks.

MELINA CHARTERS

Close to Palm Beach resorts, **Melina Charters** (Hadicurari Pier, 297/593-1550, www.arufishing.com, flexible hours, half-day $300-550) offers varied deep-sea, bottom, and inshore fishing for smaller game. They will gear trips to what is running at the time or your preference. Owner and captain Piet is a personable veteran angler who loves the sport.

KITESURFING, PARASAILING, WINDSURFING, AND SURFING

Along Palm Beach are a dozen independent operators with tents for spur-of-the-moment unscheduled activities, including banana boat rides, tubing, WaveRunners, and parasailing, usually sold in blocks of 15-30 minutes. Each resort has at least one vendor; prices and services are the same. Fisherman's Huts, north of the Marriott Resort, is Aruba's windsurfing and kitesurfing center, with kiosks and tents where lessons can be arranged or equipment rented.

ARUBA ACTIVE VACATIONS

Dedicated to extreme sports, **Aruba Active Vacations** (Fisherman's Huts, L. G. Smith Blvd. across from Bakval, 297/586-0989, www.aruba-active-vacations.com, 9am-7pm daily, windsurfing $50-135, kitesurfing $110-160, land-sailing safari 2.5 hours $60) is aptly named. Owner Wim Eehlers is the president of the Aruba Windsurfing Association, which conducts the annual Aruba Hi-Winds Pro-Am. He and his crew are enthusiastic, offering patient, expert instruction in a number of wind-based activities. Aruba has ideal conditions for windsurfing: calm waters and steady winds. Lessons can be group or private. Kitesurfing lessons are also offered, focused on beginner basics to more advanced skills such as water-based starts.

Land-sailing tours are also available and involve steering a wind-powered wheeled vehicle (outfitted with a sail) on land. This can be a thrilling experience. The tour includes pickup and drop-off from major hotels. Bring

kitesurfer

sunglasses (wrap-arounds, if you have them, are best) to protect your eyes from the blowing grit and sand. Wear clothes you're not fussy about, as they are going to get very dusty!

ARUBA SURF SCHOOL

In Aruba's calm waters, surfing does not have the thrill of surfing destinations. Only one operation is dedicated to this activity: **Aruba Surf School** (Irausquin Blvd., 297/593-0229, by appt. daily, 2.5-hour lesson and tour $95, rental $35, SUP class $60, rental $25 per hour). Owner and surfing fanatic Dennis Martinez does his best to provide a fun day of riding the waves, picking up guests at their resorts and taking them to the best surf that day at out-of-the-way coves along the north coast. Expect a combined outback and surfing experience. They also rent stand-up paddleboards (SUPs) from the beach in front of the Marriott Surf Club.

FUN 4 EVERY 1

At the north end of the Riu Palace beach is George Tromp and his tent, **Fun 4 Every 1** (Borancana 128, 297/640-6603, www. fun4every1.com, 9am-5pm daily, float rental $5 per day, banana boat and tube rides $20 per half-hour, WaveRunners $60 per half-hour, parasailing $60, beach umbrellas $25 per day, beach lounges $5 per day). George runs a friendly operation and has four fast boats. Banana boat rides offer a tour of the coastline from Palm Beach to the Westpunt. He also has beach lounge rentals by the day and shade umbrellas for those who are not guests of Palm Beach resorts. This is particularly handy for cruise ship passengers.

NATIVE DIVERS WATERSPORTS

You can always count on friendly conscientious service from Vanessa at **Native Divers Watersports** (Washington 16, 297/586-4763, book at the tent in front of the Marriott Surf Club, 9am-5pm daily, float rental $5 per day, banana boat and tube rides $25 for 20 minutes, WaveRunners $65 per half-hour, parasailing $60). She can arrange all sorts of family activities for the waves and directs clients to the most safety-conscious and reputable operators. Her tent is a hospitable place to relax, and she is a fountain of information regarding activities and operators.

VELA SPORTS ARUBA

On the beach between the Marriott Resort and Ritz-Carlton, one of Aruba's oldest and most respected operators is **Vela Sports Aruba** (L. G. Smith Blvd. 101, 297/586-3735, www.velaaruba.com, 9:30am-4:30pm daily, $60-195), with a full menu of surfing options. Two-hour beginners' group windsurfing and kitesurfing lessons are scheduled four times daily. Advanced private lessons can be set up, and kayaks, snorkeling gear, and SUPs can be rented. A unique service is a half-day kitesurfing excursion to Boca Grande, on the other side of the island, on the farthest eastern shore, away from other vendors and most of the windsurfing and kitesurfing traffic.

WATER PARKS
ARUBA WATERPARK

Affordable **Aruba Waterpark** (Hooiberg z/n, 297/585-0060, www.arubavacationpark. com, 11am-6pm Tues.-Sun., $11 adults, $8 children) houses a great collection of slides: slow, steady, shallow slides for the young and daredevil drops for thrill-seeking teenagers. Lifeguards are on duty. The high slides were ingeniously designed with a nature walk to the top rather than a climb up stairs.

The park also has a serviceable and inexpensive restaurant with a changing menu. Standard barbecue and hamburgers are always available, and the chef cooks a variety of local dishes. In the midst of the countryside, with stunning views of the surrounding landscape, the waterpark is not hard to find; head for the Hooiberg and follow the signs.

Land Tours

Choose from full-size air-conditioned buses, minibus tours, or safari-type vehicles for large and small groups. The more unique methods, such as trikes and Harley-Davidson motorcycles, take so few that they are practically private tours. Or get off the ground altogether and see Aruba on a skydiving tour.

The advantages of guided tours, large or small, are that drivers and guides know the island well, providing interesting and informative commentary, often seasoned with wit and folklore. Disadvantages include the need to keep to a schedule instead of exploring or savoring a site. This is when smaller personalized tours deliver. Aruba has a wealth of large and small tours, allowing everyone to get exactly what they want.

COACHES

DE PALM TOURS

Aruba's most prolific operator, **De Palm Tours** (L. G. Smith Blvd. 142, 297/582-4545, www.depalmtours.com, 10am daily, $40 adults, $30 ages 3-12), has a large fleet of air-conditioned buses and a variety of tours. Bus tours tend to visit the easily accessible and prosaic spots, with an obligatory shopping stop at a local souvenir vendor. These tours provide a glance at the island away from the resort centers while traveling in complete comfort. Buses take up to 65 passengers.

EL TOURS

A midsize operator, **El Tours** (Ir. Luymestraat 6, 297/585-6730, U.S./Canada 866/978-5913, www.eltoursaruba.com) uses slightly smaller buses with fewer passengers. It visits many of the standard sites, offering a 3.5-hour Aruba Highlights Tour (8:30am and 2pm daily, $41 adults, $28 children) and a 4.5-hour Explore Aruba Tour (8:30am daily, $51 adults, $38 children), which adds a stop at Arashi Beach for snorkeling (equipment is provided).

FOFOTI TOURS

Fofoti Tours (Schotlandstraat 85, 297/280-3636, www.fofoti.com, 9am daily, $50 adults, $37.50 children) offers clean, cool transport via a large, air-conditioned coach. Its 4.5-hour Best of Aruba Island Tour hits a few more spots than some of the other coach operators, and goes all the way to Baby Beach.

MINIBUSES

Several independent operators take groups of 11-15 visitors at reasonable rates and flexible schedules. Large families find it easy to arrange a private tour. Most are at a leisurely pace, allowing personalized exploration of the various sights. Vehicles are well maintained and air-conditioned. These independent bus operators are spirited tour guides with a wealth of information about Aruba. Minibus tours operate from in front of the cruise terminal in Oranjestad. They also pick up at hotels when groups hire an entire bus. During the low season, they will provide transport for groups, saving money on taxis. Minibus tours tend to stick to the more easily accessed sites and smooth paved roads.

HF TOURS AND TRANSFERS

After more than 24 years as a tour guide, Howard Folkes of **HF Tours and Transfers** (Piedra Plat 46H, 297/594-1954, http://folkestours.com, 2-hour tours $20 pp, extra time negotiable) knows every nook and cranny of Aruba. He has two buses: one for 29 passengers, the other 15. Trips are customizable. His normal point of departure is in front of the cruise terminal, but he will pick up at hotels, even if it's not a group. Depending on the departure point and time requirements, his tour includes easily accessible sites such as Santa Ana Church, Alto Vista Chapel, California Lighthouse, and Casibari Rock Formation.

KINI KINI TRANSFER & TOURS

Boasting a fleet of minibuses and luxury vehicles, **Kini Kini Transfer & Tours** (Flacciusstraat 33, 297/588-3333, U.S. 305/420-5577, www.kinikinitours.com, 9am-1pm Mon., Wed., and Fri., $45) takes up to 12 people in its minivans to hit the high spots on its four-hour Aruba's Finest Island Tour, as well as the Natural Bridge and Aruba Ostrich Farm. Kini Kini also specializes in wedding transportation and airport pickups with SUVs that you can charter.

SONNY'S TOURS

Sonny's Tours (Pos Chiquito 81B, 297/568-2028 http://sonnytoursaruba.com, $35-45 adults, $18-23 children) has a larger bus than most independent operators, for up to 28 passengers. Sonny Binns is a veteran tour guide who visits many of the popular spots on his set tours of 3.5-4 hours.

XCLUSIVE TOURS & TRANSFER SERVICES

Regmy Dubero has been a tour guide since he was 18 and has been in the business for decades, taking his responsibility as an ambassador of goodwill very seriously. **Xclusive Tours & Transfer Services** (Savanetastraat 12, 297/912-3446, www.xclusivetoursaruba.com, $25, private tour minimum 4 passengers) makes every effort to entertain while showing off his homeland. Tours can be customized, and favorite spots on the scheduled tours include Casibari Rock Formation, Bushiribana Gold Ruin, Santa Ana Church, and Alto Vista Chapel. A standard tour is two hours but can be extended. Passengers can pick the route that interests them most.

CARAVAN AND SPECIALTY TOURS

Caravan tours offer the best of both worlds: a chance to drive your own 4WD or heavy-duty safari-type vehicle and a tour guide in a lead car showing the way. Most caravans take 6-10 passengers and usually traverse the rougher roads, which are often more direct. Excursions may last a full day with a number of stops, as standard sights are mixed with out-of-the-way locations. Some operators offer shorter jaunts focusing only on off-road sights. Pickup times at resorts are 15-30 minutes prior to tour times quoted, as guests will be transported to a central departure point.

★ PRIVATE TOURS ARUBA

Private Tours Aruba (Pos Abou 2N, 297/594-4400, www.privatetoursaruba.com, 9am-1pm and 1pm-5pm daily, $80-120 pp, including meal) is a small, independent, locally owned operation. Tours are conducted in luxury air-conditioned SUVs. Guides are multilingual, knowledgeable, and personable on fixed or customized itineraries. The company also has arrangements with several excellent restaurants in Palm Beach and Oranjestad, so you can conclude your tour with either lunch or dinner. Tours accommodate 1-6 passengers for a flat rate, although couples can have a car to themselves. Prices include pickup at your accommodations.

★ TOURS BY LOCALS

Tours by Locals (866/844-6783, www.toursbylocals.com, $99-600) is perfect for personal service and ultimate comfort. The international company arranges tours connecting travelers with local guides in over 150 countries. Select your itinerary and guide on the website, then establish contact with your guide to decide if he or she will meet your needs. There are over a dozen preset itineraries, and you can filter your online search to meet your interests. Any tour can be customized, and pickup and drop-off can be anywhere. Tours might range from walking in Oranjestad and San Nicolas to swimming at secluded beaches in Arikok National Park. Tours accommodate 3-7 people for a flat rate rather than per person. More expensive tours use larger vehicles that handle bigger groups. Guides and their vehicles must meet strict standards, and vacationers will experience the kind of personal interaction that makes an island tour memorable and fun. Most guides are fluent in at least three languages. This is one of the best options for making your way around Aruba.

ABC TOURS

The first safari tours on Aruba were run by **ABC Tours and Attractions** (Schotlandstraat 61, 297/582-5600, 888/815-3577, www.abc-aruba.com, 8:30am-6pm daily, $108 adults, $70 children, includes lunch; 8:30am-12:30pm daily, $79 adults, $49 children, no lunch), and they set the standard, providing a comfortable ride in canopied Land Rovers and a barbecue lunch at the ABC-owned safari-style restaurant Waka-Waka. Owner Marvin Kelly is always innovating and making the tours better. Guides compete to make their tours the most interesting and fun. Heavy-duty vehicles can get to the more out-of-the-way spots, including Conchi, Aruba's natural pool on the north coast. Patrons do the driving while following the leader. At least one person in a group needs to know how to use a manual transmission. ABC provides a variety of half-day tours to Ayo Rock Formation, Andicuri Beach, and the Alto Vista Chapel.

EL TOURS

Using Jeep Ramblers seating only four, the **El Tours** (Ir. Luymestraat 6, Pos Chiquito, 297/585-6730, U.S./Canada 866/978-5913, www.eltoursaruba.com, daily, half-day $90 adults and $76 children, full-day $115 adults and $85 children) safari excursions are more intimate, often providing friends or family with their own car.

MADAGASCAR ARUBA ADVENTURE

Visitors rave about the charm and enthusiasm of Alfredo and his **Madagascar Aruba Adventure** (Caya Seyda 9, 297/746-0572, madagascar-aruba@hotmail.com, 8:30am-1pm and 2pm-6pm daily, $50 adults, $30 children). Tours often go over the allotted time because everyone, including the host, is having so much fun. A little young to be called "Papa Alfred," Alfredo is well informed about the island and its sights. Groups are limited to 12; his shaded safari truck is set up for taking pictures. Alfred visits all the usual sights, including Conchi (Natural Pool), but foregoes his usual schedule if passengers would like something different. Don't be shy about expressing curiosity about something outside

El Tours

the norm: He is game and his truck can handle it.

MADI'S MAGICAL TOURS

Madi's Magical Tours (Shete 19, 297/746-1397, http://madimagicaltours.com, Sunrise Conchi Tour 5:30am-8:30am daily, $75 adults, $38 children; 4.5-hour private tour $100) are run by Madi, a fifth-generation Aruban who admits to being a *bruha* (a white witch) with an encyclopedic knowledge of island folklore, bush medicine, and out-of-the-way sights. Her tours always have the feeling of *ban keiro* ("let's go tripping"), more like an excursion with family and friends. Madi takes very small groups without a set schedule or routine. Her memorable, unusual outings usually go beyond prescribed times. Pickup and return to your hotel is provided. The safari-type vehicle puts passengers in the car, so all can enjoy her running commentary. One outing is a sunrise tour to Conchi (Natural Pool), which departs before dawn. Expect breathtaking views as the sun rises on this dramatic section of the north coast. Madi is continually adding new, undiscovered areas to her itinerary.

MOTORCYCLES, MOPEDS, AND ATVS

In the past few years, tour operators have realized that getting there can be half the fun when the transportation is funky.

★ TRIKES

Show off your sense of style and see the island with **Trikes** (Noord 23, 297/738-7453, www.trikes-aruba.com, office 8am-2pm Mon.-Sat., $190 for 2 people, $95 for a 3rd person, $50 to drive with the guide). These motorcycle-car hybrids are comfortable and easy to drive. Tooling around in the hot-colored three-wheelers is fun; be ready to be noticed. A short lesson and practice precedes the tour. Some skill with a stick shift helps, but no motorcycle license is required. Three-hour tours start at 8am, 9am, and 2pm daily. Cover up for the sun and wear long pants and long sleeves.

AROUND ARUBA TOURS

Independent tour companies are meeting the demand for more exciting exploration of Aruba's off-the-beaten-path regions. **Around Aruba Tours** (Alto Vista 116, 297/593-5963, www.aroundaruba.com, 4-hour tours, 9am or 2:30pm daily, $190 per UTV, $100 pp Jeep Wrangler) is one of the few to include Philip's Animal Garden. Take a tour in a two-seater UTV or an air-conditioned Jeep Wrangler that seats six. Around Aruba Tours also offers ATV and UTV rentals without a guide. Fees range $100 for a single-seat ATV to $240 for a double-seat UTV.

ARUBA MOTORCYCLE TOURS & RENTALS

To be an Easy Rider, rent your own motorcycle or take a guided tour via **Aruba Motorcycle Tours & Rentals** (Jaburibari 16, 297/641-7818, http://arubamotorcycletours.com, 7am-7pm Mon.-Sat.). Riding two to a bike is allowed, and the company provides pickup and drop-off. Select a ride from four Harley models, ranging from the lighter Sportster suitable for "shorter ladies" and novices to the heavy-duty Road King for the experienced hog enthusiast. Whether for tours or rentals, you must be 21 and have a valid motorcycle driving license.

Four-hour tours are $25 per person and leave at 9am daily; afternoon tours are possible for a minimum two bikes, four people. Tours visit sights like the California Lighthouse and Alto Vista Chapel. Half-day motorcycle rentals range $120-140 and full-day rentals $150-180. Sportster ($375) and Dyna ($425) models can also be rented for five days.

GEORGE'S CYCLE RENTAL

For more than 30 years, **George's Cycle Rental** (L. G. Smith Blvd. 124, 297/593-2202, www.georgecycles.com, 9am-5pm daily, mopeds $55 per day, Yamaha motorcycles $95 per day, ATVs and UTVs $125-225 per day) has been the number-one choice for mopeds

and motorcycles. On the highway at the western side of Oranjestad, it has a variety of vehicles for rent, from tiny mopeds to ATVs and UTVs with automatic transmission and hardtop shade canopies. Discounts are available for three- to four-day rentals. Resort pickup and drop-off plus helmets are included.

ROCKABEACH TOURS

Visitors have come to know tour guide Frankie and his wildly painted bus over the years. **RockaBeach Tours** (Bushiri 25, booking desk at The Village in Palm Beach, 297/594-2366, www.rockabeachtours.com, 9am-1pm and 2:30pm-6:30pm daily, $125-320) offers an Aruban countryside tour via ATV or UTV, with a flat rate per vehicle. Tour prices include nonalcoholic beverages, a snack, hotel pickup, and your own personal bandana for a possibly dusty ride. Frankie has an erudite and educated staff of guides who are well versed in Aruban history, folklore, flora, and fauna, and speak excellent English. Tours include a swimming stop at Conchi (Natural Pool).

SEGWAY TOURS

SEGWAY ARUBA

All-terrain personal transporters have finally come to Aruba! **Segway Aruba** (Palm Beach 55, 297/740-7675, www.segwayaruba.com, 2-hour tours daily, flexible schedule, $50-80) has a desk next to the Hard Rock Café in Palm Beach. They will conduct a tour with as few as two people. Enjoy the exhilarating sensation of the wind in your face—without having to pedal against it. The guides are personable and well informed, and a practice session is provided before takeoff. Refreshments are included in the cost of the tour, and GoPro cameras are available to rent.

BIKING

Portions of J. E. Irausquin Boulevard and L. G. Smith Boulevard north of Palm Beach have designated official bike paths. These are

painted blue and provide cyclists with a route from Oranjestad to Malmok. The shorefront from Governor's Bay to the airport has been remodeled to provide safe biking and jogging tracks completely separate from traffic. These routes offer beautiful views of the shoreline and are often bustling with residents and tourists, particularly on weekends, early mornings, and at sunset.

ARUBA ACTIVE VACATIONS

Aruba Active Vacations (Fisherman's Huts, L. G. Smith Blvd. across from Bakval, 297/586-0989, www.aruba-active-vacations. com, 9am-7pm daily) offers mountain bike rentals from $25-35 a day to $100-160 a week, including delivery and pickup in the hotel areas. It also offers a 2.5-hour mountain biking tour ($55 pp) that goes to California Lighthouse and Alto Vista Chapel, among other sights. Private tours (from $85 pp) can also be arranged.

EAGLE BEACH BIKE RENTAL

Conveniently located to Eagle and Manchebo Beach resorts is **Eagle Beach Bike Rental** (L. G. Smith Blvd. 234, 297/587-8655, 9am-5pm Mon.-Sat., $15 per day, $70 per week). Find them on the short road adjacent to Screaming Eagle restaurant leading to Breeze Residences. Bike locks are included on request, and helmets are supplied.

GREEN BIKE

Bike-sharing program **Green Bike** (http://greenbikearuba.com, 24 hours daily, $24-89) has a fleet of 100 heavy-duty bikes and convenient stations to get around town and between the main resort areas. A touchscreen kiosk at each docking station allows you to choose a rental plan from four hours to a seven-day pass and pay with a credit card to unlock a bike. You can return it to any station. If you have problems, call customer service (297/594-6368, 8am-5pm Mon.-Fri., 8am-noon Sat.). Green Bike terminals are located at Paardenbaai Plaza (cruise terminal), Plaza Daniel Leo (behind the Renaissance Mall),

1: cycling the north coast; 2: Segway tour

Alternatives to ATV Tours

horseback riding

ATV and UTV tours and rentals are popular on the island, but they come with some environmental costs. The prevalence of vehicles designed to hold only 1-4 people means increased emissions. Noise pollution is also a problem with the large number of ATV and UTVs on the island, most dramatic at Conchi (Natural Pool), where the experience is frequently punctuated by the roar of dozens of ATVs storming the scene. Although guided ATV and UTV tours respect strictly forbidden zones closed to motorized traffic, many unguided ATV and UTV drivers have been tempted by these landscapes, such as the California Dunes; the vehicular intrusion harms delicate ecosystems and may disturb some important archaeological digs near the sea. Here are some eco-friendlier options for exploring some of the more remote sights that ATVs visit.

4WD TOURS

Safari vehicles can handle the rough roads, provide excellent panoramas, and typically have higher passenger capacities than ATVs or UTVs, offering a more environmental choice. These 4WD tours also don't contribute to the extreme noise pollution of ATVs and UTVS, which disturbs the wildlife and tranquility in the countryside. Madagascar Aruba Adventure is a good option.

MOUNTAIN BIKE TOURS

For the physically fit, touring by mountain bike is an eco-friendly choice, and you'll get in a work-out too. Rancho Notorious and Aruba Active Vacations offer mountain biking options for exploring various parts of the island. Join a group, arrange a private tour, or rent your own bike to explore places inaccessible to larger vehicles.

HORSEBACK RIDING

The best way to traverse many of the narrow rocky trails to spots like Conchi (Natural Pool) and Arikok National Park's beaches is on horseback. Enjoy the beautiful countryside in more leisurely fashion. Rancho Loco and Gold Mine Ranch are recommended.

Plaza Turismo (on the east end of Oranjestad, across from the Cas di Cultura), Costa Linda Resort, La Cabana Beach Resort, Palm Beach (South Beach Center), Paseo Herencia Shopping Mall, and Fisherman's Huts.

RANCHO NOTORIOUS

Guided mountain bike tours are offered by **Rancho Notorious** (Borancana z/n, 297/586-0508, www.ranchonotorious.com), with pickup and return to your resort. Tours are graded and grouped according to biking expertise, from novice to fanatic. Good for casual bikers are the 2.5-hour tours (9am Mon.-Fri., $55-65) that visit sights like the Alto Vista Chapel, the California Lighthouse, and Malmok Beach for a snorkeling stop. A variety of more advanced and customized rides ($85-265 pp), including night rides and trips into Arikok National Park, are also available. Riders must be at least 14. Basic bikes are included, but you can upgrade to premium TREK Superfly models ($30-50). Tours are conducted by Geert Herbots, a certified mountain biking coach and Master Mountain Biker of the Year 2015.

VELOCITY BEACH BIKE RENTAL

Velocity Beach Bike Rental (J. E. Irausquin Blvd. z/n, 297/586-3656, 8:30am-4:30pm daily, $15 per day) serves the Palm Beach area with new bikes and mountain bikes, including a tandem. A bargain for weekly rentals: Rent for seven days and only pay for five.

HORSEBACK TOURS

★ RANCHO LOCO

Whether you're experienced or not, you're bound to enjoy a ride with **Rancho Loco** (Sombre 22E, 297/592-6039, www.rancholocoaruba.com, $75-105). Offerings include tours to Conchi (9am and 3:30pm daily) along paths not usually taken by ATVs, other trips into Arikok National Park (9am and 4pm daily), and sunset rides (around 5:30pm

daily). Tours last 1-2.5 hours and include resort pickup and return. Private tours are also available.

Riders will appreciate the warm hospitality of ranch owners Annette and Constantine as well as the loving care they provide their horses. The animals roam free in large fields. Annette is living her dream: She and her husband, Steve, were married in Aruba on horseback. When they returned to relive the event, they found the ranch abandoned, and bought it to return it to its former glory, with new equipment and healthy horses.

GOLD MINE RANCH

Alternative north coast destinations via horseback are on the tour route of **Gold Mine Ranch** (Matividiri 60, 297/586-4954, www.thegoldmineranch.com, departs 9am and 4pm daily, $85 adults, $65 children). Tours make 10 stops along the way, with a beach trot through the waves. They take in the Bushiribana Gold Ruin, Natural Bridge, and Black Stone Beach, where few other stables go. These tours are for experienced riders, who are paired with a horse that matches their skills. Rates include pickup and return to the major hotels.

SKYDIVING

★ SKYDIVE ARUBA

If you have an adventure bucket list, **Skydive Aruba** (Noord z/n, 297/735-0654, http://skydivearuba.com, 8am-4pm daily, skydives by appt., $299) is a way to check off an item without extensive training. It's the only skydiving operation on the island. Jumps are strictly tandem—attached to a veteran instructor—so you can relax and enjoy the view. From nowhere else on Aruba will you catch such a vista; it is a once-in-a-lifetime experience. Instructors film the entire jump, which you can purchase on DVD to relive the experience (or prove that you really did it).

Hiking and Running

RUNNING AND JOGGING

Naturally pounded dirt paths border the west shore along **J. E. Irausquin Boulevard** between Manchebo resorts and Palm Beach, an exhilarating backdrop for a morning jog. The same paths are found along **L. G. Smith Boulevard** from the Marriott Resort to Arashi Beach. Sunsets are beautiful along these routes.

The **Linear Park Trail** offers 3 kilometers (1.9 mi) of groomed jogging and biking paths alongside the A1 road extending from the Reina Beatrix Airport to Wilhelmina Park in Oranjestad, bordering L. G. Smith Boulevard. It provides a pleasant route along the water, safe from the busy traffic. The length is bisected by the Plaza Turismo, with cafés and restrooms. An extension to Malmok's shore is currently in the works.

HIKING

Arikok National Park

Aruba's largest natural preserve, **Arikok National Park** (San Fuego 70, 297/585-1234, www.arubanationalpark.org, 8am-4pm daily, $11, free under age 17) occupies 18 percent of the island's landmass. It was designated as a formally protected area in 2000. The park provides 32 kilometers (20 mi) of hiking trails with various degrees of difficulty. Paved and dirt paths are clearly marked, with flora and fauna identified as well.

The park is a showcase of native species and Aruba's geological formations. Trails take visitors to the coastline or the island's heights. Paved or gravel roads with parking areas parallel many of the hiking paths, so routes can be reduced according to ability. Quoted distances are calculated from the visitor center at the park entrance. Free trail maps are available at the visitors center. Tour rangers

will call for a vehicle to pick up hikers who become exhausted. It is always advisable in Aruba's tropical heat to hike as early in the day as possible, and take plenty of bottled water to rehydrate frequently.

CUNUCU ARIKOK TRAIL

Cunucu Arikok Trail (3.5 km/2 mi, 1.5-2 hours) leads to an authentically preserved farm with a centuries-old dwelling. It is one of the most popular of all the Arikok hikes and the easiest. The route passes Aruba's famous kibrahacha trees, which only blossom a few days of the year in a burst of intense yellow flowers. Typical desert flora, including a multitude of cacti with spiny thorns, line the trails.

MASIDURI TRAIL

The **Masiduri Trail** (7 km/4.4 mi, 5 hours or more) is an alternate route to the top of Seroe Jamanota, Aruba's highest point at 188 meters (617 ft), for the extremely fit; it's one of the physical trials used to test Dutch Marines. It circles around the south side of the hill. You first have to climb and descend Seroe Largo, 114 meters (374 ft) high, before the steep trail to the top of Jamanota. Park rangers describe it as a true endurance test.

NATURAL POOL TRAIL TO CONCHI

Conchi can be reached via the **Natural Pool Trail** (5.5 km/3.4 mi, 4-5 hours). It heads north to the pool, then circles back following the rugged north coast before turning west to the park entrance. Natural Pool Trail offers the widest variety of scenery of all the trails, passing through cacti and scrub, as well as along the rocky coast. The trail begins at the park's main entrance.

However, there's also an **alternate route** (2.4 km/1.5 mi, 1-2 hours) to Conchi possible from the park's secondary entrance at Shete, a bit farther from the visitors center. It's an appealing hiking option since it's closed to

---

1: skydiving; **2:** hiking in Arikok; **3:** SUP Yoga with Vela Sports Aruba

motorized vehicles—so you can avoid the ATVs, UTVs, and other motorized traffic heading to Conchi via the trail from the main entrance. To get to this secondary entrance, take the A4 following the sign for the Natural Pool, continuing on until the road forks, at which point you'll take a right. Continue for about a quarter mile until you reach another junction; turn left up the sharp incline onto the paved road. Keep going until you reach the summit, where you'll find an Arikok National Park booth and pay your entrance fee.

As the Natural Pool can get crowded, visit early in the day. You have the option of beating the motorized crowds since hikers (and bikers) are allowed to enter the park before the park's 8am opening time (so long as an entry ticket is purchased post-hike).

ROOI PRINS TRAIL

The **Rooi Prins Trail** (5.5 km/3.4 mi, 3-4 hours) takes hikers through a dried-out creek bed and on to Phantage Prins. Go left to circle back to the park entrance, or continue east to the expansive beach area of Boca Prins.

ROOI TAMBU TRAIL

Following **Rooi Tambu Trail** (5.5 km/3.4 mi, 2-3 hours) east to the sea takes hikers directly to Dos Playa, a lovely place to sunbathe. Although this spot is popular with bodyboarders, rangers warn about swimming here because of the riptides and undertows. The white sand, surrounding ocher cliffs, and turquoise Caribbean present a stark contrast and make for beautiful photos.

SEROE ARIKOK TRAIL

Aruba's second-highest point, Seroe Arikok, is 185 meters (606 ft). The **Seroe Arikok Trail** (4.4 km/2.7 mi, 3 hours) offers an easy ascent by paved road to the summit. Close to the height of Seroe Jamanota, it offers an equally thrilling view.

SEROE JAMANOTA TRAIL

Seroe Jamanota is Aruba's highest point at 188 meters (617 ft), offering a remarkable panorama of the island, from San Nicolas to Westpunt; you can see the curve of the world from its peak. There are two paths to the top, but the **Seroe Jamanota Trail** (4.5 km/2.8 mi, 2-2.5 hours) is the easiest and follows a gradual winding road, paved all the way to the summit. Visitors can park at the base and walk this road to the top.

Conchi (Natural Pool)

Golf and Tennis

GOLF

Until 25 years ago, golfers had to make do with the funky San Nicolas Golf Club, where the greens are oiled sand and Astroturf, an interesting challenge that no one took very seriously. Since 1990, two world-class courses have been built on Aruba, both surrounded by luxurious communities, with regular international tournaments.

DIVI LINKS

In 2004, **Divi Links** (J. E. Irausquin Blvd. 93, 297/581-4653, www.divigolf.com, $90 with $39 replay winter-spring, $75 with $34 replay summer-fall) opened a gorgeously landscaped nine-hole course with Prince Albert of Monaco hitting the first ball. Although part of the Divi complex, Divi Links is open to nonguests. It has a pro shop, state-of-the-art clinic, and two very appealing restaurants in the clubhouse. Do two rounds to get in your 18 holes. When carving out the course, the designers preserved the natural wetlands, home to many bird species. These pools and dramatic formations provide a very unique backdrop. Thousands of birds continue to nest here, oblivious to the golfers.

TIERRA DEL SOL COUNTRY CLUB AND GOLF COURSE

Tierra Del Sol Country Club and Golf Course (Caya di Solo 10, 297/586-0978, 866/978-5158, www.tierradelsol.com, Apr. 24-Dec. 17 $139 before noon, $109 afternoon, Dec. 18-Jan. 1 $169 before noon, $139 afternoon, Jan. 2-Apr. 23 $159 before noon, $129 afternoon) is in Malmok, at the northwest tip of the island. Designed by Robert Trent Jones Jr., the 18-hole desert course is renowned for breathtaking vistas and challenging winds. Amenities include a pro shop, a day spa, a gorgeous pool deck, tennis courts, and a gourmet restaurant. Villa rental on-site includes greens fees, round-trip airport transport, and use of all facilities.

TENNIS

All the major resorts in Palm Beach and Manchebo Beach maintain tennis courts. Courts and lessons should be reserved well in advance. Nonguests can use the courts by taking lessons with the tennis pro contracted by the hotels. Aruba's tennis scene has changed dramatically recently: Traditional tennis has declined as beach tennis has become a local craze. Beach tennis resembles a supercharged version of badminton, as balls don't bounce. The game is physically demanding, and killer shots are the norm.

ARUBA RACQUET CLUB

Close to the Palm Beach and Malmok resorts, **Aruba Racquet Club** (Rooi Santo 21, 297/586-0215, www.arc.aw, 8am-10pm Mon.-Sat., 4pm-8pm Sun., $10 pp per 30 min. daytime court, $20 pp per 60 min. nighttime court, $60 lessons with a pro, $5 equipment rental) is an elegantly designed facility with gardens and eight courts. Amenities include a swimming pool, a restaurant (3pm-close Mon.-Sat.), and a locally priced spa, perfect for a massage after a couple of hours on the courts. Day passes ($20 adults, $10 children) are available and allow use of the gym, showers, and pool. The club is a social place, making it a good spot to meet local tennis enthusiasts.

BEACH TENNIS ARUBA

Beach Tennis Aruba (J. E. Irausquin Blvd. 248, 297/587-7076, www.beachtennisaruba.com, 7:30am-10am and 4pm-11pm Mon.-Wed. and Fri., 7:30am-10am and 3pm-11pm Thurs., 7:30am-noon and 4pm-11pm Sat., 4pm-11pm Sun., $5 pp per hour) offers 16 groomed courts, brightly lit at night. It is easier to book a court for daytime, as it will be busy with local club members at play after work. If you've never played beach tennis before, this is a good place to try it out. The courts are convenient to Manchebo and Eagle Beach resorts and have a full bar and a snack bar.

MOOMBA BEACH BAR & RESTAURANT

Close to all the Palm Beach resorts and a popular local spot are the courts at **MooMba Beach Bar & Restaurant** (J. E. Irausquin Blvd. 230, 297/586-5365, www.beachtennisaruba.com, 7:30am-11pm daily, $5 pp per hour), run by Beach Tennis Aruba. The six courts have lights for night play. Learn beach tennis or attend the frequent weekend tournaments to take part in the general merriment that arises from the connection to MooMba, a popular bar-restaurant. Competitions are exciting, with enthusiastic spectators fueled by frequent visits to the bar, which often offers specials.

Spas and Yoga

Aruba has an inordinate number of day spas and *estheticas*. Every major resort boasts a luxurious spa. One extremely popular service is the couples massage with champagne, chocolates, and a private whirlpool bath. Local facilities may not be quite as glamorous, but they are usually far more economical. Priced for local repeat guests, some are also conveniently located near small guesthouses.

SPAS, MASSAGE, AND BEAUTY

CLINICAL MASSAGE ARUBA & SPA

At two locations, **Clinical Massage Aruba & Spa** (Casa Del Mar Resort, 297/280-5115; Playa Linda Beach Resort, 297/280-8880; www.clinicalmassagearuba.com; $75-185) has intimate spas, and a Yoga Garden at the Playa Linda spa. Aside from the usual menu of Swedish and deep tissue massages, they also offer hot stone, prenatal, reflexology, and acupressure treatments as well as body wraps, facials, and scrubs, manicures, pedicures, and waxing. The spa also offers professional pain management treatments.

EFOREA SPA

Aruba's largest spa is **Eforea** (Hilton Aruba Caribbean Resort, 297/526-6052, www.3hilton.com., 9am-6pm Mon.-Sat., 9am-5pm Sun., massages $135-215), beachside at the Hilton along the Palm Beach boardwalk. It's beautifully appointed, with spacious, elegant treatment rooms, a stunning community area, and a gallery displaying locally produced art. The spa also offers a happy-hour rate on treatments (noon-2pm daily summer), with a Swedish massage for $99.

MANDARA SPA

Mandara Spa (297/586-4710, www.mandaraspa.com, 9am-6pm daily, 50-minute massage $120, couple's massage $275) is in the Marriott Ocean Club and serves three resorts. This luxurious facility has a relaxation lounge that opens to enclosed gardens for a serene environment.

MASSAGE AT HOME

Those staying in smaller guesthouses without spa facilities can enjoy a therapeutic massage, combined with a facial if desired, right in their rooms. Call **Massage at Home** (Bubali 145, 297/730-6660, www.massagesaruba.com, by appt., 1-hour massage $100, 1.5-hour $140), run by skilled certified therapist Miranda Wever. Private service in your room is likely to be less costly than the more glamorous in-house facilities.

MENA'S SKINCARE CENTER

Convenient to guesthouses around Oranjestad and Eagle Beach is **Mena's Skincare Center** (Tanki Leendert 283, 297/587-6282, 11am-7pm Tues. and Thurs., 9am-6pm Wed. and Fri., 8am-5pm Sat., 1-hour massage $54). It was Aruba's first *esthetica,* specializing in facials, body wraps, and skin treatments. Mena is a living example of the effectiveness of her procedures: She is as youthful as when she first began sharing her skills. Not as glamorous as the resort spas, the center has rates geared toward residents and are much cheaper. Besides standard massages and facials are laser depilation and permanent eyeliner procedures ($380 for both upper and lower lids). Mena has a very clean, pleasant space not far from the resorts. Hotel pickup can be arranged.

OKEANOS SPA

In Oranjestad, **Okeanos Spa** (L. G. Smith Blvd. 82, 297/583-6000, www. okeanosspaaruba.com, 50-minute Swedish massage $115, 2.5-hour couples $440) is a luxurious full-service spa. The main facility is within the Marina Tower of Renaissance Resort, and The Cove is on a secluded peninsula of Renaissance Island. Nonguests are charged an additional $25 per person fee.

The Marina outlet has full services, including a steam room and a community room with snacks and refreshments. Linger on lounge chairs on the outdoor terrace and enjoy a great view of the harbor. Select from exotic body wraps and skin treatments. The Royal Romance package is a couples session with dinner at L. G. Smith's Steak & Chop House next door.

The Cove only does massages, including reflexology and hot stone. Cove packages include a bottle of champagne or four frothy frozen cocktails and a fruit platter. Lunch is available. More than one young couple has gotten engaged after sharing a couple's massage in The Cove's romantic setting. Purchasing treatment here also grants access to Renaissance Island for the day, which normally costs $100 pp.

SHALOM BODY AND SOUL SPA & SALON

In the Alhambra Shopping Bazaar, **Shalom Body and Soul Spa & Salon** (J. E. Irausquin Blvd. 47, 297/280-0980, www. arubashalomspa.com, 9am-7pm Mon.-Sat., 10am-6pm Sun., massages $85-120) is a cozy spa with two treatment rooms and particularly friendly and skilled staff. Tika is known for her Thai massage (a workout, to be sure), while Mia gives relaxing and deep-tissue massages. Shalom offers the best rates among spas within easy walking distance of the resorts. It also provides manicures, facials, waxing, and hairstyling.

SPA DEL SOL

The Manchebo Beach area is home to **Spa Del Sol** (J. E. Irausquin Blvd. 55, 297/582-6145, www.spadelsol.com, 9am-6:30pm Mon.-Sat., 50-minute massage $95, 80-minute $125, couples $180-240), on the beach at the Manchebo Resort and the first day spa on Aruba. For the full island experience, massages are administered in a curtained *palapa* on the beach. Spa Del Sol is known for pampering combination packages that last several hours and include a healthful lunch. The surroundings are exotic teak and artistic carvings from the founder's collection, acquired from his travels.

ZOIA

The most beautiful and luxurious day spa on the island is **ZoiA** (Hyatt Regency Resort, 297/586-1234, http://aruba.hyatt. com, 8:30am-8pm daily, 1-hour massage $275, couples $390), just off the lobby of the Hyatt Resort and featuring elegant accoutrements. Relax in the community room with all-inclusive snacks, holistic drinks, and continental breakfast. A sauna is on-site, and terraces look over the resort's gorgeous gardens. Also available is a special line of products by

Dinah Veeris, famous for natural skin-care potions made from native plants and herbs.

Special all-day packages are conducted in a luxurious room with a private terrace. This is also the room for the couples massage, with a cozy hot tub. Each room has a private bathroom to help maintain the mood, allowing patrons to stay in their own space. Complete treatments, makeup, and hair packages are offered for wedding parties for both men and women.

YOGA

ISLAND YOGA

The woman who popularized yoga on Aruba is Rachel Brathen, known internationally as Yoga Girl. After establishing yoga programs for Manchebo, Vela, and others, she founded her own center called **Island Yoga** (Noord 19A, 297/580-0025, http://islandyoga.com, $20 studio class, SUP yoga $50), across from the Caribbean Palm Village. Daily classes in an array of yoga disciplines are for varying levels. One-week packages include four studio sessions and one SUP yoga class ($110). Combo packages incorporate activities such as sunset sails and treks into the northern shores for yoga sessions, and Rachel periodically runs retreats.

MANCHEBO BEACH RESORT

The original venue for yoga on the beach was the **Manchebo Beach Resort** (297/582-3444, www.manchebo.com, $15 nonguests, free for guests). It's still the only resort offering scheduled yoga classes every day, taught by five instructors in different specialties. Classes are held under an expansive beachfront pavilion or on covered decks on the beach for shade and greater stability. Offerings include vinyasa, sunset yoga, and core power flow sessions. All classes are one hour. Pilates classes are available as well.

VELA SPORTS ARUBA

Condition your body and soothe your spirits with **Vela Sports Aruba** (L. G. Smith Blvd. 101, 297/586-3735, www.velaaruba.com, 9:30am-4:30pm daily). Exercise, work on your tan, and meditate while connecting with nature during a stand-up paddleboard yoga experience. Vela's one-hour **SUP Yoga** (9am Mon., Wed., and Fri.-Sun., $45) is conducted on the water just north of the Marriott Resort. You'll learn paddleboard techniques on the beach first, and then head out to a secluded area for an hour that engages the entire body to perfect your physical and spiritual balance.

Vela also conducts **Beer Yoga** (5:30pm Thurs., $35) on the beach. Originating at the Burning Man festival (where else?), these three-hour sessions combine yoga, sunset-watching, two bottles of craft beer, and socializing. **Standard yoga classes** (8am Wed. and Fri.-Sun., $25) are held on the beach and last one hour.

Sights

While Aruba is best known for its glamorous hotels and beautiful beaches, there is much more to the island's character. Experience a different Aruba by exploring its museums, historic sites, and natural wonders.

A walking tour of Aruba's capital, Oranjestad, leads to historical insights, while excursions into the island's natural areas reward with dramatic landscapes punctuated by remnants of a prehistoric culture. Oranjestad's Aruba Historical Museum, in one of the country's oldest structures, Fort Zoutman, provides a journey through Aruba's past. Nature lovers will appreciate the biodiversity in the Aruban outback. Island trees are like giant bonsai due to the constant winds that form them into striking shapes. Stark limestone cliffs and terraces of the

Oranjestad............85
Palm Beach, Malmok, and
    Noord 89
North Coast...........91
Santa Cruz, Paradera, and
    Piedra Plat..........94
San Nicolas, Savaneta, and
    Pos Chiquito.........99

Highlights

Look for ★ to find recommended sights, activities, dining, and lodging.

★ **Fort Zoutman and the Aruba Historical Museum:** The island's oldest structure houses antiques and artifacts from colonial times (page 87).

★ **Butterfly Farm:** Escape to utter tranquility and an inspiring encounter with nature's most beautiful creatures (page 89).

★ **Alto Vista Chapel and Peace Labyrinth:** The stunning vistas at this charming cliffside chapel on the site of Aruba's first church encourage peaceful reflection and make for outstanding photo ops (page 89).

★ **Philip's Animal Garden:** This refuge offers an opportunity to interact with exotic animals from over 100 different species (page 91).

★ **California Lighthouse:** Enjoy a breathtaking 360-degree panorama of Aruba from this perch (page 92).

★ **Aruba Ostrich Farm:** This private nature reserve offers a memorable encounter with the world's largest bird species (page 92).

★ **Ayo Rock Formation:** Quartz diorite formations create a maze of caves and passages that lead to summits with stunning vistas (page 92).

★ **Arikok National Park:** Aruba's largest natural preserve is home to the island's two highest peaks, lovely beaches, and lots of flora and fauna (page 96).

★ **Conchi (Natural Pool):** Cooled lava rock has created a dramatic spot for swimming (page 96).

★ **Museum of Industry:** Situated within the historical water tower of San Nicolas, this beautifully designed museum provides great insight into the economic and social development of the island (page 99).

shorelines are a sharp contrast to the lush landscapes of the touristed areas.

A trip to the California Lighthouse and the north coast reveals a dramatic lunar landscape where the geological origins of Aruba are evident. At popular sights such as Casibari and Ayo Rock Formations or the Bushiribana Gold Ruin, rock climbing is popular and provides exceptional photo ops. Among the caves and rock formations are pictographs and petroglyphs, coded messages from Aruba's original inhabitants dating back thousands of years. Archaeologists have cataloged over 300 in various locations.

Interspersed are unexpected family-friendly delights offering enjoyable interludes, including the Butterfly Farm, the Donkey Sanctuary, and Philip's Animal Garden.

Oranjestad

Strolling the avenues and byways of Oranjestad, you can absorb a lot about Aruba's past. The island's physically small capital is home to most cultural and historic sites. The most interesting landmarks and statues can easily be toured on foot in less than a day, as most are clustered near the harbor in an area dubbed "Historical Oranjestad." Since 1996, a number of Oranjestad's colonial buildings have been returned to their original condition, providing a glimpse of the lifestyle of islanders from centuries past. There are an estimated 100 landmark buildings in Oranjestad alone, and 300 in total on the island. The town has 20 protected historic sights. A number of other landmarks are private homes or businesses. **Kok Optica Opticians** (Wilhelminastraat 11, 297/582-7237), for example, is housed in a landmark building across from Aruba's Town Hall.

Since its inception as a colonial town in the 1600s, the capital has maintained a warren of narrow one-way streets. Driving can be confusing for first-time visitors. There is a large parking lot directly behind the main bus terminal, an excellent starting point for exploring. It is adjacent to a picturesque landmark building, the **Eman House,** now the offices of Aruba Investment Association (ARINA).

MUSEUMS AND HISTORICAL BUILDINGS
NATIONAL ARCHAEOLOGICAL MUSEUM ARUBA (NAMA)

The daily life and culture of Aruba's inhabitants prior to the Spanish arrival are the focus of the **National Archaeological Museum Aruba** (Schelpstraat 42, 297/582-8979 or 297/588-9961, www.namaruba.org, 10am-5pm Tues.-Fri., 10am-2pm Sat.-Sun., free), with permanent and temporary displays and entertaining audiovisual programs. One section of the museum is a research center for archaeology students. NAMA exhibits are designed to immerse: Sit and examine cooking utensils in an authentically reproduced *maloca,* the dwelling of the Caquetios, the original people who settled on the island. Youngsters enjoy making their way through a darkened cave to observe glowing pictographs. The attractive displays transition to colonial times and portray the ethnic diversity of the Aruban people. Artifacts on display include ancient urns, tools, and works of art.

NAMA is in a once crumbling Dutch colonial building known as the Ecury Complex, now restored and pristine. The buildings have historical significance as birthplace of Segundo Jorge Adalberto "Boy" Ecury, Aruba's great World War II hero. A history of

---

the Ecury family is represented with antique photos and documents in the foyer.

★ FORT ZOUTMAN AND THE ARUBA HISTORICAL MUSEUM

Aruba's oldest intact landmark, **Fort Zoutman** (Fort Zoutmanstraat z/n, 297/588-5199, museohistoricoarubano@yahoo.com, 9am-noon and 1:30pm-4pm Mon.-Fri., $5), was built in 1796 and named for Admiral Johan Arnold Zoutman, vice admiral of Holland and West Friesland, who died in 1785 and never visited the island. Before the era of luxury hotels began in 1959, **Willem III Tower,** attached to the fort, was the tallest structure on Aruba. The tower was constructed in 1868 as a public clock and lighthouse. It was first illuminated on February 19, 1868, the birthday of the Dutch monarch for which it is named.

Fort Zoutman is now the home of the **Aruba Historical Museum.** The fort grounds and museum provide a lively overview of island culture, history, and development, including antiques and artifacts of Aruba's colonial years. Exhibits illustrate the lives of fishers and aloe producers with the everyday tools of home life and dress. The exhibit *Aruba: Milestones and Challenges* is a historical overview developed in 2001 for a royal visit. Another exhibit is on island youth and their heritage: Schoolchildren were asked to investigate the history of heirloom objects passed down through generations. The **Bon Bini Festival** (Fort Zoutman, 297/582-3777, 7pm-9pm Tues., $5), featuring traditional island music and dance, happens every Tuesday evening in the courtyard of Fort Zoutman.

BESTUURSKANTOOR (GOVERNMENT HOUSE) AND PARLIAMENT BUILDINGS

Observe Aruba's government in action at the adjoining **Bestuurskantoor and Parliament Buildings** (L. G. Smith Blvd.

1: Fort Zoutman; 2: Oranjestad's Parliament Buildings

76, 297/528-4900, 8am-noon and 1:30pm-4pm Mon.-Fri., free) facing Oranjestad Harbor. These historic edifices include the prime minister's office, where landmark decisions have been made and royalty received. Visitors may be welcomed by an important dignitary if they stop by and inquire into the workings of island government. There is a spectators' gallery to observe Parliament's sessions, which are sometimes heated and dramatic. The entrance is at the side of the building.

MONUMENTS

Aruba commemorates its history and position within the Netherlands with interesting plazas, monuments, and statues along L. G. Smith Boulevard.

PLAZA PADU

Behind the modern new oval ministry annex is the **Plaza Padu,** opened in 2017. It's named for the co-composer of Aruba's national anthem and the island's "Father of Culture," **Juan Chabaya "Padu" Lampe.** Its pinnacle is a bronze statue by noted local artist Ciro Abath in tribute to the three composers of "Aruba Dushi Terra." At the piano are the principal composers, Padu Lampe and Rufo Wever. They wrote the popular song well before it was designated the national anthem in 1976. Standing before them is another icon of island culture, Hubert "Lio" Booi, a noted composer of songs in the classic Aruban style that are popular to this day. Lio added some couplets to the song before its introduction as the national anthem. The beautiful plaza, which centers around a stage and a cascading fountain, is the site of national holiday celebrations, concerts, and special events.

MARCH 18 MEMORIAL

One block east of Parliament is a lagoon that divides the town. The northwest corner of the bridge over the lagoon is the attractive **March 18 Memorial** plaza, commemorating the petition for Aruban independence. This tranquil place is surrounded by a small park and offers a pleasant view of the lagoon and sea. Central

Memorial Statuary in Oranjestad

In its small plazas and both sides of L. G. Smith Boulevard, Oranjestad displays a sizable collection of memorial statuary, paying homage to local people who have had a great impact on the island.

On the east side of the Parliament building, facing the water, is a monument to *Jan Hendrik "Henny" Eman,* founder of the Arubaanse Volkspartij (AVP) and grandfather of Aruba's first prime minister, Henny Eman, and his brother Michiel, who also held the position 2009-2017. He initiated Status Aparte, the movement for Aruban autonomy from the other Netherlands Antilles.

A 10-minute walk east from the March 18 Monument is the statue of *Segundo Jorge Adalberto "Boy" Ecury,* Aruba's beloved World War II hero, in a triangular traffic island next to a small park. Boy Ecury was at school in Holland in 1940 during the German invasion. Rather than return to safety on his Aruban home, Boy joined the Dutch Resistance. His younger brother Nicky also stayed but was too young to go on missions. Boy's Afro-Caribbean features were unusual in Holland at the time and made his daring missions even more dangerous. He volunteered to derail trains to hinder German troop and weapon movements. Boy was captured during an attempt to rescue fellow resistance fighters and died by German firing squad at age 22. A Dutch feature film of his story starred noted actor and director Felix de Rooy as Boy's father. The film tells of the search for his son's remains after the war, with Boy's exploits unfolding as flashbacks. Boy's body was eventually found and received a hero's burial.

The far eastern end of Oranjestad is marked by the large Plaza Las Americas rotunda, fronted by Aruba's center for performing arts, the Cas di Cultura. In front of the art center is a small park with a memorial to *Lloyd G. Smith,* the first general manager of the Lago Refinery, 1933-1946. His policy of improvement for the island beyond the refinery's gates won him the respect and admiration of his hosts and exemplifies the cordial relationship Aruba has maintained with the United States for 100 years.

Wilhelmina Park is the site of the *Anne Frank Memorial,* a charming, wistful statue by Dutch artist Joep Coppens dedicated to ethnic tolerance. Its placement was the first official project of the Foundation Respeta bida . . . semper corda (Respect life . . . always remember). The bronze statue depicts Frank with her hands bound but looking skyward "in hope of a better world," according to the artist. It stands on a pedestal imprinted with a quote from her diary: "How wonderful it is that nobody need wait a single moment before starting to improve the world." Each side carries the message in one of the languages spoken on Aruba: Papiamento, English, Dutch, and Spanish.

to the plaza is a statue of Cornelius Albert "Shon" Eman, who headed the delegation that presented the Status Aparte petition to Queen Juliana on March 18, 1948, during talks in Holland to determine the future of Dutch territories in the region. The names of all 2,147 signatories are carved in the plates on each side of the memorial's statue. During the March 18 celebration in 2010, an eternal flame was placed at the memorial, lit by Prime Minister Mike Eman, "Shon" Eman's youngest son.

QUEEN WILHELMINA PARK

Directly across from the March 18 Memorial is **Queen Wilhelmina Park,** which has a

statue and plaza dedicated to the ruler of the Netherlands from 1898-1948 at its heart. She was the great-grandmother of the current Dutch monarch, Willem-Alexander. This was Aruba's first commemorative statue, unveiled in October 1955 during a royal visit by Wilhelmina's daughter, Queen Juliana. The park is beautifully landscaped, and the large plaza is the site of official ceremonies and events, most notably Koninginnedag (King's Day) on April 27, an impressive annual display of loyalty to the monarchy. Visitors are welcome to join the official event, which takes place in the morning.

ORANJESTAD MEMORIAL PARK

The pleasant **Oranjestad Memorial Park,** across from the *Segundo Jorge Adalberto "Boy" Ecury* monument, is a relaxing stop with lovely flowers and lush gardens that provide shade. The little park is named for the oil tanker *Oranjestad;* it was torpedoed by a German submarine on February 17, 1942, the first tanker sunk in the western hemisphere during World War II. Sitting 69 meters (227 ft) under the sea, the propeller of the ship was retrieved by divers in 2009 and donated to the government. The propeller now stands as a memorial to the lives lost on *Oranjestad* as well as the *Pedernales,* torpedoed and sunk off the western coast of Aruba. The *Pedernales* was refitted at a shipyard in the United States and continued to assist in the Allied war effort, leading islanders to refer to the *Pedernales* as "The Phoenix of Aruba."

Palm Beach, Malmok, and Noord

Palm Beach is a relatively modern district. Not far from the busy shopping and entertainment centers are natural areas and attractions. Some, such as the Butterfly Farm, are within easy walking distance. A short drive at dawn provides fabulous sunrise shots from the Alto Vista Chapel. The Santa Ana Church is a cultural anchor for many Arubans.

★ BUTTERFLY FARM

For exhilarating communion with nature, stop at the **Butterfly Farm** (J. E. Irausquin Blvd. z/n, 297/586-3656, www.thebutterflyfarm. com, 8:30am-4:30pm daily, $15 adults, $8 children), on the land side of the beach road between the Divi Phoenix and Riu Plaza Resorts. Trained guides explain everything you ever wanted to know about butterflies and moths. Did you know butterflies morph in a chrysalis, while moths transform in a cocoon? The most dramatically hued examples of both flitter about freely, feeding on fruit and flowers. Gorgeous species from all over the world can be seen emerging from breeding boxes. Relax on a bench and enjoy the classical music that plays in the background.

Consider visiting early in your trip, since the entry fee allows for unlimited returns, and arrive early in the day, when butterflies are most active. Wear bright clothing and citrus cologne if you want them to land on you. The souvenir shop features one of the largest collections of butterfly-themed knickknacks anywhere.

SANTA ANA CHURCH

At the first major intersection on the Noord-Palm Beach Road beyond the Sasaki Highway (it has a traffic light), **Santa Ana Church** (Noord 16, 297/587-1409, 8am-8:30pm daily), the second church built on the island in 1776, is central to the surrounding community. It was vastly larger than the Alto Vista Chapel, Aruba's first. Rebuilt in 1836 and in 1886 and restructured in 1916, it is notable for beautiful stained-glass windows and an intricate 1870 hand-carved oak altar by artist Hendrik van der Geld. The altar won an award during an exposition of religious art in Rome that year. It was donated to Santa Ana by the Antonius Church of Scheveningen in the Netherlands.

Adjacent to the church is a cemetery, comprising picturesque family vaults. Digging into Aruba's rock is daunting, so this form of burial is common. Dating back centuries, the crypts are brightly painted in the Caribbean way, with epitaphs that offer a glimpse of local family histories.

★ ALTO VISTA CHAPEL AND PEACE LABYRINTH

Aruba's first Catholic church, **Alto Vista Chapel** (sunrise-sunset daily, mass 5:30pm Tues.) was built in 1750 on what was sacred

ground to the Caquetio people. Spanish priest Domingo Antonio Silvestre led the mission to bring the native population into Catholicism. The modest chapel is on a cliff with views of Aruba's rugged north coast, and the simple natural setting encourages reflection.

As larger churches were erected, Alto Vista fell into disuse and crumbled. A community effort in 1952 spearheaded by Shon Kita Henriquez-Lacle prompted the building of a new chapel on the site. Around 2005, islander Peter Auwerda constructed a **Peace Labyrinth** nearby, modeled after the Chartres Labyrinth. Visitors can walk its 11 circuits. The turns are arranged in four quadrants, with 85 lunations around the perimeter. Annually on September 21, International Peace Day, a celebration is staged at the labyrinth to promote world and inner peace.

There's also an annual march on Good Friday along the winding road that leads to the hilltop perch; the parade stops at each of 13 large white crosses along the way to recite prayers.

To get to the chapel, turn right off the Sasaki Highway and take Noord-Palm Beach Road to the first traffic light. The Santa Ana Church is across the intersection on the right. Turn left onto the Noord-Westpunt Road for about 800 meters (0.5 mi) to a sign to turn right for Alto Vista. Follow this road to its end at a T-intersection. Turn left, and follow this road until it ends at the Alto Vista Chapel.

★ PHILIP'S ANIMAL GARDEN

At his family home, Philip Merryweather began at age 12 to create the haven for neglected and abused exotic animals that is now **Philip's Animal Garden** (Alto Vista 116, 297/593-5363, www.philipsanimalgarden. com, guided tours every 30 minutes 9am-5pm daily, $10 adults, $5 under age 10). His parents had an exceptionally large property in a rural area. His passion for protecting ocelots, monkeys, kangaroos, and macaws began when he observed how owners neglected them after they stopped being cute babies. By the time he rescued them, they were traumatized and aggressive. His patience and determination to learn about their needs contributed to their rehabilitation. Aruba has since passed stringent laws regulating exotic animals and trafficking in endangered species. Philip now houses 600 animals from 80 species, with public tours to finance their feeding and care. Philip's Animal Garden is a nonprofit, and entrance fees and donations maintain the facility.

North Coast

The California Lighthouse is the limit for touring in an ordinary car; beyond is 4WD country. The dividing line is the base of the California Lighthouse mount; beyond it are grueling gravel roads for 4WD or all-terrain vehicles. This part of the island is not well settled, and the sights are the natural formations of the dramatic landscape and a few rare historic structures. North coast sights can also be approached by regular roads passing through Paradera or Santa Cruz.

Unless otherwise specified, these sights do not have regulated hours and can be visited without fees. With the exception of Black Stone Beach and Conchi, these sights are regular stops on bus tours of the area. The harder-to-reach locations are on most safari tours. The north shore is a stark landscape of limestone cliffs carved by the waves and the speckled pillow basalt created by lava bubbling up from eruptions under the sea, a stark contrast to resort areas.

The first thing to capture your attention on the north coast road is a proliferation of purposely placed rock piles, some quite artistic.

1: Alto Vista Chapel; 2: Butterfly Farm; 3: Philip's Animal Garden

How this practice began is a mystery. A number of tour guides decided it would add some spice to their tours to tell clients it was an ancient tradition to pile the rocks and make a wish to return to Aruba. Each guide has their own version of the tale. Since the rock piles first began appearing 15-20 years ago, it's unlikely that this is true. Visitors are welcome to play along with the charade; children love it. In 2018, a group of concerned islanders deduced that moving the rocks from their natural placement was detrimental to soil and plant life. Volunteers spent a weekend overturning all the rock piles, but they are making a speedy comeback.

★ CALIFORNIA LIGHTHOUSE

The **California Lighthouse** (Hudishibana 2, 297/586-0787 http://arubalighthouse.com, 24 hours daily, $10) sits on Westpunt peak, the northwest point of the island, and has stunning views of the north and west coasts. The lighthouse opened to visitors after extensive repairs and renovations in 2017, and you can now climb to the light room for a 360-degree panorama of Aruba. Tours (8:30am-4:45pm daily) are conducted every 15 minutes for up to eight people. It's also possible to arrange a private tour ($64), which can be scheduled outside the standard hours; sunrise and sunset are popular for memorable marriage proposals.

The lighthouse, built in 1916, was named for a wooden U.S. cargo ship that sank nearby in 1898. The remains are an established dive site in shallow water. Contrary to widespread misconception, this is not the ship that refused to answer the *Titanic*'s distress call in 1912; that was the SS *Californian*, a steel-hulled ship sunk by a German torpedo in 1915. According to local oral history, the area became popular for salvaging the cargo from the ship, which would wash up on shore. Islanders began referring to the area as California Point.

BUSHIRIBANA GOLD RUIN

Impossible to miss on the north coast road are the medievalesque contours of the **Bushiribana Gold Ruin** (Mativaderi z/n, north coast road next to the junction to the Ostrich Farm, 24 hours daily, free). Built in 1874 by the Aruba Island Gold Mining Company of London, the ruins are atmospheric, weather-beaten, and look older than they are. Youngsters love climbing the terraces and rock formations. Combined with the dramatic crashing sea, the ruins and the view from their ramparts offer interesting photo ops.

The structure was a repository for ore during Aruba's gold rush. It began when 12-year-old Willem Rasmijn found traces of gold at Rooi Fluit in 1824 while herding his father's sheep. This discovery heralded a new era of prosperity and increased settlement. The ruins are also a landmark for the turnoff to the Ostrich Farm, less than a mile inland.

★ ARUBA OSTRICH FARM

A bit of Africa in the Aruban outback, the **Aruba Ostrich Farm** (Matividiri 57, 297/585-9630, www.arubaostrichfarm.com, 9am-4pm daily, Mon.-Sat. $14 adults, $7 ages 3-6, Sun. $11 adults, free ages 3-6) is a private nature preserve with tours every half hour. Interacting with these huge curious birds is memorable and entertaining. Be careful with brightly colored cameras and sparkly jewelry—the birds are attracted to them, and the adults have *very* long necks. A reasonably priced on-site, open-air restaurant offers views of the surrounding countryside along with burgers, salads, and platters with Dutch influence.

★ AYO ROCK FORMATION

Travel back to preceramic times at **Ayo Rock Formation** (Ayo z/n, signs indicate turnoff on route 7A, 24 hours daily, free), where huge quartz diorite formations form a maze of caves and passages that lead to summits with panoramic vistas. The area is easily explored on trails carved by park rangers to provide

---

1: California Lighthouse; 2: Aruba Ostrich Farm; 3: Ayo Rock Formation

clear paths to the summits. The Arawak people sought shelter here, and their shamans used this place to commune with the spirit world. A few spectacular cave paintings are in the hollowed-out formations. This is Aruba's gold country, and gold dust can be seen in the soil around Ayo's formations. Picnic tables and public restrooms are available.

Santa Cruz, Paradera, and Piedra Plat

For the most part these inland areas offer a glimpse into everyday island life, with its dense residential communities. But impressive rock formations are here as well, such as those at Casibari, a busy stop on most tours. You'll travel through these areas to reach Arikok National Park. The Hooiberg (Haystack Mountain), often mistaken for Aruba's highest point, dominates the skyline.

HOOIBERG (HAYSTACK MOUNTAIN)

The distinctive profile of the Hooiberg is one of the first things that catches your eye when leaving the airport. **Hooiberg peak** (Hooiberg z/n, accessible from roads 4A or 7A to Santa Cruz, a sign indicates the turn to the base of the stairway, 24 hours daily, free), which means "haystack" in Dutch, offers a remarkable panorama of Aruba from the middle of the island, a unique perspective from its third highest point. No roads or easy paths lead to the top. A 563-step stairway to the summit is challenging, with steps that are not comfortably sized or spaced, but there are places to rest along the way. Climb to the top only if you are in excellent shape. The reward is fantastic vistas of all of Aruba and the mountains of Venezuela.

CASIBARI ROCK FORMATION

The fantastical quartz diorite formations at **Casibari** (Casibari z/n, off of Santa Cruz-Paradera Rd., 24 hours daily, free) are lots of fun and an easy climb for all ages. Casibari is just off the principal Santa Cruz-Paradera Road, and the turnoff is clearly marked. The formations are more concentrated and organized than at Ayo. Tunnels and byways through the rocks have been tailored and trimmed and are strung with ropes for safety. One passage is a tight fit, allowing only one person at a time, which might be difficult with very small children. Surrounding the principal attraction are gardens and paths for exploring indigenous flora. This is a stop on nearly every tour, making it crowded at most hours. Across from the entrance is a snack shop and lavatories. There is a little snow cone wagon by the entrance that sells coconut water straight from a freshly opened nut, an interesting and invigorating treat.

DONKEY SANCTUARY

Animal and nature lovers will enjoy the **Donkey Sanctuary** (Bringamosa 2C, Donkey Distress Hotline 297/593-2933, www.arubandonkey.org, 9am-4pm daily, free), a refuge and natural park. The donkeys are intelligent, gentle, and friendly, and they eagerly nibble carrots or apple pieces; if the free-wandering donkeys spot you walking in with a bag of carrots, they will surround you instantly and follow you everywhere. Children especially enjoy getting to know the donkeys. There are always some young donkeys around. The Donkey Sanctuary is a nonprofit supported by donations and gift-shop purchases, and their efforts have allowed Aruba's donkey population to survive.

Brought to Aruba by the Spanish 500 years ago, *buricos* (donkeys) were a principal mode of transport for centuries. They were abandoned for internal combustion vehicles with the advent of the Lago Refinery. When the first car was brought to Aruba in

1: Casibari Rock Formation; 2: stairs leading to the top of Hooiberg

1915, the island had a population of 1,400 donkeys. Owners released their donkeys into the countryside. They are hardy animals, but by 1970 only 20 were left. The two families living in the wild were in serious distress when concerned islanders founded the nonprofit Fundacion Salba Nos Burico (Save Our Donkeys) in 1997.

To get to the sanctuary, take the Frenchman's Pass turnoff on the Santa Cruz main road, which is clearly marked. It is a steep decline. Once you get past the residential area and are surrounded by only *cunucu* houses, a road to the left has a prominent sign for the sanctuary. Follow this road until you spot the donkeys and a big sign.

NATURAL BRIDGE

Many tours stop at what used to be one of Aruba's most popular sights, the **Natural Bridge** (24 hours daily, free). This huge rock formation came about from the sea pounding the limestone into a unique shape. Erosion resulted in the bridge collapsing in 2005. What remains allows visitors to venture some distance out over the water on the **Baby Natural Bridge,** as it's known, a smaller version attached to the fallen section; from here you can enjoy the dramatic landscape and take interesting pictures. There is a refreshment stand and a souvenir shop at the bridge, as well as clean toilets ($1).

The Natural Bridge is easily accessible by paved road. Follow the signs to the Aruba Ostrich Farm from the Paradera traffic circle on A4. Take it to a T-intersection ending on the north coast; turn right and follow the road to its end at the Natural Bridge.

TOP EXPERIENCE

★ ARIKOK NATIONAL PARK

Aruba's largest natural preserve, **Arikok National Park** (San Fuego 70, 297/585-1234, www.arubanationalpark.org, 8am-4pm daily, $11) occupies 18 percent of the island's landmass. The park offers more than 32 kilometers (20 mi) of trails for hiking and biking, lovely beaches along the north shore popular for bodyboarding, and attractions including Conchi (Natural Pool) and the Quadirikiri and Fontein Caves. Aruba's two highest peaks, Jamanota and Arikok, are also within the park. You can get information about the flora and fauna in the area at the visitors center.

Most sights can be accessed by car. In a 4WD vehicle, Arikok National Park can be reached by continuing along the road from the Donkey Sanctuary. It is also accessible over better roads via Santa Cruz, with a pass through Paradera and Piedra Plat on the way from the main resort areas.

★ CONCHI (NATURAL POOL)

The Papiamento name for one of the north coast's most breathtaking sights, **Conchi** (Arikok National Park, follow the road to the summit of Seroe Arikok then down its back directly to the entrance), means "bowl," owing to the bowl shape of lava rock that forms this dramatic pool. A wall of pillow basalt protects the cove from huge waves, forming a calm spot for swimming. Various terraces are popular for climbing and jumping in the water, creating a natural water park. You can also snorkel here; tours often provide snorkel gear, or bring your own (though you'll likely just see a few fish).

While the rocks lining the Natural Pool aren't slippery, be wary of climbing to the top of the rim; the sea splashes against the bowl sometimes with great force, and if you're directly in the way of these rugged waves, you'll be knocked around the rocks.

The beauty of this site is definitely worth the effort, but getting here and back is an adventure. Rugged winding roads approaching Conchi are impossible to traverse with an ordinary car. Leave the driving to an experienced guide with a reliable vehicle. Another option is to arrive on horseback; **Rancho Loco** (www.rancholocoaruba.com), bordering the park, conducts a trek to the Natural Pool. There are also trails to Conchi from Arikok National Park's main and secondary

Arikok National Park

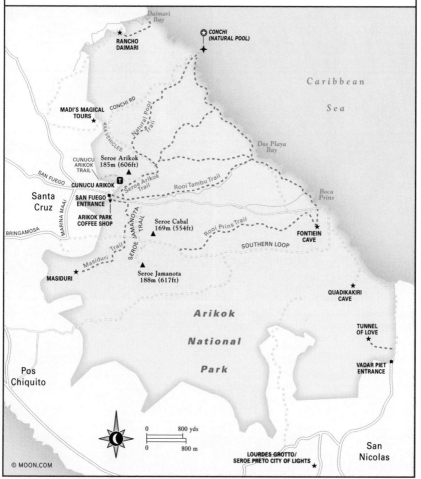

entrances; take the trail from the secondary entrance at Shete if you're hiking or biking—it's closed to motorized traffic. Also, be prepared for a long climb down a stairway to access the pool.

Since many tours stop here, Conchi can get congested. Visit the area early in the day to avoid the crowds. Note that hikers and bikers have a better opportunity to beat the crowds here as they're allowed to enter the park before the official 8am opening (so long

as an entry ticket is purchased post-hike or -ride).

A couple of privately owned snack wagons set up at the top of Conchi's stairway; purchase a light lunch, sandwiches, snacks, and cold refreshments. There are no restrooms around the pool.

QUADIRIKIRI AND FONTEIN CAVES
The **Quadirikiri and Fontein Caves** (Arikok National Park, San Fuego 70)

provide easy and safe spelunking opportunities. In the caves you can see pictographs left by the Caquetio people and early European settlers, as well as dramatic stalagmites and stalactites. These can be enjoyed without a flashlight as the caves are filled with light from natural openings in the ceilings. Park rangers guide visitors for no extra fee (although tips are appreciated); they are equipped with flashlights to illuminate some of the more interesting aspects. The chambers are connected by easily traversed passages, with more hazardous and poorly lit areas blocked off. Some are only 1.2 meters (4 ft) high, and most adults will have to bend down to crab walk through them. There is a bat population that's closely monitored; they present no dangers to people.

San Nicolas, Savaneta, and Pos Chiquito

Aruba's "Sunrise City," San Nicolas, has an authentic Caribbean feeling. Known as the site of the Lago Refinery and Colony, it has a distinct character. The inhabitants are proud of their multicultural roots. In the late 1920s, people from around the Caribbean came to work at the refinery, enriching Aruba's culture by infusing it with their traditions. Most visitors come to San Nicolas to explore areas such as Baby Beach, but there are also interesting sights such as Lourdes Grotto. Heading back west toward the hotels, you pass a number of attractive shore areas in Savaneta and Pos Chiquito.

LOURDES GROTTO

The natural formations of **Lourdes Grotto** (turn left on Pastoor Hendrikstraat at the San Nicolas YMCA, where a sign indicates the turnoff, dawn-dusk daily, free) are dominated by a 700-kilogram (1,540-lb) statue of the Virgin Mary, a shrine to Saint Bernadette, the Lady of Lourdes. Many believe it offers healing properties like its namesake in France. The grotto is a natural formation in the rock cliffs on the road to Seroe Preto, or Black Point, clearly indicated by road signs.

Local oral history reports islanders having a vision of Mary at this spot. A community effort maintains this tribute with candles and fresh flowers. Each year on February 11, the Feast Day of Our Lady of Lourdes, **St. Theresita Church** (St. Theresitaplein 8, 297/584-5118) in San Nicolas organizes a pilgrimage to the site, culminating with a mass. The site was unveiled 150 years after Bernadette had her vision, in 1958.

★ MUSEUM OF INDUSTRY

The **Museum of Industry** (Bernhardtstraat 164, 297/584-7090, 9am-6pm Mon.-Fri., 10am-2pm Sat., $5) is in the town center in San Nicolas's landmark *watertoran* (water tower), high above other buildings. It traces the economic development of Aruba, bringing many other aspects of its history to light. The island's commerce and the iconic individuals who enabled its development are told through interactive exhibits and documentaries made just for the museum.

SAN NICOLAS COMMUNITY MUSEUM

Opened in 2018, **San Nicolas Community Museum** (van de Veenzeppenfeldstraat 27 297/280-0018, 9am-6pm Mon.-Fri., 10am-2pm Sat., $5) is in the landmark Nicolaas Store, named for its owner, an emigre from Sint Maarten and one of the key figures in

1: Fontein Caves; **2:** Quadirikiri Caves; **3:** Arikok National Park

Seroe Preto City of Lights

Seroe Preto is a must-see at holiday time.

One of Aruba's most attractive sights can only be seen in San Nicolas from the first weekend in December to Three Kings Day (Jan. 6): **Seroe Preto City of Lights** (Seroe Preto z/n, 24 hours daily, free). Volunteers build a fantastical town out of colored lights with a different theme each year, taking up the entire hillside. Walkways allow visitors to climb the hill and immerse themselves in the experience. The festival includes at least one notable Aruban landmark. For impressive pictures, bring a tripod to keep your camera steady. The display is a labor of love by the **Stichting Hunbentud Uni Seroe Preto** (United Youth Foundation of Seroe Preto) and costs $12,000 each year to construct, not including the utility bills. The project is funded by donations and fund-raising events through the year. The first efforts began in 1957 and were simple compared to the elaborate work today.

Most weeknights, Seroe Preto is relatively quiet, and you'll be able to snap photos without crowds. During the holiday break and on weekends, it gets very busy. Friday-Saturday nights see musical performances by seasonal *gaita* singing groups until late. *Gaita* originates from Maracaibo in Venezuela, and *gaita* groups consist of 8-12 female singers accompanied by native instruments such as a *cuarto* (a small guitar) and *tambora* (goatskin drums).

Wagons sell snacks and refreshments. On the final night, a blowout farewell bash is held before the lights go off. Everyone brings food and drink, and the live music goes until dawn. The tone seesaws from "Silent Night" to "Don't Stop the Party" as Carnival bands take over to mark the beginning of the season. This is a joyous, authentically Aruban holiday experience.

To get here, head north off Pastoor Hendrikstraat street in San Nicolas toward the Lourdes Grotto church; at a signed fork in the road, you'll make a left to Seroe Preto.

the economic development of the island. The museum explores the enormous impact the development of San Nicolas had on the island. The multicultural sense of community across so many groups is an essential element to the character of the town and Aruba.

This is a new incarnation of the Aruba Antiquities Museum, which closed in 2010. The Odor family accumulated a number of antiques that chronicled life on Aruba from the 18th century to the present, including documents, newspapers, and artwork, and the museum exhibits some of these, along with modern artwork. Since the Aruba Antiquities Museum had such a huge collection of artifacts, this much smaller community museum has rotating exhibits of the vast inventory, in addition to some permanent displays.

The museum faces the main rotary on main street, across from the bus station. It's at the back of the restored Nicolaas Building on the 2nd floor. Entrance is through the rear doors, inside the cute snack shop on the first level.

San Nicolas Community Museum

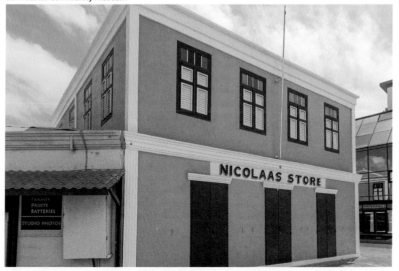

Food

Oranjestad.............104

Eagle Beach and Manchebo
    Beach 116

Palm Beach, Malmok, and
    Noord 122

North Coast............132

Santa Cruz, Paradera, and
    Piedra Plat............132

San Nicolas, Savaneta, and
    Pos Chiquito.........135

Aruba's repeat visitors say it's the food that

keeps them coming back to the island. The superb quality and selection of restaurants has generated loyal clientele.

Fine dining used to be the ken of the hotels without much competition from independent restaurants, and the hotels were relatively pricey. Now many excellent spots for breakfast, lunch, and dinner are within easy walking distance of the resorts. As a result, hotels have reevaluated their menus to compete in both pricing and innovation.

An explosion of eateries over the last 20 years continues as the island's population diversifies. You can choose a different cuisine every night. An influx of classically trained chefs from Europe and the United States has also resulted in fusion cuisine producing tantalizing original

Highlights

Look for ★ to find recommended sights, activities, dining, and lodging.

★ **Excelencia:** Find authentic Aruban cuisine, including fresh fish, for reasonable prices inside a landmark building in Oranjestad's historic district (page 104).

★ **Carte Blanche:** Aruba's originator of the prix fixe dining experience crafted for a small group each night delivers a memorable evening (page 105).

★ **Smit & Dorlas Coffee House:** Aruba's first coffee shop is still its most charming. Relax with a good cup of joe and a complimentary cookie (page 114).

★ **Yami Yami:** With good Chinese food at local prices, this is Aruba's favorite fast food (page 117).

★ **Red Fish:** This authentic Aruban fish shack is within walking distance of the Manchebo Beach resorts (page 118).

★ **Elements:** This beachfront restaurant is unquestionably one of the most romantic dining spots on the island, with excellent food and a tranquil ambience. (page 119).

★ **Terrazza Italiana:** Indulge in hearty pastas and pizzas at this reasonably priced restaurant with stunning shoreline views from its beachfront terrace (page 120).

★ **Senses:** Limited seating and delightful presentation make a fine meal a culinary experience (page 121).

★ **Salt Life:** Dine with the locals at this eatery specializing in fresh fish and other seafood (page 132).

★ **Zeerover:** This lovely spot on the water has authentic Caribbean ambience and the freshest of fish (page 135).

★ **O'Niel Caribbean Kitchen:** Chef O'Niel draws on his classic culinary training and regional roots to create a delectable and moderately priced gourmet menu (page 136).

dishes with Caribbean flair. Regional seasoning and indigenous fruits and vegetables liven up menus, including passion fruit sauces and mango salsas. Aruba's clean, abundant waters of course mean this is also a seafood lover's paradise, and beachside dining—particularly at sunset—is a part of the Aruban experience. Americans looking for familiar fare can still find a steak, hamburger, or pizza, never far from major resorts.

Oranjestad

Unlike Manchebo Beach and Palm Beach, most restaurants in town are filled with islanders, and dining is a different experience than at the resorts. Oranjestad has regional ambience, and food is more reasonably priced. Most Arubans also do their supermarket shopping on the western end of Oranjestad, helpful to note for self-caterers staying in a rental apartment, condo, or time-share.

ARUBAN

★ EXCELENCIA

A charming venue for island cuisine is **Excelencia** (Wilhelminastraat 21, 297/583-0021, 11:30am-10pm Mon.-Sat., $6-22), in the heart of Oranjestad a five-minute walk from the Renaissance Resort. With an elegant, cozy dining room in a landmark building, the waitstaff is friendly and ready to impart information about the island. Classic Aruban dishes include *stoba* made with *cabrito,* beef, or pigtail, among changing daily specials, including a fresh catch of the day. Highly recommended is the whole fresh snapper. Entrées are served with favorite Aruban sides. You'll also find more "American" fare on the menu such as filet mignon and lobster tail. A soup and main course of the day are featured, and a lunch combo with ice cream dessert runs about $6. A more elaborate dinner is $13.50.

CAFÉ MARYLI

A bastion of authentic *cuminda criollo,* **Café Maryli** (Caya Ernesto Petronia 72, 297/583-1889, 11am-6pm Mon.-Sat., $10-14) is a clean tiny place at the northern border of town in the front corner of the small Heimee shopping mall. The specialty is Aruban stews and soups made from whatever is fresh and available. The menu changes daily and is posted on a chalkboard. Platters come with pan-fried pork chops, roast chicken or ribs, and fresh fish grilled, fried, or creole-style. Find authentic local dishes such as *pan bati* or *funchi,* usually served with fish or soup. Islanders usually order takeout, as the tiny dining room offers few tables, which open up after the lunchtime rush.

SEAFOOD

AQUARIUS

A favorite lunch spot for island movers and shakers is **Aquarius** (L. G. Smith Blvd. 82, 297/523-6195, 7am-11am, noon-3:30pm, and 5:30pm-11:30pm Mon.-Sat., 7am-11am and 5:30pm-11:30pm Sun., breakfast buffet $18, Sunday brunch $30, lunch buffet $15-20, dinner seafood buffet $39), next to the reception desk of the Renaissance Marina Tower. The restaurant has chic decor and extremely accommodating staff. Bank presidents and parliamentarians may be dining at the next table or lining up for the fabulous lunch buffet. The two choices are: cold, which is just the salad bar, soup of the day, the dessert table, and unlimited iced tea; or the full buffet, with a selection of local dishes and a pasta station. The cold option has a diverse array of all-you-can-eat sushi, a cold fish dish, ceviche and seasoned salads, and all the greens and

---

Previous: whole red snapper at Excelencia; beachside meal at Bugaloe; Carte Blanche.

accompaniments you could imagine, with fresh-made dressings. The dessert assortment changes daily. Dinner adds to the buffet a fresh fish station where you choose from a few kinds of fish and shellfish to be sautéed before your eyes. Try the yummy mango salsa.

THE OLD FISHERMAN

For fresh fish, islanders will tell you to go to The Old Fisherman (L. G. Smith Blvd. 100, 297/588-3648, http://oldfishermanaruba.com, 11:30am-10pm daily, $22-44), once a tiny hole-in-the-wall on the water at the harbor where local anglers would drop their catch. Food was only to take out. It was so popular that the eatery moved into more spacious surroundings across from the cruise ship terminal. Platters of fresh fish and seafood are named for friends and family and prepared as you like: sautéed, breaded and fried, with creamy garlic sauce, or meunière. The signature dish is the "Claudio Wolfe"—a whole red snapper fried, grilled, or stewed. The dining room is filled with locals, and there is always a feeling of being with family and friends.

CARIBBEAN FUSION
★ CARTE BLANCHE

Chef Dennis van Daatselaar originated in Aruba the concept of an intimate experience shared by a small group of diners when he opened Carte Blanche (Wilhelminastraat 74, 297/586-3339, www.carteblanchearuba.com, seating 7pm Tues.-Sat., $109). It was revolutionary for the island's dining scene and rocketed to success, which has not affected personable Dennis and fellow host Glen, the restaurant's wine and drinks specialist. Frequently imitated, the excellent cuisine and innate charm has not been surpassed. The five-course meal is ever-changing and consists of a balance of seafood and meat dishes. The dinner comes with a complimentary glass of sparkling white wine, or add a full wine pairing for $89. Only 16 spots are available for each night's 7pm seating, so reserve online up to several months in advance during high season.

FRED

A short walk from the Renaissance Resort, Fred (Wilhelminastraat 18, 297/565-2324, www.fredaruba.com, 7pm-10pm Mon.-Fri., $100), named for its chef, has taken over the second level of a charming historic building. A maximum of 10 guests are served a fabulous five-course meal prepared by Fred while his partner, Tommie, "glues the night together" by mixing drinks, pouring wine (pairing available at additional cost), and chatting. Meals include an appetizer, a soup, a fish course, a meat course, and a glorious dessert, which usually consists of three different sweet dishes (always including something chocolate). The meal begins at 7pm and finishes around 10pm, but guests are invited to join their hosts on the rooftop terrace to chat and sip a fine vintage until they care to go. Reserve in advance online.

IGUANA JOE'S

A trendy Caribbean menu is the signature of Iguana Joe's (L. G. Smith Blvd., 297/583-9373, www.iguanajoesaruba.com, 11am-midnight Mon.-Sat., 5pm-11pm Sun., $15-25), on the second level of the Royal Plaza Mall, first in a local franchise that includes Smokey Joe's and Iguana Cantina in Palm Beach. Famous for island potions, they also serve traditional local favorites, including *keshi yena* and Aruban-style fresh fish. Regional specialties include jerk chicken and jambalaya, and the ribs are popular. It has funky decor and a great view of the harbor and boulevard for observing island life.

QUE PASA

A longtime Oranjestad favorite with an eclectic menu, Que Pasa (Wilhelminastraat 18, 297/583-4888, www.quepasaaruba.com, 4pm-11pm daily, $19-33) features regional cuisine with European flair. In a landmark building, it has lively Caribbean decor and showcases original art. Fresh specials of the day might be fish or steak. Loyal patrons rave about the tomato soup and ribs. The exceptionally friendly staff is happy to offer recommendations. Que Pasa features an appealing three-course menu ($40) that changes regularly. Every Wednesday is a three-course Indonesian meal ($30). Deep discounts for early birds can be had 4pm-6pm daily.

WILHELMINA

Part of the three-restaurant complex at the head of the Wilhelminastraat is the appropriately named **Wilhelmina,** (Wilhelminastraat 74, 297/583-0445, www.wilhelminaaruba. com, 6pm-10pm Tues.-Sun., $26-46), an elegant eatery sandwiched between Maroc and Carte Blanche. Prices are higher, but patrons consider the fine food worth the expense. At the low end of the main menu is a goat cheese falafel on tomato carpaccio and baby spinach; at the opposite is dover sole, dramatically prepared tableside. On Saturday nights, a five-course tasting menu ($57) is available. Wilhelmina also has a fabulously tempting dessert selection, including caramelized whole apples with ice cream and a dessert martini. Dine indoors or in the charming garden in the back.

BEACHSIDE DINING

At the very eastern border of L. G. Smith Boulevard is Surfside, the principal spot for beachside dining in Oranjestad apart from the boardwalk at Governor's Bay.

BAREFOOT

Uniquely designed, **Barefoot** (L. G. Smith Blvd. 1, 297/588-9824, www.barefootaruba. com, 5pm-10pm daily, $25-43) takes its name from the central dining room, a sandbox with tables, where patrons are encouraged to take off their shoes. (There are also no-sand options.) The circular dining area is an open-air terrace great for sunsets. The elegant gourmet cuisine from European chef-owner Gerco earns rave reviews. Dishes emphasize seafood, such as fresh crab cakes and seafood ragout. A reasonably priced three-course meal varies daily. Preparation and presentation are beautiful, but expect somewhat smaller portions in the European fashion.

PINCHOS GRILL AND BAR

A distinctive menu and memorable location mark **Pinchos Grill and Bar** (L. G. Smith Blvd. 7, 297/583-2666, www.pinchosaruba. com, 5pm-midnight daily, $24-44), one of the most romantic places to dine on Aruba. The ultracool ambience and live mellow music on weekends make it popular for businesspeople to stop for a cocktail. Veteran restaurateurs Robby and Anabella Peterson realized a dream when they opened Pinchos, named for the skewers cooked over an open wood grill that are the restaurant's claim to fame, along with distinctive dipping sauces and unique marinades. The chicken kebabs and black Angus rum-infused blue cheese tenderloin are delicious, as are the jumbo shrimp and chunky fish kebabs.

REFLEXIONS BEACH RESTAURANT AND LOUNGE

Adjacent to Barefoot, **Reflexions Beach Restaurant and Lounge** (L. G. Smith Blvd. 1A, 297/582-0153, www.reflexionsaruba.com, 10am-10pm daily, $20-43) is a longtime favorite for beachside dining among Aruba's Dutch population. The all-day spot has a shaded club area and a pool on the dining terrace. The beach and restaurant are lined with stylish couches and lounges. Snack service on the terrace or the beach allows for soaking up the island ambience. Most local weekend patrons linger well into the night. The dinner menu features gourmet appetizers and seafood. During the day, enjoy platters of assorted local and Dutch snacks. When available, a fresh snapper platter ($20) is prepared in classic Aruban fashion. On weekends they host high-decibel music events during a two-for-one happy hour (4pm-6pm), and the party continues until late, transforming this quiet beachside eatery into a trendy club.

SURFSIDE BEACH BAR

Surfside offers a tranquil beach despite being adjacent to the airport, and the **SurfSide**

1: Aquarius buffet; **2:** Carte Blanche

Beach Bar (L. G. Smith Blvd. 21, 297/280-6584, www.surfsidearuba.com, 9am-8pm daily, $6-14) makes the most of it. Open for moderately priced breakfasts, lunches, and dinners, you can eat while watching jumbo jets taking off and landing. Attracting islanders as well as a diverse tourist crowd, this charming place has a nicely shaded dining area to savor the view of the sea and sunset while munching on fish fingers, paninis, hot wings, or burgers. An ample barbecue platter ($9) is featured Sunday, drawing lots of locals. Drink offerings are reasonably priced, from exotic martinis ($5) to a bucket of beer ($20).

THE WEST DECK

The upgrading of the Oranjestad shorefront has resulted in a charming eatery at the center of the town called The West Deck (L. G. Smith Blvd. z/n, at Governor's Bay, 297/587-2667, www.thewestdeck.com, 10:30am-11pm daily, $13-46). Diners can sit on the expansive deck overlooking the water or at picnic tables on the sand. The eclectic menu includes Bahamas-style conch fritters, jerk chicken wings, West Indian samosas, enormous burgers, or fresh whole baby red snapper, Aruban-style. Finger-food appetizers can be ordered by the dozen. A single menu offers options for lunch, dinner, or snacking. A meal can range from inexpensive to pricey, especially if you order side dishes priced à la carte. Food is prepared and presented with flair, and The West Deck attracts lots of tourists but is also popular with a chic local crowd. Islanders come in large groups for extended social evenings by the water. Reservations are a must; the location and congenial staff have made it a hot spot, particularly around sunset. It is not nearly as crowded for brunch or lunch.

CUBAN

CUBA'S COOKIN'

Cuba's Cookin' (L. G. Smith Blvd., in the Renaissance Marketplace, 297/588-0627, www.cubascookin.com, 7am-11pm daily, $27-43) strives to create the carefree vivacious ambience of prerevolutionary Havana in the 1950s. Aside from a lively menu, the restaurant features a live band nightly, plus a salsa show and lessons every Monday. The open-air eatery has congenial staff and an atmosphere that encourages you to linger past dinner. The menu emphasizes Caribbean-style seafood and classic Cuban *ropa vieja* and ribs. It is the only restaurant on Aruba to have matzoball soup, if you have a hankering. The chef is attentive to some dietary requirements with tasty vegan and gluten-free dishes, including the "Mean Women's Pasta."

DUTCH

DE SUIKERTUIN

Long a charming place for an authentic Dutch meal, De Suikertuin (Wilhelminastraat 64, 297/582-6322, www.desuikertuin.com, 11am-10pm Mon.-Sat., $16-33), "The Sugar Garden," is aptly named. In a landmark *cunucu* house, it features a beautifully landscaped patio in the backyard for outdoor dining and quaint, air-conditioned, authentically maintained indoor rooms. A Dutch-European lunch and dinner menu has some Aruban touches. Luncheon baguettes might contain peanut butter with sprinkles (a Dutch treat) or smoked salmon with dill dressing. Try the pumpkin soup, a local delicacy, or the Aruban dish *keshi yena*. Once or twice a month, De Suikertuin hosts theme nights with wine tastings and amuse bouche samples from a visiting or local gourmet chef. These events can be found on the Facebook page for Aruba Promote Your Business. This is also where a secret password is posted for patrons to enjoy a special night when prices are in florins instead of dollars, meaning deep discounts.

FLOR DE ORIENTE

In the heart of Oranjestad just behind the courthouse is Flor de Oriente (Kerkstraat 6, 297/583-9808, 3pm-midnight Mon.-Sat., 2pm-midnight Sun., $4-17), one of Aruba's oldest rum shops. It was purchased by a Dutchman who converted it into this atmospheric and traditional "brown bar," a tiny pub-like Dutch establishment that specializes in dark beers.

Local Cuisine

Aruban food has been influenced by the island's history and its diverse cultures, and was often based on what could be found regionally and inexpensively. It has some surprising elements. Make sure to enjoy some *cuminda criollo* (local cuisine) while you're here.

WHAT TO EAT

Stoba (stew) is a mainstay. It can be made of *galena* (chicken), *carne* (meat), *cabrito* (goat), or *konkomber* (a sort of local squash).

Favorite Aruban side dishes include *pampona* (pumpkin), fried plantain, or *funchi* (a version of polenta, firm cornmeal that can be sliced or cubed). *Funchi* is often fried and served with melted cheese (you can feel your arteries hardening as you eat it), a beloved treat. Another

bami

standby is *pan bati,* meaning beaten bread; it's a firm cornmeal pancake.

The Dutch influence integrated into island cuisine traditional dishes from Indonesia, another former colony, and the seasonings are part of Aruba's everyday diet. Basic Indonesian dishes are *bami* (lo mein noodles) and *nasi goreng* (fried rice), traditionally made from leftovers. Most Asian restaurants also serve a *bami* or *nasi* special, which includes a sampling of Indonesian dishes with a local touch; the noodles or rice are surrounded with small servings of *sate* (pork, chicken, or beef mini skewers) with *pinda* (peanut) sauce, coconut shrimp, chicken, fish, fried sweet banana, sometimes breaded, and other traditional items.

Another colonial holdover is a snack called *loempia,* large egg rolls second in popularity only to *pastechi,* tender, half-moon-shaped, fried pastries filled with cheese, chop suey, curried chicken, fish, or beef. They are distinct from empanadas, which are made with cornmeal and also popular. *Pastechi* is the Aruban way to start the day, usually paired with a *malta,* a strong root beer.

A dish unique to the ABC (Aruba, Bonaire, and Curaçao) islands is *keshi yena,* or "full cheese." Traditionally, edam cheese came in a large ball and was eaten by cutting or scooping out the soft cheese and leaving the hardened rind. This rind would then be filled with a stew of chicken, beef, or seafood and the halves wrapped together in foil to be slowly baked. It was served whole and opened at the table by cracking it with a ritual hammer. Today, restaurants serving local food have this on the menu, but the hours-long traditional method has been replaced by surrounding the basic stew with melted gouda, which is milder than edam.

Aruban food shines in the assortment of fresh Caribbean fish available, a revelation if you've never had it. The sweet, moist, clean taste can convert the most ardent fish hater. Ciguatera, a type of food poisoning from species high on the food chain such as snapper or barracuda, is not an issue here—fish from local waters are completely safe to consume. *Moochi* is the favorite Aruban preparation style—the catch is cut into fish steaks and flash fried.

WHERE TO EAT

- **Excelencia, Café Maryli,** and **O'Niel Caribbean Kitchen** for *stoba*

- **Yami Yami** for *bami* or *nasi*

- **Flor de Oriente** for *loempia*

- **Djespie's Place** for *pastechi*

- **De Suikertuin, The Old Cunucu House,** and **Papiamento** for *keshi yena*

- **Red Fish, Salt Life,** and **Zeerover** for Caribbean fish

FOOD
ORANJESTAD

There are also 21 brands of European beer and a food menu with Dutch cheese sandwiches, cheeseballs, *loempia, sate,* and *bitterballen* (fried balls of meat and sauce). A house specialty is gigantic burgers served with a stack of Dutch fries. The beautiful snack platter with Dutch finger foods goes perfectly with a beer or chilled glass of wine. Fancy coffees and sweet snacks are also available. A large open-air terrace is where most are seated, with the interior holding little more than the bar, along with some displays featuring artifacts from its time as a rum shop. Friday evenings, Flor di Oriente is a favorite gathering place for young professionals.

THE PADDOCK

Popular with Dutch students interning abroad, **The Paddock** (L. G. Smith Blvd. 13, 297/583-2334, www.paddock-aruba.com, 9am-2am Sun.-Thurs., 9am-3am Fri.-Sat., $7-23) occupies a prime spot on the water with funky decor. You can't miss the velociraptor hanging out on the roof next to the Volkswagen. The reasonably priced menu attracts students on a budget, and the ambience appeals to all ages. Dutch baguette sandwiches are standard, from local favorite cheese and pickles to paper-thin carpaccio. *Tosties* (the

local version of grilled cheese), hamburgers, and "sharwarma" (their spelling) are considered specialties. The diverse dinner menu emphasizes fish and seafood. Wednesday and Saturday evening is an all-you-can-eat rib special (5pm-close, $13). The Paddock becomes a hangout for younger folks after the dinner hour. Visit the website for an amusing hint of what to expect from this distinctly Dutch eatery.

ASIAN

ASIAN DELIGHT

Particularly busy for takeout although there's a small dining area, **Asian Delight** (Wilhelminastraat 68, 297/583-7751, 11:30am-9pm Tues.-Sat., $8-20) is the top choice among islanders for the value-priced Yami Yami special. Yami Yami is a combo meal of appetizer and main course served on a bed of either *bami* or *nasi*. Choose from mini spring rolls or a variety of soups for your appetizer, then select from a number of main courses. The chicken and fish dishes are particularly good, or try the Tjap Choy, a fresh blend rich with crispy vegetables and tender chicken in mild sauce. The regular menu is diverse, with Indonesian and Thai dishes, Japanese teriyaki chicken, and "old-fashioned" fried rice with

Dutch finger foods are a favorite at Flor de Oriente.

absolutely everything. Asian Delight is not far from L. G. Smith Boulevard and is best reached by walking up the street on the west side of the lagoon that divides the town (aptly named Lagoonweg), which takes you directly to their door.

FUSION DELI

Try cuisine from Suriname at **Fusion Deli** (Caya Betico Croes 49A, 297/588-3588, 8:30am-7pm Mon.-Sat., $3-6), a country on the northern coast of South America that also experienced Dutch colonialism. Indonesian dishes are a staple, and because the plantations in Suriname had many East Indian laborers, the substantial Hindu population impacted the national cuisine. Curried foods are typical, wrapped in large flat Indian breads called roti. Fusion Deli is a center for this hearty dish, which attracts office workers during lunch. Diners select from tasty, filling, and inexpensive meals of roti and Surinamese *broodjes,* Dutch for "small breads." Interesting typical drinks of coconut, ginger, or almond milk complete this exotic experience. This is many islanders' top choice for Surinamese dining.

YANTI

Aruba's most high-profile Surinamese restaurant is **Yanti** (L. G. Smith Blvd. 122, 297/583-6359, 10am-8pm Mon.-Sat., $5-14), on the main highway on the western outskirts of Oranjestad. Its large noisy dining room is typically filled with Dutch clientele. Portions are ample, the food is delicious, and daily specials are fresh and abundant. Dishes include *gado gado* (steamed veggies) with a choice of chicken, pork, or beef and lots of *pinda* sauce. Try some *bacalao* or *pom,* a classic Surinamese casserole.

SUSHI

A bit off the beaten track, **Tatami Sushi House** (L. G. Smith Blvd. 124, 297/582-9945, www/tatamiaruba.com, 11:30am-2:30pm and 5:30pm-10:30pm Tues.-Fri., 4pm-11pm Sat., 5:30pm-10:30pm Sun., $10-16) is a cozy

place hidden at the back of a modern building at the west edge of town. CMB Loan Division is out front as a landmark. Tatami Sushi House offers a personalized selection of sushi made to order, with some interesting creations. There are conventional items such as California rolls as well as exotic combinations and reasonably priced assortment platters. Some have Papiamento names like "Bon Bini" (Welcome), with 12 pieces of sushi, or a big "Mi Dushi" (My Sweetheart) special for two. The dining room is tiny, so reservations are recommended.

COLOMBIAN

CASA VIEJA

Among Aruba's numerous Colombian spots is the authentic **Casa Vieja** (Cumana 8, 297/588-1627, 7:30am-11pm daily, $6-22), on the eastern end of town along the Caya Betico Croes. Dine on a small covered patio with a thatched roof. This is a good spot for inexpensive breakfasts, served all day. The food is simple, there is a lot to eat, and it is dead cheap. The delicious soups can be a first course or a whole meal. Friday is for house specialty *sopa de mariscos* (seafood soup). Two or three can share the enormous traditional mixed meat platters, heaped with beef, chicken, pork, bacon, chorizo, steak fries, and authentic *tostones,* flattened plantain chips, like crispy flat potatoes. Many of Aruba's Colombian community come to enjoy their Sunday meal here.

LA ESQUINA

There is a cluster of budget-priced eateries in the middle of the Caya Betico Croes, the main shopping street. **La Esquina** (Caya Betico Croes 49A, 297/588-0108, 8:30am-5pm Mon.-Sat., $6-20) is a cute little Colombian hole-in-the-wall on a corner with just a few tables. The popular soup of the day usually runs out by afternoon. Mixed meat platters range from the smaller "Peasant" to the "Big Mixed Platter" for 3-4 people. Fish stews or shrimp and fish platters, grilled or fried, are also available. The menu has translated names for the dishes, but not a thorough explanation, which makes the mixed platters challenging, as they include lots of organ meat. The crew tends to be a bit weak in English, but you can point at what you want.

PERUVIAN

DELIMAR

Authentic cuisine from Lima, which relies on seafood, cilantro, and regional dried peppers, distinguishes **Delimar** (Wilhelminastraat 4, 297/582-6139, 11:30am-9pm Mon.-Sat., $18-35) from other fish and seafood restaurants. Chef Marco and his wife, Lorena, import ingredients from their homeland for authentic flavor. Dishes are made to order, so you can specify the degree of spiciness. Generous portions of seafood are served as *arrisotado*, the Peruvian version of risotto; *tacu-tacu*, with rice and beans; or *cau-cau*, seafood only. After dinner, try the fresh passion fruit mousse. The bar is stocked with Peruvian beer and liquor. The restaurant is just behind the Renaissance Resort.

LA GRANJA

The Floridian franchise **La Granja** (Hospitaalstraat 2, 297/583-5602, www.lagranjarestaurants.com, 11:30am-10pm daily, $6-20) began in Aruba. Originally specializing in barbecue chicken, it expanded to include ribs, chops, steak, shrimp, and Peruvian fresh ceviche. An average meal is half a bird cooked over a wood-fired grill in classic Peruvian rotisserie style. Other main courses are a full pound of steak or grilled pork. Try the Peruvian condiments, more like relishes, for new flavors. The restaurant features quick cafeteria-style service and a rustic setting with picnic-type tables. Find it by going inland from the far eastern end of Caya Betico Croes, where the tram rails end. The building takes up a corner just a block beyond Coffee Break.

ITALIAN

CASA TUA

Casa Tua (Renaissance Marketplace, 297/583-1990, www.casatuaaruba.com, 11am-11pm daily, $12-36) was Aruba's first gourmet pizzeria. The Oranjestad outlet (there is also one in Palm Beach) has an elegant vibe and a terrific location by the water end of the mall. Dine indoors or outdoors to enjoy the free nightly shows at the bandstand. Patrons rave about the pizza and reasonably priced pasta. Order a medium pizza for two to share rather than the personal pizza special, which is often premade and reheated. Other dishes are seafood and a few meat dishes, but no veal.

ITALY IN THE WORLD

Italy in the World (Oranjestraat 2, 297/585-7958, 3pm-10pm Mon.-Fri., 4pm-10pm Sat., 5pm-9pm Sun., $19-29) is in Aruba's oldest landmark building, the Hart House, across from Fort Zoutman, with only two or three tables inside—the space is mostly occupied by a vast collection of wine bottles—so most seating is outdoors. The family-owned restaurant's focus is on pasta dishes, with other items on the menu including osso buco, baked salmon with honey and lime, chicken parmesan, and beef braciola. Since seating is limited, be sure to make a reservation. The restaurant is a block from the Renaissance Resort.

PORTUGUESE

GOSTOSO

For a long time **Gostoso** (Caya Ing Roland H. Lacle 12, 297/588-0053, www.gostosoaruba.com, noon-3pm and 6pm-10pm Tues.-Fri., noon-4pm and 6:30pm-10pm Sat.-Sun., $25-40), which means "delicious" in Portuguese, was rated Aruba's number-one restaurant online, with fish and shellfish big on the menu. The owner-operated eatery also features some Aruban dishes. It also makes great white sangria, and steaks are prime black Angus. Particularly recommended is the Espetada Marinara, a unique presentation of surf and turf, or order Catch of the Day in Mango Sauce, made with grouper or Chilean sea bass; portions are very generous and the food is excellent. This charming little place is tucked away on a side street and gets quite noisy. Its popularity can result in long waits for a table after 7pm. Don't have a heart attack when first perusing the menu; prices are in florins, not dollars.

MEDITERRANEAN

MAROC

More a hip hangout than a dinner destination, **Maroc** (Wilhelminastraat 74, 297/583-0404, www.marocaruba.com, 4pm-10pm Tues.-Sat., 5pm-10pm Sun., $4-25) has become Oranjestad's trendy evening spot to socialize and savor an extensive wine list paired with fresh hot and cold tapas, ordered individually or by platter, which might include meat, fish, cheese, hummus, and other dips and spreads. The Chef's Platter ($25) is enough for two to share.

MIDDLE EASTERN

SULTAN

Aruba's original Middle Eastern restaurant, still considered the best, **Sultan** (Caya Betico Croes 229, 297/588-2598, www.sultanaruba.com, 11am-3pm and 5:30pm-11pm Mon.-Sat., 5:30pm-11pm Sun., $9-18) is beyond the eastern edge of Oranjestad on the Cumena traffic circle. Arabic pop videos play on a big screen, and a party room in the back is for groups to lounge on colorful cushions and dine while reclining. Main courses feature kebabs of chicken, lamb, or tenderloin or a platter of large falafel for vegetarians. Shawarma is the specialty. All mains are accompanied by hummus, tabbouleh, and saffron rice or baba ghanoush and pita bread. For a large group, try the expansive sample platter ($55). Every dish comes with homemade sauces, including the tasty mild creamy garlic sauce. Approach the very spicy tomato-based salsa with caution.

STEAK HOUSES

EL GAUCHO

Aruba's first and foremost Argentine steak house, **El Gaucho** (Wilhelminastraat 80, 297/582-3677, www.elgaucho-aruba.com, 11:30am-11pm Mon.-Sat., $37) is pricier than it used to be, and there are mixed reviews on the short ribs and fish, but the *churrasco,* the Gaucho Steak, is a 16-ounce hunk of boneless sirloin that is consistently excellent. A kids menu has hamburgers and macaroni and cheese, and there's a video-game room to keep the little ones busy. Mariachi singers perform every night.

L. G. SMITH'S STEAK & CHOP HOUSE

At **L. G. Smith's Steak & Chop House** (L. G. Smith Blvd. 82, 297/523-6115, www.lgsmiths.com, 5:30pm-11pm daily, $30-65), every dish is superlative. The à la carte menu specializes in Angus prime beef steaks, from a petite filet mignon to a massive 20-ounce porterhouse. There are also fine wine pairings, vegetarian dishes such as a vegetable Wellington, and elegant desserts. Friday is Kobe beef night, when prices can more than double ($45-150). Occasionally a celebrity chef is brought in from Europe or the United States to devise a limited-time menu of unique and impressive dishes; a three-course special with wine pairing costs $75-90. On the Renaissance Mall mezzanine level, a wall of picture windows provides a view of the harbor, and decor is elegant island chic. Attached to the Crystal Casino, the restaurant also has a lounge bordering the gaming area, where light fare is served after midnight. Okeanos Spa next door offers a "treatment and dinner" package.

YAMANJA WOODFIRE GRILL

Regulars rave about **Yamanja Woodfire Grill** (Wilhelminastraat 2, 297/588-4711, www.yemanja-aruba.com, 5:30pm-10:30pm Mon.-Sat., from $25, prix fixe $43-55), behind the Renaissance Resort Marina Tower in a landmark building with indoor and outdoor dining. Meat is grilled over mesquite wood, imparting a singular flavor. U.S.-certified Angus beef makes the à la carte menu somewhat pricey, and though it's ostensibly a steak house, Yamanja offers fish and seafood dishes from the grill, as well as vegetarian dishes. There is a less expensive kids menu, and a three-course early-bird special for the budget-conscious.

Aruban Supermarkets

desserts at the supermarket

Supermarket shopping on Aruba is an interesting experience: Expect diverse goods from around the world, including those not seen in U.S. markets. Some may lament the paucity or expense of American brands, but this is to be expected, as everything is imported. Compensating for higher prices is the opportunity to sample how some of the rest of the world eats.

Aruba's diversity is evident in what is carried by most markets. You will find Dutch butter, coffee, chocolate, and tea are far superior and less expensive than their U.S. counterparts. European foodstuffs can't contain dyes; try European breakfast cereals for a more natural product. Products from China, India, Indonesia, and the Philippines are stocked, making an inexpensive source of souvenirs for the cooking enthusiast. Attractively priced and packaged exotic spice packets, local relishes, and other unique items are easy to travel with.

One drawback of island life is the once-weekly shipment of fruits and vegetables, dairy, and other fresh food. Shopping the day before they arrive can be disappointing, as it can be difficult to find things like fresh milk and lettuce. This is especially an issue during busy holiday weeks. If you arrive on a weekend and plan to cook, it's best to stock up immediately.

BREAKFAST, LUNCH, AND COFFEE SHOPS

★ SMIT & DORLAS COFFEE HOUSE
Aruba's first coffee shop, **Smit & Dorlas Coffee House** (De La Sallestraat 30-A, 297/588-4888, http://coffeehousearuba.com, 9am-6pm Mon.-Fri., 9am-2pm Sat., latte $2.50) offers 14 freshly ground coffees from around the world and 40 loose teas, both black and herbal, in the most delightful surroundings. Styled after vintage Viennese pastry shops, it serves excellent coffee, delicious paninis, a quiche of the day, and baguette sandwiches. It's famous for its freshly made cakes, all reasonably priced. Hot beverages are served with complimentary cookies. This coffeehouse embodies the treasured institution of enjoying a cup with a friend; it's a place you'll want to linger. Also for sale are unique designer coffee and teapots for two that can be lovely gifts. To get here, walk to the main post office, 10 minutes inland from the Renaissance Resort, then take a right at the traffic light just past the post office, at De La Sallestraat; Smit & Dorlas is five minutes farther along on the south side.

ARUBA EXPERIENCE

Extremely popular with the coffee-loving crowd is **Aruba Experience** (John G. Emanstraat 37, 297/588-7878, 7am-7pm daily, $5-10), in a restored landmark *cunucu* house in the center of Oranjestad. Cozy couches and owner Susan Ruiter provide a delightful experience. The walls are decorated with vintage island photos and informative articles about Aruba. Designer lattes, freshly squeezed limeade and lemonade, and a wide assortment of fruit smoothies are on offer, along with gluten-free breads, vegetarian sandwiches and wraps, and tasty croissant sandwiches.

COFFEE BREAK

Local caffeine addicts choose **Coffee Break** (Caya Betico Croes 101A, 297/588-5569, 7am-6pm Mon.-Sat., lattes $2.80) as the place to get their morning fix and meet friends. This cute, clean, cozy spot is done up in old-fashioned soda shop decor with padded stools along the counter. Comfy sofas fill one corner of the café, and Wi-Fi is free. Coffee beans are roasted and ground on-site, and coffee drinks are priced for the local trade, in florins instead of dollars and 45 percent less than at the resorts and high-profile outlets. Local snacks and pastries, waffles, a pie of the day à la mode, and a changing selection of gelato are on offer with elaborate iced-coffee treats and ice cream floats. Seasonal specials are listed on its Facebook page.

DJESPIE'S PLACE

Attached to Coffee Break but separated by a door is the cute little snack stop **Djespie's Place** (Caya Betico Croes 101, 297/588-5569, 7am-6pm Mon.-Sat., $1-4), a popular hangout for islanders, with an authentic Aruban snack menu. Lunch options include *pastechis* and croquettes, well-stuffed sandwiches, and hamburgers.

STARBUCKS

If you can't live without **Starbucks** (Renaissance Mall; Renaissance Marketplace, 297/523-6750, 7am-10pm daily), you'll find one that won awards as the most beautifully designed in the Caribbean at the center of the Renaissance Mall, next to the pier for the boat to Renaissance Island. The air-conditioned Starbucks lounge area has deep couches to relax and check your email on the free Wi-Fi.

The Renaissance Marketplace Starbucks is across the main street on Oranjestad Harbor with a lovely view. Relax on the outdoor terrace and enjoy the breeze, watching the fishing boats in the morning and bureaucrats grabbing their caffeine before sessions at Parliament.

Both cafés sell Starbucks Aruba logo gear.

SUPERMARKETS

LING & SONS

Aruba has two exceptionally well-stocked markets, including **Ling & Sons** (Italiestraat 26, 297/588-7718, www.lingandsons.com, 8am-9pm Mon.-Sat., 9am-6pm Sun.), with a diverse selection of popular U.S. brands, including the generic IGA line. It has fine fresh specialty salads, bakery goods, meat, and produce, and a diverse inventory. The brisk trade ensures fast turnover and fresh products. Ling & Sons is also the largest source of kosher items year-round.

Eagle Beach and Manchebo Beach

As Aruba's center for beachfront condos and time-shares, there are lots of options for dining out and supermarkets in these areas. Most restaurants line the beach within the resorts or across Irausquin Boulevard. The malls on the Sasaki Highway have one or two eateries worth the short walk from the hotels. Farther inland along Bubali Road are a few interesting venues, such as the elegant Madame Janette and Quinta Del Carmen, and the bargain-priced Yami Yami. Most restaurants in the resorts feature typical lunch fare such as hamburgers, wraps, and caesar salads during the day but more innovative and romantic fare in the evening.

EAGLE BEACH AND VICINITY

Aruba's southwest point, Punto Brabo, ends at Costa Linda Resort, the dividing line between Manchebo Beach and Eagle Beach. Aside from Passions, resorts and restaurants along J. E. Irausquin Boulevard are on the land side of the street, across from the beach. Eagle Beach ends at Aruba's famous landmark fofoti trees. This is the base of the Bubali Road, which leads across the Sasaki Highway to some interesting places to dine.

Caribbean Fusion
MADAME JANETTE

Beautiful gardens and excellent food have made **Madame Janette** (Cunucu Abao 37, 297/587-0184, www.madamejanette.com, 5:30pm-10pm Mon.-Sat., $35-59) a favorite for seasonal menus and daily specials. Host Ramon is an expert at obtaining fresh exotic comestibles, while Karsten is the certified master chef. They have a loyal following, and reservations are required days in advance. Seafood specialties include bang-bang shrimp, catch of the day, Asian honey-soy sea bass, and whole deboned yellowtail snapper, adding a fresh twist to standard dishes. Asparagus

season, showcasing the large white stalks valued by Dutch chefs, is mid-April-late June and results in a changing menu of asparagus-based recipes. Dress is casual, and it is advisable to wear light clothing—it can get warm because of the windbreaks. Madame Janette features nightly entertainment.

QUINTA DEL CARMEN

Inland from Super Food Plaza on the Bubali Road is exceedingly charming **Quinta Del Carmen** (Bubali 119, 297/587-7200, www.quintadelcarmen.com, 5pm-10pm daily, $27-45), in a landmark building that was Aruba's first hospital. Originally built by one of the founding families as a weekend country cottage, it is named for their daughter Carmen.

From the same people who run Barefoot in Oranjestad, dining is mostly alfresco in the rear courtyard. Tables in the elegant interior rooms are not air-conditioned, and though natural breeze cools the space, some may find it warm, particularly in early fall when winds die down. The appetizer menu is reminiscent of traditional Aruban cuisine, including pumpkin and local seafood soups and cheese croquettes. A number of dishes are categorized as "Grandma's Favorites," such as Sucade Lappen, a Dutch beef stew; typical Dutch cookies and ice cream; and chicken soup Aruban-style, which means it has a little bit of everything.

SCREAMING EAGLE

Veteran visitors point to **Screaming Eagle** (J. E. Irausquin Blvd. 228, 297/587-8021, www.screaming-eagle.net, 6pm-11pm daily, $30-50) as a bastion of gourmet cuisine. Chef-owner Erwin Husker has a reputation for producing inventive fare. Prices are high, but fanatics insist the experience is worth it. The menu includes tender tournedos with pepper sauce prepared at your table, and crêpe

Service Charges

First-time travelers outside the United States are puzzled by the extra 10-15 percent service charge tacked onto the restaurant check, particularly if the waitstaff insists that it is not a tip. In most cases, this is partially true; the servers do not receive the full amount. Most restaurants keep 7-10 percent of the service charge to cover breakage and laundry. The remainder is divided among the restaurant staff, including the kitchen help and the maître 'd. This usually works on a point system, with the higher-ups getting the lion's share. The bus person who worked so hard to clear your plates and keep the water glasses filled doesn't see much of it. Some island eateries have eliminated the service charge to draw customers. If it bothers you, check websites and menus, which usually state clearly if a service charge is included, or ask before making reservations or being seated.

A good rule of thumb: If you have had satisfactory friendly service, leave half the service charge or more as a tip. This will go into a pot (or is supposed to) to be divided by the staff at the end of the night. Individual servers still don't get it all, but they are most likely being paid minimum wage and depend on gratuities, so it will be appreciated. The same applies for tour guides, boat crews, and other employees of vacation activities and services.

suzette flambéed with cognac. There is a fine wine cellar. Dine while lounging on bed-like couches or regular tables amid quirky chic decor. Seasonal offerings include a special of the day ($80), which costs as much as an entire meal elsewhere; the Screaming Eagle is for diners with expansive budgets.

Beachside Dining
PASSIONS
Next to the Bubali Road on Eagle Beach, **Passions** (J. E. Irausquin Blvd. 252, 297/587-0110, www.passions-restaurant-aruba.com, beach bar 10am-11pm daily, restaurant noon-4:30pm and 6pm-9:30pm daily, $20-39) is the only beach-side restaurant between Manchebo Beach and Palm Beach and among the most romantic spots on the west coast. The location at the Amsterdam Manor Beach Resort provides tranquil seclusion, and the Caribbean fusion menu emphasizes fresh fish and seafood, with chicken breast, shellfish, and surf and turf of filet mignon and lobster tail. Innovative sauces and presentations earn high ratings, but the real attraction is the setting and ambience, ideal for an anniversary dinner or a proposal. Mellow singers with a romantic repertoire are regularly featured.

Chinese
★ YAMI YAMI
The Bubali Commercial Center (BCC) is a small strip mall on the Bubali Road where you'll find the suburban outlet of Asian Delight, **Yami Yami** (Bubali 69C, 297/587-0062, 11:30am-9pm Tues.-Sun., $8-16) after the bargain-priced meal that is a staple for islanders. A filling and tasty combo meal of an appetizer and a main is served on a bed of either *bami* or *nasi*. Choose mini spring rolls or a soup as an appetizer, then one of a dozen main courses; the chicken and fish dishes are surprisingly good. The regular menu is also reasonably priced, offering generous portions of high-quality Chinese dishes. This outlet has a pleasant dining room and a sushi bar, with made-to-order sushi combos from $15 for a 21-piece platter. "Party Platters" are only to go, which is useful for entertaining in your suite or dining outside while watching the sunset.

International
CHALET SUISSE
Just east of Paradise Beach Villas is **Chalet Suisse** (J. E. Irausquin Blvd. 246, 297/587-5054, www.chaletsuisse-aruba.com, 5:30pm-10pm Mon.-Sat., $18-47), the first independent restaurant on Eagle Beach and

still a favorite. The decor is Old World with several cozy booths. Specialties include a variety of steaks and wiener schnitzel with some vegetarian dishes. It's one of the few restaurants with classic chateaubriand, planked and sliced at your table. Also famous is chocolate fondue for two made with Toblerone. A daily early-bird special features an excellent fresh snapper entrée. During the high season, reservations are strongly recommended.

TULIP

Tulip (J. E. Irausquin Blvd. 240, 297/587-0110, www.tulip-restaurant-aruba.com, 7:30am-10am, noon-4pm, and 5pm-10:30pm daily, $15-31) is an appealing place to dine alfresco. In addition to lunch and dinner—fish and shrimp, steaks and chops, and pastas—are some reasonably priced breakfast options: a vegetarian omelet ($5.50), continental breakfast with yogurt, fruit, cheeses and cold cuts, cereal, boiled eggs, and coffee or tea ($8.50). Tulip is north of La Quinta Resort and screened by shrubbery; the nondescript entrance is on J. E. Irausquin Boulevard and can be easy to miss.

Supermarkets

SAVEMORE

Affiliated with the U.S. SavMor franchise, **SaveMore** (J. E. Boegoroi 4, 297/587-1090, 8am-8pm daily) carries many of the exclusive brands budget-conscious U.S. shoppers know well. For canned and packaged goods and dairy products, this is Aruba's bargain-priced grocery store with an expanded inventory that includes many Dutch brands. The deli and meat department are not as varied and elegant as neighboring Super Food, but a nice bakery produces baguettes, sweet pastries, and rolls. Try the raisin ciabatta; it's the best on the island. Fresh produce and dairy, along with frozen food, are usually cheaper than other markets, as are the generic soft drinks and juices.

SUPER FOOD

Impossible to miss at the Sasaki Highway and Bubali Road is **Super Food** (Sasaki Hwy. z/n, 297/588-6040, http://superfoodaruba.com, 8am-9pm Mon.-Sat., 9am-6pm Sun.), the island's largest market with fresh food beautifully presented. It's Aruba's Dutch grocery, with the best deli and cheese departments as well as quality meat and produce and an exceptional bakery. The arcade of surrounding shops contains a fresh fish store and an attractive and reasonably priced eatery called Jack's Cafe, named for the market's owner.

MANCHEBO BEACH AREA

Within this cluster of resorts on the edge of town are some excellent restaurants and the clubhouse at the Divi Links with two fine places—one pricey, the other moderate—with views of the golf course and surrounding area. Divi Resort has advanced the quality of dining choices at the low-rise resorts.

Seafood

★ RED FISH

An authentic Aruban fish shack within walking distance of the Manchebo and Eagle Beach resorts is **Red Fish** (Orange Mall, 297/280-6666, www.redfisharuba.com, 11:30am-10pm Tues.-Sun., $13-36), named for the red snapper featured on the menu. Owner Herby Merryweather is the veteran charter fishing captain who founded the popular Driftwood restaurant and charter fishing boats in Oranjestad. This eatery has rustic charm and local prices, though its location on the highway does not particularly convey island ambience. Come for fresh grouper or snapper prepared as *moochi*. The catch of the day platter comes in half- or full-pound sizes with sweet fried bananas, fries, and *funchi* sides. The expansive menu has mixed shrimp and fish platters, whole snapper, and a lobster and filet mignon surf and turf as well as poultry and steaks.

Tips for Dining Alfresco

One of the great attractions of the tropics is a romantic sunset dinner on a beach or in a garden. A lovely meal under swaying palms is a fantasy come true—though not when the wind blows the food off your plate. Aruba is known for strong winds, and many restaurants have been designed with that in mind. Several places set up windbreaks or have buildings designed to provide a tranquil environment. Unfortunately this can lead to open-air dining areas getting uncomfortably warm. Dress lightly, but bring a sweater in case.

Dressing lightly means mosquitoes and sand fleas can be pests, particularly around sunset, when they are most active. Bare legs under a table attract annoying insects, especially if there was rainfall in the previous weeks. This is not usually an issue at restaurants with steady breeze or little greenery. Long pants with shoes and socks are suggested. To enjoy the meal with skin exposed, invest in some bug repellent, especially in mid- to late fall.

Beachside Dining

★ ELEMENTS

In the Bucuti & Tara Beach Resort, chic **Elements** (J. E. Irausquin Blvd. 55B, 297/583-1100, ext. 109, www.bucuti.com, bar 10am-10:30pm daily, seatings 6pm and 8:50pm daily, $10-39) is strictly adults-only, making it a tranquil oasis among the family-friendly time-shares that surround it. It has an expansive waterfront perch with outdoor seating and air-conditioned indoor seating with large windows for unobstructed views of the largest beach on Aruba. The menu suits the health-conscious, with vegan, vegetarian, and gluten-free dishes as well as "European portions for healthier living." Even standard lunch offerings have a gourmet touch, like a grilled chicken breast salad with kalamata olives and chickpeas served in a crusty edible bread bowl. The dinner menu is solid if not as inventive, with steaks, seafood, and pastas. A special area is set aside for romantic dinners on the beach: three thatched-roof tables for two with two seatings, 6pm and 8:50pm. The romantic dinner includes complimentary wine or champagne and three courses ($189), with the service charge included.

MATTHEW'S BEACHSIDE RESTAURANT

Casa Del Mar Resort had seen a number of restaurants come and go. **Matthew's Beachside Restaurant** (J. E. Irausquin Blvd. 51, 297/588-7300, www.matthews-aruba.com, 7:30am-10pm daily, $25-50) is a winner. Owner Stefan Legger and his wife, Milca, have loyal patrons who rave about the food, staff, and sea view. The standard à la carte menu features grilled shellfish, snapper, grouper, and various cuts of steak. The specialty nights are the real attraction, with all-you-can-eat spareribs on Tuesday ($23); reservations are recommended. Friday is an Italian menu with lots of pasta dishes and osso buco. Private dinners for two on the beach include a complimentary bottle of champagne ($150); these should be arranged well in advance.

RICARDO'S

At Aruba Beach Club (ABC), casual **Ricardo's** (Pool Deck, Aruba Beach Club, 297/587-0760, http://ricardosaruba.restaurant, 7:30am-11:30pm and 1pm-10pm daily, $25-46) offers breakfast, lunch, and dinner menus as well as an attractive wine closet and generous portions. Monday and Wednesday evenings are all-you-can-eat rib and grouper nights, respectively ($24). The fish is fresh-caught, and the ribs are tender and tasty, both served with fries and salad. The main restaurant is on a deck overlooking the beach, but there are also shaded tables around the pool bar. There's live entertainment during the evening happy hour (4pm-6pm daily). Host Ricardo Chirino was the extremely popular maître d' of

Matthew's Beachside Restaurant and emcee for its karaoke nights. He brings the same charm and energy to his own eatery. His famous Karaoke Dance Parties, held at 9pm Thursday, are known for "dancing on the bar"-level controlled insanity.

Chinese
HE'S

He's (Italiestraat 50, 297/280-0008, 11am-midnight daily, $8-22), in Orange Mall, makes up for in deliciousness what it lacks in decor, and is an excellent choice for Chinese takeout since it's close to the Manchebo Beach resorts. Portions are huge, and two main dishes will easily feed a family of four. The vast menu offers seafood, poultry, and meat dishes. Highly recommended are the mixed fried rice noodles, loaded with chicken, shrimp, beef, pork, and tons of stir-fried veggies.

Italian
★ TERRAZZA ITALIANA

Kick back with sangria, fine Italian food, and the sunset without walloping your wallet at the delightful **Terrazza Italiana** (J. E. Irausquin Blvd. 64, 297/561-1699, 11:30am-9:30pm Mon.-Sat., $16-30), popular with islanders and visitors for its excellent cuisine and fantastic location. On Paradise Beach Villas' 3rd floor, the open-air oceanfront venue (the breezes up here can sometimes be blustery) boasts incredible views of the shoreline and serves tapas, soups, pastas, pizzas, lasagnas, and risottos. Hosts Mimma and Marco were born and raised in Italy. A three-course happy-hour special ($20) is served 4:30pm-6pm daily—until closing on Saturday—and there's a daily-changing two-course combo for around $27.

ELLIOTI'S

Outside of the all-inclusive resorts are two connected Italian restaurants with the same owners. **Ellioti's** (J. E. Irausquin Blvd. 59, 297/593-6919, www.elliotisaruba.com, 5pm-10pm Mon.-Sat., $22-38), at the juncture of the Costa Linda and Bucuti Resorts, an easy stroll from the hotels, is more elegant, with a spacious air-conditioned dining room, though most prefer the pleasant outdoor deck. Executive chef Jeffrey Elliot was the sous-chef at the famous but now defunct Valentino's. He continues to get high marks for his shrimp *fra diablo* and pasta sauces. Congenial host and owner Adrianna loves fine food.

Sommelier Bas teaches all about wine pairing at Senses.

PIZZA BOB'S PUB

The Bucuti side of the Ellioti's complex houses **Pizza Bob's Pub** (J. E. Irausquin Blvd. 59, 297/588-9046, 11am-10pm daily, $17-25), more a comfortable hangout than just a restaurant. The tiny dining room is nice for lunch in the heat of the day, but the action is at the outdoor patio and bar, with a giant screen for sports events. Local singers provide mellow music nightly. Popular for its thin-crust pizza, there are also specials and build-your-own options. Slightly pricier than most island pizza joints, the early-bird special is 5pm-7pm daily, when a 14-inch pizza goes for the price of a 12-incher. The greatest asset of both Ellioti's and Pizza Bob's is proximity to the low-rise resorts, and that in a relatively quiet area they provide nighttime entertainment.

Mediterranean

IKE'S BISTRO

In the Manchebo Beach Resort is charming open-air **Ike's Bistro** (J. E. Irausquin Blvd. 55, 297/582-3444, www.manchebo.com, 5:30pm-10:30pm daily, $24-38), wrapped around a pool deck. Reserve ahead if you want one of the prime poolside tables. Ike's leans toward Mediterranean fare, with all-inclusive Paella Night ($45) on Thursday. Chef Sandro prepares a huge paella poolside, served with salad and a dessert bar, a glass of sangria, and Spanish guitar entertainment. The menu also features vegetarian dishes, including a tofu steak. A three-course vegetarian Chef's Surprise ($35) varies based on what's fresh and available.

International

★ SENSES

Senses (L. G. Smith Blvd. 55B, 297/586-0044, http://sensesaruba.resaurant, seating 7pm Mon.-Fri., $105) is run by chef Kelt and sommelier Bas, who deliver memorable dining experiences. A maximum of 16 patrons per night are seated at a curved counter for a five- to eight-course meal starting at 7pm. Kelt explains the exotic ingredients and steps in his glorious creations, while Bas regales diners with tales of the fine wines with which dishes are paired ($79 additional fee). Reservations should be made via the website months in advance; a deposit is required. Confirm your reservations once you're in Aruba. Within the adults-only Bucuti & Tara Beach Resort, Senses only accepts patrons age 18 and over.

THE CHOPHOUSE

One of Aruba's most famous upscale restaurants, the French Steakhouse, is now **The Chophouse** (J. E. Irausquin Blvd. 55, 297/582-3444, www.manchebo.com, 5:30pm-10:30pm daily, $24-54), founded at the Manchebo Beach Resort by legendary hotelier and restaurateur Ike Cohen. Ike is gone, and chefs come and go, but the restaurant has maintained its standards and loyal clients. A sleek new contemporary look and modernized menu with quality meat continues to offer fine dining. Classic rack of lamb, giant T-bone or porterhouse steaks, fresh fish, and shrimp scampi are the fare. Dinner is accompanied by mellow nightly entertainment on the piano by Eddie, a favorite for over 25 years.

MULLIGAN'S

The lower level of the Divi Links's clubhouse is home to open-air **Mulligan's** (J. E. Irausquin Blvd. 93, 297/523-5062, www.mulligansaruba.com, 6:30am-1am daily, $10-28), with a spectacular panorama of the golf course and surroundings. The more casual golfer's lounge has early breakfast before the first tee time. Lunch and dinner are reasonable, with gourmet sandwiches, burgers, and pizza. Baguettes are priced like most local Dutch sandwich houses, and the stone-oven pizza menu has some originals, like the Asian pizza with duck and cilantro-ginger sauce or a shawarma pizza with ground lamb. Golfers can take advantage of the "Friends of Mulligan's" promotion, with rewards and discounts for repeat visits. Mulligan's livens up on Thursday with karaoke night.

TWIST OF FLAVORS

In the Alhambra Shopping Bazaar is **Twist of Flavors** (J. E. Irausquin Blvd., 297/280-2518, 8am-10:30pm daily, $10-42), a cute corner shop with floor-to-ceiling windows and friendly and efficient service for casual dining. The menu is international-Caribbean with a Dutch touch, evidenced by Dutch pancakes with sweet or savory toppings, always a satisfying breakfast. A lunch special ($15) lets you select onion soup or soup du jour and pair it with a chicken caesar salad, a sandwich, or a wrap. The diverse dinner menu includes catch of the day, seafood linguini, and burgers. Daily specials are grouped in an economical three-course meal, and there's a kids menu, with most options $10.

WINDOWS ON ARUBA

Elegantly prepared food and Louis XIV decor are the trademarks of **Windows on Aruba** (J. E. Irausquin Blvd. 93, top floor of the Divi Links clubhouse, 297/523-5017, www.windowsonaruba.com, noon-2:30pm and 6pm-10:30pm Mon.-Sat., 10:30am-2pm Sun., $30-59), along with the breathtaking view. A great local jazz trio or guitarist Ivan Jansen entertains three nights a week. A popular offering is Sunday brunch ($43), featuring unlimited mimosas or champagne. Each dish is made fresh and plated, and there is a wide choice: crêpe suzette, escargot, scallops, duck breast, and smoked salmon omelets. The regular menu focuses on fine dining, and it is pricey. The restaurant has received mixed reviews of late. To truly appreciate the Windows atmosphere and assets, go for an early dinner or drinks and appetizers to catch the sunset.

Palm Beach, Malmok, and Noord

The question in Palm Beach is not, "Where will we find a nice place to eat?" but rather, "How can we choose from so many options?" According to various review sites, there are over 100 restaurants in this area; new eateries open regularly while others close. A recent phenomenon is a cluster of independent eateries around the Playa Linda Beach Resort, offering excellent economical breakfast and lunch choices without dressing up or leaving the beach.

The main strip, J. E. Irausquin Boulevard, a bustling area of neon and bright lights, is packed with shopping malls that contain dining options where fusion and Italian cuisine tend to dominate. Some Italian restaurants feature a regional pasta specialty prepared for two or more: A sauce incorporating vodka, tomatoes, and seasoning tossed and flamed with pasta inside a giant parmesan cheese wheel from Italy. This is done at your table and is quite a show. Not far inland, away from the heavily populated thoroughfare, are some interesting places with more tranquil genuine island atmosphere.

ARUBAN

THE OLD CUNUCU HOUSE

In a landmark 150-year-old colonial farmhouse, **The Old Cunucu House** (Palm Beach 150, 297/586-1666, www.theoldcunucuhouse.com, noon-11pm daily, $16-35) is a charming bit of authentic Aruba. The menu features traditional island dishes and reasonably priced international favorites. The indoor dining room maintains the simple decor of an old-time Aruban home, while the outside terrace is surrounded by charming gardens. On a cul-de-sac of a side road off the Noord-Palm Beach Road, a sign clearly marks the turnoff. The tranquility and picturesque surroundings are transporting; the only noise is the rustling of the trees as you dine alfresco on the terrace. The house specialty is *keshi yena* with Aruban side dishes *pan bati, hasa* (plantains), and *funchi*. The catch of the day is served various ways, including Aruban-style with creole sauce, and the succulent rosemary rack of lamb is outstanding. An appetizer plate, meant to be shared, offers several favorite Aruban snacks: *pastechi,* calamari, fish cake, and meatballs.

SEAFOOD

WHACKY WAHOO'S

Great fresh fish and a friendly vibe made **Whacky Wahoo's** (Palm Beach 33B, 297/586-7333, http://wackywahoo.com, 5:30pm-10pm Mon.-Sat., $26-42) a top-rated restaurant on Aruba. Chef-owner Harald is an enthusiastic fisherman, which guarantees fresh fish on the table every day. Harald was a master chef-in-training with Cunard Lines when he met lovely Roxy on shore leave in Aruba. Both the charms of the lady and Aruba brought him back. He established the reputations of a number of island restaurants before opening his own place. The catch of the day is two or three kinds of fish, listed on a chalkboard, served five different ways. Good-quality steak and duck with tasty sauces are nonfish options. There are also tempting desserts like fresh-baked brownies. The dining room has limited space, and reservations are strongly recommended. Whacky Wahoo's is a 15-minute walk inland on the Noord-Palm Beach Road.

CARIBBEAN FUSION

SWEET PEPPERS

The mezzanine level of Paseo Herencia Mall is home to **Sweet Peppers** (J. E. Irausquin Blvd. 382A, 297/586-0740, www. sweetpeppersaruba.com, 5pm-11pm daily, $19-39), where veteran restaurateurs Harold Paesch and Anky Paesch-Chirino are the congenial hosts sharing their native cuisine with visitors. Emphasis is on fresh fish with some regional influences. There's a ceviche bar, and an impressive seafood and fish combo platter ($58) easily feeds 2-3. Lamb chops and barbecue ribs are on the menu, and since the chef is Italian, so is a selection of pastas and parmesan dishes. Sunday night is the famous all-you-can-eat barbecue ribs night ($24). Friday night is all-you-can-eat grouper ($24). Wednesday after 9pm, the place goes a little crazy with the weekly karaoke party, which includes a free fireball and tequila shot.

BEACHSIDE DINING

Every resort in Palm Beach has an eatery to exploit the romantic setting for couples to dine on the shore at sunset with their toes in the sand. All have open-air casual restaurants along the boardwalk that runs the length of the strip, so guests need only put on a little beach cover during the day. Menus are lunch and snack-bar fare: hamburgers, hot dogs, caesar salads, chicken strips, and occasionally crab cakes or quesadillas. Most have kids menus, and several will deliver lunch to your beach lounge chair. Dinner sees more elaborate and diverse menus. Dining at the water's edge is very popular, so reservations for the high-demand sunset hours should be made well in advance. Seating is usually limited and at a set hour coordinated to sunset; some offer prix-fixe meals. A few resorts have the option of a private dinner for two with dedicated waitstaff in a more secluded part of the beach for the most romantic experience imaginable, perfect for a marriage proposal or a special occasion. Make arrangements with your concierge immediately on arrival or in advance by email.

ATARDI

At the Marriott at the far northern end of Palm Beach is **Atardi** (Marriott Resort, L. G. Smith Blvd. 101, 297/520-6600, www.marriott. com, 6:30pm-10:30pm daily, $38-60), one of the most expensive of the beachfront eateries, with a menu of standard offerings from northern waters, such as tuna, sea bass, and halibut (rather than local Caribbean fish). Lobster tail, on its own or paired with filet mignon, is typical, and local fare is a rather pricey *keshi yena.* But if you want a convenient toes-in-the-sand dining experience, you'll find it here, along with sunset views and friendly staff. It's a popular spot for wedding proposals.

Private Beachside Dining

A private dinner for two on a remote corner of the beach can be arranged at a few of the large resorts. These include a choice of preset menus with a range of prices. Additional amenities, such as private photographers, flower arrangements, and personal musicians are available. This is the dream setting for a marriage proposal. Main course choices usually include a surf and turf with lobster tail, rack of lamb, or fresh fish. Menus are standard from one resort to the next.

Marriott Resort (L. G. Smith Blvd. 101, 297/586-9000, www.marriott.com, $95-135 pp without drinks) offers three different menus. The $95 meal has four courses, and the others, $115 and $135, serve five, although whether champagne sorbet is a course is debatable. There is a $25 setup fee and an additional service charge of 18 percent.

The Hilton Aruba Caribbean Resort calls its private affair **La Playa Torchlight Dinner** (J. E. Irausquin Blvd. 77, 297/586-6555, hiltonconcierge@depalmtours.com, $65 pp), a three-course meal that must be ordered at least 24 hours in advance. There is no additional setup fee, but a 15 percent service charge and 3 percent tax are added.

Hyatt Regency offers **Pampered in Paradise** (J. E. Irausquin Blvd. 85, 297/586-1234, www. aruba.hyatt.com, $96 pp) under a private *palapa* with a four-course meal, including an appetizer, soup or salad, a choice of six gourmet main courses, and dessert. There is a 17 percent service charge for the waitstaff and an additional $50 setup fee.

These dinners require dedicated staff, so resorts usually have a limit of one or two tables nightly. It is strongly advised that you arrange such a special evening by email before arriving, or check with the hotel concierge for availability when you arrive. Seating times are your choice.

BUGALOE

At the end of the De Palm Pier is **Bugaloe** (J. E. Irausquin Blvd. 79, 297/586-2233, www. bugaloe.com, 7:30am-midnight daily, $9-27), an extremely popular nightspot with unmatched views and ambience. Come for coffee, light breakfast, lunch, dinner, or late-night snacks as well as lively, friendly service. Wraps dominate the menu and are available any time. A diverse selection of finger foods pairs with exotic frozen drinks or ice-cold beer. Main courses at dinner are fish and seafood plus a steak platter. The star item is red snapper. On Crazy Mondays, choose a fish basket, grouper platter, or red snapper ($14-20). On Saturday the sparerib platter is only $13. During the two daily happy hours (5pm-6pm and 10pm-11pm), drinks are two-for-one.

CARLITO'S SPORTS BEACH BAR

At the north end of the Playa Linda Beach Resort, abutting the boardwalk, is **Carlito's Sports Beach Bar** (Playa Linda Beach Resort, J. E. Irausquin Blvd. 87, 297/592-2065, 10am-10pm daily, $7-22), the place to catch your favorite team on dozens of flat screens without leaving the beach. The location and moderately priced menu have made Carlito's popular, and it is usually busy and noisy. The menu is typical sports bar fare with regional touches, with burgers (average $14), wraps, quesadillas, and heartier fish and steak platters. Happy hours happen throughout the day, and reasonably priced beer buckets go with wings and nachos.

EDUARDO'S BEACH SHACK

On the Playa Linda beach is **Eduardo's Beach Shack** (Playa Linda Beach Resort, J. E. Irausquin Blvd. 87, 297/592-9551, 7:30am-4:15pm daily, $7-12), offering healthy options, including many choices for vegans. Bowls feature yogurt and fruits, or veggies. Smoothies are available too. Whatever's fresh is what's featured, including tropical fruits and coconut milk. It gets busy during lunch hours. The congenial staff does their best to keep up with demand, but during high season you'll need patience. Vegans have many options here.

1: early bird special at Dragonfly; **2:** Bugaloe

KOUZINA

Another beach shack at Playa Linda specializing in breakfast and lunch with a Greek twist is **Kouzina** (Playa Linda Beach Resort, J. E. Irausquin Blvd. 87, 297/565-2456, 8:30am-3:30pm Mon.-Fri., $4-10). Fresh tomatoes and feta cheese play a part in most offerings. Breakfast burritos and bagels as well as classic souvlaki, gyros, beef kebabs, and crispy fries are on the menu. An enticing and reasonable drink menu includes creative concoctions.

PELICAN NEST

At the north end of the beach, between the Playa Linda and Holiday Inn, **Pelican Nest** (Pelican Pier, 297/582-2259, www.pelican-aruba.com, 11am-11pm Tues.-Sun., $20-38) features an open seafood grill. The ceviche is rated by some as the best on the island. The restaurant generally gets low marks on service, but the location is so pretty that you might want to linger to enjoy it.

PURE OCEAN

Formerly the Sunset Beach Bistro, **Pure Ocean** (J. E. Irausquin Blvd. 75, 297/586-6066, www.pureoceanrestaurant.com, 7am-11am and 5pm-11pm daily, $23-43) at the Divi Phoenix Resort is famous as the first restaurant in Palm Beach to offer dining at the water's edge. A limited number of tables is at the shoreline, but ample seating elsewhere on the beach and in the open-air covered terrace looks out on the sea. Reserve well in advance for a shore-side table. Fresh local fish is the focus, grilled with Aruban creole sauce and served on a bed of couscous, or with coconut curry sauce. Plain steaks and a few Italian dishes, such as osso buco, chicken saltimbocca, and rigatoni and meatballs also feature. A buffet breakfast ($17) includes an omelet station at a reasonable price considering the location.

SCOTT'S BRATS

One of the first independent food venues on Playa Linda beach was **Scott's Brats** (Playa Linda Beach Resort, J. E. Irausquin Blvd. 87, 297/593-6940, 8:30am-3pm Mon.-Sat., $3-12), best-known for its variety of sausage and hot dog sandwiches and offering quesadillas, wraps, and sandwiches. A quick and economical lunch choice, it offers a $1 discount on beer with any lunch order. And they have sauerkraut!

DUTCH

CAFÉ 080

For authentic Dutch food and ambience, head to **Café 080** (Noord 90, 297/586-2937, http://cafe080.com, 3pm-1am Mon.-Thurs., 3pm-3am Fri.-Sat., $5-10), in a renovated historic house with a tiny interior and a charming terrace. Sjoerd and Japie are the convivial hosts. The menu has an entire section dedicated to fries with various toppings, with some, like the stewed beef, meals in themselves. More substantial offerings—like a chicken schnitzel or *hutspot* (mashed potatoes mixed with vegetables) with *rookwurst* (a type of sausage)—cost $10. Friday-Sunday the café features a Dutch favorite: unlimited *kibbeling* (bite-size chunks of fried fish) and buckets of beer. The food is filling and cheap, and entire families come for the warm atmosphere of a neighborhood bar. During soccer's World Cup, if the Netherlands is in the final rounds, this is the place to watch the games. Dutch expatriates will be here in force, and the controlled insanity is contagious.

ASIAN

BLOSSOMS

On the mezzanine of the South Beach Center, a short stroll from the major hotels, **Blossoms** (Palm Beach 55, 297/586-3388, www.blossomsaruba.com, 6pm-11pm daily, $22-46) offers diverse dishes from China, Thailand, Mongolia, and Japan along with tempting lunch and early-bird dinner specials. Two teppanyaki tables should be booked well in advance. The restaurant is huge and the decor is elegant. Window seats provide spectacular views of the Palm Beach strip and nightlife. Amiable staff and service have earned dedicated repeat diners. Various specials run almost every day, including 20 percent off sushi. Check the Facebook page for the week's discounts.

For entertainment with Asian cuisine, **Dragonfly** (J. E. Irausquin Blvd. 370, 297/280-0019, www.dragonflyaruba.com, 4pm-11pm daily, $8-25) offers Pan-Asian food and primarily sushi. In the heart of Arawak Gardens on the main Palm Beach strip, the small but attractive dining room and outdoor seating allow diners to enjoy the nightly entertainment. Service is friendly and prices are reasonable for Palm Beach. An early-bird special offers all-you-can-eat sushi (4pm-6:30pm daily, $24), although it doesn't include some of the specialty rolls. Another filling three-course early-bird special includes a choice of appetizer, main course, and ice cream (4:30pm-7pm daily, $20).

INDIAN

TANDOOR INDIAN GRILL HOUSE

Tandoor Indian Grill House (South Beach Center, 297/586-0944, www.tandooraruba. com, noon-3pm and 6pm-10pm Tues.-Sun., $9-24) is the place to go for authentic East Indian cuisine, prepared in a tandoor, a cylindrical clay oven, for characteristic taste and tenderness. The northern Indian fare is reasonably priced and the menu extensive, with a dozen ways of preparing lamb, chicken, or fish in degrees of spiciness, from mild to murderously hot. Start with mild and then spice it up with some green chili sauce. Sample the purple *ras golla* (cottage cheese balls cooked in sugar syrup) for dessert. They are a sweet surprise that puts out any fire.

COLOMBIAN

LA FONDA

La Fonda (Palm Beach 164A, 297/586-1988, 11am-midnight Tues.-Sun., $7-22) is open for lunch and dinner and offers Colombian food. The daily lunch special ($7) includes fresh-squeezed lemonade, and an early-bird dinner special (4pm-7pm daily) is $14. A menu of the day features red bean casserole, meat and chicken lasagna, and a variety of soups. La Fonda is on the main Palm Beach-Noord Road, a 20-minute stroll from the main resorts.

VENZUELAN

CHEO'S CORNER

A small kiosk next to the carousel in Paseo Herencia Mall houses **Cheo's Corner** (J. E. Irausquin Blvd. 382-A, 297/562-9520, 8:30am-1pm and 5pm-midnight Mon.-Sat., 5pm-midnight Sun., $7-20), with a small collection of tables for open-air dining. The enthusiasm of the charming owner-operator Cheo provides great ambience as he serves his native Venezuelan staple, arepas. Few things are more filling than an *arepa con queso* (with cheese) or *con carne mechada* (with stewed shredded beef). Arepas are thick fried cornmeal buns cut open and filled with cheese, chicken, or other meat. Also on the menu are filling empanadas (a sealed cornmeal pastry that is fried whole) and *chachapas* (stuffed cornmeal flatbread, like tortillas). Reasonably priced coffees and exotic fruit *batidos* accompany morning arepas. For a hearty dinner, the huge family-size mixed-meat platters (beef, chicken, and sausage) with avocado and fries or arepas will satisfy 3-4 people. Cheo's Corner is an inexpensive oasis of authentic regional food in Palm Beach.

MEXICAN

KALIN'S

In the center of the Palm Beach Plaza mall, **Kalin's** (Palm Beach 21A, 297/586-9700, www.kalinsaruba.com, 11am-1am Mon.-Thurs., 11am-3am Fri.-Sat., 5pm-1am Sun., $11-23) is more than a fun bar for the evening; it is Aruba's first Mexican restaurant. Excellent generous fajitas, quesadillas, and nachos are on the menu with the best ceviche on Aruba. Kalin's also has reasonably priced drinks, is popular with tourists and dedicated locals, and has live music on weekends from local bands that play salsa, merengue, and bachata to get everyone up and dancing until closing time.

FRENCH

LA BRAISE

Occupying most of the ground-floor mall of The Cove luxury apartment complex across from the Holiday Inn, **La Braise** (J. E. Irausquin Blvd. 384A, 297/280-0300, www.rotisserielabraise.com, 5pm-11pm daily, $22-46) is a lovely spot with indoor and outdoor seating. Appetizers like the escargot, frogs legs, and French cheeses are consistently excellent, as are the decadent desserts. This is the only restaurant in Aruba serving French free-range birds prepared on a rotisserie. Considering that chicken is a common offering, whether it's worth the price—$23-32 for a quarter chicken, $69 for a whole bird—is debatable. Other delicious and reasonably priced entrée choices are rack of lamb or vol-au-vent, or perhaps a beautiful *après-dîner* dessert and latte. Although it's a French restaurant, some of the better offerings are seafood linguini and osso buco.

PAPILLON

A bastion of classic French cuisine, **Papillon** (J. E. Irausquin Blvd. 548A, 297/586-5400, www.papillon.com, 5pm-10:30pm daily, $26-43) is a cozy outdoor eatery at the rear of The Village mall across from the Hilton Aruba Caribbean Resort. Decor evokes a rustic countryside inn. There are a few indoor tables, but since it's not air-conditioned, dining under the awning is preferable. Hot and cold starters include lobster bisque, creamy roast pepper soup, and goat cheese and nut salad. Entrées include classic duck à l'orange, various cuts of steak with béarnaise sauce, and local and Atlantic fish. Service can be slow; be prepared for an evening of leisurely dining. Papillon offers a reasonable early-bird special (5pm-7pm daily, $32), a three-course meal that includes a glass of wine.

ITALIAN

ANNA MARIA'S

Authentic southern Italian cuisine prepared with enthusiasm is at **Anna Maria's** (Kamay 25-M, 297/586-2833, www.annamariasaruba.com, 6pm-10pm Mon.-Sat., $17-46), a labor of love by the chef-owners Anna Maria and her husband, Christian. He is native-born Aruban with Sicilian grandparents and describes his wife as "pure Napolitano." Starting with just a few tables on the back patio of their home, the business has grown to include waitstaff and an expanding menu. Hot and cold appetizers include *chupe de camarones,* a Peruvian

Cheo's Corner

shrimp chowder. Main courses are based on pasta dishes, from fettuccine alfredo to linguini *al frutti di mare*. Everything is made to order, and you can watch the hosts puttering in the kitchen. Anna Maria's is located in a residential area off the Avenida Frans Figaroa, north past the commercial area around the Santa Ana Church. Turn left just before Ng's market; it is a short distance down the road.

SOLE MARE

Long-established **Sole Mare** (Palm Beach 23, 297/586-0077, 5:30pm-11pm daily, $22-49) has a loyal clientele and a menu with a wide assortment of traditional dishes, including the famous "pasta in parmesan" dish prepared table-side. Portions are generous, and a house specialty is reasonably priced osso buco. A favorite is *branzino al sale,* an entire fish baked en croute with salt breading, then filleted at your table. A large selection of pasta has various sauces, and an early-bird special (5:30pm-7pm daily, $25) includes three courses and coffee or tea. This is a popular place during high season, and reservations are strongly advised.

INTERNATIONAL

BARNEY'S

A comfortable neighborhood hangout for a mature crowd and a fun place for families is **Barney's** (Palm Beach 21A, 297/586-5420, www.barneysaruba.com, 4pm-11pm Tues.-Thurs. and Sat., 4pm-midnight Fri., $15-38). Owners Ron and Elina have a congenial division of labor: He loves bartending and she provides meals. Chef Hans has a deft touch in the kitchen. Patrons praise the spicy firecracker shrimp and mushrooms stuffed with escargot, or try the smoked trout fillet for a gourmet treat. Most nights have themed specials: Monday is all-you-can-eat fajitas; Tuesday is schnitzel night, with chicken or pork schnitzel prepared five ways; Wednesday is grouper night, also featuring your choice of preparation; Thursday has unlimited ribs; Friday offers unlimited barbecue; and Saturday has unlimited rib-eye steak (until they run out, which can happen). Friday evenings also features a karaoke party from 10pm.

CHICKEN & LOBSTER

Moderately priced for Palm Beach, **Chicken & Lobster** (Playa Linda Beach Resort, J. E. Irausquin Blvd. 87, www.chickenandlobster.com, 297/586-0909, 7:30am-10:30pm daily, $10-45) has lovely ambience and pleasant waitstaff for breakfast, lunch, and dinner in the open air. Fresh-caught lobster and roasted free-range chicken are the focus of the wide-ranging menu; a whole roasted chicken ($29) can feed a family of four. Daily specials include breakfast platters with free-range eggs, breakfast meats, unlimited coffee or tea, and fresh-baked bread ($12). A lunch special ($16) features a half chicken, soup du jour, a side, and a nonalcoholic beverage. The three-course early-bird dinner special (4pm-7pm daily, $30) includes a glass of wine.

DUSHI BAGELS & BURGERS

Dushi Bagels & Burgers (Playa Linda Beach Resort, J. E. Irausquin Blvd. 87, www.dushibagelsandburgers.com, 297/586-3035, 7am-11pm daily, $19-25) features the welcoming congenial charm of hosts Carina and her husband, Fernando, who enjoy cultivating relationships with their patrons. The only restaurant on Aruba to bake its own bagels, Dushi serves over a dozen varieties that can be bought fresh every morning. Call ahead to order by the dozen or half dozen so Carina can set them aside for you. Lunch and dinner feature big burgers, inventive wraps and salads, fresh fish, wings, and quesadillas. The bar produces beautiful exotic drinks—sample a gorgeous glass of sangria or a nonalcoholic smoothie. Dining is mostly outdoors, but there's a cozy air-conditioned dining room. The distinctive decor reflects Carina's quirky humor: Her colorful paintings line the walls and have been printed on the placemats. In the evening the restaurant hosts live entertainment.

LA VISTA

For hearty eaters, La Vista (Marriott Resort, L. G. Smith Blvd. 101, 297/520-6601, 5:30pm-10:30pm daily, brunch 10:30am-2:30pm Sun., $40-65) offers an excellent-value buffet. Wednesday costs more because unlimited king crab and shrimp are included, and Saturday also costs more since it features unlimited baked whole Caribbean lobsters. Tuesday (Italian) and Sunday (international) are the least expensive nights. Monday features a live folkloric show, and Thursday features a live carnival show with regional Aruban cuisine. Friday evening is all about the grill, including prime rib, prawns, and crab claws. Expect casual dining and clean surroundings. La Vista also has a terrace adjacent to the beach, and walls of windows to watch the sunset. There are special holiday buffet brunches as well as an à la carte menu. One drawback: drinks are overpriced, including nonalcoholic ones. A 50 percent discounted happy hour runs 5pm-9pm daily.

LOCAL STORE

Along the main road from the hotels to the Santa Ana Church is Local Store (Palm Beach 13A, 297/586-1414, www. localstorearuba.com, 8am-11:30pm daily, $10-29), with a breakfast featuring traditional Aruban items and a broader international menu for lunch and dinner. Breakfast includes hearty waffle sandwiches, one with chicken and melted cheese, as well as papa di maishi rabo (cornmeal porridge) with granola and berries. The lunch-dinner menu offers hearty hero sandwiches, burgers, wraps, and coconut shrimp or chicken wings done a dozen different ways, priced by the piece or the pound. Local Store is lively on weekends. Singles gather on Friday night until closing for a wide assortment of international craft beers. Sunday evening attracts families after the beach to enjoy the sunset with a snack.

OAK

Oak (Rooi Santo 3A, 297/580-4660, www. oakaruba.com, 5pm-10pm Mon.-Sat., $25-45) is in the Waykiri condo complex, inland just off Bakval Road, with air-conditioned indoor and outdoor terrace seating. The varied menu has seafood and steaks, pastas, and a classic Argentine meat platter with skewers of chicken, steak, and chorizo. Everything is beautifully presented.

PAPIAMENTO

Among the most romantic restaurants on Aruba, Papiamento (Washington 61, 297/594-5504, 6pm-9:30pm Mon.-Sat., www. papiamentoaruba.com, $30-58) is in a beautifully restored 1886 landmark country manor. Dining is outdoors among lush gardens around a swimming pool, with a few tables in the elegant interior. Papiamento offers a perfect romantic atmosphere for a proposal. The Ellis family is famous for its gourmet savvy, and a unique and delicious version of keshi yena is offered, along with quality steaks and innovative seafood. Try the Cazuela, shrimp and rock lobster in coconut milk chowder, or the Aruban bouillabaisse. Surf and turf dishes are served sizzling on a lava stone, lightly seasoned and accompanied by dipping sauces. This technique is especially suited to produce moist tender shrimp, fish, and lobster. Reservations are strongly advised.

STEAK HOUSES

TEXAS DE BRAZIL

Aruba's single eatery featuring Brazilian cuisine is the rodízio steak house Texas de Brazil (J. E. Irausquin Blvd. 382, 297/586-4686, www.texasdebrazil.com, 6pm-10:30pm daily, $48, salad bar only $27). Patrons control the all-you-can-eat service with a gadget that displays a red light or green light. Once you have indicated that you're finished with the salad bar and are ready for the main course, congenial waiters visit your table in a continual stream offering cuts of beef, chicken, pork, and lamb, cooked over an open wood fire and served on giant swords. Diners nod or say "no" to each dish; this continues endlessly until you say "uncle." The salad bar features distinctive hot dishes such as seafood thermidor and saffron rice, unique marinated salad items, and a delicious seafood chowder, good alternatives to the parade of meat. Dessert is not included, but who has room? The cost is what steak houses charge for a main course, so if you're hungry, this is a great deal. On the second level of La Hacienda Mall, it has an elegant cocktail lounge with a lovely view. The dining room is divided by an open-air courtyard. Reservations are strongly advised at this popular spot.

BARBECUE
CHÉ BAR
For authentic Argentine barbecue and friendly family ambience, nothing beats **Ché Bar** (J. E. Irausquin Blvd. 382A, 297/586-1696, http://chebararuba.com, 11am-10:30pm Mon.-Sat., 5pm-10:30pm Sun., $10-43), on the northern sidewalk of Paseo Herencia Shopping Mall. Expect ample tasty portions of pork ribs and Argentine beef steak prepared on a wood-fired grill. The house specialty is the famous Argentine mixed meat platter, ordered as a small sample platter with bits of chorizo and blood sausage, rib-eye steak, and chicken, or as a bountiful dinner for two with the addition of short ribs. With its European sidewalk café ambience, the outdoor eatery has proved

popular and is now open afternoons for hearty grilled-meat sandwiches, and mornings for breakfast under the name World of Pancakes.

NEW WEI TAI
If you pass **New Wei Tai** (Palm Beach 4, 297/586-8864, 11:30am-10pm Sun., $8-32) on the Palm Beach-Noord Road any Sunday, you'll see islanders lined up for the weekly barbecue special ($9). Huge portions of ribs and chicken are piled on an enormous heap of fried rice in takeaway containers, to be consumed on the beach. If you're not given enough barbecue sauce, ask them to put on a bit more. Most customers take their food to go, but you can have it plated to eat in the air-conditioned dining room for a nominal extra charge. The eatery's regular menu is worth a look, but Sunday barbecue is the main event.

BREAKFAST
WORLD OF PANCAKES
Operating by night as Argentinian grill Ché Bar, by day this sidewalk eatery goes by the name **World of Pancakes** (J. E. Irausquin Blvd. 382A, 297/586-1696, http://chebararuba.com, 8am-10:30am Mon.-Sat., $7-12). Besides pancakes and french toast, the menu includes egg sandwiches and breakfast burritos.

Papiamento

North Coast

ITALIAN

LA TRATTORIA EL FARO BLANCO

Next to the lighthouse at the top of California point is **La Trattoria El Faro Blanco** (California Lighthouse z/n, Westpunt, 297/586-0786, www.faroblancorestaurant. com, 8:30am-11pm Mon.-Sat., $27-45), a delightful arrangement of open-air terraces that look out on the northwestern shore, far inland and nearly to Oranjestad. The staff is congenial and food gets mixed reviews, from excellent to mediocre and overpriced, but the location and atmosphere are unmatched. Aside from the beach, this is one of Aruba's top spots for a proposal over a romantic sunset dinner. Breakfast sandwiches and coffee are offered for the early morning tours that stop by the lighthouse. A relatively reasonable lunch menu of soups and salads makes it a nice stop while touring the island.

Santa Cruz, Paradera, and Piedra Plat

You'll find a number of small local snack shops for a quick lunch stop while touring Aruba's outback. They usually feature abundant fried foods, stews, barbecue with fries and rice, and lettuce and tomato passing for salad, but they are inexpensive and offer great value. Newly developed neighborhoods in these areas are also beginning to bring more options. Attractions such as Arikok National Park, Natural Bridge, and Casibari Rock Formation have places that sell cold drinks and a *pastechi* or sandwiches.

ARUBAN

★ SALT LIFE

Not far from the main Paradera traffic circle is **Salt Life** (Seroe Patrishi 59, 297/588-0881, 11am-8pm daily, $8-22), dominating a tiny strip mall on a major road with heavy traffic. For great local food, don't miss it; the cute spot has its own deep-sea fishing boat so it can offer the freshest of fish. Portions are large and served on a large metal tray filled with your selection and every Aruban side dish imaginable: fries, brown rice and beans, *funchi, pan bati,* fried sweet banana, and salad. The superb fish is cooked on an open grill. Try the *picuda* (barracuda) or whole red snapper. A rich seafood soup is available daily, and the surf and turf can easily feed two. Dining is outdoors under a thatched roof, though most patrons order takeout. Attached to the dining area is a tiki bar that's popular with locals. A bucket of six beers is $20, and wine and other drinks are moderately priced.

KIKORICO

Close to the Tanki Leendert traffic circle in a small modern strip mall (look for the Wendy's) is **Kikoriko** (Tanki Leendert 265A, 297/587-7177, www.kikorikoaruba.com, 11am-10pm daily, $5-25). It has the trappings of a fast-food franchise, with clean nondescript decor and a counter where staff in logoed uniforms take your order. But the food stands apart. The specialty is rotisserie chicken; select a quarter chicken with the usual yellow rice, fried potatoes, *pan bati,* salad, and fried banana ($5) or a half chicken ($8). Combos with whole chickens and a mixed grill are available.

SAVANNAH LODGE

A great place to take a lunch break while touring is the Aruba Ostrich Farm's **Savannah Lodge** (Aruba Ostrich Farm, Mativideri 57, 297/585-9630, 11am-3pm daily, $7-24), decorated in African-inspired decor with figurines from Zimbabwe and featuring a menu of Aruban cuisine with some Dutch influence. Grouper, tacos in *pan bati,* and a burger made of a locally grown bean fruit are on the menu. In season, get the biggest omelet or fried egg you have ever seen made of ostrich or emu eggs. The price for a six-bottle bucket of beer ($16) is the best on the island, making this a worthwhile cooling stop to enjoy the spectacular views of the surrounding countryside.

URATAKA CENTER

On the road to Arikok National Park, **Urataka Center** (Urataka 12, 597/585-5212, 11am-midnight daily, $2-14) is a popular local hangout with a pool table, dart boards, and domino tables. It serves what patrons claim is the best pizza on Aruba, but the real gems are local island standards off the grill, such as a chicken wing "basket," a heaping helping of crispy flash-fried wings without breading, or barbecue ribs. More substantial platters are pork chops or grilled chicken *a la plancha,* served on a wooden plank. Stop for a cold beer and an authentic slice of island life. It gets busy on weekends.

DUTCH
MACAMBA'S TUINTJE

For a remarkable evening, reserve at **Macamba's Tuintje** (Paradera 50, 297/660-8411, 5pm-3am Fri. and 1st Sat. of the month, $3-10), less a straightforward dinner than a social evening with the charming owners who are also chef and bartender, Walter and Jane Steentjes. Dutch expatriates, they share their joie de vivre in their home's huge *tuintje* (garden), with seating options from picnic tables to loveseat swings. Most patrons congregate at the wraparound bar. On the menu are Dutch treats such as *bitterballen* (meatballs), *frikandel* (a Dutch hot dog), and large orders of fries with *pinda* sauce. Walter fires up the barbecue for ribs, steaks, or chicken with heaping helpings of side dishes. A fire pit is laid out with cooking stones so diners can choose to cook their own meat around the open fire. Aside from the bar, comfy picnic tables are for enjoying the evening air.

SUSHI
NIKKEI SUSHI BAR

Next to the Tanki Flip rotunda on the east side of the Noord-Ponton road is **Nikkei Sushi Bar** (Tanki Flip 10A, 297/737-6506,

tempura at Nikkei Sushi Bar

6pm-11pm daily, $14-18), where island-ers come for good sushi, excellent tempura, and reasonably priced drinks. Geared to the local trade, prices are better than in the hotel areas. A large dining room usually guaran-tees seating. The restaurant also delivers and is not far from Eagle Beach hotels. Aside from inexpensive standard sushi rolls, it has some interesting specialty rolls; the Milan features breaded grouper, shrimp, calamari, cream cheese, cucumber, and tartar and eel sauces. Nikkei has a party platter of four specialty rolls ($40), a very good deal. The waitstaff is friendly and helpful, and an app can be down-loaded to your phone to order pickup or de-livery. When you order with the app, you get a 10 percent discount.

COLOMBIAN
LOS CAFETEROS

Between the Tanki Flip and Tanki Leendert traffic circles is **Los Cafeteros** (Tanki Leendert 249, 297/587-7004, 8am-9:30pm daily, $7-28), a classic Colombian restaurant "with a Creole flavor," rustic ambience, and a playground, making it a great choice for fami-lies. The diverse menu has a reasonably priced hearty Colombian breakfast with eggs, meat, fruit, and potatoes ($7), a daily lunch spe-cial ($7), and a large seafood selection, with a reasonably priced whole local fish ($17)

that includes side dishes. Roasted meats are served *a la plancha*, on a wooden plank, and there are some vegetarian options; portions are generous.

CAFÉS
ARIKOK PARK COFFEE SHOP

After hiking around the national park, you will find the simple fare on the terrace of the **Arikok Park Coffee Shop** (visitors cen-ter, main entrance to Arikok National Park, 297/585-5200, 8am-4pm daily, $1.50-2.50) tastes just right. A tiny place offering local snacks, *pastechis,* croquettes, hot dogs, and tuna sandwiches, the seating is on the deck, where you can relax with a gorgeous view of the park.

HUCHADA

One of Aruba's favorite stops for fresh bread, cakes, and snacks is **Huchada** (Santa Cruz 328, 297/585-8302, 6am-8pm Mon.-Fri., 6am-7pm Sat., 7am-2pm Sun., $3-4). The specialty is stuffed sandwiches on a choice of fresh-baked rolls, often still warm from the oven. The basics include ham and cheese, tuna salad, and some interesting combinations. Try items from the great assortment of cakes, pastries, and cookies, boxed up to take back to your room. Essentially a bakery, Huchada has a few tables.

San Nicolas, Savaneta, and Pos Chiquito

Aruba's eastern and southern shores have yet to be heavily developed for tourism, but it will come. Most eateries are aimed at islanders and will be busy with locals around lunchtime and weekends.

ARUBAN
BALASHI BEER GARDEN

For an Aruban dining experience, visit **Balashi Beer Garden** (Balashi 62, Pos Chiquito, 297/597-6542, 6:30am-2:30pm Mon.-Fri., $4-14), adjacent to the Balashi Brewery on the south side of the island, an expansive open-air eatery on a hilltop offering breathtaking views of the sea and countryside. Originally a canteen for the brewery's employees, it offers cheap breakfast sandwiches on rolls, johnnycakes, and lunch platters. Set-menu lunch items ($5) are burgers, crispy chicken-finger platters, and wings. Daily changing lunch platters ($10-14) include steak, fish, roasted or stewed chicken, or shrimp, accompanied by a bevy of the usual Aruban side dishes. Don't miss the brewery's own Balashi Beer! A frosty 12-ounce stein costs $3. This is a great place to refresh and refuel if you've been out touring. From Oranjestad, turn off to the right just before the Pos Chiquito rotunda on 1A. Eventually the road ends in a T-intersection on a street parallel to the sea. Turn left and take the first left onto a gravel road; a sign says "Balashi Brewery."

SEAFOOD
★ ZEEROVER

Fish and shrimp lovers cannot miss **Zeerover** (Savaneta 270, 297/592-9080, 11am-9pm Tues.-Sun., bar 11am-9pm daily, $8-15), hands-down the best place on the island for fish. Given its location right on a dock where fishing boats are moored, don't be surprised to see your meal carried in fresh while you wait to order. Patrons stand in line at one window to order food and at a second window for drinks. The menu is simple: whatever fish is on hand plus fresh shrimp. The attendant taking your order will show you what's available, and you'll pick out the fish fillet, steak, or whole fish of your choice, usually grouper, wahoo, marlin, or snapper. Shrimp can be medium, huge, or both. The selection is weighed to calculate the price. Flash-frying is the only option for preparation. Try the papaya pica relish, locally produced and very spicy, for some zing that enhances the fish.

Pick a table in the shade of the terrace or on the dock. Enjoy a cold beer while you wait, which won't be long. Your entire order is put in a single basket, family-style, with plastic plates and forks (regulars bring their own sturdier silverware). Most end up eating with their fingers, so sinks with soap and towels are located around the restaurant. Zeerover is popular for lunch; dinner is hit-and-miss as food is served only as long as fresh fish is available. The kitchen can close as early as 5pm when they run out. Even with dinner reservations, call to confirm. On an island of elegant restaurants, Zeerover is an authentic Caribbean fish shack, though more comfortable and elaborate. Popular with the seafaring crowd and churchgoers, it is mobbed on Sunday, when the wait to order can be an hour or more; choose a weekday if you don't care to stand in line for too long.

MARINA PIRATA

An original local fish restaurant, **Marina Pirata** (Spaanslagoenweg 4, Pos Chiquito, 297/585-7150, 6pm-11pm Wed.-Mon., $16-40) offers dining-on-a-fishing-dock charm with a bit more elegance. Twinkling lights and hurricane lamps prompt patrons to describe the atmosphere as "magical," and it is famed for fresh fish and prompt amiable service. This is where they brought Gloria Estefan for dinner when she wanted to eat somewhere "authentic." Kids love feeding the fish that come up to the dock in large schools, attracted to underwater lights. Marina Pirata offers a half dozen ways to sample the fresh catch of the day and is great for whole red snapper and fresh Caribbean lobster. The signature dish is the Spaans Lagoen special, a seafood mix prepared à la coquille St-Jacques in a creamy sauce ringed with cheese-crusted mashed potatoes.

Driving to Marina Pirata can be confusing because the road seems to end at nothing; the restaurant is on the water, out of sight, down some steps leading to the shore. It is clearly marked with an archway and sign, but you can't see the entrance from street level.

CARIBBEAN FUSION
★ O'NIEL CARIBBEAN KITCHEN

On the main street of San Nicolas is picturesque **O'Niel Caribbean Kitchen** (v/d Veen Zeppenfeldtstraat 15, 297/584-8700, 11am-10pm Tues.-Sun., $10-15), featuring quaint, colonial-style decor. It's worth planning a day of touring the east end of Aruba with the purpose of a lunch or dinner stop here. Chef O'Niel will likely greet you personally if he isn't too busy in the kitchen. After decades of establishing the reputations of some of Aruba's most popular restaurants, his own place serves moderately priced and hefty portions of fresh fish and Jamaican and Aruban regional favorites prepared with his deft touch. Highly recommended are the steamed mussels appetizer and whole steamed snapper, or the fresh catch of the day. Inquire about other specials, which might be *cabrito stoba* or a gourmet concoction at prices below what you would expect to pay. For a real treat, try the traditional Jamaican oxtail; it's a revelation. Wildly popular with islanders for lunch, it gets busy noon-2pm. Come earlier or later; it will be easier to get a table.

RUM REEF BAR

Located next to JADS Dive Shop, **Rum Reef Bar** (Seroe Colorado 245, 297/584-6070, 11am-5pm daily, $4-16) offers a lovely view over the expanse of Aruba's southeastern point. The open-air terrace eatery is the only one next to Baby Beach. The menu includes *sate*, grouper Aruban-style with creole sauce, and platters with typical local snacks, as well as sandwiches, hamburgers, hot dogs, and chicken wings. JP, the owner of JADS and Rum Reef, fancies himself a mixologist. Relax and linger over an exotic frozen concoction in his capable creative hands. The ambience is congenial; you'll arrive a patron and depart a friend.

BEACHSIDE DINING
FLYING FISHBONE

For the most romantic dining experience possible, **Flying Fishbone** (Savaneta 344, 297/584-2906, www.flyingfishbone.com, 5pm-10pm daily, $30-59) is a top choice, the first to establish the toes-in-the-sand concept, in a perfect secluded cove. The diverse menu has refreshing gazpacho and shrimp tempura, gourmet seafood, prime steaks, and a delectable lobster thermidor. Everything is beautifully presented, but portions tend to be small. Sunset is the optimal time to experience the locale; make reservations well ahead for that time slot. One drawback is that cab fare from major hotels is almost as much as dinner, the same as the cost of renting a compact car for the day. It isn't hard to find: Follow the 1A, which parallels the sea; signs will indicate where to turn right.

INTERNATIONAL
ANTESALA CAFÉ

An appealing option for breakfast, lunch, or a refreshing pit stop is **Antesala Café** (Savaneta 1A, 297/585-5909, 8am-3pm Mon.-Sat., $8-18), with hearty soups, elaborate burgers and salads, sandwiches, and "design your own pasta" options. Fresh arepas are offered along with several vegetarian choices. Regulars claim the café serves the best coffee on the island, and it also has organic and

Charlie's Bar

herbal loose teas. A favorite item is the breakfast bowl "smoothie" ($9) of yogurt and whatever fresh fruits are available. On the main 1A highway, which runs the length of the island from east to west, it's easy to find.

CHARLIE'S BAR

No trip to San Nicolas is complete without a stop at the legendary **Charlie's Bar** (B v/d Veen Zeppenfeldstraat 56, 297/584-5806, 11:30am-7pm Mon.-Sat., $16-30), if only for a glimpse of the idiosyncratic decor. It features a large collection of miscellaneous memorabilia; even the bathroom walls are filled with curiosities and original art. Charlie's is famous for fresh shrimp, steamed or scampi, and steak sandwiches. Dishes are served with Honeymoon Sauce by chef Rosalba (also sold by the jar). The bar is named for its founder, the late Charlie Brouns II, an island character. His son keeps his memory alive in this local hangout, where visitors are always warmly welcomed. Becoming a tourist attraction has spiked the prices considerably. In the heart of Aruba's red-light district, Charlie's Bar is more appealing for a daytime snack and drink, especially if you're traveling with children.

Entertainment and Events

Nightlife 140

Shows and Concert
    Venues 148

Festivals and Events 150

Whether you're into lounges, live music, casi-nos, or festivals, Aruba has something exceptional for you.

Top Latin, jazz, soul, and classic rock groups, including superstars such as Marc Anthony, Chaka Khan, Alicia Keys, and Crosby, Stills, and Nash, can be found in concert at Aruba's venues at ticket prices much lower than in the United States. Free shows are featured nightly at most busy entertainment centers, and scores of special events associated with national holidays and weekly festivals amuse and enlighten while sharing traditional island culture.

Most large hotels have in-house casinos and cozy lounges or sports bars for socializing after dinner. All-inclusive resorts feature organized live entertainment nightly. Although visitors need not leave the

Highlights

Look for ★ to find recommended sights, activities, dining, and lodging.

★ **Arawak Gardens:** Aruba's first entertainment center offers something for everyone, including restaurants, nightly entertainment, and late-night shopping (page 144).

★ **Bugaloe:** This night spot right on the water charms all ages with its authentic island atmosphere, great bands, and a dance floor (page 144).

★ **Carnival:** Carnival celebrations dominate the island from the first Saturday after New Year's Day until Ash Wednesday, with parades, music, and street parties (page 150).

★ **Himno y Bandera Day and International Half Marathon:** Aruba's National Day encompasses elegant events, a joyous celebration of national identity and pride, and a half marathon (page 151).

★ **May Day:** The first day of May, the Royal Dutch Marines turn their camp into a theme park, with music, food, and air- and sea-based demonstrations (page 153).

★ **Soul Beach Music Festival:** Top R&B singers and big-name comedians converge in Aruba for five days of concerts and parties (page 153).

★ **Aruba Hi-Winds Pro-Am:** For over 25 years, Aruba has been hosting the most renowned Pro-Am windsurfing and kitesurfing competitions in the world (page 153).

★ **Caribbean Sea Jazz Festival:** Aruba's last weekend in September sees local and international jazz, innovative art, and gourmet food, all at bargain prices (page 154).

★ *The Nutcracker:* The immortal ballet has become a holiday tradition in Aruba thanks to famed former Bolshoi and New York City Ballet star Leonid Kozlov (page 156).

★ **New Year's Eve:** Island-wide pyrotechnics start the new year with the biggest bang anywhere (page 157).

resorts to find entertainment, Aruba's most appealing attribute is what some dub an "all-inclusive island"—unlike at many resort destinations, travelers can easily mix with locals, who enjoy the amenities of the more populated tourist areas.

It is safe to roam the principal tourist areas at night in search of amusement. Oranjestad and Palm Beach are the hubs for lounges, discos, and free entertainment. Well-lit bustling shopping malls contain elegant and casual eateries, late-night lounges, and nightly free shows. Most are set up to provide entertainment to diners. Several shops and souvenir kiosks are open during the evening hours.

Oranjestad is the epicenter of most special events on Aruba. The biggest Carnival parades, holiday celebrations, conventions, sporting events, and concerts are here. The first months of the year are filled with a parade of Carnival events, but Aruba really begins to heat up in late spring with events like the Soul Beach Music Festival, the Caribbean Sea Jazz Festival, the Aruba International Regatta, and the Aruba International Pro-Am Golf Tournament. The island's physical attributes and weather attract world-class athletes to the Aruba Hi-Winds Pro-Am windsurfing and kitesurfing competition in July and the International Beach Tennis tournament in November.

Nightlife

In Palm Beach, every sort of nighttime activity is a short stroll from any resort. Visitors can check out clubs, restaurants, shows, and even late-night shopping. Oranjestad and Manchebo Beach have casinos and clubs, with most nightlife at the major resorts and the casinos.

ORANJESTAD

Oranjestad generally tends to quiet down at night, except for the few blocks along L. G. Smith Boulevard surrounding the harbor. The Renaissance Marketplace, right on the water, has nightly musical performances at the waterside bandstand. Many clubs in the mall have their own entertainment. Outside the mall, several venues that are cozy eateries during the day turn into hot nightlife spots after dinner. Clubs lining the water have lovely views and a distinct island feel.

CAFÉ CHAOS

Across from Wilhelmina Park, one of Oranjestad's most popular nightspots, **Café** Chaos (L. G. Smith Blvd. 60, 297/588-7547, http://cafechaosaruba.com, 5pm-2am Mon.-Thurs., 5pm-4am Fri., 7pm-4am Sat., no cover) has a cozy European pub ambience: dark wood paneling, humorous signs, and good cold beer on tap. Café Chaos morphs from a quiet place early in the evening to a raucous hangout as the night wears on. Weekends feature top island bands on the small stage. The crowd often overflows out onto the sidewalk after midnight.

CAFÉ THE PLAZA

A favorite spot to enjoy free nightly live music is **Café the Plaza** (Renaissance Marketplace, L. G. Smith Blvd. 82, 297/583-8826, www.cafetheplaza.com, 7am-midnight daily, no cover), a popular hangout with Aruba's Dutch community. The restaurant is open from breakfast to midnight, and tables are filled inside and out from the lunch hour on. The outdoor terrace is for drinks and eating platters of Dutch snacks such as *bitterballen* (meatballs) or *frikandel* (hot dog). This congenial spot is

Party Buses

When looking for a happening nighttime hot spot, you want the scene to be fun and busy. Aruba's club crowd works during the week and saves the partying for Friday and Saturday nights. Locals commonly hit the clubs following some other event or after a night shift, so places don't begin to fill up until late.

Vacationers can guarantee a hopping atmosphere by signing up for a *paranda* tour, or party bus. Wherever you go on these tours, the party comes with you. Why risk driving under the influence? Wildly painted buses pick up guests at their hotels and drop them off afterward. Party buses boast friendly hosts and drivers who add to the hilarity; the hosts are well practiced at getting the party started. One tour option is to leave earlier to enjoy a champagne toast on a secluded beach at sunset; dinner at a local restaurant follows. The rest of the evening is spent at picturesque local bars, with a drink at each stop. More drinks can be purchased at special prices—usually only a dollar or two. Another option is to dine on your own with a pickup time later in the evening, an option known as a "pub crawl" that only includes the barhopping portion of the tour.

Respected *paranda* tours are run by **Kukoo Kunuku** (Noord 28 P, 297/586-2010, www.kukookunuku.com, Pub Krawl 9pm-12:30am Mon.-Sat. $50 pp, Dinner & Nightlife Tour 6pm-midnight Mon.-Sat. $71 pp, Wine on Down the Road 5:30pm-9:30pm Tues. and Thurs. $100 pp, Beer Flights & Bites 5:30pm-9:30pm Wed. $74 pp) and the **Banana Bus** (SchubertStraat 10, 297/593-0757, www.bananabusaruba.com, Pub Crawl 8pm-1am Tues.-Thurs. $45 pp).

perfect to linger and listen to great bands on the Renaissance Marketplace stage.

FLOR DE ORIENTE

Besides reasonably priced meals, **Flor de Oriente** (Kerkstraat 6, 297/583-9808, 3pm-midnight Mon.-Sat., 2pm-midnight Sun., no cover) has become *the* island hangout on Friday after work for Aruba's professionals, especially lawyers from the courthouse next door. Opened in 1935, it's one of Aruba's oldest rum shops and has the friendly neighborhood vibe common to "brown bars"—a Dutch concept referring to tiny pub-like establishments that specialize in dark beers. Flor de Oriente has over 21 brands of European beer on the menu as well as wine. The picturesque spot gets pleasantly busy on the weekends, when it hosts live music outdoors, a great way to soak in the mellow island ambience. Typical Dutch snacks such as cheese balls, *loempia* (small egg rolls), and *bitterballen* are arranged on a beautiful snack platter.

THE PADDOCK

The Paddock (L. G. Smith Blvd. 13, 297/583-2334, www.paddock-aruba.com, 9am-2am Sun.-Thurs., 9am-3am Fri.-Sat., no cover) is a popular spot for Dutch students interning abroad. It occupies a prime spot on the water and has funky decor; you can't miss the velociraptor hanging out on the roof next to the Volkswagen. It's a reasonably priced eatery serving Dutch and other foods, but The Paddock becomes a hangout for younger folks after the dinner hour. Every night features drink specials and a happy hour. Three nights a week, local bands play until 2am.

RENAISSANCE MARKETPLACE

The open-air **Renaissance Marketplace** (L. G. Smith Blvd. 82, 297/582-4622, www.shoprenaissancearuba.com, shops 10am-7pm Mon.-Sat., restaurants and clubs 10am-midnight daily) is best known for its restaurants and nightlife. Adjacent to the water, a row of dining spots offering everything from Dutch pancakes to sushi has harbor views for breakfast, lunch, and dinner. Venues including Café the Plaza, Casa Tua, and Cuba's Cookin' provide dinner and entertainment until the wee hours. A waterside bandstand features live music from classic rock to reggae. Aruba's original multiplex,

The Cinemas, is also in this mall, showing first-run films.

7 CLUB LOUNGE

The former Jimmy's Place, long the island's unofficial LGBTQ hangout, is now **7 Club Lounge** (Windstraat 32, 297/582-2550, www.7aruba.com, 9pm-2am Wed.-Thurs. and Sun., 9pm-4am Fri.-Sat., no cover). Under new ownership, it continues to welcome diversity. The decor has been updated for a disco vibe, with mirrors, purple lights, and modern furniture. At the east end of Oranjestad, in a quaint old-fashioned house that belies the glamorous interior, internationally known DJs from Europe and the Caribbean are scheduled on weekends. Sunday nights are women only. Pleasant gardens in the rear center on a specialized Gin Bar featuring only top-shelf brands and an exotic menu of martinis. Some intimate rooms allow for private celebrations.

EAGLE BEACH AND MANCHEBO BEACH

The preponderance of time-share and family condominium resorts has kept this area quiet at night. The Alhambra Casino complex is the center for nighttime excitement, within walking distance of most Manchebo Beach resorts. A free tram from the center to more distant Tamarijn and Dutch Village runs until late. For the cluster of resorts farther north on Eagle Beach, the casinos at the Tropicana and La Cabana Resorts provide the entertainment.

CAGE

Described as a club for everyone of all orientations, **Cage** (King Plaza, Caya Harmonia 9, 297/593-3550, 9pm-3am Wed.-Sun., no cover-$14) has evolved into Aruba's definitive LGBTQ hot spot, particularly popular with yuppies. Entertainment includes male pole dancers and drag contests. The space is quite big and the decor chic. Mezzanine seating provides a place to cool off after the dance floor. Ladies Night is Wednesday and includes free drinks for women 9pm-10:30pm. Friday and Saturday nights there's a $6 entry fee, and there's a $14 cover—which includes two drinks—for special events and live music. Otherwise, entry is free. International DJs and live bands typically play Latin and regional dance music, a favorite with islanders. Cage is on the north side of the Sasaki Highway, in the large mall between the Bubali Road and the large rotary. Since it's nonsmoking, it's a literal breath of fresh air compared to most nightlife venues.

FUSION WINE AND PIANO BAR

Upscale locals have made **Fusion Wine and Piano Bar** (Alhambra Shopping Bazaar, 297/280-9994, 6pm-1am Sun.-Thurs., 6pm-2am Fri.-Sat., no cover) their favorite place for late night, with an extensive wine list, a gourmet tapas menu, surf-and-turf for two, and live music and special events on weekends, from celebrity DJs to wine tastings and guest chef dinners. Enjoy the balmy Aruban evenings in front and back open areas, along with attentive service, comfy lounges, and tasteful ambience. Check Fusion's Facebook page for coming events.

STAR KARAOKE

Indulge your inner rock star at **Star Karaoke** (King Plaza, Caya Harmonia 9, 297/594-3988, 8pm-3am Tues.-Sun., no cover), a cozy hangout with two rooms to sing the night away. Karaoke is popular on Aruba, particularly with expat Filipinos. A special VIP Room has classic KTV, which can be rented for $20 per hour. Bring your own food to the VIP room, but drinks must be purchased from the house bar.

PALM BEACH, MALMOK, AND NOORD

Palm Beach is Aruba's center for nighttime excitement, with a wealth of evening activities, mostly in the large malls that line J. E. Irausquin Boulevard. Several eateries segue into appealing cafés and popular gathering places at night. Many feature free live music.

1: Bugaloe; **2:** Renaissance Marketplace

Shopping is a prime after-dinner activity, with scores of stores and kiosks open until 10pm or later.

★ ARAWAK GARDENS

Arawak Gardens (J. E. Irausquin Blvd. 370, no phone, shops 5pm-11pm daily, dining and nightlife 11am-2am daily) is a bustling center for shopping, dining, and nightlife. It attracts a diverse crowd from young singles to honeymooners to families. You can enjoy live entertainment at no extra cost when dining here; all the restaurants have outdoor terraces surrounding a gazebo where singers and musicians perform (7pm-10pm daily, free). The music is usually mellow: classic rock, golden oldies, and show tunes, and you can choose from Salt & Pepper (Dutch-continental cuisine and tapas), Fishes N' More (seafood), Casa Tue (pizza and Italian), Tango Argentine Grill (steak house), or Dragonfly (pan-Asian food). Afterward, do some late-night shopping, or grab a drink or cigar at Sopranos Piano Bar, which also has live entertainment.

★ BUGALOE

The charming eatery **Bugaloe** (water end of the De Palm Pier, 297/586-2233, www.bugaloe. com, 7:30am-midnight daily, no cover), also recommended for breakfast, lunch, or dinner, turns into a favorite nightspot when the sun sets. A diverse all-ages crowd enjoys the casual atmosphere and authentic island ambience of the pier. This spot never gets steamy, smoky, or hot with the constant trade winds. There are great live bands Tuesday-Wednesday and weekends, plus free salsa lessons Wednesday nights. The music and mood are friendly and welcoming, with the dance floor filled with jolly people most of the night.

AZIA

Azia (J. E. Irausquin Blvd. 348, 297/586-0088, www.giannisgroup.com, 5pm-1am Sun.-Thurs., 5pm-3am Fri.-Sat., no cover) has indoor-outdoor seating, and the alfresco section offers couches and lounges and an open area for dancing. This is a good spot for late-night snacking, exotic drinks, and socializing until the wee hours. It specializes in flavorful Pan-Asian tapas from India, China, Japan, Korea, Mongolia, and Indonesia, so you can snack or order several dishes and fill up.

CRAFT BAR

At the front of The Village mall, with a cozy outdoor terrace, is tiny **Craft Bar** (The Village, J. E. Irausquin Blvd. 348, 297/586-6999, www.craftaruba.com, 8am-1am Sun.-Thurs., 8am-3am Fri.-Sat., no cover). While open early for breakfast, it's more a popular tranquil late-night spot for Aruba's stylish 30-somethings. The bar boasts an extensive selection of imported craft beers and a large cocktail menu. It also offers Nicaraguan coffee, the base for a wide assortment of lattes, and some very fancy waffles served until 6pm. The bar has a long, late happy hour (7pm-10pm daily) and frequently hosts special themed evenings; check its Facebook page.

DREAM BOWL

For some after-dinner family fun, **Dream Bowl** (L. G. Smith Blvd. 95, 297/586-0809, www.dreambowlaruba.com, 4pm-11pm Sun.-Thurs., 4pm-midnight Fri.-Sat., lanes $35 per hour, up to 6 shoe rentals included) in the Palm Beach Plaza mall offers bowling with stylish modern decor. The hall is black light and neon color, right down to the bowling balls. On Tuesday-Wednesday and Thursday, happy hour features bargain buckets of beer. Thursday is Red Pin Night—hit a strike when the red-headed pin appears and win a free drink.

Aside from bowling lanes, there are pool and foosball tables, air hockey stations, and a complete arcade. Dream Bowl also sports a pizza bar with finger food. Extend your evening in the karaoke room after the lanes.

DUSHI BAGELS & BURGERS

In addition to being a popular eatery, **Dushi Bagels & Burgers** (Playa Linda Resort, J. E. Irausquin Blvd. 87, www.

dushibagelsandburgers.com, 297/586-3035, 7am-11pm daily, no cover) is a popular nightspot drawing a mature crowd. Within the arcade of shops fronting the Playa Linda Resort, it's a nice place to linger with fancy drinks or desserts. Patrons come for a light casual dinner but stay until closing time as some of Aruba's most talented singers are showcased nightly. The repertoire is golden oldies, and the mood is mellow. Dushi has a talented bartender who crafts an exotic drink special each day; owner Carina reveals that after a few of these, patrons start singing along.

GUSTO

Islanders in their mid-20s flock to Gusto (The Village, J. E. Irausquin Blvd. 348A, 297/592-5579, http://gustoaruba.com, 7pm-1am Sun.-Thurs., 7pm-3am Fri.-Sat., no cover), a cozy bar with a chic casual atmosphere; dress up or down as you please. It is Aruba's only remaining disco convenient to the tourist areas. Check the Facebook page for themed events on weekends with celebrity DJs. Music varies widely from trance, to house, hip-hop, salsa, and merengue. There is no entrance fee except for special events, and happy hour (9pm-11pm daily) offers all drinks at half price.

LOCAL STORE

Oranjestad's former hot spot for the young crowd is now in Palm Beach. The Local Store (Palm Beach 13A, 297/586-1414, www.localstorearuba.com, 7:30am-1:30pm daily, no cover) took over a popular little rum shop and maintained that traditional local ambience with a dozen craft beers. It's currently the most popular hangout on Aruba, particularly on late Sunday afternoon. On Friday afternoon, island yuppies flock to the little cocktail tables in the front yard for happy hour, staying late into the night. The club presents live music on weekends from local Caribbean bands. Expect reggae, trance, house, and reggaeton. A diverse international menu includes ice-cold imported and local craft beers and buckets of spicy chicken wings.

MOOMBA BEACH BAR & RESTAURANT

The distinctive and funky beachfront MooMba Beach Bar & Restaurant (J. E. Irausquin Blvd. 230, 297/586-5365, http://moombabeach.com, 8am-1am daily, no cover), wedged between the Holiday Inn and Marriott Surf Club, attracts all ages but is a popular place for young people to connect. On weekends it fills with families enjoying the beach and the restaurant, along with guests from smaller resorts using the beach. The bar and outdoor lounge embody the fantasy of island life and stay busy at all hours for events, beach tennis, and great bands on weekends. The main bar is always hopping at happy hour (6pm-7pm daily and 10pm-11pm Mon.-Sat.) and well into the night. It is surrounded by shops that are open until 10pm.

SAND BAR & LOUNGE

Aruba's chicest open-air nightclub is Sand Bar & Lounge (J. E. Irausquin Blvd. 370, 297/594-4366, www.sandaruba.com, 6pm-3am daily, no cover), on the main Noord-Palm Beach Road bisecting J. E. Irausquin Boulevard. The beach-bar feeling has been transplanted to this convenient location and features a VIP section with dedicated waitstaff and a stage for live music surrounded by a dance floor. There is a nightly happy hour (9pm-11pm) as well as specials every evening, including Mojito Mondays and Wednesday Ladies Night Out, when drinks are $4. Sand also has a moderately priced snack menu of calamari, chicken wings, hamburgers, and mozzarella sticks. Special events are listed on its Facebook page. For more entertainment options, there are a plethora of screens for sporting events and a hookah lounge called I♥Hookah, with an enormous selection of inhalants, from flavored tobaccos to chunks of fresh fruit. Hookahs can include up to six mouthpieces for large parties.

SOPRANOS PIANO BAR

Sopranos Piano Bar (Arawak Gardens, J. E. Irausquin Blvd. 370, 297/586-9944, www.

Casinos

Aruba boasts 14 casinos, all with a **player's club** with a VIP card that costs nothing to obtain and brings an immediate reward of a $10 play coupon. Using the card when playing slots and table games puts credits on your account. Points can be redeemed for logo items, and for dinners, spas, and extra nights at many of the resorts.

Aruba is known for **Caribbean Stud Poker,** where you play against the house with progressive jackpots based on the returns from all the tables. This unique game has surprisingly frequent big winners of $50,000-100,000. Casinos also host **blackjack tournaments** sporadically. Check with the casino, as schedules change regularly. International tournaments are common around holidays. Most casinos also host afternoon **bingo,** which is big with locals; a small investment can reap some rewards. Bingo may not be for high rollers, but it provides a congenial break from the afternoon heat, with door prizes, drinks, and snacks.

Aruba levies no taxes on winnings, but you can only transport up to $10,000 cash when traveling. Island casinos will keep the money in an account for regular visitors.

ORANJESTAD

Oranjestad has **Wind Creek Crystal and Seaport Casino** (L. G. Smith Blvd. 82, 297/583-6000, http://windcreekhospitality.com, 24 hours daily) at the Renaissance Resort next to Oranjestad Harbor. These are the only casinos on the island open 24 hours a day. The Seaport Casino offers an elaborate sports book gallery, with real-time broadcast of races and sporting events.

EAGLE BEACH AND MANCHEBO BEACH

The Manchebo Beach area has the **Alhambra Casino** (Alhambra Shopping Bazaar, J. E. Irausquin Blvd. 47, 297/583-5000, www.casinoalhambra.com, 10am-4am daily). Eagle Beach has the **Glitz Casino** (J. E. Irausquin Blvd. 250, 297/587-3399, 10am-4am daily) in the La Cabana Resort and **Tropicana Casino** (J. E. Irausquin Blvd. 248, 297/587-9000, 10am-4am daily) at the Tropicana Resort.

PALM BEACH

Palm Beach hosts several busy gaming rooms within easy walking distance of each other. The

sopranospianobar.com, 5pm-1am Sun.-Fri., 5pm-2am Sat., 2-drink minimum) features excellent local entertainers, with the occasional imported pianist. This is an after-dinner drinks and cigars kind of place, with cozy booths on the terrace and an atmospheric interior. Named and styled after the famous TV show, it draws a mixed crowd. Request a song for a tip to determine the mood, from mellow tunes to classic rock. You will not hear house, trance, or hip-hop here. Sopranos offers special evening events weekdays as well as rotating happy hours and a 50 percent discount after work on Friday. Check the Facebook page to see what's happening.

SOUTH BEACH LOUNGE

Aruba's pretty people like **South Beach Lounge** (Palm Beach 55, 297/586-6766, www.southbeacharuba.com, 5pm-1am Sun.-Thurs., 5pm-3am Fri.-Sat., no cover). The crowd is eclectic, from young vacationers to mature resident fashionistas. The stylish contemporary open-air deck offers various seating arrangements to suit your mood; take a high stool around the bar to watch a sporting event or lounge on a couch with a cocktail. South Beach Lounge is most active 11pm-1am weekends and is quiet during the week.

If you want to dance salsa and bachata,

Riu Palace's Cool Casino

Hilton has **The Casino** (J. E. Irausquin Blvd. 8, 297/526-6930, www.tcaruba.com, 10am-3am daily), which, along with the Holiday Inn's **Excelsior Casino** (J. E. Irausquin Blvd. 230, 297/586-7777, www.excelsiorcasino.com,10am-4am daily), have dedicated poker rooms for nightly Texas hold 'em tournaments. Other Palm Beach casinos include the Marriott Resort's **Stellaris Casino** (L. G. Smith Blvd. 101, 297/586-9000, www.stellariscasino.com, 10am-4am daily), Riu Palace's **Cool Casino** (J. E. Irausquin Blvd. 79, 297/587-2993, www.coolcasinoaruba.com, 10am-6am Mon.-Sat. 10am-midnight Sun.), and Riu Antillas's **Orchid Casino** (L. G. Smith Blvd. 77, 297/525-7777, www.orchidcasino.com, 10am-4am daily). Somewhat more elegant are the **Hyatt Regency Casino** (J. E. Irausquin Blvd. 85, 297/586-1234, www.hyattaruba.com,10am-4am daily) and the **Ritz-Carlton Casino** (L. G. Smith Blvd. 107, 297/527-2222, www.ritzcarlton.com,10am-4am daily). All have standard craps, roulette, and blackjack as well as hundreds of slot machines.

popular Aruban vocalist C-Zar Olarte and his band take the stage after 10pm Saturday. Tables are moved aside to enlarge the dance floor, which is packed with couples. Even if you don't want to dance, you can feel the energy of the islanders and their love of dance and see some amazing performances; many Arubans are fantastic Latin dancers.

SANTA CRUZ, PARADERA, AND PIEDRA PLAT

Suburban areas of Aruba are being built up to cater to an influx of young professionals. The result is more restaurants, shops, and nightlife options, including pleasant open-air bars with neighborhood vibes offering a more relaxed island scene.

CASIBARI MUSIC CAFÉ

A souvenir and snack shop by day—you might stop by after climbing the Casibari Rock Formation across the street—**Casibari Music Café** (Casibari 8B, 297/586-1775, www.casibaricafe.com, 8am-10pm Mon.-Sat., no cover) transforms into a lively nightlife spot, especially on Jazz Night Wednesdays, featuring top island performers. The café is partially built on another rock formation with terraces to create unique hangout spots and vantage points. There is also a substantial dance floor for Friday Salsa Nights. Casibari hosts special events of its own and staged by local groups, from wine tastings to muscle car rallies. Check the Facebook page for a list.

MACAMBA'S TUINTJE

Open only Friday evening and the first Saturday of the month, Macamba's Tuintje (Paradera 50, 297/660-8411, 5pm-3am Fri. and 1st Sat. of the month, no cover) is the sort of place where you'll feel you've found some congenial new friends. Tending the wraparound bar are Walter and Jane Steentjes, Dutch expatriates who happily open their garden (tuintje)

to neighbors and friends. The modestly priced menu has barbecue and Dutch nibbles, and drinks are cheap: The Heineken and Balashi will flow. Early in the evening sees a family crowd, but after dinner it becomes a romantic nightspot. Aside from the bar, comfy picnic tables and loveseat swings are available for lounging in the evening air.

Macamba's is also usually open the three nights prior to New Year's Day; to experience New Year's Eve Aruban-style, with the requisite fireworks, this is the place. Check the Facebook page for special events.

Shows and Concert Venues

Aruba's primary concert venues are the Aruba Entertainment Center and Cas di Cultura, both on the western outskirts of Oranjestad. In recent years, the former container harbor has seen concerts by international performers. Scattered around the island are sports arenas and community centers that often host large concerts. Wider beaches host concerts, including Surfside Beach, which hosts the annual Soul Beach Music Festival. Concerts on Aruba are about socializing, dancing, and grooving to the music.

ARUBA RAY'S COMEDY CLUB

Once upon a vacation, New York comedian Ray Ellin fell in love with Aruba, soon spending six months of the year at his island retreat. His unflagging enthusiasm for this tropical paradise prompted his comedy cohorts to dub him "Aruba Ray," and thus was born Aruba Ray's Comedy Club (Amsterdam Room, Marriott Resort, L. G. Smith Blvd. 101, 297/749-4363, www.arubacomedy.com, 8:30pm-1am daily, $36). Ray lures some of the best talent from New York and Los Angeles for 4-6 weeks of shows four times a year, usually around Thanksgiving, New Year's, Valentine's Day, and July 4; check the website.

This is entertainment for mature audiences, and Ray is a congenial host with

lightning-fast wit. His humor engages his audience in the most inoffensive manner. His rotating roster of guest comics are familiar from late-night TV. The price of a ticket includes a promotional perk from the Stellaris Casino in the Marriott and a discount coupon for La Vista restaurant. Buy tickets online or at the door. For an additional $20, enjoy four hours of access to a premium open bar during the show and afterward at the casino tables.

CAS DI CULTURA

Aruba's Cas di Cultura (Vondellaan 2, Oranjestad, 297/582-1010, www.casdicultura. aw) is the performing arts center where classical concerts, plays, and myriad other events are staged. It has a 400-room auditorium that hosts local and imported talent. The theater is flanked by the Rufo Wever School of Music and the Da Vinci Piano School, both with frequent concerts in the auditorium. The center has no house orchestra, so programs depend on who is renting the auditorium. The Cas di Cultura annually hosts The Nutcracker by Kozlov Dance International (www.koslovdance. com) with star Leonid Kozlov. Performances are usually classical, jazz, and island music

---

1: free entertainment at Paseo Herencia Shopping Mall; 2: Aruba Ray's Comedy Club

and dance. There are usually shows Friday and Saturday night, and often during the week. It also has an exposition room for smaller events and art exhibits. Upcoming performances are posted on the website.

GUY BAVLI—MASTER OF THE MIND

Two nights a week, Alhambra Casino hosts the great **Guy Bavli—Master of the Mind** (Alhambra Shopping Bazaar, 800/554-2008, www.masterofthemind.com, 8pm-11pm Tues.-Wed., $35-70). A mentalist and Las Vegas regular, Bavli performs in the Alhambra Ballroom, usually to a packed audience. His routines will have you gasping with amazement, while his patter—family-friendly yet filled with sly humor—entertains. There is never a dull moment, even for the most skeptical. Bavli is personable and approachable, happily giving autographs and posing for pictures after the show.

PASEO HERENCIA SHOPPING MALL

Great for all ages, *Waltzing Waters* is a sound, water, and light show in the **Paseo Herencia Shopping Mall** (J. E. Irausquin Blvd. 382A, 297/586-6533, http://paseoherencia.com, 7:30pm, 8:30pm, 9:30pm, and 10:30pm daily) at the north end of the Palm Beach main drag. The mall features numerous special events on holidays. Free shows at 8pm Monday-Saturday feature a wide variety of entertainment, including violinists, folkloric dancers, steelpan drummers, and local singers. There is even a salsa night and *Cirque Aruba* fantasy program of tumblers and clowns. The mall runs a horse-drawn carriage to take you back to your hotel at the end of the evening; a ride along the boulevard is $30 for 25 minutes. Shetland pony rides for kids around the mall are $5 for 5 minutes.

Festivals and Events

After New Year's, Aruba begins a long calendar of special events punctuated by ebullient parties. Weeks of Carnival happenings heat up the winter, and the "low season-slow season" months are enlivened by festivals, sports competitions, and concerts. Something exceptional happens nearly every month.

WEEKLY FESTIVALS

BON BINI FESTIVAL

The long-running **Bon Bini Festival** (Fort Zoutman, 297/582-3777, 7pm-8:30pm Tues., $10) features traditional island culture, music, and dance. Regional instruments such as the *caha di orgal* (organ grinder), the *wiri*, and steelpan accompany enthusiastic young dancers in native costume. Performers change from one week to the next, so there is no predicting the program; count on either folkloric or carnival dancers. This is a pleasant way to spend two hours and a nice segue into dinner at one of Oranjestad's excellent restaurants.

Doors open at 6pm, so take time to browse Fort Zoutman's exhibits and the booths selling inexpensive local art, handicrafts, and snacks.

JANUARY-FEBRUARY

★ CARNIVAL

The festive events of **Carnival** (multiple venues, parades free, music contest and election $5.50) start the Saturday after New Year's Day (unless New Year's Day falls Thurs.-Sat., in which case festivities wait another week) and can last 4-10 weeks depending on the date of Ash Wednesday. A full calendar with events, times, and parade routes in English is at www.visitaruba.com.

For islanders, Carnival is the most anticipated event of the year, beginning with a nighttime parade through Oranjestad called the *Fakkeloptocht,* Dutch for Torch Parade. Carnival events take place most weekends until Ash Wednesday, except the final week, when they are every night. There are music contests, queen elections, and many parades day and night. Hear local original music composed each year just for Carnival. Live bands accompany the parades in specially designed trailers while thousands of participants garbed in sumptuous costumes dance alongside. Each group is judged for their artistic floats. The major parades after the Torch Parade are the Balloon Parade (San Nicolas), Children's Parade (San Nicolas and Oranjestad), Youth Parade and Tivoli Lighting Parade (Oranjestad), Jouvert Morning (San Nicolas), Grand Final Parades (San Nicolas and Oranjestad), and finally, the Burning of Momo (Aruba Entertainment Center, Oranjestad).

At the Aruba Entertainment Center, Carnival queens are selected during extravagant pageants in four age categories, from child to mature. Two of the biggest events are music contests: the selection of the Tumba King or Queen and the Roadmarch & Calypso King or Queen (San Nicolas). The party ends at the stroke of midnight on Ash Wednesday with the burning of an effigy of Rey (King) Momo, a pagan figure who rules over revelers and the dark of night. The commencement of the new Carnival is announced annually on November 11, at 11 minutes after 11am. That evening, an inaugural event is held at a venue close to most resorts to initiate visitors into the traditions and excitement of Aruban Carnival.

Aside from the official activities, many resorts schedule "jump-ups" for their guests. These open-air festivities usually feature one of the more popular Carnival bands, beer stands, and lively entertainment. A shorter Carnival season means more frequent events; none are sacrificed due to lack of time. Aruba's Carnival is rated second only to Brazil's. Many come every year to enjoy the spectacle and unbridled indulgence.

BETICO DAY

The first official national holiday of the year is January 25, **Betico Day** (Plaza Betico Croes, behind the Cas di Cultura, 5pm-10pm), which honors the memory of "El Liberatador," Gilberto Francois "Betico" Croes. A solemn ceremony of remembrance is followed by a cultural night of speeches, music, and folkloric dance.

MARCH

★ HIMNO Y BANDERA DAY AND INTERNATIONAL HALF MARATHON

Aruba's National Day, March 18, **Himno y Bandera Day,** begins before dawn with an **International Half Marathon** (http://registration.mylaps.com/arubahalfmarathon, Sun. closest to Mar. 18, $20 registration), which starts in San Nicolas and ends in Oranjestad. It has traditionally attracted runners from Latin America, the United States, and Europe with cash awards and trophies. The day sees an elaborate street fair and a national show at night in the Plaza Betico Croes or Plaza Padu; entrance is free. This is the best place to buy Aruba souvenirs, as the fair features authentic local handicrafts; it is remarkable how many ways Aruba's attractive flag can be incorporated into alluring garments and jewelry.

WENTE/PAPIAMENTO GOLF TOURNAMENT

The famous Wente Vineyards in California partners with local restaurant Papiamento to put on the **Wente/Papiamento Golf Tournament,** a weekend of golf and gourmet food. Proceeds benefit a different Aruba foundation each year. Events include a welcome reception in Papiamento Restaurant's elegant gardens. Unlimited Wente wine flows throughout the weekend; wine tastings along the greens are part of the competition.

Arion Wine Company (Ponton 38 Q, 297/583-3325, www.arionwinecompany.com) sponsors the event. Eric Wente, head of the winemaking family, plays host. The first prize is a trip to the Wente Vineyards in California's Livermore Valley, with a weekend of golf on the famous course. The tournament is by invitation only, but visitors can leave their name at Tierra Del Sol Pro Shop in Malmok

to participate on a stand-by basis. Contact the shop for more information.

APRIL

FLIP FLOP FESTIVAL

The **Flip Flop Festival** (Bushiri Beach Arena, just north of Costa Linda Resort, www.flip-flopfestival.com, free-$70) began as an event to introduce Chill Beer by Aruba's Balashi Brewery and has grown into a huge annual music festival and beach party. The three-day affair features a lineup of local bands, regional and international headliners, and celebrity DJs. Aside from music, there are food booths, beach volleyball, tennis courts, and lots of cheap beer, as well as exclusive parties at various island venues from nightclubs to hotel pool decks.

KING'S DAY

The month ends with the most important Dutch holiday of the year, **King's Day** (Apr. 27), with revelry and various activities. A protocol ceremony honors the monarch at Wilhelmina Park at 10am, and throughout the day are flea markets, classic car club and Harley-Davidson motorcades, kite competitions, and open houses at all island museums.

MAY

★ MAY DAY

On May 1, **International May Day,** the Royal Dutch Marines open their camp in Savaneta (turnoff for the camp from Hwy. 1A is clearly marked, 9am-6pm) and turn it into a giant theme park. The day is filled with the island's best flea market, inexpensive food stands, musical performances, boat rides, and aerial and sea-based demonstrations of mock battle. It's a great way to mix and mingle and observe island life; proceeds are donated to a local charity.

★ SOUL BEACH MUSIC FESTIVAL

The **Soul Beach Music Festival** (concerts at Surfside Beach, comedy at Aruba

Entertainment Center, www.soulbeach. net, combo package and VIP seating $420), founded by comedian and actor Sinbad, has a home on Aruba and is a Memorial Day weekend tradition for thousands. Five days of beach events and after parties culminate in three concerts by chart-topping R&B, hip-hop, and soul performers. One night is dedicated to trending comedians. Alumni include Jamie Foxx, Jennifer Hudson, Toni Braxton, Alicia Keys, L. L. Cool J, Kevin Hart, and Mike Epps; expect to see top talent for cheap. Packages and charter flights can be arranged through the website.

JUNE

ARUBA INTERNATIONAL TRIATHLON

June ends with the **Aruba International Triathlon** (IBISA, idefre@setarnet.aw, 297/585-4987), a 1.5-kilometer (1 mi) swim, 40-kilometer (25 mi) bike race, and 10-kilometer (6 mi) run with cash prizes. The main event begins at Eagle Beach across from the MVC-Club, next to the Tulip restaurant. The swim is two loops, then eight loops along Irausquin Boulevard from Costa Linda Resort to Divi Phoenix Beach Resort by bicycle, and a five-loop run along the same course. Around 400 athletes from Aruba, the United States, Europe, and Latin America compete.

JULY

★ ARUBA HI-WINDS PRO-AM

A respected amateur windsurfing and kite-surfing competition is the annual **Aruba Hi-Winds Pro-Am** (Fisherman's Huts, L. G. Smith Blvd., Malmok, www.hiwindsaruba. com, free for spectators). Expect to meet some of the great names in windsurfing, including the undefeated PWA Women's World Champion in Freestyle Windsurfing since 2008, Sarah-Quita Offringa, a native Aruban. She often lends her presence to this event, in which she first competed. The week has beach parties, fashion shows, and breathtaking demonstrations of athletic prowess, including the celebrated nighttime aerial kitesurfing

1: Carnival celebration; 2: Soul Beach Music Festival

display. Spectators can join the fun with copious cheap beer.

AUGUST-SEPTEMBER

ARUBA INTERNATIONAL REGATTA

The third weekend of August, Aruba's premier all-class sailing event is the **Aruba International Regatta** (Surfside Beach, http://aruba-regatta.com), growing in scope and attendance annually but still with the atmosphere of a grand beach party. Everyone from windsurfers to cruising-class 36-footers compete. Even if you don't sail, it is a friendly event with striking photo ops.

ARUBA INTERNATIONAL PRO-AM GOLF TOURNAMENT

At the end of August or early September, the **Aruba International Pro-Am Golf Tournament** (Tierra Del Sol Country Club and Golf Course, Malmokweg z/n, 297/586-0978, www.tierradelsol.com) attracts pros and players from around the world. The 36-hole tournament guarantees one respected pro mentoring each four-person team. Three days of competition for prizes and trophies include elegant evening events and organized activities for nongolfers.

★ CARIBBEAN SEA JAZZ FESTIVAL

The **Caribbean Sea Jazz Festival** (Renaissance Marketplace and Convention Center, 297/588-0211, www.caribbeanseajazz. com, $50 presale, $70 at the door) has become a destination the last weekend of September. Enjoy two nights of great music, cheap gourmet food, and original art created for the event. International stars join regional performers. CSJF has welcomed David Sanborn, Chaka Khan, Oscar D'León, Angie Stone, and Candy Dulfer. The party starts well in advance, with featured artists performing free warm-up events at local venues.

OCTOBER

EAT LOCAL MONTH

October offers a month-long opportunity to dine on locally inspired fare during **Eat Local Month** (lunch $15, dinner $30-40), with over a dozen island restaurants offering discounted menus. Order a three-course dinner at restaurants such as Que Pasa, Red Fish, and Ike's Bistro. Find out which restaurants are participating at the island's official website (www.aruba.com).

PRESIDENTIAL ARUBA CARIBBEAN CUP

Go for the big one in billfishing during the **Presidential Aruba Caribbean Cup** (Varadero Yacht Club, Bucutiweg no. 34, 297/588-3850, www.preschallenge.com, mid-Oct.). Island fishing fanatics and their deep-sea rigs are available as crew and for rent to team up with fishing enthusiasts from around the world. The three-day event takes place during Aruba's peak marlin season. All fishing is "catch and release" using special hooks. The tournament ends with a gala awards dinner.

NOVEMBER

ARUBA INTERNATIONAL BEACH TENNIS OPEN

The world's top-seeded players and all levels of competition are at the **Aruba International Beach Tennis Open** (J. E. Irausquin Blvd. 230, 297/592-6427, www.beachtennisaruba. com, mid-Nov.). International sports journalists credit Sjoerd de Vries, founder of Beach Tennis Aruba, as the premier promoter of the sport in the Americas. Professionals from around the globe converge on Eagle Beach for a week of matches and nightly parties. There are 30 courts and constant action. Sports tournaments on Aruba always provide a congenial party atmosphere for competitors and the audience in addition to the sporting action, and this event embodies these aspects.

1: Aruba Hi-Winds Pro-Am; **2:** Caribbean Sea Jazz Festival

Ending the Year with a Bang

As New Year's Eve approaches, fireworks bid farewell to the old and greet the new. Fireworks go on sale just after Christmas, and the nightly displays don't stop until everyone runs out of rockets. On the last business days of the year, tradition demands that businesses set off a *pagara*, a roll of firecrackers that can number from 5,000 to 5 million. The most famous is set off in Oranjestad by MetaCorp, usually stretching the entire length of the Renaissance properties and beyond. It holds up traffic for an hour and takes 20 minutes to run its course. *Pagaras* are said to chase away *fuku* (FOO-koo), ill will or bad vibes. Once a business has set off its *pagara*, it is cleansed for the coming year. At the stroke of midnight on New Year's Eve, homes and restaurants alike set their *pagaras* alight, and the new year starts with a haze of fireworks smoke. Resounding through the night, hundreds of millions of firecrackers explode. Bring earplugs!

DECEMBER

During Christmas and New Year's, Aruba is packed with visitors and the excitement of the season, with its own lively holiday traditions, music, and events. Check www.aruba.com for the calendar of ever-changing festivals, sporting meets, and concerts.

SINTERKLAAS FEAST DAY

Aruba's loving observance of Dutch traditions is never more evident than on the **Festival of Sinterklaas** (island-wide, Dec. 5). This beloved figure was the precursor to Santa Claus and based on a real person. He arrives on Aruba 2-3 weeks prior to his feast day, greeted at the port by thousands of children and their parents. On December 5, the eve of his feast day, the stately gentleman is seen everywhere, including resorts, distributing toys and sweets to children. In accordance with Dutch tradition, Sinterklaas is accompanied by Zwarte Piet, a Moor dressed in Renaissance attire. Be aware that some celebrants also dress up as Zwarte Piet, donning blackface and Moorish costume; this has been a controversial part of the tradition in recent years, but it does continue to be a part of the celebration in Aruba.

HOLIDAY SHOPPING
IN ORANJESTAD

The capital's merchants' association turns Oranjestad's Caya Grande into a festive holiday celebration on the weekends (MAMBO, Caya G. F. "Betico" Croes, 10am-6pm Sat. until Christmas). All through the day there is entertainment from seasonal local *gaita* singing groups, performing regional music. Originating from Maracaibo in Venezuela, *gaita* is lively upbeat music, and *gaita* groups consist of 8-12 female singers accompanied by native instruments such as a *cuarto* (a small guitar) and *tambora* (goatskin drums). At the beginning of the month, a visit from Sinterklaas precedes his feast day, after which Santa Claus holds court with young children at various venues.

★ THE NUTCRACKER

Russian ballet star Leonid Kozlov, formally the principal dancer of the Bolshoi and New York City Ballets, and his wife, Adriana, a prima ballerina, settled on Aruba in 2013 and opened the first academy dedicated to classic ballet; they have trained some of Aruba's most talented dancers. Leonid and Adriana annually dance the principal roles and bring in notable guest performers for Tchaikovsky's *The Nutcracker* (Cas di Cultura, 297/593-2036, www.kozlovdance.com, 7pm, weekend in mid-Dec., $20). The stunning sets, gorgeous costumes, and beautiful choreography have created a delightful holiday tradition that Aruban audiences have enthusiastically embraced. Introduce the family to this seasonal treat for a fraction of what it would cost at home. Shows are frequently sold out, so purchase tickets online in advance. The exact weekend and number of shows vary; check the website. Guests of the Barceló hotel can enjoy an abridged version of the show during the weeks of Christmas and New Year's.

ARUBA DANDE FESTIVAL

Another beloved holiday tradition is the local version of caroling, focused on the New Year. The annual **Aruba Dande Festival** (various community centers, www.visitaruba.com, 8pm, weekend between Christmas and New Year's, free) is a competition lasting almost until dawn to select the next Dande King or Queen. Many resorts host Dande exhibitions for their guests around this time.

Traditionally, the New Year's "serenade" of Dande is performed by roaming minstrels who travel from home to home. Employing inside information from an informant within the household, they usually personalize the song's lyrics to the lives and foibles of the residents, always in a humorous manner. An important part of the ritual is passing the hat and a small monetary reward from each family member for their entertainment. During the Dande Festival, lyrics are far more topical and occasionally contain scathing political and social commentary. Most often, however, they deliver a message of enjoying life and good wishes for the coming year.

★ NEW YEAR'S EVE

Those who think watching the ball drop while freezing is the epitome of New Year's Eve excitement have yet to experience New Year's on Aruba. As the year's end approaches, a frenzy of fireworks can be seen and heard everywhere. At the stroke of midnight, the sky fills with pyrotechnics in every neighborhood, after which the professional displays begin. Most hotels stage fireworks displays, especially on the beach. Most notable are those by the Divi and Tamarijn Beach Resorts in the Manchebo Beach and Eagle Beach area, the Hyatt Regency Resort in Palm Beach, and the Renaissance Resort in Oranjestad. Nearly every resort hosts a special dinner for their guests to celebrate, and many restaurants host special evenings that last until midnight, with champagne included.

Shops

Oranjestad............160
Eagle Beach and Manchebo
    Beach 168
Palm Beach, Malmok, and
    Noord 169
North Coast...........175
Santa Cruz, Paradera, and
    Piedra Plat..........175

If you want a unique memento or great bargain, Aruba offers a variety of shopping options, including designer stores, jewelry shops, and souvenir and handicraft shops.

Some of the best buys are at the open-air markets. A small group of artisans produces interesting handicrafts and original paintings and watercolors, for sale at festivals conducted by the resorts. Crafts such as macramé and appliqué are more Latin American, and many attractive items from these countries, from handwoven hammocks to embroidered garments, are common at the markets.

Smaller jewelry stores are known for their "calculator dance" when a shopper asks about a piece. Being knowledgeable about gemstones and having a taste for bargaining help in haggling for some discounts,

Highlights

Look for ★ to find recommended sights, activities, dining, and lodging.

★ **Cosecha:** Chat with island artists about their work at this center for authentic, local handicrafts (page 161).

★ **The Local Market:** Across the main boulevard from the cruise terminal in Oranjestad, this convenient covered market features dozens of kiosks with regional handicrafts and popular souvenirs at affordable prices (page 161).

★ **Mopa Mopa:** Find beautiful handicrafts made by the Quillasinga people of Colombia using the same processes as their ancestors (page 161).

★ **Gandelman Jewelers:** A respected regional family operation, Gandelman is the exclusive Aruban agent for brands like Rolex and Patek Philippe (page 165).

★ **Renaissance Mall:** If designer labels are your obsession, this is the place to indulge. The greatest concentration of top American, European, and Latin designer shops is in these elegant corridors (page 166).

★ **Super Food:** Food shopping can be gift shopping for lovers of Dutch cheeses and exotic spices (page 168).

★ **Terrafuse:** Don't go on a hunt for that unique souvenir; make it yourself at Terrafuse's glass-art classes (page 169)!

★ **Aruhiba:** This cigar store sells Aruba's own homegrown and rolled brand, and has the largest selection of Cuban, Honduran, and Dominican cigars on the island (page 171).

but it requires patience and determination. This practice is not particularly Aruban, but it has been common since the turn of the millennium.

European perfumes and high-end cosmetics are comparatively good buys, as are wines from Europe and Latin America. Canadians report that famous U.S. brands are as much as 25 percent cheaper than at home. Hard liquor is discounted at duty-free shops at the airport, but not elsewhere, except locally bottled Ron Superior and Palmera rums. Buy your favorite liquor on your way on or off of the island. Smokers declare cigarettes on Aruba cost much less than in the United States. Cigar lovers will be thrilled that Cuban cigars are widely sold. Aruba has its own brand, Aruhiba, made of locally grown tobacco, which can be taken back to the United States without fear of confiscation.

Dutch cheeses are an excellent buy, and as long as they are uncut and sealed in the original rind, they can be carried into the United States. The best places to pick these up are at the supermarkets like Super Food. More locally manufactured items come from Aruba Aloe, which offers products for hair and skin care.

Well-known brands such as Louis Vuitton, Gucci, Mario Hernandez, Montblanc, Salvatore Ferragamo, and Ralph Lauren all have dedicated outlets in Oranjestad or Palm Beach. Aruba, however, is not a true duty-free port. European designer goods are marginally discounted over U.S. prices. Other items, especially electronics like mobile devices and video games, are uniformly more expensive.

Oranjestad is best known for daytime shopping. Mall fever has struck Palm Beach, with one multipurpose mall after another cropping up. Shops at the Palm Beach malls open in the late afternoon, mindful that most visitors spend their days on the beach and offering nighttime shopping, often accompanied by entertainment.

Oranjestad

Downtown Oranjestad is Aruba's daytime shopping destination. Stores open between 8:30am and 10am and close between 6:30pm and 8pm. Not long ago, most stores closed for an extended two-hour siesta, but modern times and more competition have eliminated such island practices completely. There are only a few die-hard local shops that don't remain open all day. Nearly all stores are closed Sunday, except for a very few on L. G. Smith Boulevard that open when a cruise ship is in port.

The area around the cruise terminal could be dubbed the "diamond district": One store after another boasts well-known names of fine-quality jewelry and gemstones. Several are internationally affiliated with outlets in the United States. A few have their own on-site artisans creating original pieces.

Most stores and malls are clustered around the harbor. Within are name-brand designer shops complemented by attractive cafés and stylish surroundings. Caya G. F. Betico Croes has always been the town's main shopping street. One half has high-end stores displaying well-known brands, and the eastern end is mostly local shops with cheaper goods. A free tram to and from the cruise terminal takes you directly to the vendors in downtown Oranjestad.

Previous: L. G. Smith Boulevard on a summer day; sign at Cosecha handicrafts store; Terrafuse.

ART, HANDICRAFTS, AND SOUVENIRS

Aruba has active and talented artists whose works can be found for sale at a number of surprising venues. Newcomers to Aruba have brought native handicraft skills from Venezuela, Colombia, and other Latin American countries. Most offerings can be found at flea markets and souvenir shops.

★ COSECHA

Authentic local arts and handicrafts can be found at **Cosecha** (Zoutmanstraat 1, 297/587-8709, www.arubacosecha.com, 1:30pm-6:30pm Mon., 9:30am-6:30pm Tues.-Sat.), directly behind the Renaissance Marina Tower in Oranjestad. Find anything from inexpensive handmade costume jewelry to handcrafted skateboards made of driftwood. Each day, one of the artists on display is present to discuss their work or take special commissions. All items sold at Cosecha are officially certified "Made in Aruba"; guidelines for certification are based on UNESCO criteria, including craftsmanship, originality, aesthetics, material use, and representation of local identity.

★ THE LOCAL MARKET

The greatest assortment of souvenir T-shirts and inexpensive logo items can be found at **The Local Market** (Pardenbaaistraat z/n, 297/733-1982, 9am-6pm daily), across from the cruise ship terminal in Oranjestad. Under a protective roof and thus immune to most weather, it's Aruba's first flea market that stays open daily. Aside from an incredible diversity of handcrafted items, you'll find inexpensive beach wraps, hats, sandals, and other items. Browsing this warren of kiosks, you'll find cute gifts for friends back home without wreaking havoc on your holiday budget.

★ MOPA MOPA

Aficionados of genuine artfully crafted handiwork should not leave Aruba without visiting **Mopa Mopa** (Renaissance Marketplace, L. G. Smith Blvd. 82, 297/588-7297, www.mopamopa.com, 9:30am-6pm Mon.-Sat.). Though not produced on Aruba, the arresting and beautiful pieces are unique, the result of a complex process handed down through generations of Quillasinga people from Colombia and still created as they were before the Spanish conquest. Buds of the mopa mopa tree, a bush that grows in Putumayo province in the Amazon basin, are boiled to produce

Oranjestad

Authentically Aruban Souvenirs

Cosecha

If you're looking for a unique gift that represents Aruba, check out these places:

Since the mid-20th century, nearly all food is imported, as the harsh desert climate is inhospitable to agriculture. Recently, new technologies and green sensibility have resulted in widespread cultivation of hardier fruits and vegetables as well as production of interesting liquors and condiments, such as Madame Janette relish and Papaya Pica. You can find these at **Super Food** and the **Alhambra Shopping Bazaar** in the Eagle Beach area.

Ha'Bon (Coconuts and Van Dorp stores, hotel sundry shops, Island Breeze at the airport, 297/594-5777, www.habonaruba.com) is a line of natural soaps handmade in Aruba. This small company hires individuals with disabilities and also recycles unused soap to donate to care facilities for the elderly. The various soaps are delightfully scented with fresh flowers and herbs and are attractively packaged for gift-giving.

Collectors seeking local arts and handicrafts should visit **Cosecha,** behind the Renaissance Marina Tower in Oranjestad. Housed in a beautifully restored 100-year-old landmark building, Cosecha is government-sponsored and aims to encourage local artisans. The collection is diverse, and much of the art is recycled from debris. Find jewelry made of Djucu nuts that have floated over the sea from Venezuela, skateboards made of driftwood, and remarkable accessories fashioned from old inner tubes. Every item is officially certified "Made in Aruba." Different artists visit daily to discuss their work.

resin. Natural plant dyes give the resin distinctive colors. The artisans then chew the resin to soften it so it can be stretched and cut into intricate designs. Works take the form of ceremonial masks and figurines and convey the Quillasinga culture through flora and fauna. This traditional Colombian craft cannot be readily found outside its home country.

Besides this shop, Mopa Mopa has a table at the hotel craft shows at **Marriott Surf Club**

(4pm-9:30pm Tues. and Thurs.) and the artisan market at the **Tamarijn Beach Resort** (5pm-9:30pm Mon. and Fri.).

ARTISTIC BOUTIQUE

Eclectic giftware is showcased at **Artistic Boutique** (L. G. Smith Blvd. 90-92,

1: authentic crafts at Mopa Mopa; 2: open-air souvenir stalls near Oranjestad Harbor

297/582-3142, 10am-6pm Mon.-Sat.), a long-time favorite among islanders that carries fine and semiprecious jewelry, NAO by Lladró, and unique authentic East Indian garments, rugs, sculptures, and home decor. Artistic Boutique is Aruba's last bastion of fine table linens—always one of the island's real bargains compared to prices in the United States. If you set an elegant holiday table or need a bridal shower gift, check out the hand-embroidered and appliquéd linens. Although it is close to the cruise terminal, the store is easy to miss. The entrance is in the large Renaissance parking lot, adjacent to the Breitling watch store.

HENDRIK SCHOUTEN STUDIO

Prolific transplanted Dutch artist Hendrik Schouten performs his craft before your eyes in his Renaissance Marketplace studio. His portraiture is imaginative and his style is arresting, and there is enormous demand for his work. Stop by the **Hendrik Schouten Studio** (Renaissance Marketplace, L. G. Smith Blvd. 82, 297/585-3374, www.hendrikaruba.exto. org, 2:30pm-6pm Mon., 2:30pm-7pm Fri., 10:30am-5pm Sat.).

POST ARUBA

A visit to the post office or central bank wouldn't usually be at the top of a shopping list, but these two places have ideal gifts and mementos for stamp and coin collectors. **Post Aruba** (Irausquinplein 9, 297/528-7678, www.postaruba.com, 7:30am-noon and 1pm-4:30pm Mon.-Fri.) headquarters in Oranjestad has a philately desk where collectors can find beautiful day-of-issue ensembles of commemorative stamps. The post office issues 10-12 commemorative collections annually, each created from original artwork by local artists who also design the special envelope and cancellation stamp for a first-day ensemble.

UNOCA GALLERY

The government-funded foundation that supports cultural projects, **UNOCA** (Stadionweg 21, 297/583-5681, www.unocaruba.org, 8:30am-noon and 1:30pm-5pm Mon.-Fri.) maintains a permanent collection and hosts temporary shows with works for sale. Aruba's most respected artists thus have an excellent venue for showing their work. Art collectors interested in Aruba's artistry will be enlightened—and perhaps find a worthwhile piece.

CLOTHING AND FASHION

LA LINDA DEPARTMENT STORE

The invasion of designer-brand shops has transformed many islanders into walking fashion plates, thoroughly informed in the trendiest names in garments and accessories. Still, the island has shops that Arubans turn to first for everyday needs, and these have a special place in the community. **La Linda Department Store** (Caya G. F. Betico Croes 3, 297/585-2120, 10am-6pm Tues.-Sat.) is such an institution. It started as a tiny notions store before World War II, carrying "a bit of this and a bit of that." The family business, for decades one of the largest stores on the island, still has the same philosophy. Consumer demand has expanded, and so has the inventory. It is one of the few stores on Aruba to stock big and tall men's clothing as well as stylish plus sizes for women. Find beachwear, formal clothing, beach toys, bicycles, brand-name athletic shoes, blow-dryers, and reading glasses, all moderately priced.

PALAIS ORIENTAL

Popular with island women for trendy and timeless tropical wear, **Palais Oriental** (Caya G. F. Betico Croes 72, 297/585-1422, 8:30am-6:30pm Mon.-Sat.) offers a vast selection of casual and career clothing for sizes 6-26 at comfortable prices. It features the most diverse and stylish options on Aruba for plus-size women. The shop is also famous for exceptionally friendly and helpful staff. Free alterations are included. Return vacationers make it a rule to travel with a lighter suitcase, knowing they will be visiting Palais Oriental.

Flea Markets

nighttime shopping at Palm Beach flea market

Weekend flea markets are a Dutch tradition, though immigrants from the Caribbean and Latin America are largely responsible for their proliferation on Aruba. Flea markets dominate some shopping areas and are popular for bargain souvenirs, inexpensive resort wear, accessories, T-shirts, and decorative gewgaws. You'll find some original Latin American handicrafts, though for the most part offerings consist of mass-produced and cheap imports that you've seen elsewhere.

The Local Market is one of the fastest-growing flea markets, occupying a vast field across from the cruise terminal, a labyrinth of stalls. Every month new kiosks open under the roofed area, and the quality and assortment continues to increase. Handicrafts from the region, inexpensive casual and resort wear, and logo clothing can be found every day of the week.

Another flea market lines the waterfront along **L. G. Smith Boulevard** (8am-6:30pm Mon.-Sat.), which was the fruit and fish market in decades past.

Nighttime bargain hunters enjoy trawling the numerous kiosks that open at sunset along **J. E. Irausquin Boulevard in Palm Beach,** operating seven days a week with inexpensive sunglasses, handicrafts, T-shirts, handmade costume jewelry, and attractive accessories. **The Village** mall hosts a flea market (7pm-10pm daily) in its courtyard, with a very festive atmosphere.

JEWELRY STORES

A concentration of fine-quality jewelry stores radiates out from the cruise ship terminal. It is possible to spend an entire morning examining the inventory to find that special piece. Be prepared to spend another hour bargaining for it. Shoppers who know their gems and understand current trends in the market can do well. Haggling over prices is not a practice at the finer stores.

★ GANDELMAN JEWELERS

One of the best-known names for fine designer goods and watches is **Gandelman Jewelers** (Renaissance Mall, L. G. Smith Blvd. 82, 297/529-9900, http://gandelman.net, 10am-8pm Mon.-Sat., branch stores in Hyatt Regency and Marriott Resort 9am-midnight Mon.-Sat.), a family business with a superlative reputation. For generations this has been where residents of Curaçao and Aruba shop for high-quality jewelry. Gandelman is the exclusive agent for Rolex, Cartier, Patek Philippe, Carrera y Carrera, Bulgari, Breguet, and David Yurman. They also have the largest collection of Baccarat jewelry and giftware. Accessories are 5-20 percent lower than U.S. prices.

NOBLE JEWELERS

Nash, the owner of Noble Jewelers (Westraat 4, 297/583-8780, www.noblejewelersaruba. com, 9am-6pm Mon.-Sat.), is an icon of the jewelry trade on Aruba, with return clients who swear by his quality, prices, and service. Noble is the exclusive dealer for Hearts on Fire diamonds in Oranjestad. Nash is also community-minded, providing numerous volunteer foundations with fine-quality items for fund-raising raffle prizes.

PERFUME AND COSMETICS

Still one of the traditionally great buys of the Caribbean, European perfumes can be found at shops in the main tourist areas. Prices are the same on the island as at the airport, so you don't have to wait to purchase a favorite fragrance or discover a new one. Exclusive brands such as La Prairie are also cheaper than U.S. prices.

DUFRY

One of the best-known names for duty-free scents and cosmetics is Dufry (Caya G. F. Betico Croes 29, 297/582-2790, www.dufry. com, 9am-6pm Mon.-Sat.), with three stores in Oranjestad and two at the airport. An enthusiastic crew of cosmetic artists is always ready to provide patrons with a new look and to advise on skin care.

MAGGY'S EMPORIUM

Since 1955, Maggy's Emporium (Caya G. F. Betico Croes 59, 297/582-2113, www. maggysaruba.aw, 10am-6:30pm Mon.-Thurs., 9am-6:30pm Fri.-Sat.) has been Aruba's place to shop for cosmetics and fragrances. A fully trained staff of enthusiastic makeup experts

awaits, ready to provide the latest tips on makeup trends and new scents. During the first week in June, the shop conducts a week-long beauty festival, with workshops by visiting specialists from top cosmetic companies. Sessions are usually free with a purchase. Glamorous bachelorette parties end the day here with wine, hors d'oeuvres, and cocktails.

PENHA

A well-established name in the Dutch Caribbean, Penha (Caya G. F. Betico Croes 11, 297/582-4160, www.jlpenha.com, 9am-6pm Mon.-Sat.) has a full selection of sought-after fragrances and brand-name cosmetics. It is also the exclusive agent for Karen Kane resort wear and MAC cosmetics. The dedicated MAC boutique has expert cosmeticians ready to do hair and makeup for weddings and special occasions. Penha and MAC stores are in the Royal Plaza Mall near the cruise terminal and at Palm Beach Plaza mall.

SHOPPING MALLS

★ RENAISSANCE MALL

Aruba's greatest concentration of signature designer stores is in Renaissance Mall (L. G. Smith Blvd. 82, 297/582-4622, www. shoprenaissancearuba.com, 10am-7pm Mon.-Sat.), an enclosed mall within the Renaissance Resort, with designer brands Louis Vuitton, Adolfo Dominguez, Carolina Herrara, Gucci, Michael Kors, Façonnable, Dolce & Gabbana, and Diesel. Among the clothing shops are fine jewelers Chopard Boutique, Colombian Emeralds, and Gandelman Jewelers. Aruba Aloe and Dufry outlets are also here. The mall is on the ground floor of the Renaissance Marina Tower. The focal point is a Starbucks that won awards as the most beautifully designed in the Caribbean. The hotel restaurants also offer excellent dining.

RENAISSANCE MARKETPLACE

The open-air Renaissance Marketplace (L. G. Smith Blvd. 82, 297/582-4622, www. shoprenaissancearuba.com, shops 10am-7pm Mon.-Sat., restaurants and clubs

10am-midnight daily) hosts shops with standard souvenir stock. Some of the more interesting include **Mopa Mopa,** with unique handicrafts from Colombia. **Rage** is famous for its sterling silver jewelry, including a huge selection of stylish studs for piercings. **Champagne** has an attractive collection of costume jewelry and moderately priced accessories. **City Fashion** outfits men and women with tropical resort wear. Souvenirs and sundries can be found at **Captain Cook's,** open late. **Hendrik Schouten** maintains an art store and studio, where he also gives painting lessons. Renaissance Marketplace is better known for dining and nightlife. Adjacent to the water, a row of dining spots offer harbor views for breakfast, lunch, and dinner, and a few spots offer entertainment into the wee hours.

ROYAL PLAZA MALL

Aruba's first giant multiservice mall was **Royal Plaza Mall** (L. G. Smith Blvd. 94, 297/588-0351, 10am-6:30pm Mon.-Sat.), architecturally a frothy confection dominating the boulevard and the harbor. The first thing to catch the attention of arriving cruise ship passengers is its ornate facade and the sun glinting off the golden dome. Three floors house 50 shops, restaurants, and nightclubs that overlook the harbor. The large courtyard is populated with kiosks selling bargain-priced knickknacks. Respected jewelers such as Shiva's, Pearl Gems, Little Switzerland, Royal Jewels & Diamonds, and My Time and Spare Time watch stores are here. **Dufry** is famous for fine cosmetics and perfumes. **Bula Surf Shop** is Aruba's center for the popular names in surfing gear, sandals, sunglasses, and board shorts. Among the souvenir and resort wear stores are Fantasea, Little Holland, Yellow Submarine, Souvenir Outlet and More, Bob the Fish, Del Sol, Shipwreck, Beach n' Wear, and Alcy's Boutique. The mall is also home to a cigar store, Casa Del Hubano.

Royal Plaza Mall

Eagle Beach and Manchebo Beach

Because of its easy access on foot to Oranjestad shopping, this area was traditionally more resort- and beach-oriented. The proliferation of condominium complexes is resulting in a rash of malls along the Sasaki Highway. They have not yet, however, been populated by interesting enterprises, aside from a couple of restaurants. The sleek Alhambra Shopping Bazaar houses some interesting shops and a gourmet mini market. A few local stores can be found on Bubali Road once you cross Sasaki Highway, but they carry few souvenirs and gifts. Most resorts have newsstands with small sundry and souvenir shops attached. A few facilities—the Divi, Tamarijn, and Casa Del Mar—have arcades with resort wear, jewelry, and perfume outlets.

ART, HANDICRAFTS, AND SOUVENIRS

THE CENTRAL BANK OF ARUBA

Aruba's financial agency, **The Central Bank of Aruba** (J. E. Irausquin Blvd. 8, 297/525-2141, www.cbaruba.org, 8am-noon and 1pm-4pm Mon.-Fri.) regulates the island's commerce and is the agent for stunning commemorative coin collections, beautifully boxed for display and gifts. The proofs are high-quality silver or gold limited issues. Special collections celebrate various events, beginning with Status Aparte. Two gorgeous, colorful 2018 issues commemorate 60 years of Carnival and island fauna, featuring Aruba's *prikichi*, a small parrot.

MANA AT LA CABANA RESORT

La Cabana Beach Resort in Eagle Beach turned the main lobby and mezzanine into a giant local art gallery. **Movimiento di Arte Nobo Aruba** (MANA, J. E. Irausquin Blvd. 250, 297/594-2233, 24 hours daily) is the curator for the exhibits that change every three months. Aruba's top artists are challenged to create fresh works around particular themes. The works can be viewed at any time, but to purchase, call the contact number 1pm-6pm daily.

SHOPPING MALLS

ALHAMBRA SHOPPING BAZAAR

The sleek and stylish center for shopping and dining in low-rise areas is **Alhambra Shopping Bazaar** (J. E. Irausquin Blvd. 47, 297/583-5000, shops 10am-10pm daily, dining and entertainment 7am-2am daily). Peruse **The Lazy Lizard** for tasteful knickknacks and resort wear. An **Aruba Aloe** outlet meets all your needs for locally produced sun protection and hair and skin care products. There is an official Aruba logo shop, with a distinctive graphic emblazoned on garments for all ages. **Bijoux Terner** has big floppy beach hats and other great accessories at $10 per item. **R. Glass** has a wide assortment of handcrafted costume jewelry and accessories. You will also find Shalom Body and Soul Spa here. **The Market,** a very well outfitted mini market, has an excellent wine selection and prepared foods. An expansive and charming dining patio is surrounded by a budget-priced food court.

GOURMET GOODIES

★ SUPER FOOD

Aruba's first building designed to be totally energy self-sufficient through renewable sources houses **Super Food** (Sasaki Hwy. z/n, 297/588-6040, http://superfoodaruba.com, 8am-9pm Mon.-Sat., 9am-6pm Sun.), impossible to miss at the Sasaki Highway and Bubali Road intersection, across from the Tropicana Resort. More of a mall than a market, it is Aruba's Dutch grocery, known for its inventory from Holland. This is Aruba's most complete source of gourmet and exotic food, including Dutch cheeses and an array of spices.

Aruba Aloe

Since the late 1800s, Aruba has been one of the world's top producers of aloe vera products. The extract from this cactus has remarkable healing properties and is a natural product for treating burns and irritated skin. The world lost interest in aloe in the 1950s, but a resurgence in holistic healing and skin care has prompted a thriving industry.

The **Aruba Aloe Museum and Factory** (Pitastraat 115, 297/588-3222, www.arubaaloe. com, 9am-5pm Mon.-Fri.) in Hato welcomes groups and individuals, providing a fascinating history of aloe harvesting on the island. Its R&D department developed a prescription-strength product that has been tested and praised by burn wards across Europe. **Aruba Aloe** produces several lines with varying scents and concentrations. There are sun blocks, after-sun soothing gels and creams, body and face lotions, and hair care products. Outlets are around the island, including the airport next to the departure lounges, the cruise ship terminal, Alhambra Shopping Bazaar, Palm Beach Plaza, Paseo Herencia Shopping Mall, Renaissance Mall, and The Village. Store hours vary by location. These products can also be found in most hotel mini markets.

Palm Beach, Malmok, and Noord

Palm Beach after dark has been enlivened by a nightime shopping phenomenon. Savvy entrepreneurs figured out that most vacationers would rather spend their days on the beach, and the ploy has proven successful. Most malls host special evening events, and dining venues offer free entertainment to make nighttime shopping even more attractive.

ART, HANDICRAFTS, AND SOUVENIRS

★ TERRAFUSE

Make your own mementos to remember Aruba at **Terrafuse** (Turibana 14, 297/592-2978, www.arubaglassceramics.com, 3pm-6pm Tues., 9am-noon Thurs., $85 pp), offering classes in glass bead-making with imported Moretti glass from Italy. Participants learn a new skill and create a unique souvenir. Workshops are held twice a week, and special arrangements can be made for groups of 4-6. You will also be treated to a glassblowing demonstration.

Internationally recognized artists Ciro and Marian Abath conduct the workshops. Ciro's work greets island visitors at the airport in the *Water* exhibit, and he created the memorial statue of the composers of Aruba's national anthem, the centerpiece of the Plaza Padu in Oranjestad. Both he and his wife have traveled the world and studied with masters of glass art. Their studio is on the grounds of their quaint *cunucu* house. Not far from the hotels, it is on the way to the Alto Vista Chapel. Ciro and Marian have a boutique on the premises with a collection of their original glass pieces, one-of-a-kind mementos from Aruba. A taxi ride to the studio is $7; they will provide transportation back to your resort. Returning students receive a discount on the class fee.

DUSHI BAGELS & BURGERS

More than a place to find a good meal, **Dushi Bagels & Burgers** (Playa Linda Resort, J. E. Irausquin Blvd. 87, www.dushibagelsandburgers.com, 297/586-3035, 7am-11pm daily) is an art gallery and source for fun souvenirs. In the shopping arcade that fronts the Playa Linda, the walls of the dining room are covered with entertaining artworks by the proprietor, Carina Molina. A talented and creative artist, she has also translated her funniest paintings to vinyl placemats and thermal mugs for sale. It's also possible to purchase her original paintings, which can be viewed by appointment.

I ♥ HOOKAH

I ♥ Hookah (L. G. Smith Blvd. 370, 297/744-2424, http://i-love-hookah-aruba.business. site, 11am-1am Mon.-Thurs., 11am-3am Fri.-Sun.) is a fun and funky mini market that sells and rents hookahs and smoking gear, including Cuban cigars. The shop also carries over-the-counter medicines and condoms, and is the only spot open late. The inventive owners have a startling selection of fruits, spices, and other non-nicotine inhalants for their hookahs.

THE MASK

The Mopa Mopa outlet for Palm Beach, The Mask (Paseo Herencia Shopping Mall, J. E. Irausquin Blvd. 382 A, 297/586-2900, www.mopamopa.com, 10am-10pm Mon.-Sat., 5pm-10pm Sun.) offers night shoppers these unique and impressive pieces.

POST ARUBA

Post Aruba (Palm Beach Plaza, 297/528-7678, www.postaruba.com, 8am-6pm Mon.-Sat.) is near the major resorts and sells commemorative stamps plus personalized Aruba stamps, only available here. Bring your camera's memory card and have your photos digitally inserted into one of seven designs of usable stamps. Beautiful illustrations feature Aruba's most famous landmarks. Sold in sheets of six, they can be used to send postcards.

CIGARS

★ ARUHIBA

Cigar aficionados recommend Aruba's own Aruhiba (L. G. Smith Blvd. 330, 297/585-7833, www.aruhibacigars.com, 9am-6:30pm Mon.-Sat., 9:30am-4pm Sun.) for a good buy and a pleasant surprise. The cigars are cultivated and rolled on the island, with no chemicals to hurry the fermentation process. Aruhiba produces 16 different cigars of varying length, strength, and thickness. Aficionados report an enjoyable smoke. Lack of import and shipping costs make them a bargain compared to imported stogies from Cuba, Honduras, and the Dominican Republic. A diverse selection of cigars from the Caribbean is offered in the shop, with one of the largest inventories on Aruba. Find it among the cluster of kiosks next to the Olde Molen. Join a tour of the cigar factory in Moko by appointment.

JEWELERS

Palm Beach does not have the same concentration of jewelers as Oranjestad, but there are enough in the shopping centers and hotels, frequently close to the casinos: They know big winners need a way to transport those big cash payoffs. Colombian Emeralds, Gandelman Jewelers, and Little Switzerland, all well-known regional franchises, are in the major hotels.

GEMSTONES INTERNATIONAL

The congenial woman giving expert advice during a visit to Gemstones International (J. E. Irausquin Blvd. 370, 297/583-0663, http://gemstonesaruba.com, 10am-10pm daily) is the owner, Sarita, who knows her stones and has exquisite taste. Her artisans can create original new pieces. She carries a diverse collection of loose precious and semi-precious stones and guarantees all work.

KRISTIE'S JEWELS

A cozy family operation dedicated to quality, Kristie's Jewels (Paseo Herencia Shopping Mall, J. E. Irausquin Blvd. 382A, 297/586-0598, kristiesjewels@gmail.com, 4pm-10pm daily) is the Palm Beach agent for Hearts on Fire diamonds, unique items designed and manufactured in Italy. As agents for Silverado charms, they have an "I Love Aruba" charm with a divi tree crafted exclusively for this shop. Kristie's also carries the island's largest selection of items crafted with the larimar stone, a semiprecious pectolite mineral found only in the Dominican Republic.

1: original and amusing artwork by Carina Molina at Dushi Bagels & Burgers; 2: cheeses at Super Food

Diamond Shopping

THE FOUR C'S

If you're shopping for diamonds, know the "Four C's": carat, cut, color, and clarity. In these times, a new C, country, may also be a consideration. Most consumers usually have another C in mind—cost.

Carat: This refers to a diamond's weight or size.

Cut: Cut refers to the fashion in which the stonecutter has tried to enhance the natural virtues of the gem. Multiple facets and the depth of the cut affect the brilliance and scintillation. When a round or pear-shaped diamond is well cut, light enters through the flat part of the stone and travels to the angled underside, reflected repeatedly before bouncing to the observer's eye. This light is the scintillation—the flashing, fiery effect that makes diamonds so mesmerizing. A stone of a high carat may be poorly proportioned and heavily discounted. This gives a false impression of a great deal. The brilliant fire that dazzles is the measure of a quality stone.

Color: Diamonds are graded against a white background. Grade is calculated by the hue of the stone compared to a set of master stones graded by the Gemological Institute of America (GIA). There is a wide range of color designations, starting with the purest white, letter D, and working down the alphabet to Z, the deepest yellow, referred to as canary-yellow diamonds. Jewelry fashions change to deploy champagne, chocolate, and black diamonds, their value dictated by current trends. The diamonds most used in multistone pieces are the "near colorless" categories G and H.

Clarity: An important factor that makes a simple one-carat stone cost thousands more than a gem three times the size is clarity. It is a description of the stone while still in the rough uncut stage. Clarity is rated on a scale:

- **FL**—Flawless, the rarest and most valuable.

- **IF**—Internally flawless, with only external flaws in the rough stage.

SHOPPING MALLS

The Palm Beach area has Aruba's greatest concentration of malls, and concentrated they are. Shopping, dining, and entertainment are contained in bustling beehives spread along J. E. Irausquin Boulevard. The promenade attracts islanders and tourists equally. Shopping hours uniformly end at 10pm, but clubs and cafés stay open until at least 1am, and 2am or later on Friday-Saturday nights.

ARAWAK GARDENS

Though principally a dining and entertainment center, **Arawak Gardens** (J. E. Irausquin Blvd. 370, shops 5pm-11pm daily, dining and nightlife 11am-2am daily) hosts a plethora of cozy shops and kiosks with a diverse selection of souvenir items. Piles of T-shirts, beach covers in bright colors, and

Aruba logo gear are found in the various venues.

DE OLDE MOLEN

When they enter the modern area of Palm Beach, visitors can't help noticing an authentic Dutch windmill, over 200 years old. **De Olde Molen Foundation** (L. G. Smith Blvd. 330, 8am-2am daily) is the site of a strip of nightspots and a number of kiosks that include **Prima Casa Real Estate** and the official **Aruhiba** outlet for Aruban-made cigars. The windmill was built in 1804 and used in Friesland for draining sub-sea level land. After being damaged in a storm in 1878, it was disassembled and rebuilt in Holland as a grain mill but fell into disuse after storm damage in 1929. A Dutchman with dreams of living in the tropics purchased what remained

- **VVS1-VVS2**—Very, very slight inclusion: Only an expert can detect flaws with a 10X microscope.

- **VS1-VS2**—Very slight inclusion: You need not be an expert to see flaws with a 10X microscope, but it takes longer than 10 seconds.

- **SI1-SI2**—Slight inclusion: You can easily see flaws with a 10X microscope.

- **I1-I3**—You can see flaws with the naked eye.

There are wide varieties of flaws; many do not affect the integrity of the gem. A diamond doesn't need to be flawless to be gorgeous. Flaws can be crystal growth, which sometimes looks like a diamond within the diamond. The extent of the flaw and how it detracts from the beauty of the diamond affect its investment value. Buyers beware of I1-I3 level diamonds.

ETHICAL CONSIDERATIONS

The term **blood diamond** refers to gems that are mined under repressive regimes with forced labor. African countries in political upheaval are known for this. Famous personalities have endorsed certain brands of diamonds with ethical practices of avoiding blood diamonds. These stones may be more expensive, but the people in the mines work in humane conditions under labor laws. These diamond companies have invested in and bettered the communities near the mines, providing schools and scholarships. These gems are engraved with a microscopic logo to prove their pedigree.

in 1960, and it was rebuilt on Aruba on a two-story foundation.

PALM BEACH PLAZA

The largest shopping center in the area is **Palm Beach Plaza** (L. G. Smith Blvd. 85, 297/586-0045, www.palmbeachplaza.com, shops 10am-10pm Mon.-Sat. and 5pm-10pm Sun., dining and nightlife 7pm-2am daily). The three floors shelter numerous stores, the island's largest movie theater, a bowling alley, a video game center, restaurants, cozy bars, and family entertainment. Unique to Palm Beach Plaza are Salvatore Ferragamo, Montblanc, and Lalique outlets. Jewelry stores include Shiva's, Monarch Jewels, Rage Silver, and My Time for budget-priced timepieces. Fashionistas will love Panache and Giordano. San Marino and Basinger are the shops for elegant shoes, while Goofy Gecko and Art Fusion provide unusual souvenirs.

PASEO HERENCIA SHOPPING MALL

The first major mall in Palm Beach, **Paseo Herencia Shopping Mall** (J. E. Irausquin Blvd. 382A, 297/586-6533, http://paseoherencia.com, shops 10am-10pm Mon.-Sat., 5pm-10pm Sun., dining and nightlife noon-2am daily) offers several unique shops. Most notable about this mall is its community spirit, with walls filled with displays that showcase important moments in Aruba's history and internationally famous Arubans.

For European couture, **DGL** specializes in Diesel, Gaastra, and Villebrequin. La Langosta sells exclusive lines of Latin designer swimwear. **Mario Fernandez of Colombia**

Sales Tax

Aruba's sales tax is 6 percent, comprising a 3 percent turnover tax called "Belasting op Bedrijf-somzetten," or BBO, and a 3 percent "health tax" (BAZV). Additional augmentation of the turnover tax and some other tariffs are being considered. Certain enterprises and goods are exempt, such as prescription drugs. Commercial enterprises, particularly supermarkets, apply the sales tax. Other venues, such as jewelers, that cater specifically to tourists usually build the tax into the cost of goods rather than adding it on to a purchase.

is one of the most respected names in designer leather goods. Jewelers include Kristie's, Little Switzerland, Pandora Boutique, Pearl Gems, Times Square, and Sparkles. They offer a range from handcrafted costume jewelry to top-of-the-line precious gemstones. A two-story **Maggy's Emporium** has a complete menu of spa treatments and salon services along with all popular brands of scents and cosmetics. The Palm Beach outlet for mopa mopa crafts is also here at **The Mask.**

SOUTH BEACH CENTER

South Beach Center (J. E. Irausquin Blvd. 55, shops 10am-10pm daily, dining and nightlife noon-2am daily) occupies a large complex at the corner of J. E. Irausquin Boulevard and the Noord-Palm Beach Road. Look for the giant Hard Rock Café neon guitar. This is an amalgam of local and international eateries, with a few shops and a spa. Most shopping is at the kiosks lining the sidewalk, with all sorts of bargain-priced souvenirs. Formal shops include a **Lazy Lizard,** for stylish resort wear and amusing gifts. **Island Treasures** stocks inexpensive beach bags, sandals, wraps, and other tropical gear in flowery prints. Restaurants include Rembrandt, with a distinctly Dutch pub vibe, and pan-Asian restaurant Blossoms and Tandoor Indian Grill House.

THE VILLAGE

A standout from the standard Miami Beach architecture of the area is **The Village** (J. E. Irausquin Blvd. 348A, shops 5pm-10pm daily, dining and nightlife noon-2am daily), a mall modeled to look like a community of classic

---

Paseo Herencia Shopping Mall

Aruban *cunucu* houses. Aside from the massive flea market occupying the main courtyard at night, The Village is lined with some souvenir and resort wear shops. This is a happening place as it also includes Gusto, the area's only disco; Craft Bar for craft brews; and restaurants including Papillon, for classic French cuisine.

North Coast

Aruba's traditional wilderness offers little shopping besides a few tourist sites where small shops offer standard factory-produced souvenirs like flowery beach covers and logo T-shirts. The shops of the Donkey Sanctuary and Ostrich Farm offer some unique mementos and giftware.

GIFTS AND SOUVENIRS

AFRICAN ART BOUTIQUE AT OSTRICH FARM

After taking a tour of the Aruba Ostrich Farm, make sure to visit the farm's unique **African Art Boutique** (Matividiri 57, 297/585-9630, www.arubaostrichfarm.com, 9am-4pm daily) for a surprising collection of home fashion, furniture, carvings, kitchen linens, and the like. A unique item is artwork made from hollowed-out ostrich eggs. Collectors of the unusual will find these hand-painted creations most intriguing.

DONKEY SANCTUARY

In addition to an entertaining encounter with the charming residents, the **Donkey Sanctuary** (Bringamosa 2Z, Donkey Distress Hotline 297/593-2933, www.arubandonkey. org, 9am-4pm daily) has a shop of unique crafts and gifts to support the work. The collection of donkey paraphernalia is large, with custom-made crafts and original paintings donated by top island artists. A charming wall calendar with great donkey photos is issued annually. All proceeds assist in the care and feeding of the denizens of the sanctuary.

Santa Cruz, Paradera, and Piedra Plat

The best of Aruba's shopping is in the commercial areas of Oranjestad and Palm Beach, which serve both tourists and residents. The dedicated residential areas of Santa Cruz, Paradera, and Piedra Plat have some souvenir shops offering logo shirts and tropical resort wear at places like the Casibari Rock Formation. The inventory is the same as elsewhere. The most unique shop here is the Rococo Plaza, a must-visit for collectors and those who enjoy antique hunting.

ANTIQUES

ROCOCO PLAZA

Aruba's only antiques center is **Rococo Plaza** (Tanki Leendert 158-G, 297/741-5640, http:// antiquesaruba.com, 9am-1pm and 3:30pm-5:30pm Mon.-Fri., 9am-1pm Sat.), which can be seen from afar by its unique dual-tower entrance. It is on the way to Arikok National Park and worth a stop. The store is enormous: Allow time to peruse the 20 rooms of curios from diverse eras. Most of the inventory is from Europe, and there are some truly fascinating items: vintage cameras and photos, standup pianos, art deco sconces, and authentic Louis XV furniture. Naturally, some chaff surrounds the gems. There is a lot to work through, but unique treasures await collectors. On the first Sunday of the month, Rococo hosts a diverse flea market, always with a few surprising items.

Where to Stay

Oranjestad............181
Eagle Beach and Manchebo
    Beach 183
Palm Beach, Malmok, and
    Noord 187
Santa Cruz, Paradera, and
    Piedra Plat...........193
San Nicolas, Savaneta, and
    Pos Chiquito.........194

Some of Aruba's greatest attractions are the

glamorous resorts that line Palm Beach, Eagle Beach, and Manchebo Beach. The pioneers of Aruba's tourism industry had a vision of the atmosphere that would best suit each area, and their vision set the tone for later projects.

There are large full-service resorts with casinos and nightclubs or smaller tranquil getaways to relax. Most are members of the Aruba Hotel and Tourism Association (AHATA), offering excellent service and quality accommodations. Independent non-AHATA facilities often deliver the same standards but without the marketing resources of the big resorts, so they rely on guest endorsements. Thanks to the Internet, these places are becoming easier to discover. Wherever you

Highlights

Look for ★ to find recommended
sights, activities, dining, and lodging.

★ **Wonders Boutique Hotel:** This elegant guesthouse is convenient to shopping, dining, and entertainment in Oranjestad (page 181).

★ **Renaissance Resort:** Oranjestad's only full-service resort has excellent restaurants, a beautiful spa, and the amenities of a Palm Beach resort for far less money (page 182).

★ **Divi Dutch Village:** Surrounding a lush golf course and a gorgeous pool deck, these apartments cater to golfers and their families (page 184).

★ **Beach House Aruba:** Hosts Ewald and Doris provide guests with incredible hospitality at their cozy inn on the Malmok Coast (page 187).

★ **Boardwalk Small Hotel Aruba:** This tranquil oasis has 13 spacious casitas featuring homey touches and surrounded by lush gardens (page 191).

★ **Aruba Reef Apartments:** Find your vacation fantasy come true at this converted seaside home with a private beach (page 195).

★ **Aruba Ocean Villas:** Elegant dining on the beach combined with individual thatched bungalows makes this secluded resort unique (page 197).

Where to Stay if . . .

YOU WANT TO BE IN THE HEART OF ALL THE ACTION:
Palm Beach is where the big beachfront resorts cluster; water activities, restaurants, shops, and nightlife are at your fingertips.

YOU WANT TO STAY IN A RESORT AREA BUT HANG WITH LOCALS:
Eagle Beach affords access to the amenities of a prime tourist area with the benefit of a beach where islanders congregate on the weekend.

YOU WANT TO GET AWAY FROM IT ALL:
Savaneta, on Aruba's quieter south side, offers tranquil getaways near lovely beaches.

YOU WANT EASY ACCESS TO CARNIVAL EVENTS:
Oranjestad is well situated for the parades and nighttime festivities.

YOU WANT TO USE YOUR TIME-SHARE (OR RENT ONE):
Manchebo Beach is the center of time-sharing on Aruba.

stay, the famed hospitality of the island is a consistent element, and there are accommodations to suit all tastes. The main tourist areas of Palm Beach, Manchebo Beach, Eagle Beach, and Oranjestad are close enough to each other to make all the amenities easily accessible. Resorts welcome nonguests to the shops, restaurants, and casinos.

CHOOSING WHERE TO STAY
Location
ORANJESTAD
Aruba's capital, Oranjestad, is populated with guesthouses and apartments, plus two AHATA members: Renaissance Resort and Talk of the Town. Less expensive lodgings are in a similar price range, but some rent only by the week. A few are converted homes that are exceptionally charming. Generally, staying in Oranjestad is far less expensive than the beach areas of Palm Beach, Manchebo Beach, and Eagle Beach.

Staying in the island's capital provides an authentic feeling for island life, with restaurants minutes from your door and priced for locals. Many historical sights are within walking distance. For fans of Carnival events, Oranjestad is ideal to take in the parades and nighttime festivities.

What accommodations in Oranjestad lack is immediate access to the beach. There are a few public beaches within walking distance of most guesthouses. Renaissance Resort compensates with regularly scheduled boat transport to its private island's beautiful beaches.

EAGLE BEACH AND MANCHEBO BEACH
The resorts run by Divi Properties dominate the Manchebo Beach area. Divi also runs The Links golf course, condos, and time-shares, and the Alhambra Shopping Bazaar. Divi started when Wally Wiggins, a lawyer from upstate New York, brought his family to Aruba on vacation in 1965. He built the first Divi resort to have a place to stay on the beach where zoning laws forbade a private home. It opened the same day Neil Armstrong walked on the moon in 1969. One small step for Mr.

Previous: Playa Linda Beach Resort; Aruba Ocean Villas; beachfront at Aruba Reef Apartments.

Wiggins became a giant step for Aruba's tourism.

Manchebo is also the center of time-sharing on Aruba. Time-share rooms are usually more luxurious and larger than standard hotel rooms and come with a full kitchen or well-equipped kitchenette. Most rooms have at least one separate bedroom and a sofa bed in the living room.

Eagle Beach is a center of condominium development, and many complexes offer unoccupied units for rent in an area that is quieter than Palm Beach. Note that those staying at Eagle Beach accommodations must cross J. E. Irausquin Boulevard to get to the beach.

Resorts here don't have long lines for beach towels, lounge chairs, or *palapas* for shade, which the large Palm Beach resorts often require guests to reserve. On weekdays, nearby undeveloped beaches are empty, but can get busy with islanders on weekends.

PALM BEACH, MALMOK, AND NOORD

Palm Beach is a mile-long strip of glamorous high-rise resorts bustling with activity day and night. These 300-plus-room mega-resorts offer every amenity and service imaginable. Rates and amenities vary slightly among them, but all conform to their large international hospitality brands and star ratings. The elaborate facilities are designed so that guests never have to leave the premises, with myriad dining choices, cocktail lounges, spas, shopping arcades, casinos, shows, game rooms, beautiful beaches, stunning pool decks, and catering for weddings and conventions.

With its concentration of rooms, travel agencies and package wholesalers mostly work with these AHATA member resorts. During holidays such as Christmas and New Year's, many have 10-day minimum stays and must be booked more than a year in advance. For a quiet guesthouse far from the crowds with a more personal touch, look beyond Palm Beach to adjacent Malmok.

SANTA CRUZ, PARADERA, AND PIEDRA PLAT

Beyond the main tourist areas, accommodations are fewer. Investors are still focused on Aruba's west coast and beachfront, so in these inland areas, you will find small guesthouses and apartments for rent. These offer personal service and vastly lower rates than the western shore resorts and are typically outfitted with full kitchens and surprising amenities, like attractive pool decks.

The mile-long strip of Palm Beach is lined with glamorous resorts.

SAN NICOLAS, SAVANETA, AND POS CHIQUITO

It is rare to find accommodations in Aruba's more rural areas, which are either deserted scrubland or national park. Some intimate guesthouses and villa rentals are near the scattered coves of Savaneta and Pos Chiquito, with access to lovely beaches that see little traffic. These residential areas have relatively inexpensive facilities. Some are aimed at those who want to get away from it all, and most provide an apartment setting for budget travelers with full kitchens, as restaurants are few. For a sense of isolation on a tropical island, these places deliver, but a rental car is definitely required.

Accommodation Type
GUESTHOUSES

Cozy guesthouses with 12-20 rooms are scattered around Aruba, a good choice for a local vibe, interaction with islanders, and lower rates. In most cases, guesthouses require walking some distance to the beach; rarely are they at the beach. Some are close to tourist areas offering access to restaurants, shops, and nightlife, but in many cases a car is required. Some guesthouse owners assist with car rental reservations or delivery. They can also procure discounts on weekly rates. A few guesthouses are located on Aruba's south side, around Savaneta, which offers tranquility and seclusion. For privacy, these are ideal.

LOCAL HOTELS AND RESORTS

Few Aruban hotels and resorts are locally owned, and are either leased to the chains (like the Hilton) or at least carry the name of the chain (like the Renaissance). Bucuti & Tara Beach Resort and Brickell Bay Beach Club & Spa are both locally owned and have more amenities and activities than guesthouses and boutique resorts. They also have larger swimming pools.

INTERNATIONAL CHAIN RESORTS

Aruba's tourism is dominated by international chains. Most are in Palm Beach, are members of AHATA, and partner with the Aruba Tourism Authority marketing entity. International chain resorts comprise 350 rooms or more and are huge in every way: large pool decks, multiple restaurants, in-house casinos and spas, shopping arcades, and activities directors to keep children busy. Several are all-inclusive, though they offer a European (no meals) or modified American (breakfast only or breakfast and dinner) plan if you don't want to be tied to the resort for every meal. Rooms are quite basic, however, with just a mini-fridge and a coffeemaker. These hotels might be anywhere and have no local ambience, but their advantage is proximity to the beach.

AIRBNB AND VRBO RENTALS

Aruba is a resort destination but has an array of lodging options, from small guesthouses to luxurious villas. Many listings can be found on **Airbnb** (www.airnbnb.com), with the most extensive listings and some great deals on short-term rentals. **VRBO** (www.vrbo.com) also offers direct owner-to-renter arrangements for condominiums, houses, apartments, and time-shares. A benefit is that both parties save on the commissions typically paid to intermediaries.

APARTMENTS AND VACATION HOMES

Small apartment complexes are great to be immersed in the local environment, away from the tourist scene. A number of vacation apartment complexes around the island boast hospitable staff and quality rooms. Families or groups on a budget could explore the option of renting a house. Several gated communities offer the privacy of condos, town houses, and villas. Other freestanding homes rent by the week. Some are near the beach, and nearly all have swimming pools. Prices range from $650 per week for a one-bedroom home to $10,000 for the luxurious mansions at the Tierra Del Sol Country Club. Minimum one-week rental is required, and longer rentals of a month or more have better rates.

Four reliable brokers for rentals on the island:

- **Aruba Happy Rentals** (Boegoeroei 13-D, 297/586-2662, U.S. 866/978-6986, http://arubahappyrentals.com)

- **Aruba Palms Realtors** (J. E. Irausquin Blvd. 370, 297/566-0339 or 877/586-8962, www.arubapalmsrealtors.com)

- **Aruba Villa Rentals** (Salina Cerca 35E, 297/586-4290, www.arubavillarentals.com)

- **Prima Casa Real Estate** (J. E. Irausquin Blvd. 330, 297/583-3350, http://aruba-realty.com)

TIME-SHARES

Time-share rooms are a hybrid of hotels and condos, usually with housekeeping and beach access. They provide concierge desks, activities coordinators, laundry rooms, and mini markets. Families with young children find these facilities ideal for their privacy and having meals in the room.

It isn't easy to trade a time-share at another location for one on Aruba, particularly during holiday weeks. Each time-share has a rental office with listings, although many owners prefer to rent directly to keep the commission. Direct listings can be found via classified ads in Aruba's English-language newspapers or the numerous Aruba bulletin boards online, including www.aruba.com, www.visitaruba.com, http://aruba-travelguide.com, http://arubabound.com, and http://aruba-bb.com. There are also individual bulletin boards from the various time-share resorts. If you don't find a listing that fits, join the bulletin board and post what you're looking for, including the dates and location. There are also a number of independent travel brokers specializing in renting out time-shares. Manchebo Beach is a central area for time-shares on Aruba.

Oranjestad

$50-100

ARUBA HARMONY

In Ponton, bordering north Oranjestad, **Aruba Harmony Apartments** (Palmitastraat 9, 297/593-7661, www.arubaharmony.com, studio $89, 2-bedroom suite $179) is in an upscale neighborhood surrounded by attractive homes. Ten rooms circle a courtyard with a small pool. Abundant picnic tables and deck chairs are for dining outdoors, and all rooms have full kitchens. The clientele is largely European. One unique aspect is that the place takes its name from owner-operator Barbara Arends's enthusiasm for feng shui. Room placement takes this into account to benefit your chi. Barbara offers packages attuned to your zodiac sign that include treatments in the on-site spa to create harmony and balance. Less expensive European spa treatments are also available. Activities packages with scuba and deep-sea fishing can also be arranged, along with ecotours. When making reservations, send your flight and arrival time, and you will be greeted at the airport.

$100-200

★ WONDERS BOUTIQUE HOTEL

On a well-maintained property, **Wonders Boutique Hotel** (Emmastraat 63, 297/593-4032, www.wondersaruba.com, $119-149) is an exceedingly charming alternative to the resorts, with 10 large air-conditioned studio rooms, from a Cozy Colonial to Supreme Style, all with spacious baths. Each room has a well-stocked minibar and a coffeemaker. A warm welcome with an exotic cocktail sets the mood for your stay. Formerly a two-story home, the hotel is decorated with original art. The pool is just big enough for a cooling dip, but the courtyard features lush gardens. A grill and a well-equipped shared kitchen are available. The clientele is mixed but generally European, and the hotel is a short walk to a several fine Oranjestad eateries, shopping, and attractions. Breakfast is available but not included in the room rates; it's pricey compared to the nearby cafés geared to locals. The owner provides round-trip transport to and from the airport for a fee, as well as shuttle service to Eagle Beach or Palm Beach departing at 10:30am daily.

ARUBA SURFSIDE MARINA

Clean, modern **Aruba Surfside Marina** (L. G. Smith Blvd. 7, 297/583-0300, www. arubasurfsidemarina.com, $194, minimum 4 nights) has only a few rooms: three studios and two suites on the upper level, all with oceanfront terraces. Each unit has a fridge, microwave, coffeemaker, and utensils. The 1st floor is meeting and conference rooms, so there is some daily traffic, and it is popular with business travelers. Room rates include continental breakfast served on your room's balcony. The expansive courtyard is popular for local weddings and catered events. There is a gazebo, gardens, and a view of the sea but no pool; instead, you have access to a quiet semisecluded beach area. This is a good spot for a destination wedding away from the tourist crowds, and management specializes in arranging weddings.

CADUSHI APARTMENTS

A pleasant collection of 15 apartments close to the airport, **Cadushi Apartments** (Stadionweg 4B, 297/593-1770, www. cadushiapartments.com, $140) is a short walk from the main part of town, and from Surfside Beach, with beach lounges for guests. The decor is clean and contemporary, and there is a small pool. Apartments are spacious and include a living room, a separate bedroom, a kitchen with a cooktop, a small fridge, and free Wi-Fi. Snorkel equipment and a cooler to take to the beach are included. Cadushi offers laundry (no ironing) and prearrival cupboard-stocking. Arrange to have your breakfast and lunch prepared by the De Suikertuin restaurant and delivered to your room.

CAMACURI APARTMENTS

Camacuri Apartments (Av. Milio J. Croes 46B, 297/582-6805, www. camacuriapartmentsaruba.com, $134-204) is a hideaway with 39 apartments tucked behind houses bordering a major stadium, found by turning down a dirt road across from the Aruba Entertainment Center. No signs point the way, but once you know, it's easy to find. The surprisingly tranquil oasis is on the eastern outskirts of town, with sprawling gardens and a nice pool. Extensive grounds include rooms around a courtyard and two-story casitas with suites. The largest suite has a master bedroom in a loft with its own separate bath. All rooms have kitchens. The main part of town is a 15-minute walk away; for grocery shopping, a small market is in a nearby commercial area.

$300-400

★ RENAISSANCE RESORT

Oranjestad has one full-service resort: the smoke-free **Renaissance Resort** (L. G. Smith Blvd. 82, 297/583-6000, U.S. 800/421-8188, www.marriott.com, Marina Tower $360, Beach Tower $458), which dominates the harbor and L. G. Smith Boulevard. Though operating under the Renaissance name, it is wholly owned by a local family. The resort has two elegant shopping malls, two casinos, a convention center, Oranjestad Harbor, and—offshore—Renaissance Island. The two sections of the resort are separated by L. G. Smith Boulevard and the Renaissance Marketplace, but both have appealing views. A free tram runs between them. Each section has a dedicated concierge, activities desk, and car rental service. Discounts up to 40 percent on room rates are sometimes available. Count on paying less than the full rate, except for holiday weeks.

The Marina Tower is adults-only and looks over the harbor. The lobby doubles as a mall with designer stores. Central to the mall is the dock for ferries to Renaissance Island. Clientele is diverse, but on weekends primarily made up of wealthy South Americans. The pool deck is on the mezzanine and overlooks the harbor and L. G. Smith Boulevard. Beach Tower is family-friendly, with one- and two-bedroom suites with full kitchens. It has its own attractive lagoon, a huge pool deck, and an artificial beach.

Renaissance Island is a beautiful facility with a restaurant and spa, a water-sports operator, and three beaches (including a secluded adults-only section for topless sunbathing) included for all guests. It is popular for elegant weddings. The island is accessed by speedboats departing from two locations every 15 minutes; it takes 15-20 minutes to reach the island. Day passes are sold to nonguests at the concierge desks for $100, which includes lunch, a drink, and a choice of water-activity equipment.

Eagle Beach and Manchebo Beach

$100-200

ARUBA BEACH CLUB AND CASA DEL MAR

Although it looks like one large resort, **Aruba Beach Club and Casa del Mar** (J. E. Irausquin Blvd. 53, Aruba Beach Club 297/582-3000, Casa del Mar 297/582-7000, www.arubabeachclub.info, www.casadelmararuba.com, studio $150, 1-bedroom suite from $225) are two separate entities, each with their own reception, pool decks, activities directors, guest lounges, and waterfront restaurants; they share tennis courts and other facilities. Each has pleasant and reasonably priced independently owned beachfront restaurants. Lounge chairs and the pool decks can be used interchangeably by all guests. A separate section away from the beach is called the Ambassador Suites, with a small pool and lower rates.

Aruba Beach Club (ABC) was the island's first time-share facility in 1979. Devoted clientele stay for months during winter; most bought in during the groundbreaking, and now are vacationing with their grandchildren. Both ABC and Casa del Mar (CDM) have creative and energetic activities directors who keep kids entertained and moonlight as babysitters, with activities such as daily bingo. CDM has a more contemporary pool deck, but both have plain rectangular pools, not the freeform styles that are standard now. If you need to be near the action and nightlife or around other singles, stay somewhere else.

GOLDEN VILLAS

In a quiet residential area, **Golden Villas** (Washington 30C, 297/592-5533, www.goldenvillasaruba.com, $169) offers tranquil luxury accommodations with access to beaches. Hosts Ricard and Bel live in one of the apartments and provide personal attention. The eight apartments, surrounding a splash pool and hot tub, are one-bedroom units that comfortably fit a family of four. Each has a full European-style kitchen with utensils, giant TVs, and climate control. A giant community gas grill is on the patio. Ricard is the concierge and arranges quality tours and outings.

QUALITY APARTMENTS

Many time-share owners extend their stay at **Quality Apartments** (Schotlandstraat 70, 297/582-0697, www.arubaqualityapartments.com, from $143), a family-run facility with a nice pool and large, comfortable, clean studios with loft bedrooms and one-bedroom suites. The 73 units are on a busy commercial thoroughfare not far from supermarkets and shopping, but most rooms are set back from the street. Amenities include a multi-machine laundry, a fitness room, free Wi-Fi throughout, plus a computer station. Over the years guests have left behind books, resulting in an extensive lending library of beach reading in several languages.

Hot Water

At guesthouses and alternative accommodations, travelers might be taken aback to see only one faucet in the sink and shower. The island relies on the tropical sun to heat the water, and it does a fine job. A shower from around noon till sunset has surprisingly warm water—perhaps even too hot. It depends on the weather, which is usually reliable. But if you're into colder showers, first thing in the morning is the time to take one.

While major resorts do have hot-water heaters, what comes out of the cold-water tap is the same sun-heated water the rest of the island uses—so there is no truly cold water to temper the hot. Running the cold tap will not bring colder water; it will likely get warmer. Keep this in mind when stepping into the shower or filling a bathtub; you'll want to check the temperature before stepping in to make sure it's not scalding. And if you need cold water to drink, find the ice machine down the hall.

TROPICANA RESORT & CASINO

Tropicana Resort & Casino (J. E. Irausquin Blvd. 248, 297/587-9000, www.troparuba. com, 1-bedroom suite $147) was originally an annex to the La Cabana Resort and is now is owned by the Tropicana chain of Atlantic City. The 360 rooms wrap around an attractive pool deck, with a waterfall, a waterslide, and a swim-up bar. Whirlpools and kids' pools are separate. The pool deck is the only outdoor space, but you can't beat the bargain rate. Spacious rooms have full kitchens. The affiliated casino, tennis courts, and restaurant are in the vast parking lot. There is a small snack bar around the pool, a Dunkin' Donuts and Baskin Robbins on the premises, and a mini market. It is a long walk to the beach.

$200-300

ARUBA BREEZE CONDOMINIUMS

Luxurious but reasonably priced, **Aruba Breeze Condominiums** (J. E. Irausquin Blvd. 232A, 297/732-2788, www.arubabreeze. com, from $225) is a complex that rents rooms at a nightly rate in a cul-de-sac where Manchebo and Eagle Beaches meet, with 25 identical two-bedroom duplex town houses. Two spacious bedrooms are upstairs, each with a bath, and a half-bath is on the ground level, along with beautiful kitchens, spacious living rooms, and a terrace on each level, all with high-quality furniture and fixtures. Balconies overlook two utilitarian pool decks, which are rarely crowded. Conference and fitness rooms are off the lobby, and two grills are by the large shade *palapa* at the main pool, along with an ice machine to fill coolers for the beach. Amenable concierges in the lobby assist with tours, car rental, and more. Daily maid service is included, rare for a condo complex. This is a quiet place, and Eagle Beach is only five minutes away on foot.

PARADISE BEACH VILLAS

An attractive and intimate time-share renting by the night is **Paradise Beach Villas** (J. E. Irausquin Blvd. 64, 297/525-4000, www. paradisebeachvillas-aruba.com, studio $175, 1-bedroom suite $265), on the south side of La Cabana Resort. Saved from a bankrupt developer by the owners to salvage their investment, it has a strong sense of community. The general clientele is long-term repeat visitors who have a tangible stake in the facility, and there is a palpable relationship between staff and guests at this family-oriented resort. Rooms are spacious and nicely appointed, and there is an excellent on-site restaurant, Terrazza Italiana. Guests must cross J. E. Irausquin Boulevard to access the beach.

$300-400

★ DIVI DUTCH VILLAGE

The huge, rambling **Divi Dutch Village** (J. E. Irausquin Blvd. 93, 297/583-5000 or 800/367-3484, www.dividutchvillage.com, Dutch

Village $299, Divi Golf Village $388) is ideal for golfers and their families. The closer to the course, the more expensive and newer the rooms are. Substantial discounts during off-weeks (as little as $167) can be had by booking online early and directly.

Dutch Village is adjacent to the Tamarijn on the water side of J. E. Irausquin Boulevard, which allows direct access to the beach. Buildings are arranged around three swimming pools with lush gardens. The top two floors are duplexes with bedrooms and private baths on the upper level. All rooms have hot tubs on the terraces. As time-shares, the crowd is mature, with grandchildren around during peak holiday weeks.

The Divi Golf Village consists of two sections across the road from the beach, each with its own pool deck. The older of the two sections has a tennis center. The other section is adjacent to Divi Links golf course, with apartments set far back from the main road and the beach. Its sumptuous infinity pool has an expansive deck overlooking the fairway. These buildings are also closer to the clubhouse, an attractive facility with two fine restaurants, Mulligan's and Windows on Aruba.

AMSTERDAM MANOR BEACH RESORT

The unique architecture of Amsterdam Manor Beach Resort (J. E. Irausquin Blvd. 252, 297/527-1100 or 800/969-2310, www.amsterdammanor.com, studio $335) carries hints of Bavaria; it looks a bit like a cozy turreted castle. Rooms have been redecorated in sleek modern style, and the resort is EarthCheck certified for its ecofriendly practices, including being nonsmoking throughout. The pool deck is tiny, but the beach is easily accessed by crossing the road. With few rooms but a long stretch of beach, the resort is never crowded. An excellent romantic restaurant on the beach is called Passions.

OCEANIA RESIDENCES

A huge complex on Eagle Beach, Oceania Residences (J. E. Irausquin Blvd. 238, 297/594-6827, www.oceaniaarubarentals.com, 1-bedroom suite $394) stretches over several blocks and has beachfront to match across the Irausquin Boulevard. Three very large pools are on an enormous pool deck. All rooms have terraces, some with oceanfront views and others looking out onto other buildings. Since these are individually owned condos, the decor of each is highly personal. All come with fully equipped kitchens. The smallest units comfortably accommodate a family of four. Most apartments have their own washer-dryer. Oceania's beachfront is never crowded, and a Super Food supermarket, Oranjestad, and the bus to Palm Beach are nearby. There is excellent security, but no concierge desk or in-house restaurants.

$400-500

COSTA LINDA

Costa Linda (J. E. Irausquin Blvd. 59, 297/583-8000 or 888/858-0845, www.costalinda-aruba.com, 2-bedroom suite $378-589) is one of the most luxurious timeshares in Aruba. All units are spacious and beautifully appointed two- to three-bedroom suites. Ocean-end rooms have enormous patios for outdoor entertaining, with their own gas grills and whirlpool tubs. This large facility has a wide beachfront, and the attractive freeform pool deck has an adjacent restaurant. It is family-oriented and quiet at night, but Alhambra Shopping Bazaar is just outside. Most units for rent are offered by the owners; the website has a bulletin board for listings. This is the best place to find a room at the best rate, typically for less than through an online booking engine.

OVER $500

Two sister resorts, Divi and Tamarijn, were built on the same concept: two-story casitas with terraces or patios facing the sea, separated by a small stretch of sand. Guests can use the restaurants and bars interchangeably, along with fitness rooms, tennis courts, and more. Frequent tram service takes guests between the two day and night.

BUCUTI & TARA BEACH RESORT

Owner-operated boutique resort **Bucuti & Tara Beach Resort** (L. G. Smith Blvd. 55B, 297/583-1100 or 888/428-2884, www.bucuti. com, $507-797) is adults-only, with 104 rooms in the original Bucuti section, with balconies, and the 40 suites of the more luxurious and spacious Tara. All Tara rooms have an ocean view. Room rates are on a modified European plan, with a gourmet American buffet breakfast, taxes and service charges, and free local calls, usually charged at $5 or more. Each room includes a netbook computer with Skype, and throughout the resort is free Wi-Fi. A unique perk at Tara is a huge bathroom with a TV in the mirror. Guests are greeted with a complimentary champagne toast. Souvenir water bottles, part of the environmental care policy, can be refilled at water stations on the beach. The resort and its owner, Ewald Biemans, have been cited internationally for pioneering sustainability policies.

Bucuti & Tara Beach Resort has two gourmet adult-only restaurants offering quiet seclusion. Guests are given a red flag to hold up to order food or drinks on the beach; servers don't interrupt to take an order. The resort also houses an Intermezzo Spa, with massages and skin treatments, and an air-conditioned fitness room. The pool is very small, but the resort is on a wide beach.

DIVI MEGA ALL-INCLUSIVE

Divi Mega All-Inclusive (J. E. Irausquin Blvd. 45, 297/525-5200 or 800/554-2008, www. diviaruba.com, garden view $630, ocean view $675), dating to 1969, is a rambling resort with rooms on the beach or set within lush gardens. This and the newer Tamarijn—Divi's sister resort—are considered honeymoon hotels. Rooms are not large, but common areas are elegant, a chic pool deck abuts the beach, and the lobby has an Internet center and shops. Nightly entertainment and family-oriented activities are offered daily. Aside from the family buffet center near the beach, the famous Red Parrot Restaurant features fresh fish and international cuisine. The themed restaurants require advance reservations. For an all-inclusive facility, the quality of the food is above par. Congenial groups gather during happy hour (which, this being an all-inclusive resort, is all day) at the Bunker Bar at the Tamarijn, hanging out over the water.

MANCHEBO BEACH RESORT

Manchebo Beach Resort (J. E. Irausquin Blvd. 55, 297/582-3444, 855/837-1168, www.

Tamarijn Beach Resort

manchebo.com, $527) is a cozy, full-service resort with a superior beachfront. On the island's southwest point, it has the widest beach on Aruba and dates to 1969, reflecting that era with an informal open-air lobby. All rooms have an ocean view. The clientele is mostly comprised of mature American and European repeat guests. The informal open-air restaurant becomes Ike's Bistro at night. The poolside bar has a stunning view for sunset happy hour, and the deck is a small extension of the restaurant, with an appealing setup for dining. The Chophouse restaurant is a great value, and chamber music recitals are hosted once a month on Sunday morning. Spa Del Sol massages are done in curtained kiosks on the beach. Daily yoga sessions are held in the shade of the spa.

TAMARIJN BEACH RESORT
The Divi's sister resort, **Tamarijn Beach Resort** (J. E. Irausquin Blvd. 41, 297/525-5200 or 800/554-2008, www.tamarijnaruba.

com, ocean view $603), is south of the Divi and closer to Oranjestad. Extensive renovations provide a contemporary look. Adjacent to the Divi Dutch Village time-shares, the grounds boast lush landscaping. The Bunker Bar offers beautiful views of the Caribbean at sunset. Guests from both resorts gather here at day's end. Rooms at "the Tam" are small but provide terraces and patios open to the tranquil shorefront. There are no elevators, so if necessary, specify a ground-floor room when you make reservations.

Most of the themed restaurants shared by the two resorts are within the Tamarijn. Paparazzi is for Italian cuisine, Ginger is for Pacific Rim, and Palm Grill is for fresh stir-fried dishes as well as all-day stone-oven pizza. The restaurants only serve dinner, and reservations are required well in advance. The Cunucu Terrace, adjacent to the pool deck, serves breakfast, lunch, and dinner buffets and is the spot for nightly entertainment.

Palm Beach, Malmok, and Noord

$50-100
VILLA SUNFLOWER
Villa Sunflower (Salinja Cerca 25E, 297/593-0409, studio apartment $50), in a quiet residential area adjacent to Palm Beach, provides a "guest in a home" experience. Your hostess, Rienk, lives on-site and is a delight, as are her six apartments, each artistically decorated. Rienk is an enthusiastic mosaic artist, and the entire complex is connected by a labyrinth of her mosaic walks. Walls, doors, and every tabletop are mosaic masterpieces, frequently depicting sunflowers and underwater seascapes. A good-size pool is surrounded by art, and a communal barbecue and dining area is completely adorned with mosaic tiled surfaces. Lush greenery provides ample privacy for each unit. Rienk will even give free mosaic instruction.

Rooms are airy and spacious, each with

a kitchenette and a full-size fridge, air-conditioning, cable TV, and free Wi-Fi. All-day courtesy coffee and tea as well as inexpensive laundry machines are available. Fisherman's Huts are close, about a 15-minute walk away. Villa Sunflower is on a narrow street, and there is no dedicated parking, inconvenient if you rented a car. Two guard dogs quickly warm up to guests. Villa Sunflower is pet-friendly for smaller dogs.

$100-200
★ BEACH HOUSE ARUBA
Among the Palm Beach guesthouses, **Beach House Aruba** (450 L. G. Smith Blvd., 297/593-3991, www.beachhousearuba.com, $130-395) is one of the few with its own shorefront just across the boulevard. Hosts Ewald and Doris are known for their hospitality and dedicated clientele. This converted

home is on the Malmok strip just north of Fisherman's Huts. Units vary in size; all have an air-conditioned bedroom separate from the kitchenette-lounge area. Rooms have terraces to take advantage of the breeze. Most units are around a common area in the back of the house, where yoga sessions are held. A few front units have ocean and pool area views. Decor is eclectic and quaint. Coolers to take to the beach, storage for windsurfing equipment, a *palapa* for shade, and lounges at MooMba Beach are included. Ewald is known to offer cappuccino while socializing with his guests. As a former windsurfing instructor, he can share insights into the sport.

ARUBA BEACH VILLAS

In Malmok, **Aruba Beach Villas** (L. G. Smith Blvd. 462, 297/586-1072, U.S. 800/320-9998, www.arubabeachvillas.com, studio suite $178-238) is a favorite destination for windsurfers. Aruba Sailboard Vacations and Fiberworx board shop are attached for equipment and spare parts. During high season, room rates include unlimited equipment rental; during the off-season, room rates drop by half and don't include equipment. The sport takes several hours to master. Owner Phil is an expatriate American providing spacious rustic rooms with big closets and baths, even in the studios, all with fully equipped kitchens. Oceanfront rooms have wooden decks, and the beach is just across the road. There is a small pool in the back. Less expensive rooms are bare-bones for those who will be on the water most of the time. A charming open-air common area faces the sea to kick back and talk windsurfing.

BANANAS APARTMENTS

A popular spot with Europeans and families, **Bananas Apartments** (Malmokweg 19, 297/586-2858, www.bananas-resort.com, 1-bedroom $125) is a short distance down the Malmokweg, perpendicular to the beach road. Converted from two adjacent houses, each has a small pool and a whirlpool spa. The older section has a sprawling backyard and lovely gardens with shade trees. Don't balk at an "older" room: They have more charm and big wooden picnic tables on the patios. All rooms have fully equipped kitchens. Maid service and fresh towels daily are included, with oversize beach towels provided by the pool.

BRICKELL BAY BEACH CLUB & SPA

Close to, but not on, the beach, adults-only **Brickell Bay Beach Club & Spa** (J. E. Irausquin Blvd. 370, 297/586-0900, U.S./Canada 866/238-4218, www.brickellbayaruba.com, $169) is a good value, with an unimpressive exterior and lobby masking 98 pleasant rooms. In the heart of Palm Beach, it's well situated for nighttime action. Brickell has a spacious attractive pool deck and bar. At the Orchid Day Spa, guests enjoy a pool view during a massage, facial, manicure, or pedicure at reasonable rates. Also on-site is the glamorous night spot Sand Bar & Lounge, with nighttime beach tennis courts. The bar is surrounded by shops that stay open late, and there's an Italian restaurant with a terrace dining room. Rates include continental breakfast and an airport shuttle.

BRISAS STUDIO APARTMENTS

Far, but not too far, from the crowds is **Brisas Studio Apartments** (Keito 8B, 297/592-8631, www.brisasaruba.com, studio apartment $105), a secluded serene hideaway. *Brisas* means "quiet" in Papiamento. On the eastern outskirts of Palm Beach, it shares ownership with Wonders Boutique Hotel and comprises two charming apartments. Mini markets and some nice restaurants are close by, but you will need a rental car. Amenities include coolers, snorkeling gear, beach towels, and folding lounges to take to the beach. A grill is on the premises, and each apartment has a nicely equipped kitchenette. Rooms are spacious and have a queen bed; extra occupants can request a fold-out. Note that the room rate doesn't include a 19.5 percent service charge. For an additional fee, you can arrange transport to and from the airport.

Resort Hopping

The major resorts, with the exception of the all-inclusive hotels, welcome nonguests to their restaurants, spas, casinos, shops, and shows. In Palm Beach, where resorts are in close proximity, this is especially convenient and part of the experience; walking the strip from one resort to the next, on the beach boardwalk or the boulevard promenade, is a favorite nighttime activity. Pool decks, however, are for guests only.

Riu and Barceló are all-inclusive, so you won't get in without a guest bracelet, but visitors are welcome at their casinos. Ask at the concierge desks about day passes.

CARIBBEAN PALM VILLAGE

Across the street from Santa Ana Church and in the middle of a commercial area with a supermarket, a department store, and a drugstore, **Caribbean Palm Village** (Noord 43E, 297/526-2700 or 813/322-3667, www.cpvr.com, studio $171), has studio rooms and spacious 1-2-bedroom suites as well as two attractive pool decks. A community lounge, barbecue and picnic areas, a day spa, a fitness center, and an independent restaurant serving breakfast, lunch, and dinner also feature.

CARIÑAS VACATION HOME & APARTMENTS

Cariñas Vacation Home & Apartments (Palm Beach 360, 297/592-8631, www.arubacarinas.com, studio $127, bungalow $183) offers a two-bedroom bungalow with a private entrance, and five spacious studio apartments with kitchenettes. In the residential area of Palm Beach, the main hotel area is nearby, and it's a 10-minute walk from the beach. Each apartment has a spacious terrace. The bungalow has a large living room and a private outdoor patio; it sleeps six comfortably. Laundry machines are available. The neighborhood is quiet but convenient to the action of busy Palm Beach, including restaurants, stores, and casinos. It does not have a pool but offers charming common areas for relaxing in the sun. The clientele is mostly sociable Europeans along with North and South Americans.

COSTA ESMERALDA VILLAGE

Convenient to the Palm Beach action, tranquil **Costa Esmeralda Village** (Washington 61B, 297/567-5611, www.costaesmeraldaaruba.com, $120-175) is in a quiet neighborhood minutes from nightlife, casinos, dining, and beaches. Rooms are attractive and contemporary, from hotel studios to one-bedroom suites and a duplex town house with two bedrooms and two baths. Rooms are light and spacious, and baths are huge. Suites have complete kitchens. Two moderate-size pools include a lap pool and a whirlpool. The community area has a gas barbecue for guest use. Management is personable and assists with car rentals and arranging tours. Costa Esmeralda Village is next door to Papiamento Restaurant's superb gourmet dining.

DEL RAY APARTMENTS

Off the beaten track north of the Santa Ana Church in Noord is a side street with **Del Ray Apartments** (Caya Calco 13D, 297/586-3309, www.delreyaruba.com, $118), minutes from the beach by car, close to shopping, and a few doors from Anna Maria's Italian restaurant. Twenty-six comfortable, clean apartments surround the large pool deck and playground, a good value for spacious rooms. The mom-and-pop operation has a largely European and Latin clientele. It has an arrangement with MooMba Beach for lounge chairs for guests.

LA BOHEME

Inland along the Bakval Road, across from the Marriott Resort, is **La Boheme** (Bakval

2E, 297/593-6512, www.labohemearuba.com, $165-185), a delightful guesthouse comprising four one-bedroom apartments around a lovely pool deck. Each has a kitchenette, a giant TV, and a spacious terrace. Grills are on hand for a cookout, and coolers for trips to the beach. La Boheme has an arrangement at MooMba Beach Bar to provide lounges for its guests. In a quiet residential area within easy walking distance of all the major Palm Beach action, all units are standard, and friendly relations with other guests seem to develop naturally. The clientele is a mix of North Americans, Europeans, and Latin Americans.

VILLA BOUGAINVILLEA

At the main sea road, a short walk from the beach at Boca Catalina, staying at **Villa Bougainvillea** (Malmokweg 4, 297/526-1055, U.S. 646/502-8510, www. villabougainvilleaaruba.com, $119-149) is a unique experience stamped with the character of hostess Rona. Three charming apartments with mini kitchens are attached to the proprietor's home. Each has its own entrance and a key to the gate for security. Rooms are spacious and decorated with fine and eclectic taste, creating a unique ambience. Baths have tubs as well as showers, unusual at budget places, and each room has a terrace looking out on a charming backyard with a pool and a grill. "When the spirit moves her," Rona will cook up a storm of gourmet snacks and mix a pitcher of sangria to treat her guests to a get-acquainted happy hour. Three big *cunucu* rescue dogs (a local mixed breed) have the run of the property. They warm up to renters, but you should be completely comfortable with dogs if you stay here.

$200-300

BLUE RESIDENCES

On the border of Eagle and Palm Beach, directly across J. E. Irausquin Boulevard from the Baranca Plat beach, is **Blue Residences** (J. E. Irausquin Blvd. 266, U.S. 866/728-4910, www.bluearuba.com, $280 double, 2-3-bedroom $320-400), attractive condos rented out as hotel rooms. Those selecting the $280 option get a queen bed and bath with a full kitchen. Larger groups can opt for a beautifully appointed apartment with two or three bedrooms and baths, full kitchen, exceptionally spacious living room, and terrace with ocean views. Decor reflects the taste of each owner. Ground-floor apartments each have whirlpool spas on the terrace but no privacy. There is an attractive pool for swimming laps. Other services include an on-site day spa, a mini market, a restaurant, and a fitness room. Aside from holiday weeks, the facility is not busy. The resort has not placed *palapas* or lounges on the beach, so it remains a quiet spot. Next to Blue Residences, Azure is under construction and will add hundreds of rooms to make this the largest condominium group on Aruba with a relatively small beach front.

THE MILL RESORT

Across the street from the beachfront resorts, **The Mill Resort** (J. E. Irausquin Blvd. 330, 297/526-7700, U.S./Canada 800/992-2015, www.millresort.com, $229) is next to the signature landmark for which it was named. The unique sprawling facility is low-rise and has studios, junior suites, and royal suites, each with full or mini kitchens. Royal suites have a private whirlpool in the middle of the room. Families can combine junior or royal suites with a studio for the kids, with its own bath. Up to two children under age 13 stay free in the same room with parents. Two hundred rooms surround a spacious attractive pool deck with three freeform pools, a restaurant, and a bar, popular with locals on Friday evening for the lively happy hour and local bands. A shuttle to the beach is provided. A section of beach just south of the Riu has The Mill's lounge chairs. A mini market and the Intermezzo Day Spa, with a luxurious couples' room, are on-site.

OCEAN 105

Adjacent to Boca Catalina, popular with islanders on the weekend, **Ocean 105** (L. G. Smith Blvd. 105, U.S. 866/978-6986,

1-bedroom $216-325) is the one Malmok guesthouse on the water with direct access to the beach. Guests have a small patch of beach, bordered by two nice snorkel spots for beginners, with easy shore access. Sailboats stop in the bay daily with charter trips. The two-story guesthouse has four apartments: a one-bedroom and three two-bedroom units, all spacious and elegantly decorated. Sofa beds are in the living rooms, and kitchens are fully equipped, with terraces or patios hanging over the sea, but there is no pool. Maid service is twice a week.

$300-400

★ BOARDWALK SMALL HOTEL ARUBA

The first of the Malmok off-the-beach resorts is **Boardwalk Small Hotel Aruba** (Bakval 20, 297/586-6654, www.boardwalkaruba.com, studio suite from $335), which feels like a tropical paradise. A tranquil place with 13 casitas surrounded by lush gardens, it is close to the Palm Beach action, with the Marriott's Stellaris Casino just across the road. Rooms are spacious enough to sleep four comfortably, with high ceilings, large closets, dressing rooms, and fully equipped kitchens. Each has its own patio or terrace with an individual

grill. There's a small pool and a whirlpool, and guests can use the lounge chairs at MooMba Beach Bar, between the Holiday Inn and Marriott Surf Club. A shuttle to the beach includes individual coolers for ice and refreshments. The owners are twin sisters Kimberly and Stephanie Rooijakkers, and their enthusiasm is infectious. The hotel is pet-friendly; expect the sisters' adorable longhaired dachshund to greet you in the lobby.

ZENTASY VILLA

Zentasy (Ruby 17, 297/733-0108, www.zentasyaruba.com, $375-625) is a beautiful four-bedroom, four-bath house with basic decor in the bedrooms, but the common areas are attractive and appealing. The house has a small saltwater pool and a deck with a charcoal barbecue, curtain-covered lounges for two, and lounges in the pool. There's a roof sundeck with vistas to the sea for spectacular sunset views. Baths are modern and spacious. Amenities include a full kitchen and a laundry room. The house is in a residential community close to Tierra Del Sol Country Club and Golf Course, far enough from the beach and shops that you'll have to rent a car. Minimum stay is 3 nights, and 14 nights during Christmas and New Year's weeks.

Divi Phoenix Beach Resort

$400-500

DIVI PHOENIX BEACH RESORT

Divi Phoenix Beach Resort (J. E. Irausquin Blvd. 75, 297/586-6066, www.diviresorts.com, $425-499) has two sections with disparate configurations and rates.

The older section is composed of suites with fully equipped kitchens, a simple pool deck, and the Pure Ocean restaurant, which provides a toes-in-the-sand waterfront dining experience.

The newer, more sumptuous section has higher prices. It houses the main lobby and a luxurious pool. All rooms have spacious balconies facing out over the pool or ocean. The poolside restaurant and swim-up bar are beachfront.

The resort also has a mini market, a casual sandwich spot, a business center, concierge and car rental desks, a day spa, and friendly accommodating staff. Set apart from the strip of resorts, it has a more tranquil atmosphere at the beach.

OVER $500

CASA DEL VIENTO

Casa del Viento (L. G. Smith Blvd. 125A, 297/525-2525, www.casadelvientoaruba.com, $1,275-1,450) is a luxurious, stylish five-bedroom, five-bath home a five-minute walk from Boca Catalina beach in Malmok, Aruba's most exclusive residential community. The cost of a daily rental divided by five couples is only $255 per day per couple, a rate that beats the most luxurious time-share and condo complexes. Bedrooms are spacious, each with TV and climate control, and several have private entrances. One bedroom includes a sub-bedroom ideal for parents and children to share connected quarters; each has its own bath. The master bedroom is on a floor of its own, with a wraparound terrace and stunning views of the sea and the coast, all the way to the lighthouse. An enormous pool deck with two entertainment areas has large tables and chairs and a gas barbecue. Other amenities include a laundry room and a fully equipped kitchen with top-of-the-line appliances and a large double-door fridge.

HILTON ARUBA CARIBBEAN RESORT & CASINO

Aruba's first major resort, the **Hilton Aruba Caribbean Resort & Casino** (J. E. Irausquin Blvd. 81, 297/586-6555, www.hilton.com, $522) retains the charm and elegance of a bygone era, having gone through several incarnations since first opening as the Aruba Caribbean in 1959. Rooms in the main section are well maintained, with unconventional dimensions—spacious, with high ceilings and huge dressing rooms and closets—a throwback to when people like James Bond actor Roger Moore regularly stayed here. The pool deck, one of the most gorgeous on Aruba, creates the feeling of sitting on the beach and has lushly landscaped paths. It's also home to one of Aruba's most interesting unofficial attractions: Victor the Birdman, who cares for the exotic birds around the gardens.

The Plaza Club on the upper floors offers more elaborate rooms and suites, a personal concierge, complimentary continental breakfasts, afternoon tea, and happy hours, with snacks and drinks included.

All interior areas are nonsmoking. Accessibility for people with disabilities include lowered sinks in rooms and hoists in the pools. The hotel has also taken care to include braille elevator and room numbers as well as visual information for the hearing impaired.

OCEAN Z

A boutique resort that deserves that label is **Ocean Z** (L. G. Smith Blvd., 526, 297/586-9500, U.S./Canada 800/299-0472, www.oceanzaruba.com, studio or 1-bedroom $690-750), with an elegant aesthetic, a reflection of its owner and founder, fashion designer Eva Zissou. A boutique shop with her creations is here, along with 13 guest rooms, two of which share an infinity pool overlooking the sea. A larger pool is at the center of the resort. Rates include gourmet breakfast in the cozy dining area with no set serving hours; wake up whenever you want. The warm welcome from the accommodating staff includes a glass of champagne. Ocean Z is adjacent to the turnoff for Malmokweg, across from the beach.

PLAYA LINDA BEACH RESORT
Playa Linda Beach Resort (J. E. Irausquin Blvd. 87, 297/586-6100, www.playalinda.com, studio or 2-bedroom $380-736) is one of the most luxurious time-share resorts on Aruba, with a mini market, several shops, and restaurants on the street side and the beach boardwalk. A nice day spa, a fitness room, tennis courts, and a beautiful pool deck give it a family-oriented feel. The independent Playa Linda forum on the website has sections tailored to those seeking trades or rentals, and another for those offering them, where great discounts can be found. An ambulance and EMT center are in the parking lot.

Santa Cruz, Paradera, and Piedra Plat

$100-200

CUNUCU VILLAGE
Cunucu Village (Calabas Plaza, 297/594-6338, www.arubacunucu.com, 2-bedroom suite $150-195) was a residential community with homes built in the classic *cunucu* style. Each villa is picturesque and attractively decorated, painted in bright colors in the island tradition. Most circle a community pool, with rear entrances onto the pool deck. Some have their own hot tubs. Full kitchens include utensils. There is a shared laundry with washer and dryer. Hosts Ursula and Rudger take pride in their villas and provide a memorable Aruban vacation.

CUNUCU VILLAS
Lia Lopez is the sweet friendly host at Cunucu Villas (Santa Cruz 63, 297/585-1616, www.cunucuvillasaruba.com, 1-bedroom suite $150), with 12 identical units on two levels. Upper rooms have a view of the surrounding countryside. Set back on a dirt road at the end of a residential street, Cunucu Villas has an attractive pool deck with a common grill and picnic tables under a shaded terrace. Rooms have simple decor and full kitchens. Despite its out-of-the-way location, it is a 10-minute walk to Huchada bakery, and Santa Cruz's principal commercial area is only a bit farther. It is close to Arikok National Park.

PARADERA PARK APARTMENTS
Providing quick access to Arikok National Park, Paradera Park Apartments (Paradera 203, 297/582-3289, www.paraderapark-aruba.com, studio $189) is a friendly family-run operation with a dedicated following. A surprising number of long-term guests have been vacationing on Aruba for years, as the accommodations are clean and attractive with personable owners. A small complex of 17 studios and one- or two-bedroom suites, Paradera Park Apartments is down a side street in a residential area. The turnoffs are clearly marked. One duplex suite has a bedroom and master bath on the second level. All rooms include full kitchens. The focus of the complex is a small pool with an attractive deck and garden.

What Exactly Are *Cunucu* Houses?

a traditional *cunucu* house

A *cunucu* house is considered the traditional architecture of Aruba, distinctive for its cultural and practical details and built piecemeal over time. The characteristic peaked roof at the center delineates the original home erected for newlyweds. As the family grew, rooms were added to the front, back, and sides. City homes of wealthier families had a 2nd floor for offspring, usually adorned with dormer windows, which distinguishes the houses in town from their country cousins. Having a dozen children in a family was quite common, and boys and girls would have separate sleeping areas. Placement of the rooms took advantage of Aruba's steady northeast winds. Sleeping rooms caught the breeze and provided cool comfort, while the west end was the cooking space with the *facon,* a fireplace and chimney where meals were prepared. This placement allowed the wind to blow the heat and cinders away from the house. Islanders have such affection for this particular style of architecture that many new homes are still planned this way.

The word *cunucu* is frequently used to describe anything considered rural, though *mondi* is the actual word for "deep woods." *Cunucu* also indicates something native to the island, such as a *cunucu* house or *cunucu* dog, the local mixed breed. Charles Croes, who has extensively studied the Papiamento language, claims that *cunucu* does not mean "country"; it was the word applied to the perimeter of sand placed around rural homes, smoothed out each night before bedtime. Residents examined the sand in the morning for telltale footprints, indicating unwanted visitors such as scorpions or millipedes that may have entered the house during the night.

San Nicolas, Savaneta, and Pos Chiquito

$50-100

SEABREEZE APARTMENTS

Perfectly situated to enjoy the beaches of Pos Chiquito, **Seabreeze Apartments** (Malohistraat 5, 297/593-5043, www. seabreezearuba.com, $80) is a delightful complex of 10 studio and one-bedroom units, each with a kitchenette, cable TV, and free Wi-Fi, a five-minute walk from Mangel Halto Beach and sensational snorkeling and diving. Free coolers are provided. Owner Joey enjoys the company of his guests. The charming complex has an appealing common area with a pool and a whirlpool, all designed to encourage congeniality. Next door is a small supermarket and a Chinese restaurant, and Marina Pirata restaurant is within walking distance.

$100-200
★ ARUBA REEF APARTMENTS

Aruba Reef Apartments (Savaneta 342 C, 297/735-2053, www.arubareef.com, $187) is as close as you'll get to a fantasy tropical island getaway. Parts of this expansive waterfront home have been converted into delightful apartments where you can roll out of bed (or your hammock) onto a private beach. Each of the five units has a kitchenette with a full-size fridge, a terrace, and a spacious bath. Former owner Fred had a house in Bali, so the ambience is a mix of Caribbean and South Pacific, filled with art from around the world. He had the word "Paradise" engraved at the home's quaint entrance—and it does truly feel like a slice of paradise here. The current host is his son, Raffy, who took over when Fred passed in 2016. He lives on the premises and is a congenial host, full of information about the island. The beach here has a volleyball court and plenty of lounges. Common areas have a grill and a meditation zone on a deck next to the water. Free kayaks and snorkel gear are on hand to explore the stunning waters along Aruba's south coast. And the complex is adjacent to Flying Fishbone restaurant, a few doors down from Zeerover.

VISTALMAR

Out-of-the-way **Vistalmar Apartments** (Bucutiweg 28, 297/582-8579, www.arubavistalmar.com, $781 per week) has dedicated clientele but no beach, just a private dock along a pretty section of the south shore. Close to two yacht clubs, it is handy for deep-sea fishing. Rooms have fully equipped kitchens and terraces over the sea

for sunsets. Breakfast is provided the first day, fresh bread is delivered daily, and an airport shuttle is provided. Other amenities include snorkel gear, coolers, and bicycles. Car rental can be arranged as part of the package.

$200-300
CLUB ARIAS BED & BREAKFAST

The surreal facade of **Club Arias Bed & Breakfast** (Savaneta 123K, 297/593-3408, U.S. 917/508-7210, www.clubarias.com, $135-250)—named for its owner, Arias Schwarz—disguises a charming courtyard with surprisingly large pools and attractive gardens. The courtyard is surrounded by 10 spacious rooms, each uniquely decorated with original art and knickknacks. Each room has a kitchenette, and one has a full kitchen. The common area sports a cozy open-air restaurant where Cordon Bleu-graduate chef Gabriel prepares omelets for breakfast 7:30am-10:30am. Nonguests can come for breakfast, which is included for guests. Gabriel is also available for private dinners. High tea with fresh pastries is served at 4pm daily. Club Arias is on the main highway from Oranjestad to San Nicolas, a busy thoroughfare, but it's set back enough to be quiet, particularly the back rooms.

FORTUNA VILLA

Fortuna Villa (Savaneta 364, 297/593-3408, www.aruba-villas.com, $212) is across the street from the beach and Flying Fishbone restaurant and a five-minute walk from Zeerover. Owned by a friendly English couple, it was previously the home of author Daniel Putkowski, who lived here six months of the year and made a career of writing popular quasi-historical fiction about Aruba, sprinkled with real-life characters. The attractive home can accommodate up to nine guests in three bedrooms, plus sleep sofas in a second living room. It has a fully equipped kitchen and a laundry room. A charming pool deck with a tiki bar is great for entertaining and barbecuing.

SERENE BY THE SEA

Another Savaneta guesthouse is **Serene by the Sea** (Savaneta 354, 297/594-0289, www.serenebythesea.com, $235), a stunning property on the beach with only four rooms, disguised by a bland street front. Each room is decorated in tropical style, equipped with a mini-fridge and a patio overlooking the sea. A popular restaurant is here, and the included breakfast is served on the picnic tables on the beach. A communal barbecue is available, and kayaks and snorkeling gear are provided free.

$300-400

THE HIDEAWAY

A bargain for a large group or a few families, **The Hideaway** (Pos Chiquito 273F, 297/596-0197, capeskris@aol.com, $319) feels like a luxurious villa. The two-story home has three apartments, each sleeping six or more, with beautifully outfitted kitchens. The top unit has a "nanny's room," and the terraces have stunning views. Rates are per room with no additional fees for extra people. Each apartment closes off completely from the others. The property is made for entertaining, with a spacious patio, pool, spa, gas grill, and spectacular sound system. A rental car is necessary in this secluded location, but the beaches of Savaneta and Pos Chiquito are five minutes away by car. Housekeeping service is available at extra cost.

OVER $500

★ ARUBA OCEAN VILLAS

Epitomizing the tropical island getaway is **Aruba Ocean Villas** (Savaneta 356A, 297/594-1808, U.S. 917/391-4327, www.arubaoceanvillas.com, studio or 1-bedroom suite $350-650). Six thatched-roof bungalows are scattered along a large beachfront on the south shore, three built on the water so you can relax on your private deck; the others are on the beach. Ocean Villas began as the eatery The Old Man and The Sea, and the restaurant and bar are the resort's common areas. Evenings around the bar can be an education as bartender Hector espouses the wine selection or reveals the recipes of exotic concoctions. Hostess Osyth is a respected artist, and her creative touches are evident in every detail. Gather around the gorgeously painted piano in the lounge or peruse her hand-painted menus. Rates include buffet breakfast. Lunch and dinner can be arranged. The menu changes daily with delicious local fish. You can also arrange a private dinner in your bungalow. A special lounging-dining area over the water for a private dinner for two can be arranged; it is an ideal location for a wedding proposal. Osyth will arrange flowers or anything else you need to make it more memorable.

1: Aruba Reef Apartments; **2:** Club Arias Bed & Breakfast

Background

The Landscape. 198

Environmental Issues . . 200

Plants and Animals. 203

History 208

Government and
    Economy 218

People and Culture 219

The Landscape

A phrase from Aruba's national anthem, "Aruba Dushi Tera" ("Sweet Land Aruba"), describes this island nation as *Nos baranca tan stima* (Our beloved rock). This simple phrase conveys the self-awareness and affection Arubans have for their unique desert island. Aruba is a relatively flat island with three major peaks: Seroe Jamanota (188 m/617 ft), Seroe Arikok (184 m/606 ft), and Hooiberg (165 m/541 ft). Constant winds buffet the island from the northeast after traveling thousands of miles across open sea. In terms of geological makeup, Aruba's north coast is a lunar landscape of limestone outcroppings interspersed

The Caribbean

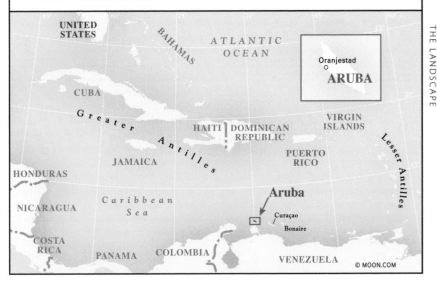

with quartz rock and pillow basalt. All were formed when undersea volcanoes created the submerged landmasses that would become the ABC islands of Aruba, Bonaire, and Curaçao. Along the north coast, heavy waves crash and spume dramatically, occasionally broken by small coves and beaches. The land resembles an elongated triangle. The south shore is dotted with small beaches, mangrove formations, and limestone cliffs. The western or leeward side is home to the miles-long stretch of beaches that attract visitors and real estate developers. Areas from Palm Beach south have been exclusively zoned for tourism.

Located north of the equator at 12°32'28" N, 69°57'30" W, Aruba is 31 kilometers (19 mi) long and 9.65 kilometers (6 mi) wide at its widest point. Approximately 179 square kilometers (69 square mi), the island is divided into seven zoning districts, each containing multiple barrios. The closest major landmass is the Paraguaná Peninsula of Venezuela, 19 kilometers (12 mi) south; Caracas is 400 kilometers (250 mi) from Aruba. Sister islands of Curaçao and Bonaire are 88 kilometers (55 mi) and 103 kilometers (64 mi) east, along the 12° latitude line. Aruba is the physically smallest of the ABC islands, but it has a population of 107,000 compared to only 15,000 on Bonaire, which is 293 square kilometers (113 square mi) in size. Curaçao, at 453 square kilometers (175 square mi), is the largest of the three and has a population of 141,766. It takes 20 minutes to travel from Aruba to Curaçao by prop plane, but the sea voyage is a challenging 15 hours in very rough waters.

GEOLOGY

Studies propose the initial undersea landmasses were formed around 95 million years ago, making their way to the surface through tectonic activity around 30 million years later. Aruba was formed from three kinds of rock: igneous, which is a cooling and solidification of magma; metamorphic, a rock formed from a previously produced rock; and sedimentary,

---

Previous: The Hooiberg is one of Aruba's tallest peaks.

resulting from the continual deposit and hardening of other rocks. The fantastical pillow lava formations primarily around the north coast confirm the underwater accretion of the land. After the original volcanic eruptions, a continuation of the magma flow over the rock, a process called plutonism, created layers.

The majority of the island's landscape, named the Aruba Lava Formation, is part of a huge geologic formation called a batholith. Of this, only a minor portion has been exposed after weathering, erosion, and being pushed up by the earth's movement. The carved limestone cliffs in the coves along the shore are the most recently accumulated rock. Close examination of the terraces reveals a wealth of interesting marine fossils and coral impressions.

CLIMATE

One of Aruba's great assets is reliable weather: a sunny 28-33°C (82-92°F) year-round. Its proximity to the equator defines it as a tropical island, but constant breezes and sea currents keep the temperature comfortable. The sea is cooler than expected. Temperatures are ideal for coral growth and a proliferation of colorful fish life.

Aruba is south of the Hurricane Belt and therefore is rarely subject to devastating Caribbean storms. Aruba's weather is most unstable mid-August-November, when named storms are more likely to form in the Gulf of Mexico. Each year, weather experts predict increasing numbers of storms of greater strength in the Atlantic, Caribbean, and Gulf of Mexico, but records show they rarely approach Aruba. Storms usually turn north for the gulf as they make their way west across the Atlantic. Storms that were large enough to cause heavy seas and hard rain on Aruba include Hurricanes Dean (2007), Ivan (2004), Frances (2004), and Lenny (1999). Sometimes faraway storms will produce small occlusions that can result in rough waters or occasional squalls. Still, it is unheard of for flights to be canceled because of weather on Aruba. The most common effect of big storms is that the ever-present wind dies down, causing it to become oppressively humid. This effect can't be predicted much in advance.

Environmental Issues

OVERDEVELOPMENT AND POPULATION

Aruba faces the conundrum of many Caribbean islands: making economic and technological progress while maintaining its cultural identity. Unbridled construction and development create jobs and business opportunities, but at what cost to the island's character? This has become a concern not only for the government but also ordinary citizens. Islanders are dismayed to see developers callously bulldozing habitats of endemic flora and fauna. Coastal areas and essential mangrove formations with their delicate ecosystems are particularly endangered. Aside from cases of unwarranted waste, other projects raise the question: Does the island really need another shopping mall or upscale housing complex? There is already an overabundance of both. Another dilemma for property owners is generating profit from undeveloped land that has been in the family for generations. Legislation requiring environmental studies and prohibiting threats to endangered species is not in place to curb these actions. Aruba's enormous success with tourism has exacerbated its sustainability issues, and it doesn't help that tourism has been the island's primary financial pillar for decades.

Aruba has also been a land of opportunity, attracting immigrants from other islands and South and Central America. The rapidly growing population on a small island naturally created stresses on the infrastructure, although the native population readily accepted and socially integrated newcomers from disparate cultures. Aruba's advanced system of water distribution and an attractive social and educational system under the Dutch have provided benefits and support that many immigrants from the region could not find at home. Much of this came with the Lago Refinery, along with skilled labor that tripled the island's population after 1925.

In the years since the 1986 achievement of Status Aparte, immigrants could count on jobs in tourism, construction, and unskilled labor. In 1986 the population was 72,000, and the 2010 census counted 107,000 legal residents. The demands on infrastructure, the loss of natural land to housing, as well as the boom in development of tourism has caused great concern among environmental groups. Add the additional strain of 1.5 million visitors per year. Much waste is produced with limited land to store it.

TRASH AND RECYCLING

Aruba lags behind Europe, Canada, and the United States in environmental attitudes, recycling, and waste disposal. Many people are sensitive to these problems, and serious legislation was enacted in 2012, including severe penalties for illegal dumping. In 2017 plastic shopping bags were banned, and in 2019 legislation will outlaw single-use plastic straws, cups, and Styrofoam containers. Regular Caribbean travelers report that Aruba is far cleaner than most other destinations in the region.

Aruba maintains a landfill on the south shore at Parkietenbos, where trash is burned. Regular weekly collection is conducted in almost all communities, and private operators collect trash from businesses and hotels more frequently. Large appliances and debris are not carted away by the public service, and individuals must transport it to the dump themselves for recycling. Not all households have the means, and frequently they remain in backyards, rusting eyesores that can become breeding grounds for mosquitoes.

Collaborating with private waste haulers, various foundations and companies have organized island-wide cleanups. At least three annual beach cleaning efforts see hundreds or thousands of volunteers; tourists are welcome to join in.

Ecotech, which collects 50 percent of Aruba's trash, sorts and ships recycled materials. A biogas plant, slated for expansion, processes all the organic refuse. The island's water and power plant, WEB, uses the recycled fuel, expected to provide 9 percent of Aruba's energy needs. Incentives reward residents to sort waste to win prizes. The Caribbean Waste Collective (www.caribbeanwastecollective.com) is a collaborative initiative for Aruba, Bonaire, and Curaçao, supported by the Dutch Ministry of Infrastructure and the Environment. Its first project, *Ayo Sushi* (Good-bye Garbage), focuses on education on recycling.

AIR POLLUTION

In 2008 the U.S. Department of Energy's Carbon Dioxide Information Analysis Center (CDIAC) showed that Aruba was number 9 among 214 nations in carbon dioxide emissions per capita. The refinery in San Nicolas was the reason for this high rank. The Netherlands Antilles, dissolved in 2010, was rated number 4 in carbon dioxide emissions per capita, likely due to the huge Shell refinery in Curaçao.

Aruba's refinery has been idle since 2012, which has proven beneficial to Aruba's emissions, and all refining ceased in 2014. Currently Aruba is used as a transshipment station, loading oil from lake tankers onto larger oceangoing vessels. Recurring rumors have yet to result in refinery production restarting, and informed parties hold that the antiquated facilities won't be viable again due to the cost of repairs and modernization.

Despite refinery, power plant, and trash-burning emissions, visitors have always found Aruba's air delightfully fresh, carrying only the scent of salty seas. Prevailing northeasterly winds push emissions away from the island.

Even at Baby Beach or Roger's Beach, in the shadow of the refinery, emissions weren't noticeable even in the refinery's heyday.

RENEWABLE ENERGY

The WEB power plant, Aruba's other great carbon emitter, is working to reduce and possibly eliminate petroleum use. Their concern is not necessarily the environment but the turbulent speculative oil market. Cleaner air will be a positive side effect. Other renewable energy sources include the Vader Piet Wind Farm, 10 giant wind turbines on the far northeast coast. A second planned wind farm at Urirama, near the Alto Vista Chapel, met with strong local resistance over noise and zoning issues, and the government canceled the project in 2017. The possibility of doubling the size of the Vader Piet Wind Farm is now under discussion.

A large solar farm was built at Aruba's airport that also acts as shade for the parking lot. It provides all the airport's power and 3 percent of Aruba's overall energy needs. Import tariffs on clean-energy equipment have been drastically reduced, encouraging residents to power their homes and feed energy back into the grid. WEB has switched to reverse-osmosis water purification, which requires far less energy. Island administrators have declared the goal of making Aruba completely oil independent, supported by international organizations such as Richard Branson's Carbon War Room. This will require new means of harnessing energy and education to change residents' wasteful energy habits.

Dutch energy think tank TNO set up an experimental community on Aruba with 15 homes that will operate solely on renewable energy sources and 5 control homes that do not in order to provide comparative statistics. TNO describes Aruba as the perfect springboard for markets in the United States and South America. TNO and the Aruban government hold that investment in renewable technologies can provide jobs, profit, and improved quality of life in the region.

Islanders have been encouraged to switch to electric or hybrid cars. Small electric cars were included in some condo sales. Aruba's power distributor, ELMAR, is promoting electric cars and solar energy structures to house and charge them. Tariffs on electric cars have been reduced from the 40 percent levied on conventional vehicles to 2 percent.

LITTER ON BEACHES

Efforts continue to raise awareness of the multiple consequences of plastic cups, plates, and straws as well as Styrofoam containers on Aruba's environment. Resorts have typically provided meal and drink services on the beach in disposable containers, cutlery, and cups which, when not disposed of properly, are blown into the sea by trade winds. Various marinelife, particularly turtles, feed on jellyfish, and plastic and Styrofoam is easily mistaken for food. Plastic and Styrofoam debris accumulates underwater. Legislation banning the import and sale of single-use plastic food items such as straws and Styrofoam containers was passed in Aruba in 2018.

Paper goods are at least biodegradable, but these should also be disposed of properly, especially newspapers, which tend to blow around. Conscientious guests at resorts should not hesitate to speak up if there aren't enough convenient disposal bins. If bins are filled to capacity, bring it to management's attention; they will respond. Certain resorts, such as Bucuti & Tara Beach Resort and Amsterdam Beach Resort, have made great strides in becoming green certified; Amsterdam Beach Resort has been cited as a champion by Green Globe International. Visitors can encourage all resorts to go green by selecting green-certified resorts.

Plants and Animals

PLANTS

Trees

Year-round tropical temperatures and little rainfall produce a plant population heavy with thorny succulents, flowering plants, and trees. Thorns range from microscopic to inches long as natural protection from herbivores. Hiking in the countryside requires care to avoid them.

Island trees are best known by their Papiamento names. **Kwihi** are prolific and valued for their wood. After these have been felled to build houses, stumps often end up as arresting tables, maintaining their original configurations. Kwihi germinate easily in the slightest bit of soil, with huge thorns to protect the young green plants, and grow into majestic shade trees.

When full grown, **Watapana** or **divi** trees *(Caesalpinia coriaria)* resemble bonsai; continual northeast winds bend and carve them in dramatic gnarled formations. Common advice if you get lost in the outback: Follow the direction the divi trees point, and you will end up back in Oranjestad.

A tree that is abundant and green year-round is the **Crown of Thorns** *(Acacia tortuosa),* called *hubada* by islanders; give these a wide berth. They produce an appealing yellow ball flower but have long painful spikes even when full grown.

In May or June, the rare **kibrahacha** *(Tabebuia billbergii),* commonly known as yellow poui, is in bloom for a few days and only when there have been showers. The foliage of the hills around Arikok National Park and the Hooiberg turns into a riot of brilliant yellow blooms, which disappear in less than a week. The tree gets its local name (*kibra* means "break" and *hacha* means "hatchet," literally "break the hatchet") from the extreme hardness of the wood.

Fruits

A number of regional wild fruit trees produce an impressive harvest in wet years. **Sea grape** *(Coccoloba swartzii)* is a sweet snack providing welcome shade along many beaches. **West Indian cherry** *(Malpighia emarginata),* locally known as *chimarucu*, is sometimes sold in markets. Cultivated in gardens or growing

brilliant blooms of kibrahacha trees

The Aruban Orchid

Aruba has a native strain of orchid, *Brassavola nodosa*. In the 1940s Esso executive Russ Ewing, who lived in The Colony, produced a unique hybrid by cross-pollinating the hardy Aruban *Brassavola nodosa* with the Venezuelan *Encyclia cordigera*. The result was larger than both. He registered this new species with the Royal Horticultural Society of the United Kingdom as *Brassoepidendrum arubiana* on January 1, 1950. The common name is the "Aruba good friend." The **Aruba Orchid Society** (sociedaddiorquidiaaruba@yahoo.com) is very active and stimulates interest in cultivating orchids with regular shows. It has published some how-to books in Papiamento on growing orchids.

Aruban orchid Brassavola Nodesa

wild are **kenepa** *(Melicoccus bijugatus),* known as Spanish lime. This regional tree produces clusters of green-skinned fruit the size of a lychee. Inside is a large seed coated with delicious pulp that is a beloved treat, eaten by sucking on the seed. It's a tasty non-fattening way to stop smoking.

Aruba has a variety of cacti and prickly flowers growing wild or cultivated, not the least of which is aloe vera. The most common endemic varieties are the towering *cadushi,* better known as **candle cactus** *(Stenocereus griseus).* It produces a tasty, deep-red fruit, attracting birds that manage to avoid the thorns and then eat and spread the seeds.

With a delicate yellow flower, the tuna or **prickly pear** *(Opuntia wentiana)* eventually produces a sweet fruit with many seeds. The comical *bushi,* or **Turk's cap cactus** *(Melocactus macracanthus),* has brilliant neon-pink flowers sprouting from spongy white centers. These become a tart bright-pink fruit, shaped like a small pepper to attract lizards and birds.

Flowers

Among the many wild flowering plants, one of the most noticeable is *Passiflora* or **passion flower,** known in Papiamento as *shoshoro.* The bulbous pods open into a delicate purple flower with green stigmata. It is a tenacious vine, often twining around other plants. A garden left to grow naturally will eventually produce an abundance of desert foliage, scrub, and cacti. Though brilliantly hued tropical flowers such as dewdrops, azaleas, hibiscus, frangipani, flamboyan, and begonias are imported, they are commonly seen decorating landscaped resort gardens and homes. Recycling wastewater from septic tanks is commonly used to maintain these gardens.

ANIMALS
Insects

Since this is a tropical climate, insects of every type are found in abundance. Desert denizens such as scorpions and millipedes are common in outlying areas but have a distaste for populated neighborhoods, and the chance of seeing one at a resort is highly unlikely. During a 2003 study of the ABC islands, 29 species of butterflies were collected on Aruba, with **Lycaenidae, Pieridae,** and **Hesperiidae** the most common families. **Monarch butterflies** *(Danaus plexippus)* are seen everywhere, as milkweed, their chosen plant for laying eggs, grows abundantly. Known as the athletes of the insect world, they travel thousands of miles, often hitching rides on boats at sea. It is likely that Aruba was a welcome rest stop along the way to South America, where they established a home. Most butterflies are a tasty treat for birds, but monarchs are foul and poisonous because the caterpillars feed on milkweed. They display their dramatic colors without fear of being eaten.

Birds

Aruba is an important rest stop and haven for many migrating species. Several have stayed and made Aruba their home. The native **Caribbean brown-throated parakeet,** or *prikichi,* was declared the national bird in 2017 after strong petitions by island bird enthusiasts and conservationists. While 249 species of birds nest on Aruba, this small, brilliantly green parrot is found only on Aruba. The Aruban *prikichi* is a variant of the order that has developed particular characteristics that make them endemic to Aruba.

The **shoko,** a burrowing owl, is also found only on Aruba and is the national symbol. It has distinctive large golden eyes. A pair protects their hole-in-the-ground nest. When they anticipate being disturbed, one will fly off to draw attention away from the nest. As ground-dwelling birds, their habitats are extremely vulnerable to boa constrictors and the ill effects of bulldozing and construction.

A brilliantly colorful common species is the **trupial.** The **yellow oriole** is a cousin of the trupial, and on the ABC islands has earned the name *trupial kachù.* On Aruba, it is better known as a *gonzalito.*

Aruba's more common predatory birds, **eagles, falcons,** and **hawks,** are known by their charming local names, *caracara, falki,* and *kini kini.* Common to the Caribbean is the **tropical mockingbird** *(chuchubi).* This dramatically marked gray bird nests on rooftops and ferociously defends its home against intruders. It wakes the neighborhood with its beautiful song. The **bananaquit,** a bold, tiny bird that loves sweets, is called *barica geil,* meaning "yellow belly."

The **brown pelican** is common to all three ABC islands, but researchers find Aruba is where they breed. During breeding season, the hind neck plumage turns dark reddish-brown. It remains white at other times and in winter. Wetlands are home to herons, egrets, cormorants, and ducks of various species. The yellow feet of the **snowy egret** has earned it the name "the lady with the golden slippers," which differentiates it from the great egret.

Flamingos are usually associated with Bonaire, and a thriving flock can be found on Flamingo Beach on Renaissance Island. They are very accommodating in posing for photographs. The characteristic deep salmon color is a result of their diet of brine shrimp. They eat small marine snails and the larvae of flies and mosquitoes, making them a worthwhile creature to preserve and protect.

Reptiles

As one would expect in a desert climate, the island is home to a wide variety of lizards *(lagadishi),* from tiny geckos to iguanas of all sizes. It is not uncommon to find birds and lizards gathered at the edges of outdoor restaurants ready for crumbs and fruit or bread to be tossed their way.

Iguanas *(Iguana iguana)* are plentiful and can be seen around hotel gardens, particularly on rock formations. While adolescent, they maintain a brilliant jade-green hue. As they grow, they develop the characteristic striped tail. Eventually they fade to dusky camouflage colors. The **Aruban whiptail lizard** *(Cnemidophorus arubensis)* or *kododo blauw* is an endemic species named for the striking aqua coloration of the mature male; females and the young are varying shades of brown.

Visitors to Arikok National Park will see a display of the **cascabel** *(Crotalus durissus unicolor),* Aruba's endemic and endangered rattlesnake, and the santanero, the Aruban **cat-eyed snake** *(Leptodeira bakeri).* Only the cascabel is venomous and is rarely seen outside the wilds. The **santanero** can be found anywhere, even in domestic gardens, but is absolutely harmless; both snakes help control vermin.

INVASIVE BOA CONSTRICTORS

A nonnative predator threatening indigenous mammals and birdlife is the boa constrictor.

How it was introduced is unclear; many point to the practice of buying snakes as pets, or perhaps they came in bunches of bananas on small boats from Venezuela. First noticed around 1990, they consume threatened native birds, rabbits, lizards, and, on rare occasions, pet cats and dogs. Herpetologist Andrew Odum from the Toledo Zoological Society has studied the impact on the native cascabel. The largest boa constrictor found on Aruba to date measures 2.9 meters (10 ft) long.

Boa constrictors give birth to up to 64 young snakes at any time of year; they are immediately viable and out hunting for food. Their preferred method is to wait in ambush for prey, which they crush and kill. They can be found on the ground, under bushes, in trees, and on cacti. The snakes are found mostly in Arikok National Park and in rural areas, and one section of Arikok is reserved for the study of the snake and its habits. A Boa Task Force headed by Arikok National Park biologist Diego Marquez began a training program for the public, conducting regularly scheduled boa hunts on weekends. About 100 boas are caught at a time, but the task force assumes that for every boa found, there are another four in the bush. To tackle this problem, Arikok National Park placed bounties on boas.

In 2011, **Arte Sano Studios** (297/733-5232, artesano@setarnet.aw) opened a workshop producing various accessories made from boa skin. Each item is handcrafted and unique. This new industry is a social project, teaching a trade and rehabilitating young delinquents. The project is endorsed by Aruba Bird Conservation and the Boa Task Force, turning a liability into an asset by establishing an industry of singular fine-quality products made in Aruba. They expect to produce two limited collections annually.

Marinelife

The island's tropical marine environment includes extensive reefs at depths from less than a meter to over 60 meters (200 ft) populated with countless brilliant tropical angelfish, triggerfish, wrasses, and parrotfish, as well as colorful corals. Fortunately there is no industry to spoil these waters with toxic runoff. Aruba has minimal predatory fish, and shark attacks are unheard of. Barracuda are plentiful, but their ferocious reputation is undeserved.

Divers and snorkelers should be mindful

Young iguanas are bright green.

Saving Aruba's Turtles

A baby leatherback turtle slowly struggles to the sea.

Every year, March–November, sections of beach are cordoned off, particularly around Eagle Beach, to protect the eggs and hatchlings of local and migrating sea turtles, which mate and nest here. Four species are the concern of **TurtugAruba** (297/592-9393, http://turtugaruba.org), the local foundation that works to protect the island's turtles. The green sea turtle and the hawksbill are native to Aruba and can be spotted year-round while snorkeling and diving; the hawksbill is considered critically endangered. Leatherbacks and loggerheads feed and live in the far distant North Atlantic but travel thousands of miles to mate in the Aruban waters where they first entered the sea. Females lay their eggs on the same beaches where they hatched years before, most often under cover of night, a remarkable sight.

Once the eggs are buried, mom returns to the sea, and the hatchlings face survival to adulthood on their own. Many things, including human actions, are a threat to newborn turtles. Driving on the beach is discouraged for this reason. TurtugAruba asks that observers report, but not disturb, a female laying her eggs. The area will be cordoned off to protect the nest and monitored during the two-month gestational period. Volunteers maintain a vigil when the young turtles emerge, helping them make it safely to the sea.

that they are much larger than any fish they will encounter. Humans are the largest and most dangerous predator. Most fish will dart away at your approach, except in the few areas where they have become accustomed to being fed. Spearfishing is illegal in Aruba, and any equipment for this pastime will be confiscated at customs.

INVASIVE LIONFISH

The influx of nonnative lionfish threatens indigenous animals on every island from the Bahamas south. They began showing up in Aruban waters around 2010. Speculation is that the invasion began as a result of the destruction wrought by Hurricane Andrew in 1992. Lionfish are native to the Indo-Pacific and Red Sea, where natural predators such as large groupers and certain sharks consume them. The fish do not reproduce as often or develop as quickly in their natural habitat as they do in the Caribbean's warmer waters. Their fins are distinctive, containing highly venomous spines, so few fish will feed on them; they can extend the spines into the throat of any fish attempting to eat them. Lionfish are prolific and ravenous predators. They have been observed literally vacuuming schools of smaller fish into their large maws, which extend for the purpose. They also hunt in packs, cooperating to drive prey toward the jaws of larger dominant lionfish.

Though beautiful, they are a real pest, reproducing at an alarming rate: 2,000,000 eggs annually. Devouring the many fish that play an important role in the delicate reef environment has serious ramifications. Within a year, they can strip a reef area of 80 percent of its small fish. A number of small fish species feed on the algae that grows on coral, which is necessary to keep the reef healthy; lionfish disrupt this marine cycle, potentially causing the reef to die.

Various solutions have been initiated, including fishing tournaments directed at lionfish. Diving operations are encouraged to hunt them when they are spotted or to notify the agency charged with their control. A group called Lionfish Hunters regularly hunts them and provides instruction on how to do so properly. Island restaurants are even adding lionfish to their menus. The local fishing organization Centro di Pisca Hadicurari and the Aruba Marine Park Foundation teach consumers how to clean and prepare lionfish. They are quite tasty, despite the paltry edible flesh for their size.

It took no time for islanders to imbue lionfish soup with the magical properties of expensive medications such as Viagra, a greatly desired effect long attributed to iguana meat. Perhaps now lionfish can prove useful and give that endangered species a respite from poachers.

Mammals

Most indigenous mammals are small desert creatures such as rodents, tiny hares (some will fit in a soup spoon), and several bat species, found mostly in caves at the eastern end of the island. The bats are being monitored to ensure that their population remains constant, as they perform the vital role of feeding on insects and pollinating fruit plants. None of the bats are rabid; rabies does not exist on Aruba.

Aruba also has a marine mammal population of dolphins and the occasional whale pod passing by on their migrations. The organization dedicated to monitoring and protecting them is the **Aruba Marine Mammal Foundation** (http://arubadolphins. wordpress.com).

Aruba has a notable population of undomesticated donkeys and goats, not native species but brought to the island and allowed to roam freely. It is not unusual in Arikok National Park and other undeveloped areas to come across a family of donkeys or goats living in the wild.

History

Perhaps the fact that the Spanish conquistadors did not find minerals spared Aruba from their attention. They labeled Aruba, Curaçao, and Bonaire "Islas Inutiles" (Useless Islands), and the records of European contact are vague. Alonso de Ojeda is credited as the first European to see Curaçao, and presumably also Aruba and Bonaire, around 1499, describing them as *"islas adyacentes a la costa firme"* (islands adjacent to the mainland).

Ojeda returned to Spain in 1501 to be appointed governor over the coastal regions of Coquibacoa and Guajira, with the "adjacent islands" under his administration. Aruba also earned the title "Isle of the Giants," ironic considering the unearthed remains of Aruba's indigenous people reveal they were quite short by modern standards.

Historians are unsure of the origins of the modern name Aruba; the discovery of gold in 1824 fuels speculation that it is an adaptation of the Spanish word for gold, *oro*. Some assert it means "Island of Shells." The lack of documented early history makes it difficult to ascertain.

EARLY HISTORY
Caquetio People and Spanish Rule

The fortunes of the ABC islands were always tied to their proximity to the mainland under the rule of the local indigenous caciques (chieftains) or the Spanish. The Paraguaná Peninsula, east of Lake Maracaibo, was a seat of power for the caciques, and during the 1500s the fate of Aruba was closely tied to what is now Venezuela. The Caquetio people, a small subgroup of the peaceful Arawak people, lived nomadic lives in small villages along the coast and in the caves at the island's south end, harvesting food from the sea. Over 300 of their pictographs and a few petroglyphs (rock carvings) can still be seen. The population was eventually enslaved by the Spanish, and by 1515 nearly all were transported to Hispaniola to work in the mines.

Juan Martínez de Ampiés was appointed administrator of the ABC islands in 1525. Under his relatively benevolent administration, an agreement was made with Manaure, Caquetio chieftain of Coro, which allowed the Caquetio people to return to the islands and awarded them protected status; in a sense, Aruba became a reservation. De Ampiés declared slave-hunting illegal on the ABC islands; his intentions, however, were far from altruistic. His treaty with Manaure meant that in exchange for protection, the chieftain was to enslave people from other tribes to be sent to the mines.

Eventually, to settle his enormous debt, Spain's Charles V awarded trade rights to the region to the Welsers, a German banking family. Their 30-year administration, ending in 1559, proved particularly harsh for the indigenous people of the peninsula, prompting them to flee to nearby islands. Beginning in 1529, Aruba was set up as a rancho, one great pasture for goats, pigs, cows, sheep, horses, and donkeys. Most indigenous people left on the island tended the herds. This has spurred speculation as to what the original flora of the island was like, compared to the cacti that dominate today.

Introduction of Christianity

During the mid-1500s, conversion of the Caquetio people to Roman Catholicism by missionaries began in earnest. In 2002 archaeologists unearthed remains in a communal gravesite that were buried in a mix of Caquetio and Christian styles. Grave artifacts confirm the graves date from the mid-16th century. The mix of cultural elements indicates the conversion process had not yet fully taken hold. Aruba's first Christian church, the Alto Vista Chapel, was built in 1750 on what had been sacred ground to the Caquetio people. Spanish priest Domingo Antonio Silvestre led the mission to convert the sparse indigenous population to Roman Catholicism.

The Dutch Conquer Aruba

Aruba's defining relationship to the Netherlands was established during the 80 Years' War for Independence between the Dutch Republic and Spain (1568-1648). The Dutch conquered Spanish and Portuguese colonies in the Caribbean, with direct Dutch trade beginning around 1593. Merchants in Holland were eager to establish a Dutch trading company similar to the highly profitable Dutch East India franchise. Dutch trade in the area was restricted by a treaty until 1621. When the treaty expired, a group called the Heren XIX (19 Gentlemen) actively sought private investors to open trade routes. Encouraged by the Dutch Republic, they founded the West Indian Company (WIC). Many were interested in this high-risk enterprise, which included substantial financial assistance from the government.

Dutch trade in the region was a way for the Dutch to interfere with their Spanish enemies, a desirable offshoot of any enterprise. They also sought to "free the natives" from religious

210

oppression, a pretext for the war. Holland defeated Spanish forces in Curaçao in 1634, taking possession of all three islands. Despite the involvement of the Dutch in the slave trade from Africa, the indigenous population of the ABC islands was treated the same as the colonists under Dutch law. It was prohibited to enslave indigenous people. Despite nominal equality under the law, documentation proves it was not so in practice. Discrimination made life harsh for the indigenous population.

The Napoleonic Wars resulted in Aruba falling under control of England 1799-1802, and again 1804-1816. Very little is written about this period, and the effect on island culture or tradition is undetectable. Aruba soon reverted to Dutch control.

Slavery

It was long believed that since Aruba did not have the extensive agriculture of other islands and was sparsely populated, enslaved African laborers were not imported by the colonists. Careful investigation by a new generation of historians has disproved this. Historical documents reveal that in the late 1700s and early 1800s, an estimated 10 percent of the population were enslaved people working as maids, nannies, cooks, gardeners, and handymen. It is believed they were better treated than field hands, and Aruba did not experience a slave revolt like Curaçao—home of the notorious slave markets—did in 1795. By declaration of the king of the Netherlands, all enslaved people were freed in 1863. Records show Aruba had almost 500 enslaved people living on the island at the time.

Settlement on Aruba

Actual settlement in Aruba was forbidden until at least 1750. The concern was about the security of the area and Curaçao, an important port and commercial center, if there was overdevelopment and population on its sister islands. Only a few personnel of the WIC, including the lieutenant governor, his entourage and enslaved workers, plus about 20 soldiers, occupied the island. Being virtually ignored by administrators

encouraged smuggling, as Aruba was a tax-free port, and it became a hideout for privateers and pirates, the Zeerovers.

Aruba's isolation ended when Mozes Maduro, a Sephardic Jew from Portugal, was granted land and became the first European settler. The WIC deployed a system of tenure, with land leased in exchange for various services or fees, with WIC continuing to own the land. From around 1780, European settlers began changing the makeup of the population. According to Jan Hartog's history of Aruba, a report from the early 1800s has population at 1,732. Of this, 564 were the indigenous inhabitants, 584 were freed "colored people," 37 free "black people," 133 "colored slaves," 203 "black slaves," and less than 100 European colonists. Accounts from the 1800s described the islands as unsuitable for agriculture and basically useless. Even then, however, it states that "Arubans displayed great pride and love for their island, despite the barren, infertile soil."

As the colonial influence grew, the indigenous population and culture declined. The colonial era is defined as 1724-1924, ending with the establishment of the oil refineries. The departure of Esso and the first closing of the San Nicolas refinery coincide with Aruba's independence from the five other islands of the Netherlands Antilles.

STATUS APARTE: ARUBAN INDEPENDENCE

Aruba's achievement of independence from the five other islands of the Netherlands Antilles, while remaining an autonomous entity within the Dutch kingdom, is inspiring in that it was achieved without bloodshed or revolt, setting an example for other islands. The Aruban model paved the way for Curaçao and Sint Maarten in 2010. The other islands of the Netherlands Antilles—Bonaire, Sint Eustatius, and Saba, now called the BES islands—chose to become Dutch municipalities, with status more closely related to Holland than before.

Monuments to "The Liberators"

GILBERTO FRANCOIS "BETICO" CROES

Gilberto Francois "Betico" Croes helped establish Aruban self-rule within the Dutch kingdom, called Status Aparte. Originally a member of the Arubaanse Volkspartij (AVP) political party, he founded the Moviemento di Electoral di Pueblo (MEP) in 1971. As party leader he became the principal negotiator of Aruba's independence from the Netherlands Antilles, earning him the informal title "El Liberatador." Plaza Gilberto Francois "Betico" Croes is one block inland from Plaza Las Americas, the huge rotunda marking the eastern end of Oranjestad. Directly behind the Cas di Cultura is a statue of Croes, holding the nation's flag high over his head. Croes relentlessly pursued Status Aparte and Aruban national pride. In 1976 he advocated the creation of an Aruban flag and national anthem.

Despite his pivotal role in the negotiations resulting in Aruban autonomy, Betico and his party did not earn the majority during Aruba's first independent elections, and he was denied the title of Aruba's first prime minister. The eve of Aruba's independence from the Netherlands Antilles, on December 31, 1985, saw instead the inauguration of Jan Hendrik "Henny" Eman as prime minister. On his way to the ceremony, Croes was gravely injured in a traffic accident. He was in a coma for 11 months and died on November 26, 1986. After dedicating the last 15 years of his life to Aruba's Status Aparte, he never witnessed the realization of that goal. His birthday, January 25, was declared a national holiday.

SIMÓN BOLÍVAR

The statue of Betico Croes gazes upon the most impressive monument in Oranjestad: Across the street from his plaza, Simón Bolívar majestically salutes his admirers from his rearing stallion in the Plaza Bolivariana. "The Great Liberator" of Latin America is immortalized in a striking sculpture donated by Aruba's expatriate population from Venezuela, Colombia, Peru, Bolivia, Ecuador, and Panama. Venezuelan and Colombian consuls welcome fellow compatriots and island dignitaries here to observe their independence days, July 5 and July 20.

July 5, 1811, was when Venezuelan independence was called for by a revolutionary congress; in 1813 Bolívar took up the cause instigated by Francisco de Miranda in 1810. Miranda died in exile in 1816. After leading the war for independence through many bloody battles, Bolívar finally ousted the Spanish colonists in the famous Battle of Carabobo on June 24, 1821. Bolívar dedicated his life to fighting for the independence of Colombia, Peru, Ecuador, and Panama. Eventually, he founded the nation of Bolivia. Bolívar died in Cartagena, Colombia, in 1830 after a life devoted to achieving freedom from Spanish control for most of Latin America. He was buried in Colombia, but in 1942, after years of petitioning, Venezuela finally received his remains with great pomp. He now lies in state at the National Pantheon in Caracas.

The AVP and PPA

The concept of Status Aparte starts with Jan Hendrik "Henny" Eman, founder of the AVP political party, who nurtured the idea of decentralization and organized a petition to separate from the Colony of Curaçao. Getting signatures was a monumental task in prewar Aruba, often carried out by donkey cart traveling from home to home. The 2,147 signatures confirmed that Eman had obtained majority support for this movement. Eman's son, Albert "Shon" Eman, presented

Aruba's formal proposal to Holland's Queen Juliana on March 18, 1948, during roundtable talks with Suriname and the other Dutch islands at The Hague. The crown "took it under advisement," and the talks resulted in the Constitution of the Netherlands Antilles, enacted in 1951. Eventually, Arubans sought more independence from the other islands, as it was frustrating to have Aruba's economy and development in the hands of Curaçao politicos.

Particularly dissatisfied by the events of

1951 was Juan "Juancho" Irausquin, also a member of the AVP. Irausquin went on to establish the Partido Patriotico Arubano (PPA) political party and built Aruba's first major resort in Palm Beach, the Aruba Caribbean. Henny Eman died in 1957, and his son "Shon" Eman took over leadership of the AVP. The PPA began to acquire influence until Irausquin's death in 1962. "Shon" Eman died in 1967, and the influence of both parties waned with the founding of MEP by Gilberto Francois "Betico" Croes.

Betico Croes and the Path to Independence

The ascendancy of Betico Croes in Aruba's political arena began in 1967. Originally part of the AVP, he founded his own political party, Moviemento di Electoral di Pueblo (MEP), while taking up the cause of autonomy. He is credited with the name of Status Aparte, making national identity and self-determination a priority. During the 1960s and 1970s, with the decline of the refinery, Aruba began to focus on tourism, soon to become the principal pillar of the economy. The desire to construct more hotels and acquire additional flights was hampered by control from Curaçao.

Aruba's acquisition of Status Aparte was not entirely without incident. Agustus Scur (Dark August) in 1977 was marked by civil disobedience and protest marches. Work stoppages by ELMAR, which regulates and distributes electricity, brought business to a standstill. Lights were out for several nights during the summer months as a show of solidarity for Holland to respond to the will of the people. Those who witnessed these events describe it as "exciting, adventurous times."

Betico Croes led the successful talks with Holland in 1981-1982 that resulted in Aruban self-rule under Dutch supervision for 10 years. It was enacted January 1, 1986, with Aruba to be fully independent from Holland in 1996. Surprisingly, elections in 1985 resulted in Henny Eman, son of Albert and leader of the AVP, becoming Aruba's first prime minister. During his administration, Aruba's independence from Holland was renegotiated. Aruba remains an independent part of the Dutch kingdom, and islanders retain Dutch citizenship and passports. Coalition administrations consisting largely of AVP party members dominated the government until 2001, when the MEP won a clear majority of seats in parliament. The MEP, headed by Nelson Oduber, held sway until the 2009 elections, with Oduber occupying the office of prime minister. Michel Godfried Eman, the younger brother of Henny, became prime minister when the AVP party won a record 11 parliamentary seats in 2009. They remained in power after winning 12 seats in 2013.

Contemporary Times

The 2017 elections resulted in the MEP winning nine seats and forming a coalition with two smaller parties, Pueblo Orguyoso Respeta (POR) and Red Democratico (RED). POR was founded in 2016 by former AVP party member Otmar Oduber, who resigned his position as Minister of Tourism, Transport and Labor to begin the new party in opposition of his former colleagues; POR means "can do" in Papiamento. The new party won two seats in parliament during the 2017 elections. The RED party, led by former priest Armando Lampe, ran on a platform of legalizing medical marijuana, to which AVP was opposed. They won one seat, occupied by Lampe, now Minister of Education, Science and Sustainable Development. The 2017 elections are notable for a historic event: the election of Aruba's first female prime minister, Evelyn Wever-Croes.

ECONOMIC DEVELOPMENT
Gold and Phosphate

Aruba's economic elite in colonial times established their fortunes shipping and importing goods. Others eked out a living farming, fishing, and breeding horses and livestock. Change came when 12-year-old Willem Rasmijn discovered gold in 1824 while herding his father's sheep along the north coast. A century earlier the crown had sent surveyors to search for minerals on all the ABC islands, but nothing of consequence was found. The gold at Rooi Fluit started a gold rush, increasing the population and facilitating the designation of Oranjestad as the capital of Aruba. Some argue Aruba's first capital was Savaneta, on the south side, as it was the headquarters of the Dutch marine commander and is where their camp is still located today.

Everyone who could afford a pickax went looking for gold, but regulations were in place to control its sale to the government at fixed prices. This encouraged attempts to smuggle the gold to more lucrative markets. Finally the government prohibited free prospecting, awarding mineral rights to the highest bidder. The initial rush died down after five years, but new veins found in 1854 revived interest in the economic development of the island. Gold mining rights passed from one company to another, ending with the Aruba Island Gold Mining Company of London.

The discovery of phosphate during the early 19th century provided another economic stimulus. Aruba Island Gold Mining Company of London demanded the harvest rights, claiming it already had exclusive rights for the extraction of minerals. The courts denied the claim, and rights went to the Aruba Island Phosphate Company. It did not fare very well, and eventually evolved into the Aruba Phosphaat Maatschappij. The establishment of gold and phosphate industries stimulated immigration and settlement in areas such as San Nicolas, where the phosphate works were established, previously virtually ignored. In 1833 Aruba had a population of 2,476, which increased to 8,065 by 1893. The collapse of the gold and phosphate industries reduced immigration to a trickle, with an increase of only 1,000 people by 1923. However, Aruba's fortunes changed radically with the inception of the Lago Oil Refinery.

Aloe Vera

The cultivation and processing of aloe also contributed to prosperity and an influx of population in the 1800s. Introduced to the island in 1840, aloe vera thrived in Aruba's arid climate to produce a high-quality extract, which was in great demand. The aloe industry became profitable in 1890 when Cornelius Eman founded Aruba Aloe Balm. At one point two-thirds of the island's agricultural production was aloe. Aruba became the world's number-one exporter of aloe products. Interest waned in the early 1950s,

aloe vera plantation

and Aruban production and export dropped dramatically. New methods of manufacture and a renewed interest in the natural healing properties of aloe prompted Louis Posner to acquire the factory and fields in Hato in 2000. He replaced the old plant with a modern facility that accepts visitors for tours and provides a history of the industry.

Refinery Era

No island historian would deny that the opening of the Lago Refinery was a defining moment in Aruba's history. It brought employment, prosperity, and technology, resulting in a noticeably higher standard of living and education than in other nations in the region.

ARUBA'S FORGOTTEN REFINERY

Two refineries opened at almost the same time: Lago was preceded by a collaboration of British Petroleum and Royal Dutch Shell. First to begin production was Arends Petroleum Maatschappij, better known by the English translation *arend*—Eagle Oil Company. It was located on the western outskirts of Oranjestad, where an exclusive gated community was constructed for management. Eagle Oil Company occupied a vast expanse of land, from what is now Bubali, where the company's medical facility was housed at Quinta Del Carmen, to the turbo rotunda now situated at the far west border of Oranjestad, and extended about a quarter mile inland. Within its borders were a social club, a tennis club, a private golf course, and private train lines to transport construction materials. A pier was built for the tankers where the Tamarijn Beach Resort now stands; Oranjestad Harbor had not yet been dredged and refitted for large ships. The pier was demolished in 1974. The end of World War II reduced demand for the Eagle Refinery products as it did not produce jet fuel, and it closed in 1954. Most employees were relocated to Shell's Curaçao refinery. The land was sold back to the Aruban government, with the housing purchased by islanders to become an upscale community. The beach areas were zoned for tourism.

THE SAN NICOLAS REFINERY

The discovery of oil in Lake Maracaibo, Venezuela, in 1918 heralded a change of lifestyle and standards for Arubans. The Venezuelan dictator Juan Vicente Gómez purposely generated great interest among U.S. and European oil companies to relieve the country's extreme debt, spurring development of the industry by granting concessions and selling oil cheaply. An impediment to development was that it was not possible to fill the large oceangoing tankers with crude at Maracaibo. Smaller ships called lake tankers could be used, and a more suitable transshipment station was sought, where the loads of the smaller tankers could be transferred to oceangoing vessels. In 1924, Captain Robert Rogers of the British Equatorial Oil Company began scouting a site for such a terminal. Originally he had Curaçao in mind, but the Dutch government was not cooperative about competition for its Shell refinery. Powerful U.S. oil companies wielded strong influence in the region at the time. They were reluctant to build refineries in Latin America because of the constant political turmoil. Aruba attracted their attention for its stable government and close proximity to the source. During negotiations, Gómez pressured the Dutch government to concede to the construction of a facility.

Although San Nicolas harbor would require dredging and preparation at great cost to accommodate the big ships, the existing infrastructure from the phosphate industry made it attractive to Rogers. A few savvy local businesspeople were also involved in convincing him of the wisdom of putting a facility on Aruba. They pointed out the advantage of Aruba being closer to Maracaibo than Curaçao, whose port was already occupied by the Shell refinery. Rogers was convinced that the money saved with the shorter distance for the lake tankers justified the expense of creating the deep-water harbor at San Nicolas. Within a year of the contracts being signed, British Equatorial Oil was purchased by Canadian Lago Oil & Transport.

What Is a Lagoite?

From 1925 until 1986, San Nicolas was home to what was the world's largest refinery during World War II, operating under Esso, then Exxon, as the Lago Refinery. Adjacent to the refinery was The Colony, an elite and fully equipped community for refinery executives with its own hospital, school, restaurant, bowling alley, and bachelors quarters as well as elegant homes for the married executives. Many executives lived on Aruba for decades; children were born and raised in this unique multicultural community, graduating from the school. They came to call themselves Lagoites. The refinery closed and the employees scattered, but some retained interest in Aruba and have nostalgia for growing up in such singular circumstances. Lagoites have recounted much of their history on www.lago-colony.com. Input and scrapbooks from the children of the 800 executives who resided in The Colony during its 60-year history have evolved into a tapestry of island life during its development. These privileged children lived with stunning seas, beautiful beaches, and a rich social life. It was a more innocent time, when the arrival of the first jet airplane on the island was a landmark event.

An anchor marks the entrance to the Lago Colony.

The original transshipment terminal idea became a full-blown refinery during the planning stages. Lago Oil & Petroleum Company began operations in January 1929.

The first refinery radically affected Aruba's economy. The refineries provided jobs locally and brought in workers from around the world, as operations required specific skills not found among islanders. Once construction was completed, the need for new skills and personnel brought 7,000 new residents from 56 countries. In 1945, only 32 percent of the employees at the refinery were native born. Eventually, the refinery was taken over by the Rockefellers' Standard Oil of New Jersey, which became Esso and Exxon. The refinery and adjacent residences continued to be referred to as Lago and Lago Colony—a name still used today.

The influx of immigrants and near doubling of Aruba's population prompted construction of one of the first modern large-capacity water desalination plants in the world, accompanied by a complex and efficient clean-water distribution system. Experts assert these advances in production and distribution as key to the higher standard of living enjoyed by Arubans over many other Caribbean nations.

WAR STORIES OF ARUBA'S FAMOUS SHIPWRECKS

The *Antilla* was a German cargo ship, one of three along with the *Heidelberg* and *Troja* moored in the neutral waters of the Aruban coast, but believed to be used to supply U-boats. Curaçao harbor had German ships hiding out from British destroyers before Holland was invaded in May of 1940, thus ending their policy of strict neutrality. German sailors were well aware that their homeland was going to invade Holland and were given orders to either make a run for it or scuttle their ships. The *Heidelberg* and *Troja* managed to escape Aruba's waters but were unable to break through the British blockade and scuttled far out at sea, while *Antilla* returned to anchor when it encountered a British destroyer just outside the three-mile limit. Seven German ships were captured in Curaçao. When Germany invaded, island authorities attempted to board the *Antilla* at night and claim her, but the captain refused to lower the gangway. The machine gun backup on shore was unable to sight the ship in the dead of night, so they came back at first light, which gave the ship's Captain Ferdinand Schmidt time to prepare.

Rather than turn over the ship, Schmidt ordered the sea cocks opened, which flooded the vessel. The crew set fires in many of the cabins. The *Antilla* eventually listed to port and sank in 18 meters (60 ft) of water off the coast of Malmok. It became a haven for sealife and a favorite dive and snorkel spot since it can easily be seen without scuba gear. Its large open compartments allow scuba divers to enter the wreck without risk. The captain and crew surrendered and were placed in a temporary internment camp on Bonaire, then transported to Jamaica in July 1940, to a POW camp maintained by the British for the rest of the war.

The *Pedernales* was a British-registered Italian oil tanker anchored off San Nicolas when it was torpedoed by a German submarine, *U-156*, along with the *Oranjestad,* on February 17, 1942. The *Oranjestad* sank in deep water off the south side, the first tanker sunk in the western hemisphere during the war. This was part of a concerted effort by Axis powers to cripple Allied fuel supply routes, deploying seven German and Italian submarines attacking tankers and refineries. The long-range gun on *U-156* fortunately malfunctioned, so it was unable to damage the Eagle refinery. The same night, two other Lago tankers, the *San Nicolas* and the *Tia Juana,* were torpedoed 40 kilometers (25 mi) southwest of Punta Macolla in the Gulf of Venezuela by *U-502*. Four days later, a torpedo ended up on Eagle Beach, an attempt to blow up the refinery, and a team of four Dutch soldiers died trying to defuse it. The final death toll of crewmembers on tankers was 47. This event prompted a greater U.S. military presence on Aruba for the remainder of the war.

The *Pedernales* was towed to dry dock, where the bow and aft sections were removed and transported to a U.S. shipyard, joined with a new midsection, and put back to use; it was finally retired in 1959. What remained of the wreck offshore was used by troops stationed on Aruba for target practice. Some of the giant unexploded ordnance can still be seen underwater. Because of Aruba's strategic position in the war effort, it was officially under British protection for two years. Troops from Britain and the United States were stationed on the island to protect the refinery from the Germans, their submarines continually attempting to sink tankers and destroy the refineries.

The end of World War II signaled the gradual decline of the refinery's place in the island's economy. Automation resulted in a drastic reduction in personnel. In the final decades, only 700 employees staffed the refinery. Peripheral companies cropped up around San Nicolas to perform repairs and maintenance. Farsighted island leaders, entrepreneurs, and legislators had already turned their attention to Status Aparte and tourism as priorities for Aruba to advance and prosper.

TOURISM TAKES OVER

Simultaneous with the realization of Status Aparte came the closing of Lago Refinery, seemingly abandoned overnight. The 60-year contracts for crude oil from Venezuela had expired, and Venezuela had constructed numerous refineries; there was no need to transport oil to an outside facility. The refinery was aging and the cost of improvements prohibitive. By this time, tourism had a foothold on Aruba, with several large resorts in Palm Beach and time-shares proliferating like bunnies. The first major resort, the Aruba Caribbean, now the Hilton Aruba Caribbean, opened in 1959. It was built by Juancho Irausquin, a force in the development of Aruba's tourism industry. Prior to that, Chaven Neme, who built the first tourist hotel in Oranjestad, had opened the tiny Basi Ruti Resort in Palm Beach—its first—where the Playa Linda Resort was erected in 1985.

By 1980, large resorts had altered the Palm Beach coastline. Visionary developers like Ike Cohen, a Holocaust survivor from Holland, and Wally Wiggins, a New York lawyer, founded the Manchebo Beach Resort and Divi Hotel, respectively. These established the low-rise concept at Manchebo Beach. In the late 1970s, Sun Development opened the first time-share on Aruba in that area, heralding a highly successful industry catering to annual returnees. Statistics have shown time-share owners account for 40 percent of Aruba's visitors.

Island leaders saw tourism as Aruba's future and offered attractive conditions to developers. These are criticized now, as guarantees signed by the government cost millions in failed plans. Huge projects were begun at the southern and northern ends of Palm Beach at the same time; each experienced labor and materials shortages. Numerous delays, rather symptomatic of the region, resulted in three unfinished projects declaring bankruptcy. Despite this, Aruba's reliable climate, political stability, and reputation for cooperative and hospitable people attracted developers and the attention of hospitality franchises. The Marriott chain was rewarded for acquiring and completing one failed project by opening the most successful resort in its stable. The chain then claimed another failed project, which became the Marriott Ocean Club, and constructed the Surf Club, both time-share operations. A Ritz-Carlton opened on the north side of the Marriott in 2014.

Ever practical, Cohen and Wiggins also realized that the numerous small resorts operating on shoestring budgets could not afford to market individually. They formed a cooperative that became the Aruba Hotel and Tourism Association (AHATA), a successful public-private collaboration working with Aruba's official tourism marketing entity, the Aruba Tourism Authority (ATA). The combined efforts provided the marketing brain trust that saw the fledgling industry become the main pillar of the island economy it is today.

THE REFINERY IN THE 21ST CENTURY

There is a footnote to the refinery's role in Aruba's economic well-being. A number of businesses came and went since the departure of Exxon, interspersed with periods when the refinery sat idle. Valero Corporation of Texas took over the facility in 2004 and invested hundreds of millions of dollars in modernizing it, but circumstances resulted in stoppage of production in 2009. This was two months prior to a crucial national election that resulted in a complete change of Aruba's political landscape. All employees were kept on salary, and not long after, Valero and the new government announced the reopening of the refinery, which recommenced operations in 2011. The rise of crude oil prices precipitated the announcement of a number of closings of Valero refineries, Aruba included, in 2012. Employees were kept on salary while a solution was sought. That year Valero announced the refinery would shut down entirely and serve as a transshipment station, downsizing the workforce by 90 percent by 2014. The government signed a 25-year contract with CITGO, the U.S. subsidiary of Venezuela's PDVSA, in 2016. CITGO committed to investing $685 million in refitting the refinery, but progress on the antiquated facility remains at a standstill.

Government and Economy

GOVERNMENT

Parliament and Ministries

Aruba is an autonomously ruled entity within the Dutch kingdom. Arubans are Dutch citizens and carry Dutch passports. The government is a 21-seat Parliament with elections every four years, one year after the U.S. presidential elections. There are a president and vice president of Parliament, positions occupied by elected officials. For a political party to be in power, it must capture an 11-seat majority or form a coalition with other parties to hold a majority. The individual heading the dominant party of the coalition assumes the title of prime minister and appoints a cabinet of ministers. The various ministries administer island operations, headed by the ministers appointed from among those elected to Parliament. Aruba also has ministers-plenipotentiary to Holland and the United States, appointed positions that serve as ambassadors to these countries. The elected officials of the cabinet each have multiple interrelated ministries under their jurisdiction.

Dutch Representation

The island maintains strong ties with Holland. Despite its distinctly Caribbean-Latin culture, the official language of schools, contracts, legislation, and official notifications is Dutch. The Dutch monarch's official representative on Aruba is the governor, an appointed position lasting six years. They may serve up to two terms. Governor Alfonso Boekhoudt took office in 2017. The governor ratifies national ordinances and resolutions, awards decorations in the name of the monarchy, signs off on passports and visas, and considers extradition requests. His presence is required at all official functions related to Holland, and he swears in ministers, members of the Common Court of Justice, the public prosecutor, the Advisory Council, the General Audit Office, and the Central Bank of Aruba. From

the governor's official website (www.kabga.aw.en): "The Governor is inviolable, immune, and carries out his powers as a national organ under the responsibility of the Ministers of Aruba, who, in their turn, are accountable to the Parliament of Aruba." Until she abdicated in 2013, Queen Beatrix was Aruba's monarch. Her eldest son, King Willem-Alexander, is the first male monarch since 1890.

The Judiciary, Foreign Affairs, and Defense

Holland still has jurisdiction over the judiciary, partly to maintain impartiality. Judges and prosecutors are appointed within the Dutch system. Foreign affairs fall under Dutch control, and Aruba is bound by Dutch treaties. Aruban administrators have the power to negotiate agreements for the island that don't directly affect Holland. Aruba's national protection is also Holland's responsibility, and a division of the Royal Dutch Marines is stationed at the camp in Savaneta. Aruba has a subordinate branch of service at the camp, the ArubaMil.

Dutch Immigration to Aruba

For decades there were rules against unfettered Dutch immigration to the island, but these have been eased in recent years. This had to do with old Dutch laws preventing miscreants from escaping to the colonies after committing crimes or accumulating debt in Holland. Government policy is that jobs should first go to qualified Arubans before someone is brought from outside to fill the position. Individuals who want to retire on the island must be able to prove they are financially independent and don't need to work.

ECONOMY

Aruba's economy is a free-enterprise system with entrepreneurship and fair trade heavily encouraged. Tourism is the primary pillar of the economy, accounting for 86.5 percent of the island's GDP and 87 percent of jobs. Although tourism can be volatile in the face of global events, aside from small setbacks from the world financial crash of 2008 and the 9/11 attacks, Aruba's tourism has grown steadily since it achieved Status Aparte. In December 2012 the Reina Beatrix International Airport welcomed its millionth paying passenger, and cruise ship tourism broke passenger records that year. Statistics show Aruba welcomes over 1.5 million visitors annually.

Aruba's government is mindful that dependence on tourism alone is not in the best interest of the economy and seeks methods to diversify. In 2012 Repsol, a Spanish energy development conglomerate, was allowed to start seismic exploration for natural gas in Aruban waters north of the island. In 2013 Aruba hosted an international "Europe Meets the Americas" Conference in a bid to become a liaison and business hub between the European Union and the Latin America-Caribbean region.

Aruba is highly dependent on imported goods. Agriculture is encouraged, and the Santa Rosa Center of Agriculture and Animal Husbandry and Fisheries has begun a program instructing islanders on how to grow and harvest their own food. A small commercial agricultural industry has been established using unique methods of desert reclamation and aquaculture. Some small manufacturing exists on the island, such as Office Systems, the local and regional manufacturer and distributor for Dauphin, a famed European brand of office furniture. Freezone Aruba has proved innovative in providing product storage and services, increasing Aruba's export statistics.

Generally, the standard of living is high for the region, with salaries averaging around $22,000 annually; retirement pensions are among the highest in the Caribbean. The cost of consumer goods is relatively high due to import duties and shipping costs. Aruba has a progressive tax system and is one of the most highly taxed nations in the world.

People and Culture

The description "One Happy Island" is apt for this small island where the inhabitants understand the need to get along. The past and its legacy are treasured, while sustainability is a paramount concern. Arubans have enormous pride in their island and a strong sense of community. The most beloved time of year is Carnival, when weeks of revelry consume the island's attention. Festivities are frequent and happen for the simplest of reasons.

Arubans are also proactive, with strong community concerns. Service organizations such as Rotary, Kiwanis, Women's Club, Lion's Club, and Quota, among others, play a strong role in community events. Visiting members of organizations like Rotary are welcome to sit in on meetings. Aruba has over 1,000 registered foundations, many recently established to recruit, organize, and educate.

POPULATION

In the 2010 UNESCO worldwide census, the population was 106,000 officially registered residents, of which over 35 percent were immigrants. Many have been nationalized and received Dutch passports. According to the statistics bureau, there are 90 distinct ethnic or national groups harmoniously inhabiting this little rock, including substantial East Indian, Filipino, and Chinese populations who have integrated while maintaining aspects of their native cultures. Each group has a community organization to continue traditions among generations born on the island, including the Aruba Indian Association (IAA), United Filipino Community of Aruba (UFILCOA), and the Chinese Center in Bubali, where classes are taught in Chinese language and culture. Important celebrations of these groups have been integrated into Aruban life. IAA organizes a community event for Diwali, and the honorary consul of the Philippines and UFILCOA conduct a protocol event at Wilhelmina Park for Filipino Independence Day. Aruba's prime minister and important dignitaries usually attend. The Lion Dance, performed by members of the Chinese community, is a welcome part of many island celebrations.

During a visit by the royal family in October 2011, Queen Beatrix was accompanied by then-Crown Prince Willem-Alexander and Crown Princess Maxima, who became king and queen in 2013. They were treated to the first official event at Aruba's Plaza Turismo in Oranjestad, comprising authentic performances by a dozen of Aruba's various ethnic and national groups, with offerings of native food and beverages. Informative displays regarding each group's culture and history were part of the event. It was a vibrant demonstration of pride in the multicultural nature of island society. Aside from these groups, there were authentic cultural programs by expatriates from Portugal, the Dominican Republic, Venezuela, and Colombia.

RELIGION

The Spanish influence is evident, with the majority of islanders being Roman Catholic, and each district has a large Roman Catholic church. The Dutch Protestant Church is well established, with a landmark building in Oranjestad. There is also a synagogue, Temple Beth Israel, erected in 1962. The Jewish cemetery in Oranjestad has historic headstones dating back centuries. The present congregation is perhaps 35 families. Every year, the congregation of Temple Beth Israel, as well as the Chabad Aruba community center, conduct First Seders for Passover. Jewish vacationers are welcome and regularly participate. Chabad Aruba is a particularly young, vibrant group, frequently staging exciting events for local and vacationing Jewish people on important holidays. San Nicolas has a large Anglican church, and there are a few Methodist and Baptist churches on the island. Evangelical Christianity has had a strong influence on the island over the past 20 years, and Evangelical ministries have cropped up in all sorts of venues, with too many storefront churches to count.

Aruba's university is located in a former Jesuit monastery.

EDUCATION

Attending school is compulsory for children ages 5-15. Elementary schools comprise kindergarten through sixth grade. English and Spanish are in the curriculum from fifth grade. After sixth grade, students are streamed into academic or vocational schools based on an IQ test, their grades, and observances by teachers and principals. Island children begin learning Dutch in kindergarten. Many island schools are under the authority of a Roman Catholic school association, SKOA, or are Protestant-affiliated. Aruba has two private schools without religious affiliation, the Skagel, with instruction only in Dutch, and the International School of Aruba (ISA), in English but with a distinctly multicultural flavor, using Montessori methods in the younger grades and providing education from kindergarten to the equivalent of 12th grade.

Exceptional students may qualify for Brugclasse (Bridge Class), an introductory year testing their performance and ability to progress to higher levels of learning. Diplomas are called degrees. Attaining a HAVO degree is the equivalent of a U.S. high school diploma, thus qualifying for university. The VWO program is accelerated learning for the gifted and determined. It is very academically demanding, and VWO students in their freshman year at U.S. universities report they are already at a sophomore level. Students graduating from elementary school who are not yet ready for an accelerated program are directed toward MAVO, a four-year school. Graduates can later acquire their HAVO or VWO degrees. They may also elect to take professional training courses at EPI, Educativo Professional Intermedio, four faculties that award an associate degree in technology, business administration, social work, or tourism and hospitality management. The faculty of EPI includes the renowned Aruba Culinary School, where graduates receive certification from the American Culinary Federation. This school accepts students from around the world. EPI also receives students from Aruba's Educativo Basico Professional (EPB) who have gone through four years or more of dedicated vocational training. EPB classes are divided into three levels of academic accomplishment, with only the top level qualified to go on to EPI. Students can work their way up the ladder from the lowest to highest level, but that is rare. After completing four years of the lower levels of EPB, graduates may decide to join the workforce in apprentice positions in mechanics, electrical repair, woodworking, or as beauticians and caregivers. EPB also has a highly acclaimed school of culinary training where students continue to the EPI culinary school to become certified chefs. The HORECA (HOtel, REstaurant, CAfé) program also trains youngsters for the tourism and food industry as waitstaff, bartenders, and managers.

Aruba has one institution of higher learning, the University of Aruba. Fields of study include hospitality and tourism management, accounting, financing and marketing, arts and sciences, and law. Graduates earn a bachelor's degree. The **University of Aruba** (www.ua.aw) accepts students from abroad, and tuition is considerably less than at U.S. schools. Most Arubans travel abroad for advanced degrees, primarily to Holland, the United States, or Latin America.

NOTABLE ARUBANS

Aruba has heroes and heroines who have contributed to the island's advancement in education, sports, culture, and technology. Some who have received worldwide recognition for their achievements.

Juan Chabaya "Padu" Lampe

Best known for his musical compositions, Juan Chabaya "Padu" Lampe was the coauthor with Rufo Wever of Aruba's national anthem, "Aruba Dushi Tera." He is truly a Renaissance man: a painter, musician, composer, and author. Padu made his living at ALM airlines and contributed to the island's culture out of love of the arts. His work required that he travel extensively, and he was an unofficial

Why *Himno y Bandera*?

Aruba's **National Day** is March 18, often referred to as *Himno y Bandera*—**Anthem and Flag Day,** a celebration of the establishment of Aruba's self-identity, 10 years before autonomy was achieved, marking the day Aruba's official flag and national anthem were introduced. An open contest was held to design the nation's flag, and it got more than 700 entries. The desired concept was to represent the island culturally and physically and be easily recognized from a distance. Like many flags, stripes and stars were included, and many Arubans felt the sun was important to Aruba's lifestyle. The color most commonly suggested was blue, representing the sky and the sea. Other popular colors were yellow for sunlight, white for Aruba's beaches, and red for sunsets, the island's clay soil, progress, or the blood of Arubans, though none was actually shed in attaining autonomy. A bold and unique four-pointed star, something unheard of for flags, was settled on as the primary symbol. The four points represent Aruba's four main languages: Papiamento, English, Dutch, and Spanish. The yellow stripes, sometimes attributed to the discovery of gold that initiated island posterity, symbolizes Aruba's movement to the future.

"Aruba Dushi Tera" ("Sweet Land Aruba") was a popular and patriotic song composed by Juan Chabaya "Padu" Lampe and Rufo Wever 20 years earlier. It was immediately considered for the national anthem. A few couplets were added to the end by the founder of the Instituto di Cultura, composer and musician Lio Booi, before it was first performed as Aruba's national song, accompanying the raising of the flag.

ambassador of Aruba, performing to appreciative audiences and establishing goodwill. His enormous diverse body of work and influence on the island earned him the popular title "Father of Culture."

Never charging for musical performances, his presence elevated any event. Padu gave many concerts in Venezuela, where he finally began recording LPs in the 1960s. Some won Golden Piano awards, the equivalent of a Grammy. "Padu Del Caribe" was his recording name, and he still has a loyal following in the region. Born in 1920, he earned his nickname in honor of his *padu,* his grandfather and namesake, who had died the week he was born. His mother called him Padushi (Sweet Little Grandfather); the nickname stuck and was later shortened to Padu. He began his love affair with the arts as a painter. While he was just a teenager, one of his works was selected to be shown at the 1939 World's Fair in New York as an example of Caribbean art. He authored metaphysical treatises in English titled "The 3rd Element" and "Harmoniology—The Art and Science of Living in Harmony with the Universal Laws." They were published in 1960 and 1978, respectively.

"Sir" Dr. Edward Cheung

On the Sasaki Highway heading to Palm Beach, you may spot the Dr. Edward Cheung Center for Innovation. When he was still a relatively young man, he actually sent Aruba into space. Born and raised on Aruba by immigrant parents, Cheung obtained his PhD in electrical engineering, specializing in robotics, from Yale University, with a scholarship from Phillips and NASA. He joined NASA, and in 1995 was assigned to the Hubble Space Telescope maintenance project. His work with NASA electrified his homeland when Hubble experienced a failure in the NICMOS cooling system that threatened to send it crashing to earth. When it became clear that a substitute system was problematic, Cheung and his team had three months to devise a solution. It was named the ASCS/NCS Relay Unit Breaker Assembly, or ARUBA box. Its installation during a 2002 mission saved the Hubble. In photos taken during space missions, it can be seen attached to the outside of the Hubble, with the word *ARUBA* clearly visible.

Cheung's was one of the voices heard during broadcasts of the final mission to the telescope, when they installed his invention, the

Wide Field Camera III. This revolutionary equipment is delivering images of space never possible before. Cheung was also part of the team present for the last crewed NASA space mission, working the "Tweet Tent" at Kennedy Space Center during the blastoff. Cheung now heads a new division at Goddard Space Center in Maryland, devising robotic means of in-space repair of satellites. The new technology extends their useful life and saves tens of millions of dollars in prematurely replacing equipment.

During his annual visits to his family in Aruba, Cheung has made it a regular practice to give free lectures about space and the Hubble. It is his stated goal to inspire young Arubans to consider careers in science and to continue their education to the highest levels. In 2010, NASA reported that its principal engineer was dubbed a Knight in the Order of the Netherlands Lion. This is the highest honor the monarchy bestows on a civilian subject, and it is a rare occurrence. His colleagues at NASA affectionately refer to him as "Sir Ed," though the title "Sir" is not part of being a knight in the Dutch system.

Sarah-Quita Offringa

An exemplary role model for island youth

is Sarah-Quita Offringa, the reigning Professional Windsurfing Association's (PWA) Women's Freestyle Windsurfing World Champion since 2008. At the time she won her first world championship title, she had just turned 17, setting a world record for the youngest champion ever. Sarah-Quita, "the girl with big hair," turned the windsurfing world around when she burst onto the professional scene, going pro at age 12. At 15 she won her first gold medal, also setting a new PWA record for the youngest to do so.

Since claiming the Freestyle title, she has never lost a competition heat or elimination round. In 2011 she was crowned Women's World Champion in Slalom. For the remarkable achievement of earning two world champion titles in a single year, she was selected as a contender for the ISAF Rolex World Sailor of the Year Award. Since then she has held both titles four times. She has also taken a number of championship titles in the Waves competition category, proving herself a unique triple threat in the windsurfing world.

Although the life of a sports champion offers fame and travel, Sarah-Quita is aware of her position as a role model for young Arubans. She put her studies first, and in 2014 obtained her bachelor's degree in science

Sarah-Quita Offringa

and innovation at the University of Utrecht, Holland. Before going for her master's, she decided to show the windsurfing world her true capabilities, successfully maintaining her status as Freestyle champion in 2014 and 2015, winning the Slalom title in 2015 for the second time, and placing third worldwide in wave sailing. Her ultimate goal is to be the first triple crown winner for the sport's three major international competitions. Sarah-Quita is such an important figure in the sport that her 2015 windsurfing pilgrimage around the world was made into a documentary by French filmmaker Julian Robinet, titled *Cabeibusha*, which means "bushy hair" in Papiamento, after her iconic profile.

Xander Bogaerts

Probably Aruba's best-known international celebrity at the moment is Xander Bogaerts, shortstop for professional baseball's Boston Red Sox. He rocketed to fame in 2013, when he came up from the minors, and two months later adorned the cover of *Boston Magazine* after the team won the World Series. The victory was all the sweeter as the team had come in dead last the year before. Arubans like to think it was all because of Xander. He was born on Aruba in 1992, making him one of the youngest players ever to compete in a World Series.

Two years prior to his participation in the World Series, Xander and his Aruban compatriot, Shawn Zarraga, were part of the Dutch team that won the Baseball World Cup. This was the first European victory since 1938, as Cuba dominated the competition for decades. Following this victory, Xander and Shawn received decorations from the Dutch Crown as knights in the Order of Oranje-Nassau.

Xander has also received a star on the Aruban Walk of Fame, which adorns a Palm Beach sidewalk. In 2016 he was selected to play in the MLB All-Star Game as a shortstop, and that year he was awarded the American League's shortstop Silver Slugger Award for the second year in a row. He has also lent his name and status to the Xander Bogaerts Dare to Dream Foundation to inspire island youngsters to healthier pastimes, particularly Little League, providing funding and assistance to participate.

Boston reprised their World Series win in 2018, again catapulting Xander into the headlines. He was the only player on the team on the roster for both the 2013 and 2018 wins. He was named the American League Player of the Week for July 2-8, 2018, hit three grand slam home runs in April, and hit another in July. Xander was again welcomed home a hero when he returned to the island.

THE ARTS
Regional Music and Traditions

During national holidays, Carnival, and the end of the year celebrations, Arubans put their idiosyncratic cultural traditions on display. European and regional influences on what is considered authentically Aruban can be observed in the festive music and dance performances. Ties to **Holland and Dutch traditions** are evident in the celebration of **King's Day** and at the end of the year when **Sinterklaas** comes to visit. Families look forward to *oliebollen,* a typically Dutch holiday treat, and fireworks on **New Year's Eve.** Christmas means the manifestation of *gaita* singing groups who perform at dozens of public events. *Gaita* originates from Maracaibo in Venezuela and has very lively upbeat music. *Gaita* groups consist of 8-12 female singers accompanied by native instruments such as a *cuarto* (a small guitar) and *tambora* (goat-skin drums).

The end of the year is also the time for **Dande,** traditionally performed by wandering minstrels. Dande has a distinctive repetitive chorus with lyrics that change to personalize the song to each household visited. Dande minstrels come with hat in hand for each family member to ritualistically drop in a little *propina* for luck. Just before the end of the year is the annual Dande competition to crown a new king or queen. It starts in the early evening, and there are so many bands, and the songs are so long (with each one sounding *exactly* the same, except for slight variations in lyrics), that it doesn't end until dawn. Those who make it through this marathon musical event are truly devoted to the art form.

Carnival time produces three important musical competitions: the Roadmarch (Soca) Contest, the Calypso (Caiso) Contest, and the crowning of a Tumba king or queen. These entail several nights of concert competitions, as winners are declared in three age groups: child, youth, and adult. Costumes are an important part of the event, as well as the quality of performance and the suitability of the piece, which must be an original composition. The winning song of the adult Roadmarch contest will be the official theme for that year's Carnival season, performed endlessly during parades and events. This is selected by judges as the best piece to inspire participants and spectators to dance along. It is usually a classic example of Afro-Caribbean polyphonic music, making it impossible to resist shaking the hips and guaranteed to start shoulders twitching. A second song, likely more popular with the public than the judges, is heard just as frequently. Dubbed the "Road Jam," this is an unofficial winner, as no one ever completely agrees with the judges' decision.

Tumba is the island's music most steeped in the roots of slavery and African culture, brought to Aruba and Curaçao in the 1700s. It has evolved to incorporate more Latin harmonics in recent times. **Calypso** is a traditional regional music originating from Trinidad and Tobago. Songs are not only judged for their musicality but also for their lyrics and pithy social commentary. They are usually quite humorous and topical, wry observances of human behavior based on events of the previous year.

Beyond these, islanders consider the pieces derived from more **classic European music** such as waltzes, *danzas,* and mazurkas to be typical of their culture. Most folkloric dance is performed to such pieces, usually composed by well-respected artists such as Juan Chabaya "Padu" Lampe and Rufo Wever (coauthors of Aruba's national anthem, an excellent example), and Lio Booi, founder of the Aruba Institute of Culture, who also contributed to the national song. **Steelpan** is another musical art form integrated into island culture, which arrived with the great migration prompted by the opening of the refinery. The Connor family is particularly noted for this, and Lee and Nico Connor carry on a tradition of their father. Steelpan music is regularly

Aruba's Carnival

heard at events, and there are concerts dedicated to it at least once a year. It is an integral part of the Bon Bini Festival.

Aruba has been described as "an island of dancers." Every weekend, several bands perform around the island, often giving free concerts. At nearly any party or gala, the dance floor will be full, particularly when the band plays merengue. Islanders dance with complete abandon during Carnival and other events.

Performing Arts

Aruba has several centers for performing arts and concerts as well as a number of galleries. **Cas di Cultura** (Vondellaan 2, 297/582-1010, www.casdicultura.aw), "House of Culture," is where most dance recitals and classic concerts are staged. On the large traffic circle at the east end of Oranjestad, it has been Aruba's theatrical and cultural center since 1958, and is booked nearly every weekend for a recital or play. It also has an exhibition room for art and exhibitions. The main auditorium seats over 400.

Holiday time on Aruba can include the seasonal favorite *The Nutcracker,* staged and choreographed by former star of the Bolshoi and New York Ballet companies Leonid Kozlov (www.dancearuba.com and www. leonidkozlov.com). Now a resident of Aruba, he has brought Tchaikovsky's fairy-tale classic to the island as a new holiday tradition. Performances run twice over the holiday week at the Cas di Cultura.

Private studios offer dance lessons and conduct recitals annually. Visual artists are regularly featured in shows and in a few galleries. The Cas di Cultura is home to the Rufo Wever School of Music, occupying one side of the building, and the Da Vinci Academy, dedicated to classical piano, on the other. Aruba is also home to several highly respected jazz musicians, many of whom teach at the Rufo Wever School. They are producing a new generation of musicians who are enthusiastic about interpretive music. Internationally known performers are brought in annually for the weeklong Aruba International Piano Festival in June and the Caribbean Sea Jazz Festival over Columbus Day weekend in mid-October. These are just two international events; at least once a month some international talent is imported to perform.

It is perhaps in the continuing tradition of original music created for Carnival where what can truly be called Aruban originates. Many of these fine self-trained musicians and composers are producing the distinctive, complex, polyphonic works that are close to the hearts of islanders.

Literary and Visual Arts

UNOCA (Stadionweg 21, 297/583-5681, www. unocaruba.org, 8:30am-noon and 1:30pm-5pm Mon.-Fri.) is a foundation dedicated to the promotion and development of literary, visual, and performing arts. It funds publication of books, both poetry and prose, usually in Papiamento; dance recitals; art expositions; and other projects that elevate the cultural awareness of the community. The offices double as a permanent exhibit hall for local artwork, and it also sells many of the publications it has helped publish.

There is an active long-established community producing work in several media. A number of foundations are dedicated to promoting education and interest among youth. Traditional painters and primitive style held sway for years, and their work is revered. Current schools of art, however, lean toward the abstract, the impressionistic, and particularly the avant-garde. Island hotels and restaurants support this community by displaying works of art on their premises, where they are offered for sale.

Essentials

Transportation

Transportation 227
Visas and Officialdom . . 235
Conduct and Customs . 238
Health and Safety 238
Travel Tips 241
Information and
    Services 245

GETTING THERE
Air
Reina Beatrix International Airport (AUA, Reina Beatrix Airport z/n, 297/524-2424, www.airportaruba.com) is the only airport on Aruba for commercial or private flights. Not typical of island facilities, visitors are pleasantly surprised by the large, comfortable terminal with air-conditioning and art. The arrivals area offers some duty-free shops for liquor and cigarettes before you officially step onto Aruban soil. Import limits are still two cartons of cigarettes and two liters of

liquor for personal use. There's a diverse shopping and restaurant arcade for departing passengers, and a graceful sculpture garden bids visitors farewell at departure control.

A separate terminal for private planes is at the south end of the airport, staffed by separate immigration and customs officials. It is modern and comfortable with several amenities.

COMMERCIAL AIRLINES

Two regional carriers, the **Aruban Insel Air Aruba** (Reina Beatrix International Airport, 855/493-6004, 297/582-1200, www.fly-inselair.com) and **Aruba Airlines** (Cumena 69, 297/583-8300, www.arubaairlines.com), are authorized to fly direct to Aruba from the United States, serving cities such as Ft. Lauderdale and Orlando. Insel now provides daily round-trip service to Miami. **Surinam Airways** (Rockefellerstraat 3, 297/582-7896, www.flyslm.com) also flies direct between Miami and Aruba, with connections across the United States and Canada.

On weekends there are additional flights to Aruba by these carriers and charter services from U.S. cities and Toronto. Weekend arrivals sometimes involve waiting on the tarmac for other flights to deplane passengers, especially at the peak mid-afternoon arrival time. All ticket offices for U.S. and Canadian airlines are in Reina Beatrix International Airport. The following airlines fly to Aruba daily:

- Air Canada: U.S./Canada 888/247-2262, www.aircanada.com

- American: U.S./Canada 800/433-7300, Aruba 297/582-2700, www.aa.com

- Copa (via Panama City): U.S./Canada 800/359-2672, Aruba 297/525-2672, www.copair.com

- Delta: U.S./Canada 800/455-2720, Aruba 297/588-5623, www.delta.com

- JetBlue: U.S./Canada 800/538-2583, Aruba 297/588-5977, www.jetblue.com

- Southwest: U.S./Canada 800/435-9792, www.southwest.com

- United: U.S./Canada 800/864-8331, Aruba 297/582-9592, www.united.com

For current regularly scheduled flights, check the airport's website (www.airportaruba.com). With its greater distance from North America, one might expect higher airfares to Aruba than other Caribbean destinations, but the difference is minimal, particularly off-season. **American Airlines,** one of the first with regular service to Aruba in the 1960s, has two nonstop flights from Miami, with connecting flights from all over the United States. A weekend flight from Miami can be as low as $227 economy and $526 business class off-season. High-season tickets can go for as little as $279 in bare-bones economy on weekends. Peak holiday rates, such as Christmas, are $1,000 or more in economy. American also has daily nonstop flights from Dallas and Chicago. Aruba's most frequent carrier is now **JetBlue,** with daily nonstop flights from New York and Boston for as little as $506 weekdays during high season and $614 round-trip from Boston, including taxes and fees.

AIRPORT TRANSPORTATION

Major resorts do not provide airport shuttles, but there are car rental agencies across from the arrivals exit, and taxis line up in the lane nearest the terminals; fares range $18-35 one-way, depending on how far your destination is. Taxis are required to display the chart of flat rates in the vehicle.

Arubus (Weststraat 13, 297/588-0617, www.arubus.com, $2.50) has a bus stop across the main highway opposite the airport, which offers a low-cost option to Oranjestad and the principal resort areas of Manchebo, Eagle, and Palm Beach.

Previous: Aruba's bike-sharing program.

Sea

CRUISE SHIPS

Cruising high season usually begins in November, with as many as five megaships arriving at the central Oranjestad Harbor two or three days a week. Arrivals slow in April. Immigration procedures for arriving passengers are handled by cruise officials on the ship, so passengers can just disembark and walk into town. Arriving by sea is under the administration of the **Aruba Ports Authority** (L. G. Smith Blvd. 23, 297/582-6633, control tower direct 297/582-1740, www.arubaports.com, 24 hours daily). The current schedule of ships set to call at Aruba, with dates and times, can be found on the website, usually no more than one season in advance. Cruise ship schedules change from one year to the next; check the Ports Authority website to find trips that interest you. A local agent for cruise companies stopping in Aruba is **S. E. L. Maduro & Sons** (Rockefellerstraat 1, 297/528-2343, 8am-noon and 1pm-5pm Mon.-Fri.), which can book passage with Aruba as the embarkation point.

Cruise lines with Aruba on their itineraries include **Royal Caribbean** (www.royalcaribbean.com), with one-week tours from Puerto Rico. **Holland American Line** (www.hollandamerica.com) runs 2-4-week excursions from Ft. Lauderdale and San Diego. **Carnival** (www.carnival.com) departs from Ft. Lauderdale and Puerto Rico regularly. **Princess Cruises** (www.princess.com) has 10-day charters departing from New York City and one-week cruises from Ft. Lauderdale. **Disney Cruises** (http://disneycruise.disney.go.com) has a 10-day excursion from Port Canaveral.

PRIVATE YACHTS

Oranjestad Harbor is the best clearing point for hassle-free immigrations and customs for private yachts. The northwest entrance to Oranjestad Harbor is 12° 31' 070° 04' W, southeast entrance is 12° 30.3' N 070° 02.' The port control should be hailed on channel 16 at least half an hour before entry; the duty officer will likely switch to channel 11 or 14 once contact has been made. Be prepared with all documentation when authorities board your vessel. All hands must remain on board until this process is completed. This is done at Hans Dock, in the second basin, west of the long cruise ship dock. It is located to port at 12°31.285' N, 70°2.709' W.

Entry forms must be filled out in triplicate for immigration and duplicate for customs,

cruise ship docked in Oranjestad and a colorful tour bus

along with an entry card for each crew member. There are no entry or departure fees for individuals. Forms can be downloaded at the Renaissance Marina website (http://www. renaissancemarina.com/forms). The boat itself must be declared to customs. Declaration forms can be downloaded from the Ports Authority website (www.arubaports.com) in English, Dutch, and Spanish, along with an immigration form. If the yacht stays in Aruban waters no more than 180 days, a temporary import permit must be acquired; this does not require a deposit. If it stays longer, up to a year, a temporary import permit must be applied for with payment of a deposit or a bank guarantee for the value of the duties on the yacht. Any stay longer than a year categorizes the yacht as an import, and duties must be paid. Once a temporary permit has expired, the yacht must leave Aruban waters for no less than 15 days before another permit can be obtained.

After clearing customs and immigration, boats can proceed to their registered berths. Visas for the other islands of the Dutch Caribbean are not valid for Aruba; a separate visa must be obtained. Pleasure yachts no less than 14 meters (46 ft) moored in Aruban waters, or registered at a slip, are immediately eligible to extend their stay, and harbor managers recommend they do so. They must be able to show proof of ownership of the boat. Aruba Ports Authority charges a port fee for yachts moored at docks in addition to the private slip fee. Fees are levied according to length and are charged per 12-hour block, with a minimum 12-hour fee. They start at $1.20 per meter (3.3 ft) to a maximum of 60 meters (197 ft). Vessels moored offshore are subject to mooring fees based on gross tonnage and are charged per 12-hour block. Vessels 3,999 tons and under are levied $109 per time block, and vessels over 9,500 tons are charged $194. Any vessel with gross tonnage between these pays $144 per time block. An official from the Ports Authority will board your vessel to calculate and collect the fees.

Harbors that accept visiting yachts are Renaissance Marina, adjacent to Oranjestad Harbor, and Bucuti and Varadero Yacht Clubs, next to each other behind the airport. Offshore protected anchorages, from west to east, beginning north of the Palm Beach resorts are: Arashi, Malmok, Eagle Beach, Surfside, Bucuti, Spanish Lagoon, Savaneta, and Roger's Beach. VHF channels used by the Ports Authority are 16 and 1.

SHIP CHANDLERS

Within the Seaport Marketplace, adjacent to Renaissance Marina, **East Wind Marine Services** (L. G. Smith Blvd. 5, 297/588-0260, http://eastwindmarinearuba.com, 8am-6pm Mon.-Sat.) handles the marina business. The shop provides nautical maps for the entire world, can arrange for parts and repairs, and has a diverse inventory for boaters, anglers, and casual water activities. The exclusive agent for Evinrude parts on Aruba is **Salas Marine** (Bushiri 37, 297/593-4706, john@ salasmarine.com, 9am-noon and 2pm-6pm Mon.-Fri., 10am-2pm Sat.). It also carries a selection of boat accessories, but no paint. If Salas Marine does not have a part in stock, it will take about a week to obtain it. Salas is not far from the harbor, on a dirt road behind the complex of large supermarkets at the west end of Oranjestad.

Offering advance service online and the most complete chandler is **Ola Ship Supplies** (De La Sallestraat 43A, Oranjestad, 297/583-6599, http://olashipsupply.com, 8am-5pm Mon.-Fri.), carrying both International Marine Purchasing Association (IMPA) and International Shipsuppliers & Services Association (ISSA) catalogs. It has in-store inventory and can order expedited shipping on other parts. Ola does garbage handling and certification every day and can be called outside store hours for emergencies.

GETTING AROUND

Not a large island, Aruba has connecting roads that eventually intersect route 1A, stretching the length of the island east to west and paralleling the southern shore, often

Road Signs and Regulations

Islanders are patient with tourists on the road who are unfamiliar with road signs and laws. Visitors are easily identifiable by the rental-car license plates, which start with V for *Verhuur*, Dutch for "rental." They expect visitors will drive slowly, and are usually understanding and helpful.

Aruba uses standard international road signs. Some that are important include a solid red circle with a white bar, which means **do not enter.** If you ignore it, you will be going the wrong way on a one-way street. Oranjestad has several narrow one-way streets. A round blue sign with a white arrow indicates traffic is **one way,** and the driver must follow the direction indicated. This can also be a square sign, which informs drivers they are traveling in the correct direction on a one-way street. A downward-pointing white triangle outlined in yellow is a **yield** sign; a white diamond outlined in yellow indicates you are on a main thoroughfare and have the **right-of-way** at upcoming intersections. If there are three parallel black slashes through the sign, it is warning that the road status has changed. At the upcoming intersection you **forfeit right-of-way.** There should be a yield or stop sign at the intersection. A **no-passing zone** is indicated by a red car on the left of a black car. Any sign with red symbols is an indication of a prohibition of some kind.

bordering the beachfront. From the major resorts to the airport, Oranjestad, San Nicolas, or the California Lighthouse, stay on the 1A. A few major roads connect to it that transect the island. Beyond these major routes, explorers will find streets are sand or dirt. Beyond the city limits or main thoroughfares, addresses are by area and building number, and most streets do not have a name. Areas with street addresses are Oranjestad and outlying neighborhoods of Ponton, Dakota, and Eagle. Other urban centers, such as Santa Cruz and San Nicolas, also have named streets.

Road signs are improving but are not always easy to understand. In rural areas, maps sometimes indicate a road where there is little more than a path. This makes getting around beyond the main roads confusing. Major destinations, resort areas, and several sights are easily reached on a few principal roads. In the Aruban outback, landmarks are a matter of interpretation. Islanders are quite familiar with their surroundings and are notoriously deficient at giving good directions. It is a common practice for them to hop in their car, or change their personal itinerary, to lead a visitor to a destination.

Car

On exiting the airport you'll find several car

rental agencies across from arrivals. Cars rented here incur a 10 percent surcharge, but it is likely equal to or less than the round-trip cab fare to and from most resorts. Several resorts host car rental agency desks, and others can be found close by. Smaller off-site agencies will meet you at the airport to transport you to their offices. Car rental rates are reasonable; third-party liability insurance is included in the rental rate, as required by law, though there is normally a $150 deductible. There are over 40 car rental agencies on Aruba, many with familiar chain affiliations. Several are associated with reliable European or Latin American agencies. All must conform to regulations, but rates vary. Daily rates for a compact start at $30, but you can find them outside high season for as little as $25. The lowest rate for a weekly rental is $145 for a subcompact, which includes unlimited mileage. Every type of driver's license is accepted.

DRIVING ON ARUBA

Traffic drives on the right side of the road, the same as in the United States, Canada, and continental Europe. Speed limits are posted regularly. Top speed on a highway is 80 kilometers per hour (50 mph); in town, 40 kilometers per hour (25 mph); and in "suburban" areas, 60 kilometers per hour (37 mph). Urban areas and busy streets are populated with marked crosswalks for pedestrians. Motorists must stop for a person standing on the black-and-white-striped crossings. On foot, look for these "zebra" crosswalks rather than braving traffic.

A chart of international road signs used on Aruba is usually provided with the map from rental agencies, so take the time to get acquainted with them. There are few traffic lights on the island, and those at important intersections on the divided Sasaki Highway can be confusing. When stopped, drivers should take note of the light on the near side of the road, not across the highway. A green light on an island in the middle of the Sasaki Highway is to allow highway traffic to turn left, not an indication for traffic at the intersection to cross the highway. Look to the near light to the right or left to see if it is safe to enter or cross the highway. Right turns are not allowed on a red light.

Rotaries or roundabouts have replaced traffic lights at most intersections, and there are plans to phase out all traffic lights. Those entering the traffic circle always yield to cars already in the circle. When stopping at a four-way intersection, motorists must yield to the car on the right regardless of which car arrived first. If you have not spotted a traffic sign indicating right-of-way at a major intersection, look at the marks painted on the road. Arrows pointing at you indicate you must yield to the cross street. Boxes painted where you are stopped mean you have the right-of-way. Left-turning traffic must yield to oncoming traffic until the way is clear. Passing on the left at intersections is forbidden. Make sure you use your turn indicator.

Aruba has a lot of motor vehicles for a small island, most of which seem to be on Oranjestad's main thoroughfares. Traffic is usually stop-and-go for a half mile along L. G. Smith Boulevard fronting the cruise terminal, especially when several ships are in port, or during commuter hours in the morning and late afternoon.

GAS STATIONS

Aruba has two chains of gas stations, Citgo and Texaco. Self-service pumps do not take credit cards. Motorists must first go into the station and prepay. Prices are in Aruban florins, but stations take U.S. currency and traveler's checks in denominations of no greater than $20. The exchange rate is 1.75 Aruban florins to the U.S. dollar. U.S. and Canadian credit and debit cards are accepted; a valid photo ID is required.

When driving around, be prepared to stop for goats!

Parking in Oranjestad

Arubus, Aruba's mass transit system, has established paid parking in Oranjestad, in effect 7am-7pm Monday-Saturday. Paid parking spots are marked with numbers, and pay stations are scattered around the principal parking areas. The cost is 1 florin ($0.57) per 45 minutes, and 30 percent cheaper after one hour. Machines only accept 1 florin pieces, not U.S. money, so come prepared. Follow the cues in English on the machine to enter your parking spot number.

Paid parking covers all the side streets around L. G. Smith Boulevard and the Caya Betico Croes, where most shops are located. It begins at Columbiastraat on the eastern end of the town and extends through the service roads on the western side to the traffic light at the Sasaki-Sun Plaza intersection. Parking spots marked in yellow are reserved for local employees.

Cars occupying a space beyond the paid time will have a lock placed on the tires. The overtime fine for less than half an hour is $43. After half an hour, the car is towed, and it costs $100 to retrieve it from the impound. All parking fees and fines support Arubus and the mass transit system. To spend a day in town, consider using the clean and well-kept buses, with frequent service to Oranjestad from all the main resort areas.

Bicycle

Biking to certain tourist sites has become popular, and a number of operators conduct tours. These areas are less crowded with cars. Caution is advised cycling in Oranjestad; the streets are narrow and crowded, with no bike paths and little room to maneuver. Portions of J. E. Irausquin Boulevard and L. G. Smith Boulevard north of Palm Beach have designated bike paths, painted blue. The route runs from Oranjestad to Malmok. The shorefront from Governor's Bay to the Reina Beatrix International Airport has been remodeled to provide safe biking and jogging tracks separated from traffic.

Bike-sharing program **Green Bike** (http://greenbikearuba.com, 24 hours daily, $24-89) has a fleet of 100 heavy-duty bikes and convenient stations to get around town and between the main resort areas. A touchscreen kiosk at each docking station allows you to choose a rental plan from four hours to a seven-day pass and pay with a credit card to unlock a bike. You can return it to any station. If you have problems, call customer service (297/594-6368, 8am-5pm Mon.-Fri., 8am-noon Sat.). Green Bike terminals are located at Paardenbaai Plaza (cruise terminal), Plaza Daniel Leo (behind the Renaissance Mall), Plaza Turismo (on the east end of Oranjestad,

across from the Cas di Cultura), Costa Linda Resort, La Cabana Beach Resort, Palm Beach (South Beach Center), Paseo Herencia Shopping Mall, and Fisherman's Huts.

Conveniently located to Eagle Beach and Manchebo Beach resorts is **Eagle Beach Bike Rental** (L. G. Smith Blvd. 234, 297/587-8655, 9am-5pm Mon.-Sat., $15 per day, $70 per week). **Velocity Beach Bike Rental** (Irausquin Blvd. z/n, 297/592-1670, 8:30am-4:30pm daily, $15 per day) serves the Palm Beach area and has brand-new bikes and mountain bikes, including a tandem. They offer a bargain for weekly rentals: Rent for seven days and only pay for five.

Motorcycle, Moped, and ATV

Motorcycles are a common form of transport, but mopeds are rarely seen. Generally 4WDs, UTVs, and sturdier vehicles providing better sun protection have become the preference. Mopeds are still available to rent for short hops to closer sights. But for a full day traveling around the island, look for a vehicle that provides a break from Aruba's intense sun. On the western outskirts of Oranjestad is **George's Cycle Rental** (L. G. Smith Blvd. 124, 297/593-2202, www.georgecycles.com, 9am-5pm daily, mopeds $55 per day, Yamaha motorcycles $95 per day, ATVs $125-225 per day), which has a variety of vehicles for rent, from tiny mopeds to ATVs with automatic transmission and hardtop shade canopies. Discounts are available for three- to four-day rentals. Resort pickup and drop-off plus helmets are part of the service. George's is located on the service road that parallels the Sasaki Highway.

Bus

Arubus (Weststraat 13, 297/588-0617, www. arubus.com, 5:40am-11:20pm Mon.-Fri., modified schedule Sat.-Sun., $2.50) is the official mass transit system. Buses are new, clean, and comfortable. The L10 route runs between Oranjestad and Palm Beach past all resorts and through Manchebo Beach and Eagle Beach along J. E. Irausquin Boulevard. It runs a round-trip route from the Oranjestad Bus Terminal daily, nearly every 10 minutes during the day. Frequency is reduced to every 20-30 minutes or longer after 6pm and Sunday. A complete schedule is on the website. Bus stops are clearly marked by a small yellow sign, with shelters at many, along J. E. Irausquin Boulevard. Stations are in front of each resort and by the hospital.

The smartcard system is for residents only; cash is accepted from visitors, who can purchase a day pass ($10) at a kiosk attached to the

bus station. Minivans are used for less busy routes and off-hours. A system of privately owned minibuses picks up the slack during night hours when Arubus service is sporadic. These are strictly regulated and clearly marked, charging less than Arubus. They are a legitimate option if one comes along first, rather than waiting for a more official-looking bus.

Taxi

Because major resorts do not provide airport shuttles, on arrival taxis are the most common way to get to your hotel. Cabs line up at the airport in the lane nearest to the terminals. Drivers are happy to give you their card so they can be summoned later. Every resort has a taxi stand at the entrance; hotel staff calls the dispatcher if one is not immediately available. Licensed cabs are clearly marked but do not use meters. The government sets the rates, and regulations require cabbies to have the fare chart on hand. You can ask hotel front desks to see the rate chart as well. A complete taxi fare chart can be downloaded from www. aruba.com.

Cabdrivers charge extra for luggage, on Sunday, and after midnight. Taxis in Aruba are rather pricey: The average rate from the

Free trams depart the cruise terminal to downtown Oranjestad.

Marriott to Playa Linda (if you don't want to walk 10 minutes along the beach) is $6; some might ask $9. Markets will be happy to call you a cab after grocery shopping.

Taxis have display lights on their hoods or dashboards, but they do not turn on or off when occupied or empty. It is always worth trying to flag down a cab if you need one, even though it's not the usual procedure. Don't be disheartened if they don't stop. If you're looking for a cab in Oranjestad, there are taxi stands at both entrances of the Renaissance Resort, and an empty cab is always waiting.

TAXI DISPATCH SERVICES

When you need a cab and one is not in sight, call **Aruba's Transfer Tour Taxi** (Pos Abao 41, 297/583-6988), **Diamond Taxi Service** (Salinja Cerca 27 A, 297/587-2300), or **Taxi Address Service** (J. E. Irausquin Blvd. 228 F, 297/588-0035). All resorts have a taxi stand, usually busy around the dinner hour. If no taxi is waiting, the front desk or concierge personnel can call a taxi dispatcher.

Tram

Aruba has a free **tram** (10am-5pm Mon.-Sat.) that departs in front of the cruise terminal and takes visitors to downtown Oranjestad along the Caya G. F. Betico Croes. There are eight set stops along the route with attractive shaded stations at key locations for sightseeing and shopping. It has a hydraulic lift for passengers in wheelchairs. Part of the Green Aruba program, it is powered by solar energy and is intended to reduce auto traffic and carbon emissions.

Visas and Officialdom

ENTRY REQUIREMENTS

All international travelers must have a passport. As an independent Dutch territory, Aruba is a signatory to agreements among NATO countries with an understanding that visitors from the United States and Canada do not require a visa for the island, but a valid passport is required. Aruban immigration officers require a return ticket be shown before approving entry. Foreign nationals residing in the United States or Canada without passports issued by these countries must be able to show valid residence permits at entry and departure. By cruise ship, immigration is usually handled by officers of the cruise lines, and passengers returning after a shore visit need only show a government-issued photo ID, such as a driver's license, and the pass they received when departing the ship.

Immigration officers at entry points may request proof of lodging reservations on Aruba or that the visitor owns a home, timeshare, or yacht moored in Aruban waters no less than 14 meters (46 ft) in size. Officers can also demand that a traveler show proof of sufficient funds for a stay on the island, or the sponsorship of a relative, friend, or employer.

EXTENDED STAYS

Travelers planning to stay more than the automatically allotted 30 days need to file a form with **DIMAS** (Paardenbaaistraat 11, 297/522-1500, www.dimasaruba.aw, 7:30am-11:30am and 2:30pm-4pm Mon.-Thurs.), the Department of Immigration. Officers at the airport issue a visitor visa for one month; anyone planning to stay longer should inform the officer while passing through immigration. Tourists are allowed to stay on Aruba a total of 180 days out of a year without a work or residence permit.

Extending a stay for more than 30 days but not exceeding 180 days can be done immediately at the airport for Dutch nationals and those of the United States, Canada, the United Kingdom, Ireland, and the Schengen countries. Those with property on Aruba can also immediately request to extend their stay if they are prepared to show proof of ownership. Officials are less cooperative in extending stays for those renting at smaller, cheaper guesthouses. The immigration officer can grant up to 90 days if the visitor shows proof of sufficient funds to cover an extended stay. All tourists applying for an extension beyond 30 days are required to have valid travel insurance (medical and liability) for the duration of the stay. To extend a stay beyond what is granted on arrival, file an application at the DIMAS offices. There is no filing fee to apply for a tourist extension. Forms can be downloaded from the website. Applicants should make copies of all completed forms before applying. The following documents must be presented:

- Original application form for extension of tourist stay

- Copy of the profile page and all written and stamped pages of your passport, valid for at least another three months from the date of application

- Copy of Embarkation-Disembarkation form (ED-Card)

- Copy of a valid return ticket

- Copy of valid travel insurance (medical and liability) for the duration of the extended stay

If the petitioner is not staying at their own residence or a hotel, they need to present a declaration of guarantee from a resident of Aruba who will accept liability for expenses incurred during the stay. Anyone planning to stay longer than 180 days in Aruba will need a residence permit and will not be considered a tourist.

CUSTOMS
Entering Aruba

Personal clothing and belongings are not charged duty upon entering Aruba; nor are electronics, computers, or cameras. Individuals over age 18 are allowed to bring in 2 liters of liquor and 200 cigarettes, 50 cigars, and 250 grams of tobacco. Cats and dogs from most countries are allowed if accompanied by valid rabies and health certificates from a veterinarian and proof of residence for at least six months in the United States or a low-incidence rabies location. Pets from South and Central America, Cuba, Haiti, and the Dominican Republic are not allowed.

Returning to the United States

Aruba has a division of the **U.S. Department of Immigration and Customs Enforcement** (ICE, Reina Beatrix Airport z/n, 297/588-7720, www.ice.gov) within its borders. This does not affect arriving passengers, but returning to the United States, travelers pass through U.S. customs and immigration on Aruba prior to the flight. This expedites arrivals at U.S. airports; passengers arrive the same way as domestic flights. This means departing passengers go through two immigration checkpoints when leaving Aruba. The Aruban immigration process is perfunctory, but you should allow time for the process when heading for the airport. Customs declarations are made prior to entering the gate area.

Travelers returning to the United States are required to declare the following on a CBP form, in U.S. currency:

- Items purchased

- Items received as gifts

- Items bought in duty-free shops, on the ship, or on the plane

- Repairs or alterations to any items taken abroad and then brought back, even if the alterations were performed free of charge

- Items brought home for someone else

- Items intended to sell or use in a business, including merchandise taken out of the United States

To avoid being charged duty, costly electronic items less than six months old should be registered on departure from the United States.

EXEMPTIONS

Travelers returning to the United States from Aruba have an $800 standard duty-free exemption, applied in the following instances:

- Items for personal or household use or intended to be given as gifts

- Items declared to CBP

- Items classified as accompanying baggage, returning with the traveler

- Purchases of fine art, such as original paintings or sculpture

Exemptions are applied cumulatively. Frequent travelers must take into account items declared 30 days or less prior to the present return. Items declared on previous journeys less than 30 days are deducted from the $800 exemption. Two liters of alcoholic beverages, as long as one was produced in a U.S. Insular Possession (e.g., Puerto Rico), are allowed when combined with liquor distilled and bottled in the Caribbean basin or Andean countries. Otherwise, the limit is one liter. Travelers carrying alcohol must be over age 21 and returning to a state with no restrictions on its import. No more than 200 cigarettes and 100 cigars are exempt, if they are within the $800 exemption. The same double allowance for liquor can be applied to cigarettes and cigars when half the allowance is purchased in a U.S. Insular Possession. Travelers might avoid duties for totals over $800, depending on circumstances and the items. If a piece of fine jewelry costing $700 is received as a gift, for example, while other miscellaneous goods were purchased, the official may waive the duty, even if the total exceeds $800.

Cruise ship passengers who have stopped in multiple Caribbean basin or Andean countries may receive an allowance of $1,600 for duty-free purchases. This is applicable if one of the ports of purchase was a U.S. Insular Possession such as Puerto Rico or the U.S. Virgin Islands. Duty-free purchases from the Caribbean basin or Andean countries are limited to $800. An additional $800 in duty-free purchases is allowed from the Insular Possession for a total of $1,600. A number of cruises stopping in Aruba embark from Puerto Rico. This allows travelers additional purchases from the embarkation point. It is essential to retain receipts on all purchases.

PROHIBITED ITEMS

- Cuban cigars

- Live birds of any kind—exotic, domestic, or wild

- Live fish, marine animals, and mollusks

- Meats, fruits, vegetables, plants, seeds, animals, and plant and animal products (including soup or soup products)

- Prescription drugs

Some items, such as cooked foods, may be exempt. A full declaration should be made to a customs officer. Travelers departing Aruba pass through U.S. customs prior to their return flight. If you purchased unsealed fruit, local snacks, or sandwiches to eat on the plane, inform the customs officers.

Conduct and Customs

The increased diversity of Aruba's population over the past two decades has resulted in evolving social behaviors. The predominantly Roman Catholic island's conservative attitudes are tempered with tolerance for visitors.

The multilingual talents of Aruban people are famous. Most are fluent in English, particularly those working in tourism, but they appreciate an effort to pick up a word or two of the local language. A genuine interest by visitors to understand island customs and traditions will be warmly welcomed.

ETIQUETTE

Arubans are polite and appreciate good manners. Before stating your business, a sincere *Bon dia* (Good day) will always bring a smile. After midday the greeting is *Bon tardi,* and once the sun has set, *Bon nochi. Por Fabor* and *Danki* (please and thank you) are noticed and appreciated. Shopkeepers and restaurateurs may be polite when you enter wearing a bathing suit, but they are not really comfortable with skimpy attire. Arubans are accustomed to tourists wearing shorts and T-shirts, but beachwear is not considered appropriate beyond the resorts.

Islanders' extreme politeness is suspended behind the wheel of a car on the highway or when seeking a parking spot. Islanders will park anywhere—on sidewalks and other places that would amaze—but they don't block driveways. During Carnival and special events, anything goes. But they are calm about commuter-hour snarls in town or when there is roadwork.

TIME

As with much of the Caribbean and Latin America, punctuality on Aruba is highly subjective. Influenced by Dutch timeliness and dealing daily with American expectations has sharpened the Aruban attitude. Visitors do need to learn patience, as most things are done at island speed. If you're planning a day tour, allow plenty of time for breakfast, or select the buffet, to be ready by pickup time. Dinners are usually leisurely, not always intentionally, but isn't that the purpose of a vacation?

Health and Safety

SUN PROTECTION

Aruba is only 12° north of the equator, and the sun must be taken very seriously. "I never burn" are famous last words for those hiding out in their rooms for a major portion of their vacation. Be smart about exposure and protection. There is debate about the strength of sun protection you should wear. Without a good base tan, SPF 15 should be the minimum strength. Limit sun exposure the first few days, and take a break during the peak midday hours.

Sensitive areas that many forget to cover are behind the ears, the back of the neck, and the tops of feet and the instep, which tend to be turned to the sun and get maximum exposure. Use sunblock or wear a shirt that covers your shoulders. Children require special attention as they typically wash off protection in the water. Have a T-shirt they can wear in the water and a hat for the vulnerable back of the neck. Keep dry shirts to change into when they're resting and playing on the shore. Hair braiding on the beach is popular, and makes hair easy to care for, but it exposes the scalp; strong sunblock should be applied between the rows of braids.

Aruba has laws prohibiting the sale of sun

Aruba's Pure Water

Aruba began producing freshwater from the sea in 1931, at one time boasting the world's largest desalination plant. Before that, wells and cisterns were used. **Water-en Energiebedrijf Aruba (WEB)** is Aruba's water and electricity plant, located at Balashi; hence the term "Balashi Cocktail," meaning tap water. The plant still ranks among the top 10 desalination plants in the world. Engineers at WEB are credited with innovations that have revolutionized the industry. Frequent visitors often declare the water from the tap "the best in the world" and a relief from chlorination. The water is also very soft, so less soap is required to work up a lather.

In the past, the freshwater was run over coral to imbue it with phosphorus and manganese to improve taste and provide essential minerals. Steam distillation was used until 2008, when it was replaced by far more energy-efficient reverse osmosis. The plant produces 44,000 metric tons daily to meet Aruba's demand. In 2012, a plant with a capacity of 24,000 metric tons began operation. Combined, they make WEB the largest freshwater producer in the Caribbean.

protection products containing oxybenzone, a chemical that is harmful to coral reefs. Visitors should use products without oxybenzone. Lotions labeled "for children" have used alternative ingredients for years, and there are many effective inexpensive products on the market without oxybenzone.

ALCOHOL

Restaurants entice visitors to indulge in rich meals every night, and beach bars, happy hours, and exotic cocktails encourage overconsumption of alcohol. A few days of this can seriously upset digestion; don't blame the local water. Alcohol also dehydrates, contributing to heatstroke or heat exhaustion. Take breaks in both food and alcohol consumption, and drink plenty of water, juices, and other nonalcoholic beverages.

DENGUE FEVER

Aruba is a desert island, but it does get rainfall, especially in autumn, the local rainy season. Showers mean standing water, and standing water means mosquitoes. The island's strong winds usually keep them to a minimum, but during the late fall and early winter, mosquitoes and the dengue fever they carry can be an issue. The rest of the Caribbean, with far more rainfall, reports greater numbers for dengue fever, but it should not be discounted on Aruba. The amount of rainfall is a significant

factor in dengue statistics. Dengue virus is carried by the *Aedes aegypti* mosquito, which requires clean water to lay eggs. The mosquito has distinctive white striping on its legs. Standing puddles are not breeding grounds for *Aedes aegypti*, but any sort of container in which rainwater can pool provides breeding ground. This is another reason why controlling litter is so important.

There are four strains of dengue, and each produces general malaise similar to flu but with distinctive symptoms, including severe headache; pain around the eyes, back, and joints; high fever; rash; and possibly nausea and diarrhea. Depending on the strain, symptoms can be minor to severe. It is a virus, so antibiotics are useless. A single bout of dengue can be unpleasant, but is not fatal unless, as with the flu, other chronic conditions are present. Once a person is infected with a particular strain, antibodies are manufactured in the system, and the individual will be immune to that strain for life. If bitten by a mosquito carrying a different strain, the reaction can be catastrophic. Dengue often mimics flu symptoms, so do not dismiss being ill. Go see a doctor, who can arrange for blood tests to confirm dengue.

Aruba's government pays close attention to dengue. Inspectors travel house to house and to businesses searching for breeding grounds. Homeowners and landlords are warned and

Bush Medicine

On the islands, a deep-rooted (yes, pun intended) reliance on natural, homegrown remedies is rampant. Every drugstore has a shelf of leaves and roots for steeping to produce teas. These are not in commercial packaging but fresh in individual bags, sometimes with a label describing their purpose. Ask the pharmacist how to use them. Freshly processed lotions and potions are also sold; some have to be made to order and refrigerated, such as *Lotio Alba*, a mild natural remedy for heat rash.

Most residents cultivate a few aloe plants in their gardens, cutting a piece of leaf to apply the fresh juice to burns. Many believe the beneficial properties of the plant go beyond skin care and drink the juice mixed with water. It takes determination and a healthy dollop of honey to make it even remotely palatable. Others nibble on the gelatinous meat inside the leaves, also hard to imagine for anyone familiar with the malodorous species that grows on Aruba.

cited for noncompliance in correcting conditions favorable for mosquitoes. Each year, in the fall, they mount an information and prevention campaign.

HOSPITALS AND EMERGENCY SERVICES

Doctors are on duty outside office hours at the **Dr. Horacio E. Oduber Hospital** (Dr. Horacio E. Oduber Hospital Blvd. 1, 297/527-4000, www.arubahospital.com, 24 hours daily). A number of resorts have a local doctor who they work with to make house calls at the resort or accept visitors at their offices. Inquire with the front desk. If the resort does not have a doctor, staff will advise you or call an ambulance. Emergency room service at the hospital is $316 for examination and diagnosis; X-rays and other testing are extra. Emergency services must be paid for in cash or by credit card. The hospital and doctors will not accept foreign insurance or coverage. Receipts are issued for insurance claims once you return home. The same procedure is in place for a regular policy or a travel insurance policy.

Aruba's hospital is clean and modern, continually being renovated and improved. It can perform MRIs, CT scans, and other tests. It also has a hyperbaric chamber. A recent total renovation doubled the number of beds, modernized wards, and added new diagnostic tools and treatment facilities.

Emergency Hotline

Dial 911 for emergencies, 24 hours daily. Responders dispatch police, the fire department, or ambulances.

Dialysis

Individuals requiring dialysis during their stay can set up appointments at the **Dr. Horacio E. Oduber Hospital Clinic** (Dr. Horacio E. Oduber Hospital Blvd. 1, 297/583-6952 or 297/527-4371, www.arubahospital.com, c.raphaela@arubahospital.com, 7am-7pm Mon.-Sat., $485). Substantial documentation is required for treatment; visit the website for the list of requirements. Any treatment must be arranged at least two months prior to your visit. Patients who are on the island but who have not scheduled ahead of time or submitted the documentation will be denied dialysis.

PHARMACIES

Prescriptions must be filled and paid for at a pharmacy, or *botica*. At night or on Sunday, prescriptions are filled at the venue on duty. Pharmacies are open 8am-8pm Monday-Saturday, and one on each side of the island remains open Sunday, holidays, and after hours; these on-duty pharmacies change on a rotating basis. Find which pharmacies are on duty in the newspaper or in the window of any pharmacy, or by calling the hospital. The following pharmacies are close to resort areas. All operate 8am-8pm Monday-Saturday.

- **Oranjestad: Botica Kibrahacha** (Havenstraat 30, 297/583-4908), directly behind the Royal Plaza Mall
- **Eagle and Manchebo Beach: Botica di Servicio Eagle** (Caya Punto Brabo 17, 297/587-9011), next to the Dr. Horacio E. Oduber Hospital
- **Palm Beach, Malmok, and Noord: Botica Santa Anna** (Noord 41B, 297/586-2020), next to Caribbean Palm Villas Resort
- **Santa Cruz, Paradera, and Piedra Plat: Botica Santa Cruz** (Santa Cruz 54 A, 297/585-8776), on the corner across from Mundo Nobo Supermarket

CRIME

According to statistics and the CIA Factbook, Aruba is one of the safest destinations in the Caribbean. Incidents of wallets and handbags forgotten in a store but returned intact are common. However, no place in the world is crime-free.

Petty Theft

As at any vacation destination, petty theft by a few active miscreants can be a problem. Thieves know that vacationers have extra cash, cameras, phones, and other valuable electronics and jewelry.

Safes and Deposit Boxes

Safes and deposit boxes are provided by nearly all accommodations to store passports, cash, and bank cards. The purchase of a watertight "beach box" for cash and valuables that can be worn in the water is a worthwhile investment. Don't leave your watch and wallet unattended on the beach when taking a swim.

Car Theft

If you're driving an open car such as a jeep and parking in isolated spots to swim, don't leave valuables in the car. Even a closed car should be kept in sight, as it's possible to break a window and open the trunk. Wear a waist pack or small backpack for exploring the caves and Arikok National Park. Individuals who victimize tourists know the places where they are most likely to leave valuables and cash. Carry very little and use watertight carriers or plastic bags to foil ill intentions while you're in the water. The same applies on the beach at your resort; don't leave a bag filled with valuables behind. Take only what you need and keep it in a watertight container you can wear in the water.

Car theft was once an issue, particularly of the most common rental cars. The **KPA** (Korps Politie Aruba, www.kparuba.com) police created a task force and in 2010 arrested 25 individuals in a theft and chop-shop ring, which has greatly reduced thefts.

Travel Tips

WHAT TO PACK

Aruba is decidedly casual, and typical resort wear is adequate most everywhere; fancy dresses and sports jackets are not required. Bring sweaters or blazers, as air-conditioned restaurants can get chilly, as can nights, with Aruba's gusty trade winds. Sunny tropical days require sunblock, and sunglasses are always needed. A spare pair of prescription glasses is advised, but contact lenses can easily be replaced. During the fall rainy season, pack mosquito repellent, particularly if you plan to dine alfresco.

Electricity supply is the same as in the United States, and no special adapters are required. Roaming charges on foreign cell phones can be outrageous, and a phone can be rented for far less. It is not necessary to change money for local currency. U.S. dollars, traveler's checks, and credit cards are readily accepted everywhere.

WEIGHTS AND MEASURES

Aruba uses the international metric system for all purposes. Meat, produce, and baked goods are measured by kilogram; one kilo is 2.2 pounds. A liter is 34 U.S. fluid ounces or 35 imperial ounces. There are 3.8 liters in a U.S. gallon and 4.5 liters in an imperial gallon. Prices on gas pumps in Aruba are per liter of gasoline, and it is quite expensive. Distance and speed postings on roads are in kilometers; multiply either by 0.6 to get miles and miles per hour.

Electricity

Adapters for electrical appliances and devices are not required for travelers from the United States and Canada. Aruba uses the same 110-120 volts, 60 hertz AC. European appliances require adapters, which hotels can provide. If not, they are readily available at home or hardware stores. Some facilities may not have outlets that handle three-pronged plugs, but adapters are also available. Notify your resort of your requirements before arrival to ensure they have an adapter reserved for your use.

Aruba is far less prone to power outages than in the past. The power plant, WEB, has greatly increased its output and efficiency of production, although a lightning storm can result in an outage. Unplug your devices during an outage, as the surge when the power comes back on has been known to burn out anything from laptops to refrigerator motors.

ACCESS FOR TRAVELERS WITH DISABILITIES

Aruba still has a ways to go to be completely wheelchair-friendly. Oranjestad is getting a facelift wherever you look, with the pedestrians and those with disabilities integrated into the plans. An ambulance dispatch station has been set up at Playa Linda Resort, centrally located to all of Palm Beach. A few businesses offer transportation in vans set up to board individuals in wheelchairs.

Aruba Disabled Services

Before arrival, travelers with wheelchairs can arrange for transport with **Aruba Disabled Services** (Paramira 30, 297/561-6944, http://www.arubadisabledservice.com, 6am-9pm daily). It has a fleet of vans (from $60 per hour) with hydraulic lifts that can accommodate up to two wheelchairs and five passengers. It also rents personal transport for a minimum of three days, including three- and four-wheel motorized personal transport ($57-150), as well as wheelchairs and wheeled walkers ($48-90).

Aruba Happy Wheels

Special wheelchairs designed to enter the water and travel on sand are rented out by **Aruba Happy Wheels** (Palm Beach 472, 297/568-4787, adaptedhappywheels@hotmail.com, $40 for 24 hours). A fold-up platform may also be rented to allow wheelchair access on difficult surfaces. They will deliver the equipment to resorts and offer discounts for long-term rentals.

Lite Life Medicab

One of the first and most experienced companies on Aruba dedicated to transporting the physically challenged is **Lite Life Medicab** (Hooiberg 19D, 297/585-9764, U.S. 786/955-8829, www.litelifemedicab.com, 6am-8pm Mon.-Sat., $80 round-trip from the airport). Their vans and customized sedans feature ramps and hydraulic lifts. Some deploy hydraulic lifts and have room for multiple wheelchairs, with additional seating; others are smaller vans with ramps. Service hours are 24 hours daily year-round.

TRAVELING WITH CHILDREN

Traveling with children, no matter the destination, presents some distinctive considerations and precautions. Aruba is surrounded by the sea, and many accommodations have on-site swimming pools, so water safety for children is paramount. Aruba's beaches do not have lifeguards, so parents must be vigilant.

A Fantasy Wedding on Aruba

Destination weddings are in. The advantages are numerous, including financial ones. A winter wedding can be held outdoors with clear skies, comfortable temperatures, and no coats. For the legal ceremony, Aruba's Town Hall is picturesque with a beautiful interior. Government staff perform ceremonies with grace and emotional fervor. Formal papers must be submitted a month prior to the nuptials in Dutch. This is where the assistance of local wedding planners is vital. They will translate the required forms requested of the prospective bride and groom (same-sex marriage is not currently legal on Aruba; many gay and lesbian couples wishing to marry head to Bonaire, where it is legal). The forms must be accompanied by:

- Birth certificate with the names of both parents and an embossed Apostille Seal

- Copy of passport or picture ID

- Divorce Certificate with Apostille Seal *or* Final Decree of Divorce with Apostille (if applicable)

- Death Certificate with Apostille Seal (if applicable)

- Letter of Intent to Marry

- U.S./Canada Negative Statement of Marriage or Affidavit of Single Status; must include Apostille Seal

Begin collecting the documents at least six months prior to the planned wedding date. Two witnesses must be present for the ceremony (the wedding planner can provide them if necessary). A renewal of vows does not require this paperwork. If you want to conduct only a spiritual ceremony on the beach, proof of marriage is required—religious officiants need to see a certified copy of the wedding certificate. Several nondenominational Christian ministers can perform ceremonies in any location of your choice. **Diane Keijzer** (www.dianekeijzer.com) does a fine job. The Catholic Church will not perform destination weddings because of the required spiritual preparation.

Every major resort has a dedicated wedding planner, available if you are using the resort's facilities. Veteran independent wedding planners include:

- **Aruba Fairy Tale Weddings** (297/593-0045, www.arubafairytales.com)

- **Aruba Weddings by Bonny** (297/730-0350, www.arubaweddingsbybonny.com)

- **Cayena Weddings** (973/460-0284 or 212/292-4221, www.cayenaweddings.com)

- **Ceremonies & Celebrations in Aruba** (321/473-3856, candcaruba@yahoo.com)

Aruba.com has a separate wedding section and a bridal registry, http://bridal.aruba.com, where friends and family can purchase gifts for newlyweds honeymooning on Aruba. Spa days, sailing cruises or tours, flowers, and romantic dinners can be purchased in advance as wedding gifts. Newlyweds-to-be should investigate the **One Happy Honeymoon** perks offered in cooperation with local resorts.

Utmost precaution with the tropical sun is also a priority. Better than continually annoying a squirming child to reapply sunblock, keep T-shirts for them to wear in the water, and dry ones to change into afterward.

The excitement of travel and the constant activity, along with tropical temperatures, can result in overtired, cranky youngsters. Keep this in mind when making dinner plans. Aruba has many family-oriented eateries that provide children's menus and expedite these orders. If a child appears to be ill, medical service can be accessed 24 hours a day. Resort staff will assist in contacting the doctor on duty and arranging a consultation. There are always at least two drugstores on the island providing off-hours service to fill prescriptions.

Aruba is generally a family-friendly island. Children are welcome and respected, and most resorts provide a wealth of activities to keep them engaged throughout the day. They also have a roster of vetted babysitters, and parents can dine out with peace of mind. Sensitive to the needs of families, the Aruba Tourism Authority (ATA) has devised the **One Cool Family** program, which runs June-September for ages 12 and under. Save cash on dining and accommodations by signing up through the website (www.aruba.com), then present your One Cool Family ID when reserving with participating vendors.

WOMEN TRAVELING ALONE

Despite some notoriety and misconceptions, female visitors experience no more unpleasant encounters or attention than they would at home, and likely far less. Making safe and smart decisions about new acquaintances in bars or on the beach shouldn't change under the influence of the tropical moon. Female travelers are welcome at clubs and nightspots, with plentiful opportunities to mingle with locals. Islanders are accustomed to women traveling on their own. However, don't leave an unfinished drink in a crowded club; if it has been left unattended, leave it and order a new drink.

Incidents of women being bothered while walking alone at night are rare to nonexistent, but being alert or avoiding such situations is always advisable. Larger hotels post security guards day and night to discourage intruders. Overt and hidden security cameras are installed at major resorts and along popular walkways. Stay in well-lit populated areas.

GAY AND LESBIAN TRAVELERS

Aruba has an active and open gay and lesbian community, and islanders are nonchalant about visitors' sexual orientation. There are Caribbean islands where homosexuality is a capital crime, but Aruba has no such discrimination. Frequent gay and lesbian cruises include Aruba among their ports of call; all visitors are welcome.

OPPORTUNITIES FOR VOLUNTEER WORK

Aruba Reef Care Project

What began as an underwater reef cleaning effort by young diving enthusiasts is now the long-standing **Aruba Reef Care Project** (297/740-0797, castroperez@gmail.com), which polices the shore and marine environment. In September, volunteers sign up with dive operators to use scuba or snorkeling gear while cleaning underwater as hundreds of others take to the beaches to remove trash. Volunteers are rewarded with a party (this is Aruba, after all) and lunch, plus an attractive certificate and a raffle for prizes donated by local concerns, including dinners for two and weekend stays at resorts.

Coastal Zone Clean-Up

The Aruba Hotel and Tourism Association (AHATA) Environmental Committee conducts its **Coastal Zone Clean-Up** (297/582-2607, vanessa@ahata.com) in November, targeting every beach and awarding prizes for groups that collect the most refuse.

Project Aware

Every April, Red Sail Sports carries out **Project Aware** (297/586-1603, info@redsailaruba.com), rewarding its volunteers with a cruise on one of its large catamarans after a morning of strenuous garbage collecting. The effort is smaller than others, focusing on a specific beach that needs attention.

Information and Services

MONEY
Banks and Foreign Exchange

The official currency of the island is **Aruban florins,** officially written **AWG** (and sometimes as **AFL**). The term "guilders" may also be heard among locals; this is similar to saying "bucks" instead of dollars. The official exchange rate at banks is 1.8 florins to one U.S. dollar. This can vary on the street 1.75-1.80, depending on the shop; it is completely arbitrary. Supermarkets where prices are only in florins usually exchange at 1.75. Jewelry stores most often exchange at 1.80, though prices are marked in dollars.

Aruba has three large banks, each with branches in Oranjestad. Branches in Palm Beach and Eagle Beach are close to some of the resorts; all are a short walk from the water, past the Sasaki Highway. It is not necessary to change money from U.S. dollars to florins. Stores and restaurants accept dollars, traveler's checks, and U.S. and Canadian credit cards. A valid photo ID is required when using a card or traveler's checks at shops and markets. ATMs that accept MasterCard, Visa Cirrus, and Visa Plus are located in every mall, casino, gas station, and major grocery store.

Aruba Bank

Aruba's first bank, **Aruba Bank** (Camacuri 12, 297/527-7777, www.arubabank.com, 8am-4pm Mon.-Fri.) is affiliated with the regional Orco Group. The main branch is near the airport, but there is a branch in Hato, close to the Eagle Beach and Manchebo Beach resorts.

Banco di Caribe

Banco di Caribe (Vondellaan 31, 297/523-2000, www.bancodicaribe.com, 8am-4pm Mon.-Fri.) has many ATMs around the island, but no branches except the Oranjestad head branch.

Caribbean Mercantile Bank

Caribbean Mercantile Bank (CMB; Caya G. F. Croes 53, Palm Beach 4-B, 297/522-3000, www.cmbnv.com, 8am-4pm Mon.-Fri.) is a subsidiary of Maduro & Curiel Bank of Curaçao, affiliated with the Bank of Nova Scotia. The Palm Beach branch is midway between the Sasaki Highway and Santa Ana Church on the principal Palm Beach-Noord Road. It also has a branch near the airport, in the Wayaca Falls Shopping Mall (8am-4pm Mon.-Fri., 9am-1pm Sat.).

Royal Bank of Canada

RBC (Italiestraat 36, 297/523-3100, www.rbtt.com, 8am-4pm Mon.-Fri.), the Caribbean chain of the Royal Bank of Canada, has taken over RBTT, a widespread regional bank. The main branch is close to Manchebo resorts on the Sasaki Highway.

COMMUNICATIONS
Phones and Cell Phones

Calling the United States from hotels can be an expensive and time-consuming affair. Guests have to wait for the hotel operator to make the connection and pass it through to their rooms. There are several "Call Home" phone stations around shopping centers and near resorts. These only require a credit card, but they automatically charge $15, even when there is no answer.

Roaming charges on foreign cell phones can often be outrageous. Renting a cell phone is a cheaper alternative for keeping in touch. Aruba cell phone systems charge only for calls made, with users not charged for calls received.

SETAR

Aruba's national telecommunication company, **SETAR** (Palm Beach z/n, 297/525-1000, http://setar.aw, 9am-5:30pm Mon.-Sat.) installs all landlines. It has a branch in Palm

Beach where long-distance calls can be made at minimal rates, right next to Brickell Bay resort. Phones outside the shop are available at all hours. An adjacent vending machine dispenses phone cards, required to make calls. The main headquarters is on the outskirts of Oranjestad. SETAR also has a **cell phone rental kiosk** (9am-11am and noon-6pm Mon.-Sat.) in the arrivals hall of the airport to get mobile service immediately upon arrival.

INTERNET ACCESS

Almost all resorts have Wi-Fi, and larger hotels charge for Wi-Fi use in the rooms. Communications stations can be used free of charge. Many visitors complain about the quality of connections in the bigger hotels, as the infrastructure may be antiquated and cannot handle heavy traffic and multiple devices. Most guesthouses and apartment or house rentals offer free Wi-Fi and usually a more modern and better connection. Several restaurants, particularly the fast-food franchises, provide free Wi-Fi. Data plans can be purchased at SETAR, which charges $28 for 3 GB valid for one month. A local SIM card costs $22.

MEDIA

Newspapers

Aruba has a highly literate population that likes to keep informed. Despite the ascendancy of web-based news, several print newspapers are published in the four predominant languages.

ARUBA TODAY

Aruba Today (Weststraat 22, 297/582-7800, Mon.-Sat., free) focuses on international news, with a few local pages dedicated to superficial events. On Monday, they feature an international version of the *New York Times* in an additional section. It can be found free at hotels, supermarkets, fast-food franchises, and other locations every morning.

ARUBA HERALD

Found only online, the **Aruba Herald** (297/583-2424, http://arubaherald.com) has diverse local news, covering every aspect of island life that makes the Papiamento papers, from domestic disputes to lost dogs. International coverage is generally only politics and top headlines.

Tourist Magazines

An inordinate number of tourist publications in English provide information on restaurants, services, and island happenings. They can be found free at supermarkets, hotel lobbies, restaurants, and stores. Hotels provide a hard copy of *Aruba Nights* in every room. The bible of Aruba's Carnival—*Bacchanal*—is printed in both English and Papiamento. The English magazines available are:

- *Aruba Nights*
- *Bacchanal*
- *Destination Aruba*
- *I Love Aruba*
- *Island Gourmet*
- *Island Temptations*

Radio and Television

Aruba has 18 FM radio stations and 3 AM stations. There are three island-based TV stations: **TeleAruba,** channel 13; **ATV,** channel 15; and **TOP TV,** channel 22; with two Venezuelan stations on channels 10 and 12. Television and radio programming is in Papiamento and Spanish, with some Dutch newscasts. ATV (channel 15) has an English Lifestyle and News program for local events at 7:15pm Monday-Friday. All resorts are connected to SETAR Cable or have satellite dishes to carry U.S. programming and sporting events, as do most bars and lounges.

Easy 97.9 FM radio plays easy-listening music from the United States and the Caribbean. Commentary is practically nonexistent. It is relatively commercial-free and broadcasts 24 hours daily. **Hits 100** radio station at **100.9 FM** targets the over-35 audience with Billboard hits from the 1980s and 1990s. Other radio stations are geared to the cultural tastes of the region.

STRAY DOGS AND CATS

Unfortunately spay-neuter practices have not taken hold sufficiently to control the unwanted dog and cat population of Aruba. Some take the animals to be euthanized, while others drop animals somewhere in the hope that a kind person will adopt them or that they will fend for themselves. This state of mind is prevalent throughout the Caribbean and Latin America. Most islands have no service to remove unwanted dogs from the streets, despite visitors finding it distressing to see them hungry or injured. Rabies does not exist on Aruba.

Cas Animal Foundation

Aruba's first no-kill animal refuge is the ultimate goal of **Cas Animal Foundation** (hotline 297/742-8732). Founder Kirsten Arndt has converted three homes into a temporary facility while fund-raising to build a proper shelter. Cas Animal maintains an Animal Ambulance to pick up strays. The foundation also welcomes donations, including paying veterinary bills or providing dog food. Another primary objective of Cas Animal is to facilitate the adoption of local mixed breeds by visitors. Often one of Aruba's sweet and intelligent strays will capture the heart of a sympathetic tourist. Arndt will assist in any way possible in obtaining inspection and treatment for the dog from a qualified vet, allowing it to pass U.S. standards for import. She will also assist in acquiring a carrier and arranging transport. Vacationers returning to the United States or Canada with an Aruban dog or cat is far more common than you might imagine. The pets adapt well to their new environment.

Resources

Papiamento Phrasebook

Islanders' fluency in English leaves little need to use Papiamento. It is rare to find someone working at resorts, restaurants, or shops who does not speak and understand English well. Still, when patronizing local restaurants or shops, a few phrases might be sometimes necessary. Anyone with a good working knowledge of Spanish will also do well in these circumstances, as it is more often used by those who don't know any English.

PRONUNCIATION GUIDE

Papiamento combines elements of Spanish, Portuguese, Dutch, and also English, with occasional French, such as *petit pois* for peas. Emphasis is frequently on the last syllable, but keep in mind that a shift in emphasis can change the meaning of a word, morphing it from a verb to an adjective, for instance.

Consonants

Only a few consonants differ from standard English pronunciation:

dj as in "join"—"djispi" is a precocious child; "djucu," a good luck charm

g can be normal, as in "go," but is frequently soft "h" as in "hello"

j is a "y" sound, as in "year"; June and July are "Yuni" and "Yuli"

ñ is a "ny" sound, as in the Spanish words "señor" or "aña"

zj is a soft "j," such as "zjilea" (jelly), but rarely seen

Vowels

Standard vowel pronunciation is very different. The long vowels of English never come up.

a as in "papa"
e as in "they"
i as in "police"
o as in "blow"
u as in "dude"
u as in "buck"

The influence of Dutch can be seen in the oft-used *ij*, the Dutch way of writing *y* as in "ray." An example is *Tamarijn*, with the final syllable pronounced "rain."

TERMS OF ADDRESS

I *mi* or *Ami* (Example: "*Mi ta bai*"—"I am going"; "Who gets this?"—"*Ami.*")

You *bo* or *Abo* (Example: "*Undo bo ta biba?*"—"Where do you live?"; "Who do you love?"—"*Abo*")

he or she *e*

us or we *nos*

they *nan* (Also added to the end of words to make them plural, as in *mucha* for "child" and *muchanan* for "children.")

IMPORTANT GREETINGS AND RESPONSES

Good day *Bon Dia* (Bon DEE-A)
Good afternoon *Bon Tardi* (Bon TAR-dee)
Good evening, Good night *Bon Nochi* (Bon NO-chee)
How are you? *Con ta Bai?* (literally translates as "How does it go?")
Everything is good? *Tur cos ta bon?*
Yes, good, thank you. *Si, bon, danki.*

Good enough; OK *Basta Bon*
Welcome *Bon Bini*
Please *Por Fabor*
Thank you *Danki*
Goodbye *Ayo*

Do you speak English? *Bo por papia Ingles?*
My name is . . . *Mi nomber ta . . .*
What is your name? *Con jamabo?*
How much? *Cuanto ta?*
How do you say . . . ? *Con bo ta bisa . . . ?*
Excuse me. *Despensa.*
I love you. *Mi stimabo.*
Help! *Yudami!*
Fire! *Candela!*

USEFUL PHRASES

It is a pleasure to meet you. *Ta un plaser di conocebo.*
Until next time. *Te otro biaha.*
Have a nice day. *Pasa un bon dia.*
What time is it? *Cuant'or tin?*
I don't understand you. *Mi no ta comprende bo.*

Merry Christmas and Happy New Year. *Bon Pasco y Bon Aña.*
Happy Birthday *Cumpleaño Felis*
Congratulations *Pabien* or *Bon Suerte*
anthem and flag *himno y bandera*

Suggested Reading

PHOTOGRAPHY AND TRAVEL

Bäcker, Jennifer, and Josefa Wodl, photographers. *Wings Over Aruba*. Aruba: Wings Global Media, 2011. The ultimate coffee-table photography book of Aruba is very big and very bright, with new aerial angles of the prettiest places.

Bertsch, Werner. *Aruba Tropical Moods of the Caribbean*. Oranjestad: DeWit/Van Dorp, 2008. A picture book focused on the colors of Carnival.

Bertsch, Werner, and Charles Croes. *Aruba, I Am Your Island*. Aruba: self-published, 2012. A lovely picture book from Werner Bertsch, combined with the reflective prose and poetry of Charles Croes, well-known as the storyteller of Aruba forums, comes in a plain paperback or a handsome sleeve for gift-giving.

Bertsch, Werner, and Linda Hiller. *Aruba Picture Book*. Oranjestad: DeWit/Van Dorp, 2011. Bertsch loves photographing Aruba. This collection of his charming shots with

captions by Hiller is a smaller, budget-priced paperback.

Boland, Matt (author), and Eva Kock. *Aruba Tips for Travelers*. Vitae Publishing, 2005. This compiles a longtime resident's folksy bits of advice on what to expect when vacationing on Aruba. He clarifies all those new and funny things that make visitors scratch their heads in confusion.

Knevel, Theo. *Aruba, Ariba*. Aruba: ATA Publishing, 2011. Stunning aerial photography provides an interesting perspective.

Night, Sam. *Aruba: Including Its History, the Alto Visto Chapel, the Ayo Rock Formations, the Quadriki Caves, Fort Zoutman, and More*. Earth Eyes Travel Guides, 2012. Culled from Wikipedia articles and images under Creative Commons licensing, this guide gathers popular subjects within one portable resource.

HISTORY

Bongers, Evert. *Creating One Happy Island*. Self-published, 2009. Put out in commemoration of the 50th anniversary of the opening of the Aruba Caribbean Resort, considered the defining moment when tourism became a pillar of the island's economy, this compendium of a few island writers showcases the visionary personalities that established Aruba as a vacation giant in the Caribbean.

Dijkhoff, Raymundo, and Marlene S. Linville. *The Marine Shell Heritage.* Oranjestad: Aruba Archaeological Museum Press, 2004. The head of the museum's scientific department has edited essays on shore areas and a society dependent on marine animals, particularly mollusks. Shells were used for everything from building to decoration and money.

Kock, Adolf (Dufi). *The Story of the German Freighter E.S. Antilla.* Self-published, 2012. A longtime friend and chronicler of Lagoite culture and life at The Colony recalls World War II. This is a very detailed description of the dramatic events leading up to the sinking of the *Antilla.*

Ridderstaat, Jorge R. *The Lago Story.* Aruba: Cha Aruba, 2008. A visually beautiful and thorough accounting of Aruba's economic history prepares the reader by first painting a picture of the island's initial development for mining gold and phosphate. It passes through the years when the refinery was in its prime, World War II, and then the decline of its influence and the growth of tourism.

van der Klooster, Olga, with Michel Bakker. *Monument Guide Aruba.* Amsterdam/ Aruba: Kit Publishers/Charuba Foundation, 2013. An attractive guide to a majority of Aruba's many landmark buildings, each page is dedicated to one of the 127 structures profiled, with beautiful color plates and a detailed history of the landmark, frequently including the effort undertaken to save it from demolition. The front and back covers fold out to provide detailed maps of Oranjestad and San Nicolas. Eight lovely postcards for sending or framing are at the back of the book.

Versteeg, Aad H., and Stephen Rostain. *Archeology of Aruba: The Tanki Flip Site.* Oranjestad: Aruba Archaeological Museum Press, 1997. This book profiles Aruba's first major archaeological dig and the revelations it contained.

Versteeg, Aad H., and Arminda C. Ruiz. *Reconstructing Brasilwood Island: The Archeology & Landscape of Indian Aruba.* Oranjestad: Aruba Archaeological Museum Press, 1995. NAMA administrators and archaeologist Versteeg delve into the significance of artifacts.

NATURE

De Boer, Bart, with Eric Newton and Robin Restall. *Birds of Aruba, Curaçao, and Bonaire.* Princeton, NJ: Princeton Field Guides, 2012. The first comprehensive field guide to the birds of the region, this compact and portable book contains close to 1,000 color illustrations on 71 color plates, helping to identify the more than 200 species.

Roll, Barbara. *Explorer's Guide to Aruba.* Beckenham, UK: Loft Publishing, 2010. The author has a charming way of introducing Aruba and its endemic animals to children, with highly entertaining artwork and prose.

MISCELLANEOUS

Croes, Robetico. *Anatomy of Demand in International Tourism: The Case of Aruba.* Saarbrücken, Germany: Lap Lambert Academic Publishing, 2010. A must-read for tourism executives from Aruba's former Minister of Tourism, who now holds a chair at the UCF School of Hospitality Management, the book examines the dynamics of a small island and the impact of international tourism, based on statistics from an extended study.

Fenzi-Thayer Sargent, Jewell. *This is the Way We Cook!* Oranjestad: DeWit/Van Dorp, 1971. Already in its 14th printing, this is a compendium of recipes from the outstanding cooks of Aruba, Bonaire, Curaçao, Saba, Sint Eustatius, and Sint Maarten, for those who wish to try their hand at preparing some of the regional cuisine.

Viana, Carlos. *Prescriptions from Paradise.* Merritt Island, FL: Healing Spirit Press, 2012. Viana, a holistic healer certified in Chinese medicine, presents a compilation of more than 10 years of health columns. The easy-to-understand entries are organized alphabetically. His years of practice have resulted in some surprising insights. This book is the winner of the 2012 International Book Award in Alternative Medicine from USA Book News.

Internet Resources

GENERAL INFORMATION

Aruba Online
www.arubatourism.com
This is one of the earliest Aruba websites. It has been around since 1992, founded by a frequent visitor to the island. The site includes information and visitor reviews with links to websites. This is an impartial, basic site. It is left to the visitors to rate and comment on services. Home of a long-established and popular Aruba forum, an excellent resource for current information and input, the site also provides a booking engine for lodging through Travelocity and has webcams set up in various locations around Aruba.

Official Tourism Website of Aruba
www.aruba.com
Aruba's official website is conscientious about providing complete information on every aspect of island life. It has booking engines for room reservations, activities, and dining out. There is a bridal registry allowing family and friends to purchase excursions, romantic dinners, and shopping as gifts for newlyweds honeymooning on Aruba. Newlyweds can also take advantage of the "One Happy Honeymoon" special discounts on lodging, dining, and activities. Other packages include "One Happy Family."

The Official Aruba Travel Guide, a downloadable app for smartphones and available on the website, has features for planning activities. Users can review and rate attractions and services, and even upload the information to social media later. A GPS locator provides directions to sites and amenities. A very busy forum section is an excellent place to pose queries and obtain firsthand advice.

VisitAruba
www.visitaruba.com
This extremely thorough venue is one of Aruba's longest-established websites, in operation since 1997. It maintains impartiality but offers reviews by users and a busy forum. Frequent and first-time visitors are welcome to file trip reports, which can be highly informative.

Find a complete schedule of island events, including all Carnival events, posted here. The site strives to stay topical and up-to-date, including useful links to restaurants, car rentals, and weather reports. Visitors can purchase a VisitAruba discount card ($14). This does not include postage or delivery to your resort on arrival, which can be arranged for $4. Cardholders get discounts from over 100 island vendors for shopping, dining, accommodations, car rentals, and other activities.

ARUBA GOVERNMENT AGENCIES

Aruba Airport Authority
www.airportaruba.com
This complete guide to the Reina Beatrix International Airport includes arrival times, amenities, clearing customs, and the latest notice of restricted items and luggage allowances.

Aruba Department of Foreign Affairs
www.arubaforeignaffairs.com/afa/home.do
An interesting site for travelers to learn about consular affairs and Aruba's international treaty partners, it provides information about all the various international organizations with which Aruba is aligned. Anyone interested in the extent of Aruba's international relations will find the information here.

Aruba Ports Authority
www.arubaports.com
This website offers a complete listing of all cruise schedules and port information, including shore safety regulations and communications, cargo services, and cruise statistics.

Arubus
http://arubus.com
The official website of Aruba's mass transit system features complete bus schedules to every route on the island.

Central Bureau of Statistics
www.cbs.aw
The Central Bureau of Statistics posts complete statistics on every aspect of island life. This is where the CIA Factbook gets its figures.

DIMAS in English
www.aruba.com/sigma/Entry_Req-Eng.pdf
Find full information on entry requirements for visiting Aruba, as well as residency requirements and permit procedures, with downloadable forms, from Aruba's immigration site.

Government of Aruba
www.overheid.aw
The official site of the government of Aruba is in Dutch, but Google can translate it to English. Every aspect of government authority is explained, and current government news is posted. The translation is somewhat stilted but informative.

Korps Politie Aruba
www.kparuba.com
The official site of Aruba's Police Department shares a history of the service, the location of its various branches and districts, and travel advisories.

ISLAND LIFE

The Bent Page
http://bentpage.net
Novelist Daniel Putkowski used to live part-time in Aruba. His ramblings around the island took him anywhere and everywhere. While he no longer lives here and hasn't updated the site since 2015, it remains a handy resource. An entire section is dedicated to videos of driving directions to out-of-the-way beaches, rum shops, and sights.

Lago Colony
www.lago-colony.com
This is an active site where a dedicated group interacts. They have the unusual bond of having been born or raised in the Lago Colony during the Esso-Exxon heyday. Posters share recollections, old photos, and current news. Interesting stories and discussions bring alive this important time in Aruba's history.

Temple Beth Israel Aruba
http://bethisrael-aruba.blogspot.com
Visitors curious about Aruba's synagogue, wishing to attend services while on vacation, or curious about a destination bar or bat mitzvah should visit this site.

Vacations by Aruba
www.vacationsbyaruba.com

Angelo Limon, in his own words, can "be found probably drinking a beer at the beach right now. So feel free to find your way around Aruba with my travel tips." When he is not investigating a new restaurant or nightclub, he is updating this site or putting together his free weekly newsletter. It keeps subscribers updated on island life, from legislation to news about resorts and facilities. There's quite a bit of advertising to wade past, some of it not even Aruba-related, but it's worth it; Vacations by Aruba is far more current on what's happening than most other sites.

Vegan Aruba
www.veganaruba.com

Vegan visitors can look to this website for recommendations on dining and shopping. Meredith, a devout vegan and former New Yorker who relocated to the island with her Aruban husband in 2016, hopes to encourage more eateries and shops to cater to vegans.

RECREATION
Arikok National Park
www.arubanationalpark.org

Everything you want to know about Arikok National Park is here: maps, hiking trails, park news, and information about island flora and fauna.

Aruba Cruising Guide
www.aruba-cruisingguide.com

This is one of the best sources of need-to-know facts and advice for private yachts. Run by sailors for sailors, it has everything from bottom clearances and how to handle harbor entries to the best places for supplies and repairs. Find downloadable forms for customs and immigration especially for yachts.

Noonsite
www.noonsite.com

Labeled "the ultimate cruiser's planning tool," Noonsite covers nearly the entire world but has a very complete guide of Aruba and the Caribbean. This is a handy site for sailors, featuring a wealth of input by cruisers who have visited the island and other suggestions based on personal experience.

TRAVEL
Cruise Critic
www.cruisecritic.com

This is the most complete site for finding and booking cruises with Aruba as a port of call.

BUSINESS
Department of Economic Affairs
www.arubaeconomicaffairs.aw

Details of what it takes to do business in Aruba, like investing, economic reports, acquiring a business license, economic relations, and Aruba's Freezone, are explained in downloadable forms for applying for business and investment permits.

Aruba Chamber of Commerce
www.arubachamber.com

The Chamber of Commerce, or Kamer Van Koophandel, plays an important role if you're interested in establishing a business on Aruba. The website goes into great detail about tax responsibilities, necessary forms to be filed, and upcoming events, including workshops during the year to assist fledgling enterprises.

REAL ESTATE
Casnan.com
http://casnan.com/realestate

Every real estate agent on Aruba and their listings are consolidated into this site. View houses, condos, and apartment sales and rentals on the island via agents, without the need to jump around from one website to the next.

U.S. GOVERNMENT SITES
CIA Factbook Aruba
www.cia.gov/library/publications/resources/the-world-factbook/geos/aa.html

The go-to guide for statistical information on every aspect of Aruba. Factual and impartial, it lists everything from geographic details to the number of Internet subscribers.

U.S. Department of Agriculture
www.aphis.usda.gov

Listed here is exactly what is and isn't allowed to be brought back to the United States from Aruba, including live animals, plants, and foodstuffs, and why. It explains what diseases, fungi, or parasites are problems in certain areas and what to watch out for.

U.S. Travel and Customs Regulations
www.cbp.gov

Find a complete description of all taxable purchases, allowances, and exemptions, plus explanation of duties charged when bringing home purchases over allowances.

WEATHER

Departmento Meterologico Aruba
www.meteo.aw

Aruba's official site for all weather warnings and forecasts provides five-day forecasts, alerts, and live weather maps in English, Dutch, and Papiamento.

Index

A

accessibility: 242
accommodations: 34, 36, 176-197; Eagle Beach and Manchebo Beach 183-187; Oranjestad 181-183; Palm Beach, Malmok, and Noord 187-193; San Nicolas, Savaneta, and Pos Chiquito 194-195, 197; Santa Cruz, Paradera, and Piedra Plat 193
air travel: 227-228
alcohol: 239
Alhambra Shopping Bazaar: 27, 162, 168
Alto Vista Chapel: 29, 89, 91
Andicuri Beach: 49-50
animals: 204-208
Antilla shipwreck: 28, 58, 61, 215-216
Aquarius: 28, 104-105
Arashi Beach: 28, 49
Arawak Gardens: 27, 30, 34, 144, 172
Arikok National Park: 18, 29, 77-78, 96-99; map 97
arts: 224-226
Aruba Active Vacations: 30, 32-33, 66-67, 73, 74
Aruba Aloe Museum and Factory: 169
Aruba Beach Club: 27, 183
Aruba Dande Festival: 157
Aruba Historical Museum: 28, 31, 87
Aruba Hi-Winds Pro-Am: 153-154
Aruba International Beach Tennis Open: 154
Aruba International Pro-Am Golf Tournament: 154
Aruba International Regatta: 154
Aruba International Triathlon: 153
Aruba Kayak Adventures: 30, 64
Aruba Motorcycle Tours & Rentals: 38, 71
Aruba Ocean Villas: 36, 197
Aruba Ostrich Farm: 29, 37, 92, 175
Aruba Ray's Comedy Club: 148
Aruba Reef Apartments: 36, 195
Aruba Surf School: 30, 33, 67
Aruba Waterpark: 30, 37, 67
Atlantis Submarines: 28, 61-62
ATMs: 245
ATVs: 38, 233-234
auto travel: 231-232, 233
Ayo Rock Formation: 29, 92, 94

B

Baby Beach: 29, 37, 52
Baby Natural Bridge: 96
banana boats: 33, 64, 66, 67
banks: 245

Baranca Plat: 47
beaches: 17, 35, 40-54; Eagle Beach and Manchebo Beach 45, 47; North Coast 49-50; Oranjestad 42-43, 45; Palm Beach, Malmok, and Noord 47, 49; San Nicolas, Savaneta, and Pos Chiquito 52, 54
Beach House Aruba: 34, 187-188
Bestuurskantoor (Government House) and Parliament Buildings: 87
Betico Day: 31, 151
bicycling: 73, 74, 75, 233
birds: 205
Black Stone Beach: 50
Boca Catalina: 49, 57
Boca Grande: 52
Boca Prins: 50
Bon Bini Festival: 31, 87, 150
Bucuti & Tara Beach Resort: 28, 29, 186
budgeting: 34
Bugaloe: 27, 124, 144
Bushiribana Gold Ruin: 29, 92
bus travel: 234
Butterfly Farm: 28, 37, 89

C

Café Chaos: 27, 140
California Dunes: 49
California Lighthouse: 28, 92
camping: 54
caravan tours: 69-71
Caribbean Sea Jazz Festival: 31, 154
Carnival: 31, 150-151
car travel: 231-232, 233
Casa Vieja: 34, 111
Cas di Cultura: 148, 150
Casibari Rock Formation: 94
casinos: 146-147
cats, stray: 247
caves/caverns: 97, 99
cell phones: 245-246
Ché Bar: 27, 131
Cheo's Corner: 29, 127
children, activities for: 37
children, traveling with: 242-244
churches/temples: 89, 91, 99
climate: 200
coach tours: 68
concert venues: 148-150
Conchi (Natural Pool): 18, 28, 29, 39, 77-78, 96-97
crime: 241

cruises: 35, 229
culture, local: 20, 31, 219-226
Cunucu Arikok Trail: 29, 39, 77
cunucu houses: 194
currency exchange: 245
customs regulations: 236-237

D

Daimari Beach: 50
dengue fever: 239-241
De Palm Island: 62
De Palm Pier: 27, 62, 124, 144
diamond shopping: 172-173
disabilities, access for travelers with: 242
Dive Aruba: 28, 32, 60, 61
Divi Links: 27, 79
diving: 32, 60-61
dogs, stray: 247
Donkey Sanctuary: 37, 94, 96, 175
Dos Playa: 50
Dream Bowl: 37, 144
Driftwood Fishing Charters: 33, 65
Druif Beach (North Coast): 49
Druif Beach (Oranjestad): 42

E

Eagle Beach: 45, 47, 116-118, 142, 146, 168, 183-187; map 10
Easter Week: 54
Eat Local Month: 154
economy: 218-219
education: 221
electricity: 242
Elements: 28, 119
Eman House: 85
emergencies: 240
entertainment: 34, 138-150
entry requirements: 235
environmental issues: 200-202
etiquette: 238
events: 150-157
Excelencia: 28, 104, 109
experiences, top: 16-21
extended stays: 235-236

F

family activities: 37
fauna: 204-208
festivals and events: 150-157
Fisherman's Huts: 47
fishing: 33, 64-66
Flamingo Beach: 43
flea markets: 165
Flip Flop Festival: 153
flora: 203-204

Fontein Cave: 97, 99
food/restaurants: 34, 35-36, 102-137; Eagle Beach and Manchebo Beach 116-122; North Coast 132; Oranjestad 104-115; Palm Beach, Malmok, and Noord 122-131; San Nicolas, Savaneta, and Pos Chiquito 135-137; Santa Cruz, Paradera, and Piedra Plat 132-134
Fort Zoutman: 28, 87
4WD tours: 74
Fun 4 Every 1: 33, 67
Fusion Wine and Piano Bar: 27, 142

G

gay and lesbian travelers: 244
Gemstones International: 30, 171
geology: 199-200
Gold Mine Ranch: 29, 39, 74, 75
golf: 79
government: 218
Government House (Bestuurskantoor) and Parliament Buildings: 87
Governor's Beach: 42-43
gratuities: 117
Gusto: 28, 145
Guy Bavli—Master of the Mind: 150

H

Hadicurari Pier: 65-66
Haystack Mountain (Hooiberg): 94
health and safety: 48, 238-241
hiking: 39, 77-78
Hilton Aruba Caribbean Resort: 36, 192
Himno y Bandera Day: 31, 151, 222
history: 208-217
holiday shopping festivities: 156
Hooiberg (Haystack Mountain): 94
horseback riding: 39, 74, 75, 96
hospitals: 240
hot water: 184

IJK

insurance, travel: 236
International Half Marathon: 151
Internet access: 246
itineraries: 27-30
JADS Dive Shop: 29, 32, 52, 61
J. E. Irausquin Boulevard: 77
Kalin's: 30, 127
King's Day: 153
kitesurfing: 32-33, 66-67
Kok Optica Opticians: 85
Kozlov Dance International: 148

L

land tours: 68-75
La Playa Torchlight Dinner: 36, 124
La Trattoria El Faro Blanco: 36, 132
La Vista: 30, 130
lesbian and gay travelers: 244
L. G. Smith Boulevard: 77
Linear Park: 43, 77
Lourdes Grotto: 99

M

Madagascar Aruba Adventure: 38, 70-71, 74
Madi's Magical Tours: 28, 71
magazines: 246
Malmok: 47, 49, 89-91, 122-131, 142, 144-147, 169-175, 187-193; map 11
Malmok Beach: 47, 49
Manchebo Beach: 45, 47, 118-122, 142, 146, 168, 183-187; map 10
Manchebo Beach Resort: 27, 82, 186-187
Mangel Halto: 30, 54, 57-58
March 18th Memorial: 87-88
Masiduri Trail: 77
May Day: 153
measurements: 242
Melina Charters: 33, 66
memorial statuary: 88
minibus tours: 68-69
money: 34, 245
mopeds: 71-73, 233-234
motorcycles: 38, 71-73, 233-234
Museum of Industry: 31, 99

N

National Archaeological Museum Aruba (NAMA): 28, 31, 85, 87
Native Divers Watersports: 33, 67
Natural Bridge: 96
Natural Pool (Conchi): 18, 28, 29, 39, 77-78, 96-97
Natural Pool Trail: 39, 77-78
newspapers: 246
New Year's Eve celebration: 156, 157
nightlife: 140-148; Eagle Beach and Manchebo Beach 142, 146; Oranjestad 140-142, 146; Palm Beach, Malmok, and Noord 142, 144-147; Santa Cruz, Paradera, and Piedra Plat 147-148
Noord: 47, 49, 89-91, 122-131, 142, 144-147, 169-175, 187-193; map 11
North Coast: 49-50, 91-94, 132, 175
notable Arubans: 221-224
Nutcracker, The: 156-157

OP

ocean travel: 229-230
Octopus Cruises: 32, 58, 62

Okeanos Spa: 28, 35, 45, 81
O'Niel Caribbean Kitchen: 29, 34, 109, 136
Orange Mall: 30, 118, 120
Oranjestad: 28, 42-43, 45, 85-89, 104-115, 140-142, 146, 160-167, 181-183; map 8-9
Oranjestad Harbor: 65
Oranjestad Memorial Park: 89
packing tips: 241
paddling: 64
Paddock, The: 28, 110, 141
Palm Beach: 37, 47, 49, 89-91, 122-131, 142, 144-147, 169-175, 187-193; map 11
Paradera: 94-99, 132-134, 147-148, 175, 193
parasailing: 33, 66-67
parks and gardens: 88, 89
party buses: 141
Paseo Herencia Shopping Mall: 29, 30, 31, 150, 173-174
passports: 25, 235
Peace Labyrinth: 91
pharmacies: 240-241
Philip's Animal Garden: 29, 37, 91
phones: 245-246
Piedra Plat: 94-99, 132-134, 147-148, 175, 193
Pinchos Grill and Bar: 28, 35, 106
planning tips: 22-26
plants: 203-204
Plaza Padu: 87
politics: 218
population: 219-220
Pos Chiquito: 52, 54, 99-101, 135-137, 194-195, 197
Presidential Aruba Caribbean Cup: 154
Private Tours Aruba: 38, 69
Punto Brabo: 35, 45
Pure Ocean: 29, 126

QR

Quadirikiri Cave: 97, 99
Queen Wilhelmina Park: 88
radio: 246-247
Rancho Loco: 29, 39, 74, 75, 96
recreation: 55-82
Red Fish: 30, 109, 118
Red Sail Sports Dinner Cruise: 35, 64
religion: 220
Renaissance Island: 28, 43, 45
Renaissance Marketplace: 27, 34, 141-142, 166-167
resort hopping: 189
resources: 248-254
Ricardo's: 27, 119-120
Roger's Beach: 29, 52
romance: 18, 35-36
Rooi Prins Trail: 78
Rooi Tambu Trail: 78
running and jogging: 77

S

safari tours: 38, 57, 66, 69, 70, 71, 74
safety: 48, 238-241
sailing: 32, 62, 64
sales tax: 174
San Nicolas: 29, 52, 54, 99-101, 135-137, 194-195, 197
San Nicolas Community Museum: 31, 99-101
Santa Ana Church: 29, 89
Santa Cruz: 94-99, 132-134, 147-148, 175, 193
Savaneta: 30, 52, 54, 99-101, 135-137, 194-195, 197
Savaneta Beach: 52, 54
scuba diving: 32, 60-61
Seabreeze Apartments: 34, 194-195
sea travel: 229-230
segway tours: 73
Senses: 29, 121
Seroe Arikok Trail: 78
Seroe Jamanota: 29, 39, 78
Seroe Preto City of Lights: 100
shops: 158-175; Eagle Beach and Manchebo Beach 168; North Coast 175; Oranjestad 160-167; Palm Beach, Malmok, and Noord 169-175; Santa Cruz, Paradera, and Piedra Plat 175
shows and concert venues: 148-150
sights: 83-101; North Coast 91-94; Oranjestad 85-89; Palm Beach, Malmok, and Noord 89-91; San Nicolas, Savaneta, and Pos Chiquito 99-101; Santa Cruz, Paradera, and Piedra Plat 94-99
Sinterlaas Feast Day: 156
Skydive Aruba: 30, 75
skydiving: 75
Smit & Dorias Coffee House: 29, 114
snorkeling: 32, 57-58, 60
Soul Beach Music Festival: 153
South Beach Lounge: 27, 146-147
souvenirs: 162
spas, massage, and beauty: 35, 80-82
specialty tours: 69-71
Stichting Hunbentud Uni Seroe Preto: 100
St. Theresita Church: 99
sun protection: 238-239
surfing: 32-33, 66-67
Surfside Beach: 37, 43

T

taxes: 174
taxi travel: 234-235
television: 246
tennis: 79-80
Terrazza Italiana: 34, 120
time: 238
tipping: 117
trams: 235
Tranquilo: 28, 32, 35, 58, 64
transportation: 227-235
Trikes: 38, 71
tubing: 33, 64, 66

UVWXYZ

underwater tours: 61-62
Urataka Center: 29, 133
Urirama Beach: 49
vaccinations: 25
Village, The: 30, 165, 174-175
Villa Sunflower: 34, 187
visas: 25, 235
volunteer opportunities: 244
Waltzing Waters: 30, 37, 150
water park: 67
water sports: 21, 32-33, 57-67, see also specific activity
WaveRunners: 33, 66, 67
weather: 200
weddings: 243
weights and measures: 242
Wente/Papiamento Golf Tournament: 151, 153
wildlife: 204-208
Willem III Tower: 87
Windows on Aruba: 27, 122
windsurfing: 32-33, 66-67
women travelers: 244
yachts, private: 229-230
yoga: 82
Zeerover: 30, 34, 36, 109, 135
ZoiA: 35, 81-82
zoos and animal parks: 91, 92

List of Maps

Front Maps

Aruba: 4–7
Oranjestad: 8–9
Eagle Beach and Manchebo Beach: 10
Palm Beach, Malmok, and Noord: 11

Sights

Arikok National Park: 97

Background

The Caribbean: 199

Photo Credits

All photos © Rosalie Klein except:

Title page photo © ARTN Photography; page 2 © Stephan Karg - Dreamstime.com; page 3 © Hella Brandenbruger - Dreamstime.com; page 12 © (bottom) Wings Global Media; page 15 © (bottom left) Aruba Tourism Authority; page 16 © Jason Frankle | Scott Wesson 2017; page 19 © (top) LOOK - Alamy; (bottom) Wings Global Media; page 20 © Lex Corbach; page 22 © (bottom) Meunierd - Dreamstime.com; page 23 © (bottom) Jetlag Creative Studio; page 24 © Timeless-Pixx 2009-2017; Wings Global Media; page 25 © (bottom) Chiyacat | Dreamstime.com; page 26 © Jeroen Lucas; page 27 © (top) Bugaloe Beach Bar & Grill; page 30 © (bottom right) Aruba Tourism Authority; page 32 © (bottom) Richard Mosch; page 38 © (bottom) Wings Global Media; page 40 © Timeless-Pixx 2009-2012; page 51 © (top) Timeless-Pixx 2009-2017; page 55 © Richard Mosch; page 59 © (bottom) Jetlag Creative Studio; page 63 © (top right) Jetlag Creative Studio; (bottom) Wings Global Media; page 66 © Devy | Dreamstime.com; page 69 © Wings Global Media; page 72 © (top) Timeless-Pixx 2009-2017; page 74 © Wings Global Media; (bottom) Timeless-Pixx 2009-2017; page 78 © Aruba Tourism Authority; page 83 © Timeless-Pixx 2009-2017; page 86 © (top) Alexander Meacham - Dreamstime.com; page 90 © (top left) cadosbla; page 93 © (top left) Aruba Tourism; (bottom) Mihai Andritoiu - Dreamstime.com; page 95 © (top) Timeless-Pixx 2009-2017; (bottom) De Sousa Photography - Dreamstime.com; page 98 © (top left) Gail Johnson - Dreamstime.com; (top right) Melissa Robert; (bottom) Artmando Multimedia Armando Goedgedrag; page 101 © Timeless-Pixx 2009-2017; page 107 © (bottom) Carte Blanche; page 109 © Olena Beisiuk | Dreamstime.com; page 115 © Super Food Plaza Aruba; page 125 © (bottom) Bugaloe Beach Bar & Grill; page 138 © Wings Global Media; page 143 © (top) Bugaloe Beach Bar & Grill; page 147 © Darryl Brooks - Dreamstime.com; page 152 © (top) ARTNPHOTOARUBA; page 155 © (top) Tony Filson; (bottom) Rogier ter Meulen; page 158 © Mihai Andritoiu - Dreamstime.com; page 162 © Cosecha/Chris Schouten; page 163 © (top) Mopa Mopa/Ainhoa Gogorza Gondra; (bottom) Picturemakersllc - Dreamstime.com; page 167 © Darryl Brooks | Dreamstime.com; page 170 © (bottom) Super Food Plaza Aruba; page 173 © South12th | Dreamstime.com; page 174 © David Castillo Dominici - Dreamstime.com; page 213 © Hella Brandenburger - Dreamstime.com; page 225 © ARTNPHOTOARUBA; page 229 © Byvalet - Dreamstime.com

Moon Travel Guides to the Caribbean

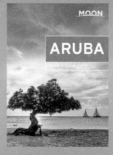

ARUBA

BAHAMAS

MARIAH ERINE MOYLE

BERMUDA

ROSEMARY JONES

CUBA

CHRISTOPHER P. BAKER

DOMINICAN REPUBLIC

LEBANIT LILY DIRMA

JAMAICA

Central & South America Travel Guides

BELIZE

LEBANIT LILY DIRMA

CARTAGENA & COLOMBIA'S CARIBBEAN COAST

COSTA RICA

ECUADOR

& THE GALÁPAGOS ISLANDS
BENJAMIN

TRIP OF A LIFETIME

GALÁPAGOS ISLANDS

TRIP OF A LIFETIME

MACHU PICCHU

RYAN DUBÉ

TRIP OF A LIFETIME

PATAGONIA

Including the Falkland Islands
WAYNE BERNHARDSON

PERU

RYAN DUBÉ

GO BIG AND GO BEYOND!

These savvy city guides include strategies to help you see the top sights and find adventure beyond the tourist crowds.

OR TAKE THINGS ONE STEP AT A TIME

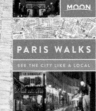

#TravelWithMoon

MAP SYMBOLS

▦▦▦	Expressway	○	City/Town	✈	Airport
▦▦▦	Primary Road	◉	State Capital	✈	Airfield
▦▦▦	Secondary Road	⊛	National Capital	▲	Mountain
-------	Unpaved Road	★	Point of Interest	✚	Unique Natural Feature
————	Feature Trail	•	Accommodation		
- - - - -	Other Trail	▾	Restaurant/Bar	🈨	Waterfall
············	Ferry	■	Other Location	▲	Park
▦▦▦	Pedestrian Walkway	Λ	Campground	▯	Trailhead
▥▥▥	Stairs			⛷	Skiing Area

⛳	Golf Course
℗	Parking Area
▆	Archaeological Site
♙	Church
⛽	Gas Station
	Glacier
	Mangrove
	Reef
	Swamp

CONVERSION TABLES

$°C = (°F - 32) / 1.8$
$°F = (°C \times 1.8) + 32$
1 inch = 2.54 centimeters (cm)
1 foot = 0.304 meters (m)
1 yard = 0.914 meters
1 mile = 1.6093 kilometers (km)
1 km = 0.6214 miles
1 fathom = 1.8288 m
1 chain = 20.1168 m
1 furlong = 201.168 m
1 acre = 0.4047 hectares
1 sq km = 100 hectares
1 sq mile = 2.59 square km
1 ounce = 28.35 grams
1 pound = 0.4536 kilograms
1 short ton = 0.90718 metric ton
1 short ton = 2,000 pounds
1 long ton = 1.016 metric tons
1 long ton = 2,240 pounds
1 metric ton = 1,000 kilograms
1 quart = 0.94635 liters
1 US gallon = 3.7854 liters
1 Imperial gallon = 4.5459 liters
1 nautical mile = 1.852 km

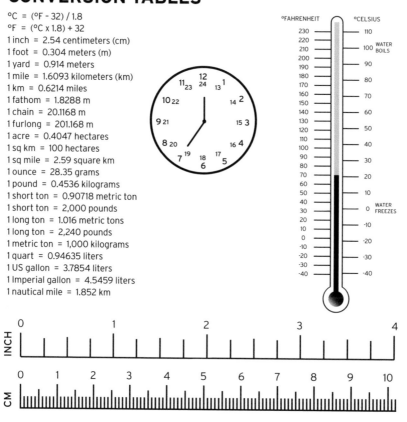

MOON ARUBA

Avalon Travel
Hachette Book Group
1700 Fourth Street
Berkeley, CA 94710, USA
www.moon.com

Editor: Kristi Mitsuda
Series Manager: Kathryn Ettinger
Copy Editor: Christopher Church
Graphics and Production Coordinator: Ravina
  Schneider
Cover Design: Faceout Studios, Charles Brock
Interior Design: Domini Dragoone
Moon Logo: Tim McGrath
Map Editor: Kat Bennett
Cartographer: Karin Dahl
Proofreader: Ann Seifert
Indexer: Greg Jewett

ISBN-13: 9781640491182

Printing History
1st Edition — 2014
3rd Edition — October 2019
5 4 3 2 1

Front cover photo: © Werner Bertsch / Huber
  Images / eStock Photo
Back cover photo: © TS Corrigan / Alamy Stock
  Photo

Printed in China by RR Donnelley